WIND
WIND

LIVING THE GOODE LIFE

AT FULL THROTTLE

Porter Press International

To Cary

It took me 18 years from our first meeting to invite Cary out to dinner, but six weeks later she persuaded me that we should be married and indeed we were a further six weeks after that! And when for that wedding she organised a sit-down dinner-dance for 220 people in our house and garden, I realised that I had made a rather good choice.

Since then, we have had an exceptionally full life restoring old houses and gardens, much driving in old cars, travelling the world, hosting and attending many parties and owning generations of dogs.

At one level a wife but, more importantly, a genuine partner in my life. Thank you so much for putting up with this book!

LIVING THE GOODE LIFE

AT FULL THROTTLE

Richard Goode

Porter Press International

First published in June 2020

978-1-913089-13-9

Published by
Porter Press International Ltd

Hilltop Farm, Knighton-on-Teme, Tenbury Wells, WR15 8LY, UK
Tel: +44 (0)1584 781588
sales@porterpress.co.uk
www.porterpress.co.uk

Design & Layout by Adrian Morris

Printed by Gomer Press Ltd

ACKNOWLEDGEMENTS

I am very grateful to the following good friends whose collective memory of events, often many years ago, has transpired to be far clearer than mine and who all have greatly contributed to ensuring that this book is reasonably accurate! In alphabetical order, they are Patrick Alexander, Harry Boggis-Rolfe, Noni Chawla, Maxim Chouvaev, Cindy Cottman, Tim Daniel, Rowena Hutchison, Chris Jamieson, Allan Johnson, Hans Jorda, Murray Kenyon, James Mehew, Vic Norman, Cressida Pemberton-Pigott, Andrew Ritchie, Nigel Rugman, Al Simkin, Sasha Tavaryan, Jon Wand, Clive Wilson, Robert Woods and Peter Wright.

I am also very grateful to my assistant Elaine Lloyd for her tireless support, secretarial work and picture research.

On the subject of pictures, my friend the noted aviation photographer Peter March has been generous in allowing me to reproduce photographs from his extensive archive, while also contributing a number of notable reminiscences.

Thanks are due to Philip Mather, archivist at the Fusilier Museum, Bury, for permission to reproduce the photograph of my great-great-great uncle, Archibald Arnott, on page 14. The cuttings from the *Sunday Express* on page 85 and *Daily Express* on pages 194 and 261 are courtesy of Mirrorpix. I would like to thank Philip Whiteman of *Pilot* magazine for permission to reproduce images on pages 175, 234 and 240, and Bauer Media Archives for the illustration on page 219.

Barbara Harrad, Global Affairs Co-Ordinator at the Commonwealth Development Corporation, has been extremely helpful in seeking out pictures and I would like to thank her and the CDC archivist for permission to reproduce the picture of the Swaziland Irrigation Scheme on page 49.

The team at Porter Press deserve special mention for transforming the Goode life into this handsome volume. Particular thanks are due to Philip Porter for his support and encouragement throughout, and to Adrian Morris for the dynamic design layout including the very striking cover. I am also grateful to motoring historian Mick Walsh for information about the Triumph Dolomite/HSM story.

I would especially like to thank Clive Dickinson, who is a proper author and who has given me absolutely invaluable help and advice during the writing of this book.

FOREWORD

I've often wondered whether Richard Goode was a genius or completely mad. It all started when I was 13 and watched the black and white biplane, a Stampe, zoom across the grass at White Waltham airfield. It would have been spectacular had it been the right way up but most notably it was upside down at an altitude of 20 feet!

I asked the pilot that immortal question: 'Please Mr Goode, can I clean your aeroplane?' Spotting an opportunity for either some youth development or more likely free labour, Richard said yes. I then spent most summer weekends cleaning his Stampe and Pitts in exchange for aerobatic lessons. It beat studying for O-levels and the distraction caused me to fail most of them.

Was he mad or a good judge of character? In 1984 when I was just 19, Richard sent me to fly solo in his Pitts. My friends wouldn't trust me on their bicycles. Two years later Richard introduced me to display flying. I remember his very short briefing by phone: 'Bonhomme, do a display, keep it simple and don't crash.'

The weekends included having a go in or on whatever vehicle Goode had at his disposal. Memorable drives with a vintage Rolls-Royce, a Jaguar XK 120, a Honda CBX1000 or the trusty Daimler Sovereign spring to mind.

Ten years later I'd forgotten that 'don't crash' guidance at an airshow and written off his brand new Yak-18T. He had seen the crash watching satellite TV news whilst in Kazakhstan. He politely phoned to ask if I was OK and was the wreckage back on the airfield? There was no hint of a whinge or moan. I went on to fly for Richard's variously-sponsored aerobatic teams, flew vintage fighters at Duxford and competed very successfully in the Red Bull Air Race World Championship.

I have Richard to thank for his 'madness' and the opportunities he gave to me. His guidance, can-do attitude and relaxed but well directed management skills all helped propel me to the more exciting side of my aviation career. Enjoy the book...

Paul Bonhomme Red Bull Air Race World Champion (and British Airways Captain), Cambridgeshire, April 2020

Для меня Ричард Гуд всегда был квинтэссенцией понятия «Британский джентльмен». Ему всегда нравились скоростные автомобили и самолеты и поэтому, когда впервые я встретился с ним в Москве зимой 1990 года, то специально заказал для него один из самых больших представительских авто, которые на тот момент использовались для перевозки советских «больших шишек». Думаю Ричарду это понравилось.

Он тогда прибыл в Россию, чтобы купить один из наших фантастических самолетов Су-26, который незадолго до этого увидел на авиационной выставке в Фарнборо. При первой встрече Ричард показался мне необычным человеком-немного эксцентричным, одним словом. Он привез с собой делового партнера и хотя был немного моложе своего друга, тем не менее показался мне значительно «более английским», чем его пожилой соотечественник.

Однако, очень скоро между нами установились добрые, дружеские отношения, что очень способствовало успеху переговоров. Тогда это было весьма непросто для таких, как я, воспитанных в советской системе, но мы быстро достигли соглашения и Ричард стал первым европейцем, который приобрел самолет Сухого.

Это стало началом нашего делового сотрудничества и добрых дружеских отношений. В последующие годы совместной работы Ричард всегда в тонкой и интеллигентной манере делился со мной своим богатым опытом в области авиационного бизнеса. Его поразительное деловое чутье и заражающая энергия позволила нам открыть новые направления бизнеса – приобретение невостребованных в то время российскими аэроклубами самолетов Як-52 и продажа их по всему миру, организация коммерческих полетов на современных российских истребителях для состоятельных западных клиентов.

Для меня английский юмор - это то, как шутит автор этой книги. В наших отношения было много интересных, забавных и подчас удивительных событий.

Хотите узнать больше? Прочитайте эту книгу, ведь Ричард поразительный рассказчик.

Александр (Саша) Таварьян Экс-коммерческий директор Сухого, Москва, Апрель 2020

To me, Richard Goode has always been the quintessence of the British gentleman. He likes fast cars and aeroplanes. When I first met him in Moscow in the winter of 1990, we had arranged to have use of one of the large cars that were only used by the big bosses in Russia. I think Richard liked that!

He had come to Russia to buy one of our fantastic new aerobatic aeroplanes, the Su-26, which he had seen at Farnborough. At first he seemed to me an unusual person, a little eccentric in a word. He had brought a business partner and although Richard was quite a bit younger than his friend, he seemed much more English than the older man!

However, very quickly good friendly relations were established which contributed much to the success of the negotiations. These were unusual for people like me who had been brought up in the Soviet system, but we reached an agreement and Richard became the first person in Europe ever to buy a Sukhoi aircraft.

This was the beginning of a close working relationship and friendship. Over the years Richard has taught me a lot about the aviation business, but always in a very gentle and polite manner. His astounding business flair and his infectious energy allowed us to explore new opportunities, including buying unclaimed Yak-52s from Russian flying clubs and selling them all over the world and organising commercial flights for wealthy Westerners on modern Russian fighters.

For me, English humour is central to the author of this book. During our relationship, there have been a lot of interesting, funny and sometimes surprising events. If you want to know more, read this book because Richard Goode is an amazing storyteller.

Alexander (Sasha) Tavaryan **Ex-commercial director of Sukhoi, Moscow, April 2020**

Aresti aerobatic symbols

Count Aresti, a Spanish nobleman from a distinguished family began display flying before the war and then became an Air Force test pilot after the war, but continued as a very keen aerobatic pilot. He recognised that there was a real need for an aerobatic sequence to be written in a simple pictorial form, and this led to his aerobatic dictionary, in which every manoeuvre could be written with a simple symbol, and a complete sequence of aerobatics through combining individual symbols into a diagram. This system, of some 15,000 manoeuvres, is now used throughout the world in every aerobatic competition so that all the pilots and judges will know exactly what each pilot is attempting to fly. At the beginning of each chapter in this book you will see an aerobatic sequence, some relatively simple but others at world championship level!

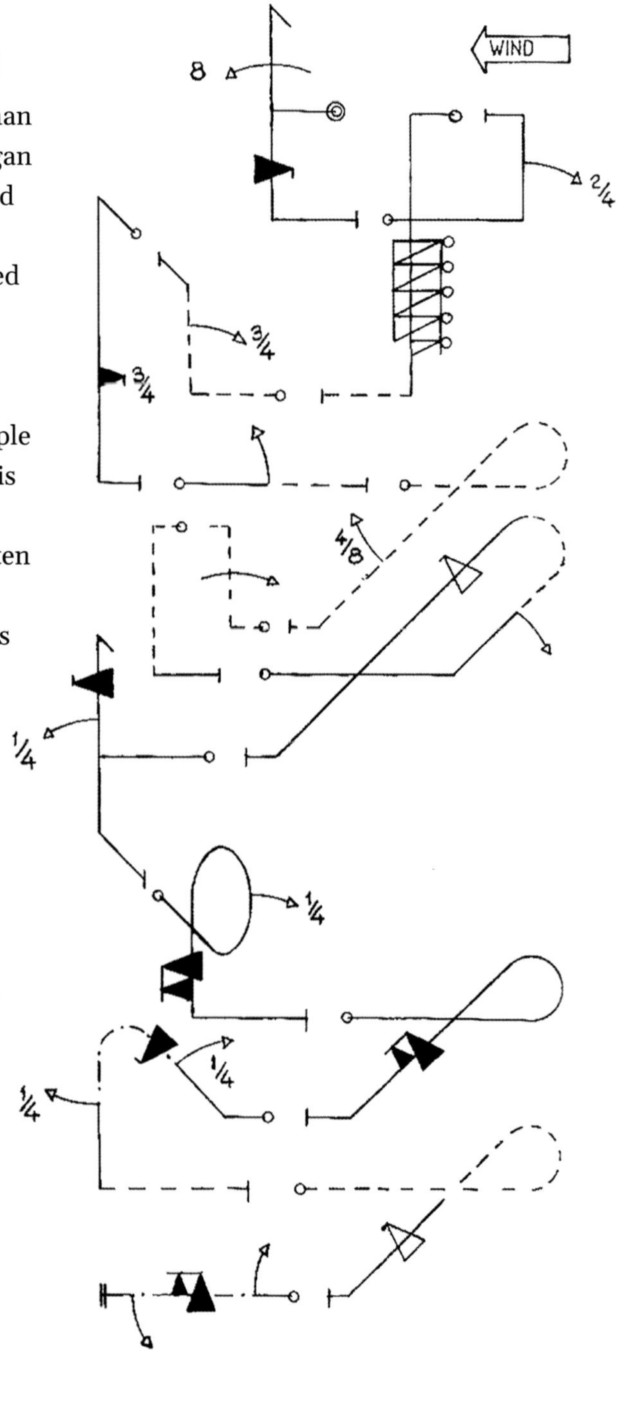

CONTENTS

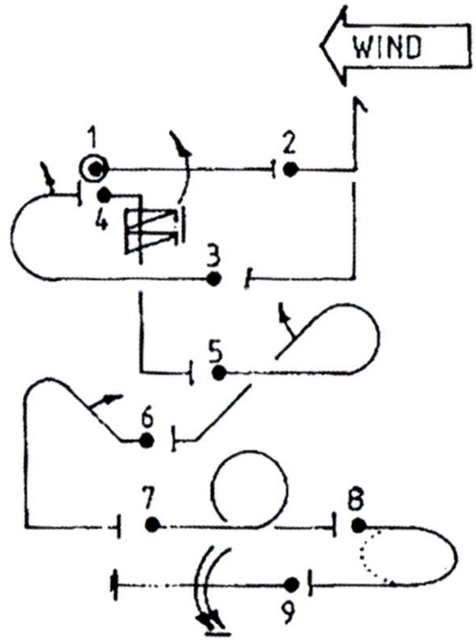

Chapter 1

SON OF THE EMPIRE

Had it not been for Adolf Hitler, or more specifically his allies in the high command of the Japanese Imperial armed forces, I would probably have been born in Malaya.

But I was not. My actual birthplace in 1946 was a maternity hospital in the dreary post-war London that Hitler, Hermann Göring and the Luftwaffe had left battered after relentless bombing campaigns. Malaya, though, was my first home and almost certainly would have been whichever of the men in my mother's life in the late 1930s had ended up as my father.

The way my mother told it, she found herself in Malaya as the result of what sounded like the aftermath of a satisfyingly boozy dinner party, during which a pig-hunting trip to Malaya had been proposed. My mother and the rest of the party (all of whom were men as it happened) lived in Cape Town, but this presented no impediment to those with the means, the freedom and the curiosity to board ship and set out to enjoy themselves in the further reaches of the British empire.

My mother was always a little vague about the success of the actual pig hunting, preferring to divert my attention and imagination to the oriental delights that she discovered. Such was her enchantment with the country that when the rest of the pig-hunting band returned to South Africa, my mother decided to stay on.

Her account depicted her as a tropical counterpart to Karen Blixen, and the *Out of Africa* analogy is strengthened by the arrival in her story of the other man who might conceivably (in both senses) have become my father.

Pat Noone was a Cambridge-educated anthropologist cast from a similar arrestingly handsome mould as Karen Blixen's lover: the big-game hunter, Denis Finch Hatton. Dashing, impeccably English and very much a man of action, my mother's portrayal of Pat Noone had him venturing deep into the jungles of Malaya to focus his intellectual talents on a tribe so detached from the 20th century that they still practised the primitive rite of headhunting. Noone's allure is enhanced by a glamorous photograph prefacing his biography, *Noone of the Ulu*, which shows him riding on his own elephant in Malaya.

(Above) Belvedere House in Calcutta where my grandmother, Jean Beatson-Bell, is thought to have spent her formative years. The house is now the National Library of India.

(Left) My great grandfather, Nicholas Beatson-Bell who is standing on the right, was the first governer of Assam.

Pat Noone on his elephant. He cuts a very romantic figure and it is easy to see the attraction he had for my mother, but however he met his end it was untimely.

Unfortunately for Noone, and quite probably for my mother at the time, the tribe he was interested in did not view him with the same degree of curiosity, or enchantment. She told me that having grown tired of Noone's constant surveillance and scrutiny they bumped him off in their time-honoured fashion, leaving her rather high and dry on the husband-hunting front.

By this stage she would almost certainly have come across the District Officer, a reserved, studious man called Andrew Goode. Describing them both to me in later life, my actual father highlighted the difference between the two men in terms he recognised that I would understand. Where Noone cruised about Malaya in the comfort and effortless power of a Ford V8 convertible, Goode was bumping about his district in an elderly MG.

However, with Noone out of the picture and, I am sure my mother told me at least once, jointed and simmering in the tribal cooking pot, Andrew Goode provided a shoulder to cry on. In the fullness of time this became an arm on which to lead his new bride down the aisle.

TRUTH BE TOLD

This is a story I have enjoyed telling over the years as much as I am sure my mother did. The only snag, as I was to discover much later and long after her demise, is that it does swerve rather disconcertingly from the truth.

Reading Noone's biography, it looks as if he and my mother met rather earlier than she would have liked me to believe; they may have got to know each other in South Africa. At the very latest, their relationship blossomed during a seaboard passage from Cape Town to Singapore. Noone had been on leave in the UK, where he had spent a couple of terms lecturing back in Cambridge.

However, their amours beneath tropical nights across the Indian Ocean could not be sustained once they reached dry land. Delving a little deeper into his book, it became clear that during the nine years he had already spent in the jungle as Field Ethnographer of the Perak Museum, Noone had developed a partiality for native teenage girls.

With their engagement broken off, Noone renewed his travels around Malaya and his former fiancée found herself faced with somewhat limited options. My mother was in a country she did not know, but where she herself was already known for slightly awkward reasons. So the presence of a nice, available man such as District Officer Andrew Goode must have made her decision to marry him relatively straightforward.

In the intimate, some might say incestuous, environment of distant colonial outposts, my mother's enforced switch of emotional allegiance could not be allowed to pass without comment. This gave rise to a celebrated episode in the Cameron Highlands Club, when a wag hailed her with the greeting, 'Hello, Goode-after-Noone.'

If these details appear sketchy, it is simply because the fleeting glimpses my parents gave me of their early life together were few and far between. Neither of them were inclined to share personal feelings, or really anything for that matter, with me. I was an only child, with no other close relatives, and I thought nothing of it when I was young. By the time it might have troubled me, I had forged my own modus vivendi which caused them so little concern that my parents and I jogged along contentedly on parallel, but never close, paths.

FORTUNE FAVOURS

Good luck, and the pattern of leave followed in the Malayan Civil Service, meant that my parents were in Cape Town, visiting my mother's family, when the Japanese invaded Malaya. For Noone, however, destiny had been less kind, although it did allow him the opportunity to show his true mettle. While the British imperial forces were swiftly driven down the Malay peninsula to their ignominious capitulation at Singapore barely a couple of months later, Noone stayed on behind enemy lines. There he rallied a guerrilla force that harried Japanese supply lines and generally caused so much turmoil and chaos for the invaders, that a hugely disproportionate number of enemy soldiers had to be deployed to combat them.

Noone would not survive this daring hit-and-run conflict. His end came, not at the hands of his Japanese pursuers, but from the jealousy of one of his girlfriend's brothers. In a way, my mother was right; Noone was killed by native Malays, just not in the way she would have had me believe.

My father came from the last generation born into the British Empire in its full, but increasingly rickety, entirety. By happy coincidence a forebear of ours, one William Goode, was working his Herefordshire farm at the turn of the 18th century not that many miles from where I work today a couple of hundred years later. But it was not long before that branch of the Goode family was on the move. William's three sons emigrated to South Australia in 1858 where they launched themselves into the burgeoning retail trade and in due course built up one of the largest chains of department stores in the state.

Among the next generation, Samuel Goode joined the Indian Civil Service after a glittering academic career first at Way College in Adelaide, and then at Cambridge University. He became Chairman of the Calcutta Corporation and the author of a worthy tome entitled *Municipal Calcutta: its institutions in their origin and growth*. It is an earnest work, filled with exhaustive research and tedious detail. It resides, somewhat reproachfully, on my bookshelf, unread.

Reproachfully because Samuel Goode was my grandfather and I fear I should have taken a greater interest in what must have been one of the principal undertakings of his career. However, we never met and I doubt that he would have taken a great deal of interest in me had we done so.

INDIAN HERITAGE

In common with many of those employed in the service of the Raj, my grandparents sent their own children back to England to be educated. As a consequence, my father and his younger brother, Richard (after whom I am named), only saw their parents during visits back to India every couple of years. To say that the two brothers barely knew who their parents were is something of an understatement, but they did have each other and formed a close bond at prep school and after that at Charterhouse.

One quality both sons inherited from their father was the formidable intellect that would earn them both first-class degrees at Cambridge. Richard would become a junior fellow at Gonville and Caius in the run-up to the outbreak of the Second World War while Andrew, a couple of years his senior, shone as a classical scholar at Trinity. Indeed, my grandparents seemed to have enjoyed parading their sons' precocious talents at an early age. I remember my father telling me that when he was three and his parents were having a dinner-party, he used to be hauled out of bed and lifted up onto the piano to recite the whole of 'Tyger, tyger burning bright' to entertain their guests, before being packed off back to bed.

Such was my father's reticence, however, that he seldom talked about himself. One detail he did reveal later in his life was that he was just pipped to the top first awarded in that year's classical final tripos, losing out by an agonisingly slim margin to the exceptional classicist and later politician Enoch Powell, who had been awarded the very rare distinction of a double-starred first. While Powell became a fellow of Trinity, my father jumped ship, so to speak, and went up to Christ Church College, Oxford to take a degree in Oriental Studies for which he achieved another first. After Oxford, he joined the Malay Civil Service, in which he soon became a District Officer and found himself running, virtually single-handedly, the 275 square miles of the very pretty part of the country that constitutes the Cameron Highlands.

Archibald Arnott, here in his British Army uniform, was the physician who took Emperor Napoleon's death mask.
Picture kindly supplied by The Fusilier Museum, Bury

By contrast Molly Arnott, my mother who later found her way to that part of the world, was anything but academic but she compensated for this with an adventurous, fun-loving disposition that would serve her very well throughout her life. The Arnotts, the men of the family that is, were largely trained as doctors. Indeed, my great-great-great uncle, Archibald Arnott, served as the British Army doctor to Napoleon Bonaparte during his final incarceration on St Helena.

Dr Arnott was the only official there that Napoleon had any time for. Prior to his death he called for a snuff box, on which he carved an 'N' with a penknife before presenting it to Arnott, along with a locket of his hair, a pair of duelling pistols and a handkerchief. And it was Archibald Arnott who took Napoleon's death mask the night after the Emperor's demise; Napoleon had given explicit instructions that Arnott was the only English physician permitted to touch his body.

MOTHER'S RUIN

Much of my mother's family history is a bit sketchy, due in large measure to a major falling out between her two brothers over a property deal involving the sale of the sizeable family home in Cape Town that had gone seriously wrong. The brothers never spoke to each other again following the incident, and such a schism split the family that whenever she was visiting back home, my mother was only able to see them individually.

Against this backdrop of seething fraternal tension, my mother seems to have enjoyed a comparatively carefree life punctuated by parties, visits to the Cape Town races and travelling. I doubt that she ever spared a thought for the burning

My father, Andrew Goode, was always keen on riding and whether in Asia or Africa he had ponies.

injustices of racial inequality that would lead to the establishment of apartheid and the ANC struggle for black liberation of later decades.

As a child, I was never really certain when my parents were born. My mother was a little guarded about her age, especially as it turned out she was a couple of years older than my father. But she was definitely getting on by the conventions of her day when they tied the knot in the early stages of the European war. In fact, soon after the war started, my father went to his superiors to ask if there was anything he should be doing. Their reply was that whatever Germany was up to in Europe was no concern of theirs, and his job was to carry on the good work in Malaya. That, of course, was brought to a halt by the arrival of his next six-month spell of leave, when he and my mother sailed from Singapore to Cape Town and the Japanese army sailed across the Gulf of Thailand to start the war in the Pacific.

Even by this early stage of the Second World War my father had become an only child after his brother had been killed serving in the RAFVR. The Hampden bomber in which Richard Goode was navigator had been shot down over Belgium during a raid on the docks at Antwerp, on 17 September 1940, 16 days before his 25th birthday.

Finding himself somewhat high and dry, my father decided to present himself to the British authorities in Cape Town to explain his predicament. They were not quite sure what to do with a member of the Malayan Civil Service, but after a bit of faffing about he was packed off to India and then to Ceylon, where he served on Mountbatten's staff and ended the war with the rank of lieutenant colonel in the Royal Corps of Signals. Meanwhile my mother found herself back home, on the opposite side of the Indian Ocean, seeing out the war in the fractured atmosphere of family life in Cape Town.

As far as she must have been concerned, the Second World War had taken a pretty big chunk of what was left of her biological breeding time. The Colonial Office too had not been slow to realise that they, too, needed to get moving swiftly. British rule had to be restored to freshly-liberated parts of the empire before the King Emperor's subjects dotted about the globe started getting ideas about self-government.

UP AND AWAY

My father was summoned back to London to select, recruit and train the new wave of post-war colonial administrators. My mother did not waste any time in joining him, because I made my appearance on 1 March 1946, which means I must have been conceived within a month of the end of the war in Europe. By

Clearly enjoying my bath, this is the period that we were living in Government House, Kuala Lumpur.

the time I was born, my father had been sent back to Malaya, this time to serve as a District Commissioner. So, when I was only six weeks old, my mother and I set off to be reunited with him, undertaking what was probably a week-long journey in the questionable comfort of a Vickers Viking: a twin-engined, ex-military transport plane.

My first experience of flying was lent added drama when the aircraft hit such violent turbulence along the North African coast that my mother was flung upwards forcefully enough to crack open her head. With me in tow and blood gushing from a deep gash in her scalp, she was rushed to hospital to be patched up the moment the plane landed to refuel in Cairo.

I cannot be sure how long this first posting of my father's lasted. But we lived in the bungalow that came with it long enough for me to register a very early memory of the punkah-wallah, who manually powered the ceiling fan, rhythmically

Pictured with my mother, it strikes me that while my parents were always somewhat distant figures, they were in their way very loving towards their only son.

tugging at his rope to create a cooling draught while my father sat working at his desk. Once he had found his feet again after his five-year absence from Malaya, my father was promoted to serve as ADC to the Governor, which brought with it a move to Kuala Lumpur and a nice flat in Government House.

This splendid residence was positioned on a hill that gave me my first taste of independent speed. I have a hazy recollection of being in my pram when it began moving down the slope, gathering pace as it did. Whether I had played any part in getting it going I cannot remember, but I do have a clear image of the amah, the nursemaid who looked after me, diving panic-struck in a desperate attempt to stop the pram and hurting herself quite badly in the process. Meanwhile I trundled down the hill emerging a little startled, but otherwise none the worse when I came to a halt at the bottom.

I got into distinctly hotter water some time later, after I took it upon myself to use my crayons to embellish the elegant silk wall coverings that decorated the public rooms in Government House. My father was hauled over the coals for that little outpouring of creative expression, but the lesson that I should not repeat it was not lost on me either.

Promotion within the Malayan Civil Service swiftly moved my father to a new post and a new house in Kuala Lumpur called West Folly, a large colonial residence set in its own two-acre tropical garden. While my father settled back into the work of a colonial administrator, life was not so easy for my mother. For one thing she had had me, although I do not think I was ever a source of too great a distraction from things she enjoyed in her early days in Kuala Lumpur. There were bridge parties, visits to the races, plus a pretty busy social round of dinner- and cocktail-parties.

For some reason, that again I have difficulty in accounting for, she began to adopt a rather more serious approach to life. Perhaps it was her way of responding to the

Looking back on these times they were a great adventure. Here with my father as I sit on the bonnet of the Willys Jeep station wagon.

war. Malaya and Singapore had witnessed some of the worst excesses of a brutal occupation. Or, perhaps it was a sense of duty brought on by motherhood. Whatever the cause, quite on her own initiative, when I was three-and-a-half she set up a half-way house for convicts newly released from prison in Kuala Lumpur. I have a very early memory of going there with her. Even allowing for my distorted perception as a toddler, it was a pretty big set up and, for the most part, proved to be a great success.

It was also a gutsy undertaking; on a couple of occasions my mother was beaten up by inmates and at times the atmosphere could get very intimidating. But, to her great credit, the majority of the men she took in really appreciated what she was doing for them and they frequently rallied round to screen her if any of the others started getting a bit overheated. Come the Queen's accession in 1953, my mother was awarded a Coronation Medal in acknowledgement of her important work with these ex-prisoners for whom, I imagine, the future would otherwise have looked pretty bleak.

LANGUAGE BARRIER

The one advantage of living at the periphery of my parents' lives is that I got a taste for pretty much unfettered freedom at a very early age. I must have played with the offspring of their friends and colleagues, but most of the time I mucked about with the children of the staff that worked in the house and garden. They spoke Malay, naturally, as did their parents and my parents. So, when I started talking, I spoke Malay too and I knew nothing else.

And I knew no difference until my first venture abroad, when I was approaching four and my father's next six-month spell of leave came around. We took a ship to Cape Town and, being a gregarious little boy, I made it my business to chat to people during the passage. I addressed them, naturally, in fluent Malay and was mildly surprised that I got no replies, apart from slightly surprised responses from Malay-speaking members of the crew. A bigger shock awaited me in Cape Town, where my one surviving grandparent, my formidable maternal grandmother, was horrified to discover that I could not speak a word of English.

It would be interesting to know how my parents explained that fundamental oversight, but it was quickly rectified. Packing them off for a couple of months to travel around South Africa, my grandmother enrolled me into a smart kindergarten and by the time my mother and father returned to gather me up, I was close to bilingual.

My parents and I returned to Africa for my father's next period of leave, when I was seven years old. I could tell that there was going to be something special about this visit because he had bought a new Willys Jeep, which was shipped to South Africa with us. Once again, we landed in Cape Town, where a rudimentary metal roof was mounted on the jeep and two jerry cans were fitted to boost our petrol reserves. My parents also fitted a trailer to carry our gear, because we were setting off to travel deep into Africa for several months entirely by ourselves. For today's security-conscious overland drivers, our transport would have looked perilously vulnerable to theft but, in those days, it just did not seem to be an issue.

Surveying the post-war world and casting her mind forward, with my father's future career prospects in mind, my mother had concluded that Asia was finished and that the future lay in Africa. It may seem hard to reconcile that point of view with what has subsequently happened in much of sub-Saharan Africa, but in the

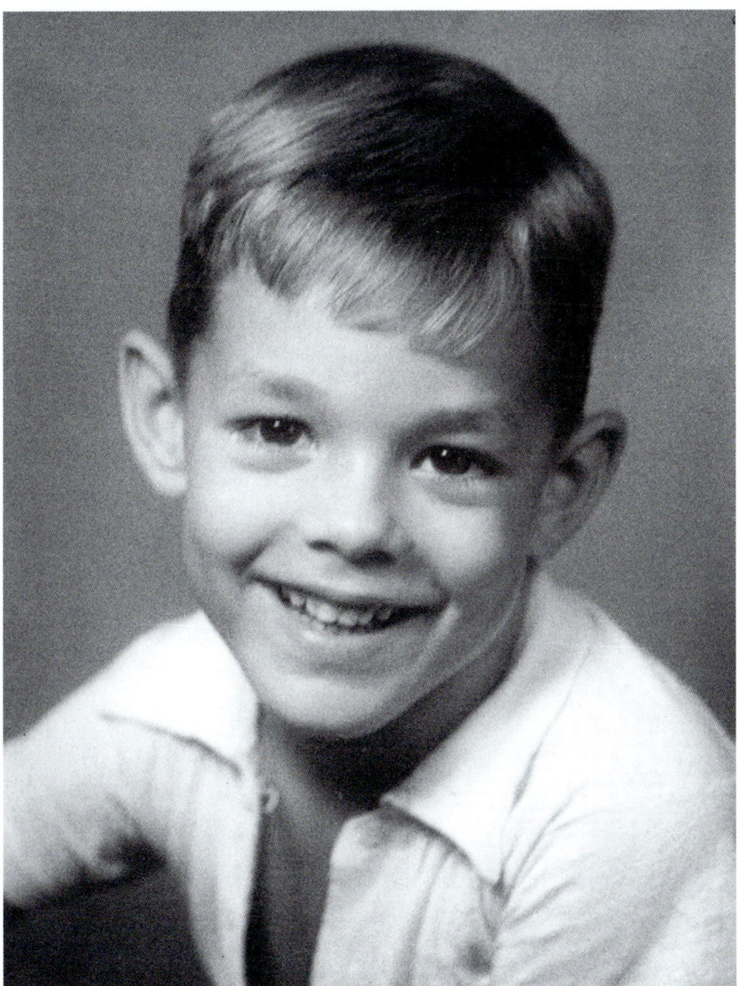

A rather charming photo, although I do say so myself!

1950s there was a very positive vibe running through the continent, generated by a lot of investment. The new Federation of Rhodesia and Nyasaland had recently come into being and looked like offering big opportunities. At the same time plans were well advanced for a massive construction project to build the Kariba Dam, which was scheduled to bring power, and the commercial development that would follow, to large areas of the territory. Although I was not told at the time, it became clear that one of my parents' objectives on this trip was to find somewhere to buy.

AFRICAN QUEST

It was Christmas time, midsummer in the southern hemisphere, when we set forth, travelling quite extensively in South Africa itself before crossing into Rhodesia, where my father had some cousins living in Salisbury. Where there were hotels in large cities, we could stay in a degree of comfort. For most of the journey, however, we either made do with whatever makeshift accommodation we could find, or were welcomed into the homes of other Europeans, marooned and cut off from western contacts.

Although the monotony of dusty, bumpy roads, did get pretty boring for me stuck in the back seat, it proved to be a trip of considerable contrasts. I remember that we spent days on the shore of Lake Nyasa, a huge inland sea as far as I was concerned. I loved swimming and spent most of my time either splashing about in the water or staring earnestly at it trying to catch fish. At higher altitudes, it became quite chilly at night and for the first time in my life I started wearing a jersey to keep warm.

From Nyasaland we travelled north visiting the Congo, Rwanda and Burundi – which I remember as a beautiful country – Uganda and Tanganyika. In all, we were travelling for four months, with quite long stop-overs in places we liked. Our quest ended in the Vumba Mountains, in north-east Rhodesia very close to the border with Mozambique and it was here that my parents settled on the property they had been on the lookout for. Quite how they found it, I have no idea, but it was incredibly pretty, with wonderful views over the Burma Valley.

At 6,000 feet above sea level, the 500 acres my father bought did not have much agricultural value. To complicate matters, 200 acres of it lay at the bottom of a 3,000-foot sheer cliff. We could look down on it and through field glasses could see a load of fantastically valuable teak. But there was not a road for 20 miles and no way any timber could be extracted.

However, there was another tree that did have commercial potential. This was the wattle, one of nature's most efficient and productive creations, which is blessed with the great commercial attraction of providing a double crop: the bark was used for tanning leather and, after 10 years' growth, the trunks were turned into telegraph poles. It was just my father's bad luck that, nine years into the growth cycle of his crop, some clever chemist developed an artificial tanning agent that did the same job as wattle bark, but far cheaper! Not that this put my father off. He kept the land for another 25 years and offered it to me, before finally selling it after I had to explain that taking it on was even more impractical for me than it had been for him.

While my father was going through the formalities of buying the land, we stayed about 12 miles away at the celebrated Leopard Rock Hotel, which lived up to its name by having outcrops of bare rock protruding into many of the rooms. It was a pretty special place to stay 60 years ago and is now among the prime tourist destinations in that part of Africa.

My first visit to the Vumba is logged in my memory for another, more sobering reason. Like almost every colonial family, our closest neighbours, a very nice American family called the Achesons, had a fair number of staff to whom I used to go and chat. One day I popped in to find that one of them had died during the night.

As a seven-year-old child, the sight of a young man to whom I had been speaking only a day or two before, laid out dead on his bed, made a powerful impression, although interestingly, this was not something from which my parents tried to shield me. I think they felt I might as well get used to the idea of mortality and meeting death face to face in this way was probably better for me than the shock of suddenly being confronted with a far more gruesome and distressing sight.

From the Vumba mountains we drove north to Uganda. There my father arranged for the jeep to be shipped back to the Far East, though not to Malaya, for he had been given a new appointment in North Borneo and that was where the jeep was heading, to be followed by us a few weeks later.

In the meantime, we boarded a Comet 1 at Entebbe and flew to the UK, where my father had meetings at the Colonial Office. We landed at London Airport (as Heathrow was then called) in early June 1953, a couple of days after the Coronation. A new job, a new country, a new jeep and my mother now needed a new car as well. So, one of the places we visited was the Longbridge motor factory, where my father bought her a Morris Minor straight off the production line. I vividly remember our being allowed inside the factory to watch the cars being built.

MINOR MATTERS

Then we ran it in, touring around England for a few weeks visiting relatives, including my godmother Aunt Muriel. A little over a decade later, she was kind enough to leave me money in her will all of which I used to buy the car that kick-started what would become my lifelong interest in classic British motors. But I am getting ahead of myself. Between my mother's new Morris Minor and the fruits of Aunt Muriel's generous bequest lay the small matter of education, of which I had not had a great deal in the orthodox sense.

But, where to send me to school? Back to England like my father and most other offspring of people posted overseas? Maybe somewhere nearer to my parents' new posting?

The choices seemed obvious, though not apparently to either of them. When I was packed off to school a year later, it was to neither of these destinations.

Eagle School was conveniently close to my father's recently-acquired land in the Vumba, and that was where I was bound. The fact that my new school was several thousand miles away from my home, on a different continent and without a single person I knew did not seem to be a consideration, at least not as far as my mother and father were concerned.

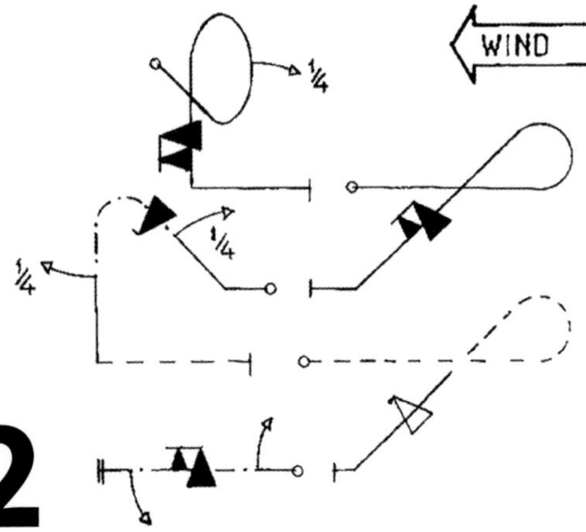

Chapter 2

WILD MAN FROM BORNEO

Although my parents' approach to child rearing was unorthodox, it is only fair to say that it did equip me surprisingly well for school and for boarding school in a different continent in particular.

I had not been at Eagle very long before I became known as the Wild Man from Borneo, which even in those early days I regarded more as a badge of honour than a term of contempt.

The nickname my schoolmates gave me was not entirely misplaced. I was more or less a stranger to shoes or shirts and certainly did not take willingly to donning the Eagle uniform of khaki shorts, blue shirts and school shoes for weeks on end. Then there was the issue of toilet habits. There were no doors on the lavatories at Eagle, so word quickly spread through the school that the new boy Goode went to the loo in a quite bizarre way. Instead of sitting on the seat in an orthodox western posture, it was natural for me to squat just like everyone I had ever seen in the Far East. Perched above the pan at Eagle like an ape attending to its alimentary business, it is hardly surprising that I attracted some comment.

By contrast I was well advanced academically. In the months before I went to Eagle, my father had farmed me out to a Roman Catholic priest three times a week, so that he could teach me Latin, which gave me a significant head start at prep school.

(Left) Leopard Rock Hotel, very near the land that my father purchased and indeed near to the Eagle School.

(Below) This is taken from the brochure about the Vumba, widely seen as a lovely holiday destination in Rhodesia.

My father's promotion that had taken him, my mother and me to North Borneo, was to serve as Financial Secretary, in other words as second-in-command, to the Governor and Commander-in-Chief, Major-General Sir Ralph Hone. Like my father, Hone had served at SEAC HQ, where his long friendship with Mountbatten had begun. He had ended the war in Malaya and had been present at the Japanese surrender at Singapore on 12 September 1945.

North Borneo had suffered more than most territories occupied by the Japanese. With 16 per cent of the population being killed during those three years, 'the whole community descended into hell', according to one historian of modern Malaya. Liberation in the summer of 1945 had been prefaced by heavy Allied bombing and wartime damage was still very evident when we moved to Jesselton, the capital, where our home was one of only three two-storey houses still standing.

HEAVEN'S GATE

While my father became absorbed in his new job, my mother wasted little time in filling her days. She was always a keen gardener and our garden at Jesselton quickly acquired a fabulous collection of orchids. She played a lot of bridge. She played a lot of golf too. In fact, she quickly established herself as one of the foremost women golfers in North Borneo, which led to her becoming an 'international', representing Borneo in Commonwealth and other international competitions for amateur golfers.

She had always been very keen on dogs and in Jesselton acquired a couple of Bornean Hunting Dogs, the kind used by the native people out hunting for game. I remember her trying to have them officially registered by the Kennel Club, which shows her enthusiasm for the breed. After a while my parents built a small weekend retreat, not dissimilar to one that I now enjoy in our Herefordshire woods. This was a simple wooden hut on a section of beach that lay between the sea and a lagoon. The sea was about a hundred yards away and our hut backed onto the lagoon. It had a rudimentary kitchen where the cook prepared our meals. The loo was a Heath-Robinson structure perched on stilts over the lagoon. I struggle to think what the authorities would make of that arrangement today, but it served our needs.

My father's position also gave him use of the official government launch, of the kind yacht brokers would term a 'fully-crewed gentleman's motor yacht'. This could comfortably sleep eight people (which meant that I had a cabin all to myself) and gave us the means to set off for a weekend, sometimes four or five days, to

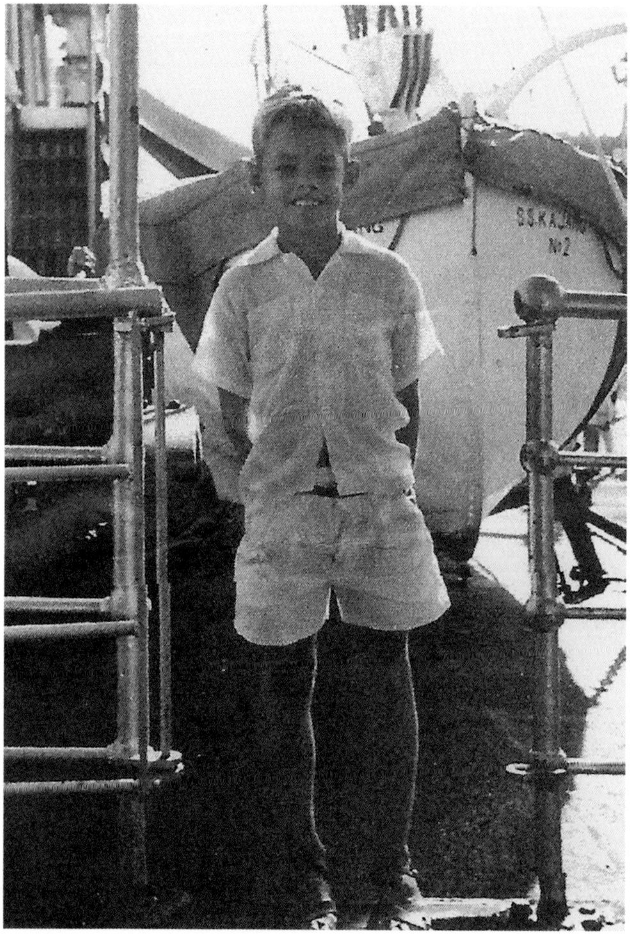

On a ship going to Africa in 1955.

explore the coastline and outlying islands. Sometimes we would anchor off a totally deserted island for the night, where the cook and crew brought ashore provisions and bedding, so that we could spend the night on the beach and under the stars.

The charity work my mother had begun in Malaya continued in North Borneo, although the focus of her attention switched from ex-prisoners to TB sufferers. There was a distressingly large number of these unfortunate people, not just in Jesselton, but in remote villages, deep in the jungle, where there was virtually no medical treatment available.

In the middle of the 20th century, less than 70 years ago, TB was the number one killer disease in the colony. Those patients who could be brought to hospital, lay on their beds suffering appallingly, while the medical staff did what they could in the face of such large numbers of very sick people. Out in the countryside, TB patients died untreated and largely unnoticed.

My mother had been one of the founders of the North Borneo Anti-Tuberculosis Association (NOBATA), to which most of the senior officials in the colony and their wives lent their support. Her hard work and commitment earned her an MBE. This and her Coronation Medal meant that officially she outranked my father, until he was awarded an OBE a few years later.

My mother's involvement extended far beyond genteel fund-raising tea-parties and the occasional ball. I remember her disappearing on horseback, for weeks on end, when she travelled into the mountainous jungle interior, seeking out TB patients and arranging for them to be brought to the hospital in Jessleton. There, treatment with streptomycine and a greater understanding of tuberculosis was beginning to turn the tide and offer hope of a lasting cure.

Sometimes when she was travelling into less remote areas, she let me go with her and we would set off on our horses, carrying everything we needed for an expedition lasting a good many days. The villages in which we stayed were incredibly primitive with simple bamboo huts thatched with palm leaves, although one village I particularly enjoyed visiting had hot and cold running water, thanks to a thermal spring and some ingenious bamboo pipework. Some enterprising villagers had channeled the constant flow of hot spring water, and another source of cold water, out of the hillside through bamboo pipes into a very large wooden bathing tub. So there, in the middle of the Borneo jungle, you could enjoy a bath with water as hot as you wanted. All you had to do to regulate the temperature was to push one pipe or the other over the side until the water was exactly as you liked it. I thought it was wonderful and I still love long, long hot baths, in which I can read and relax. That, for me, is a very great pleasure.

CLOSE SHAVES

Looking back, I can see that we lived life much closer to the edge than families in the West. Maybe this created a degree of fatalism in my parents' outlook. When I was a little boy there were certainly a couple of instances when my well-being caused them a great deal of anxiety.

Exploring one of our outhouses, I came across a wild cat skulking in the shadows. It was a big fellow, the size of a small dog. Not perturbed by this, I went to make friends with it saying 'Kitty, Kitty, Kitty' and extending my hand to stroke it. I could tell it was hungry and probably hoped that with food and friendship I could tame it. The wild cat had other ideas and made a run for it, although it did stop momentarily on its rush to freedom to give my hand a vicious bite. That rapidly became septic and produced a huge ball of pus hanging below my upper arm. The sepsis leached into my bloodstream and landed me in hospital, where I lay very uncomfortably and really quite ill for 10 days.

An even greater concern for parents was my other childhood health scare, when I caught malaria in a very remote mountain town called Ranau. We used to visit Ranau from time to time, although the place had a very dark recent history. During the war it had been the destination for a series of death marches imposed on Allied prisoners of war, of whom 2,345 had died. A decade after the end of the war, Ranau was still only approachable on foot or by flying in aboard a twin-engine, eight-seater biplane called a de Havilland Rapide. There were only two motor vehicles in the town, former US army jeeps that had been carried up in pieces from the coast on the backs of mules.

HIGH FLYING

Ranau, then, was not the best place to contract malaria and for an eight-year-old running a temperature of 106degF with only makeshift medical facilities available, the consensus was that I was going to die. A bout of malaria comes in phases. Having had it three times in my life, that is a detail with which I am all too familiar. Typically, there is a 48-hour cycle which starts with an incredible fever. That calms down for a while before returning with an even worse fever. The sufferer progresses through peaks and troughs until it gradually fades and passes after 10 days or so.

Drifting in and out of waves of soaring temperatures, I remember hearing grown-up whispers that I was not going to make it. However, one very brave pilot agreed to try and rescue me. Flying into Ranau and landing on the saturated racecourse was going to be tricky enough, but the real challenge lay in taking off again. To have any chance of doing this successfully, they needed to make the aeroplane as light as possible, so the pilot had all the spare seats removed. This also ensured that there would be space for the stretcher to which I was securely lashed, to be tied down to the floor to prevent any futher injury during the most perilous part of the mission.

With just the two of us on board, the pilot pushed the engines to maximum revs, released the brakes and set off on his first attempt. As the wheels ploughed through one huge puddle after another, clouds of spray smashed against the fuselage windows. I can vividly remember that the noise was deafening.

Our first take-off failed, as did the second, and the third. As we turned around to have a fourth go, the pilot said something as much to himself as to me that we simply did not have enough room to get clear of the sodden ground. By now anyone watching us, presumably my parents included, would have realised that my survival and that of the pilot was very much touch and go. This time the thundering from the wheels and the vibrating fuselage, and the violent lashing of spray against the windows faded as we crawled into the sky above Ranau, and set course for Jesselton, an ambulance and a hospital bed. It was another four days before conditions on the ground at Ranau improved sufficiently for the Rapide to fetch my parents and bring them down to Jesselton to be reunited with me.

Delightful as jaunts with my parents were, I have to say that they were the exception rather than the rule in the Goode household in North Borneo. My father used to start work in his office at seven o'clock in the morning, before knocking off at two. So, we would have breakfast together at around six o'clock. My mother's days were always well filled and during term time I was packed off to a kind of pre-prep day school. I was reasonably well taught there, because when I arrived at Eagle at the start of the following year, the Wild Man from Borneo, was right up with the clever boys in the school.

The obvious companion for me to play with in Jesselton would have been the Governor's son, Richard Hone. However, our friendship was brief and ended abruptly for reasons that I cannot remember. My parents were guarded about what had happened, but clearly I had committed an act of grave misconduct so severe that Richard Hone was forbidden by his parents from ever associating with me again. As it turned out, he was destined to be packed off to school in England not long after. But I am still puzzled about what exactly I had done to bring about such a stern interdiction.

HAPPY GO LUCKY

Fortunately, my Chinese truck driver friends proved to be more steadfast. There was a lot of post-war reconstruction taking place in and around Jesselton while we were there, and the Chinese drivers had a base three or four miles from our house. During the school holidays I got into the habit of setting off on my little bicycle every morning to spend the day riding in their trucks converted from wartime military vehicles, which were pretty unreliable.

I chatted away to them in Malay and I often shared their lunch. I would certainly spend whole days in their company, before bicycling home in the evening and none of this was kept secret from parents. They would ask what I had been doing, I would tell them and they would show polite interest. The one thing they did not show, at least as far as I could gauge, was any concern about who I had been with. I imagine that the idea of an eight-year-old boy getting chummy with a group of Chinese HGV drivers and spending whole days with them rattling round in pretty dodgy lorries would horrify parents today. But mine seemed to accept that I had not come to any harm and probably would not do so, as proved to be the case, of course.

This, then, was the tropical life from which schooling plucked me at the age of eight and set me off down the orthodox road of English education. I use the word 'English' deliberately, because even though Eagle School was situated in the Vumba Mountains near Umtali, in north-east Rhodesia, its ethos was very much that of an English prep school.

In fact, Eagle had the same school motto as the Dragon School in Oxford; 'Arduus ad Solem', or 'Striving towards the sun' in English. Whether it was by accident or design, the freedom my parents had given me to discover life for myself at what was still a very early age, set me up well for the rough and tumble of boarding school in a strange country and started me on a trajectory of attainment I have tried to follow ever since.

As I mentioned earlier, my mother was the prime mover in the decision to send me to Eagle. It was conveniently close to the land my father had bought, of course. The snag as far as I was concerned was that my parents were not actually living there and never would be. My mother did accompany me when I first went

Eagle school was beautifully situated if extremely isolated. During the later terror attacks in Rhodesia the school was closed.

to Eagle and she stayed in the Acheson's garden house for a month while I was settling in. After she went home I was left to fend for myself, but for the first time in my life I found myself in the constant company of a group of boys who were either my own age or just a few years older. Enclosed by hills, Eagle was also surrounded by stunning scenery, which made it an enjoyable place to be at school. Thanks to my father's quiet, but perceptive, preparation I did not seem to have any difficulty with schoolwork, while my love of swimming helped me gain a place in the Manicaland provincial swimming team.

Like most prep and public schools, we had games every afternoon, playing the usual variety of school sports; I enjoyed rugby especially. My one enduring disappointment from the playing fields of Eagle came on the cricket square. Even when I was a little boy I had been drawn to Rolex watches. To be precise, I was deeply impressed by the classic Rolex advertisements I used to see in the kinds of international magazines my father read, such as *Time*. These Rolex ads used to show a man, photographed from the neck downwards, who was clearly a major statesman. There would be a glimpse of his watch and below the picture was the statement 'Men who guide the destinies of the world wear a Rolex.'

It was incredibly good advertising and certainly made such an impression on me that I was given a Rolex for my ninth birthday. It was an Air-King Rolex, the cheapest model they made, but it was a Rolex – a real Rolex. (Interestingly, the company has reintroduced the Air-King back into the range in the last few years, but this time as a rather up-market watch.)

It was my pride and joy. I wore it everywhere. I wore it swimming. I wore it playing cricket and that was my undoing. It was when I was batting that I must have misjudged a delivery and the ball thudded into my wrist. Despite wearing batting gloves, my watch was smashed beyond repair. I cried and cried, not believing that I could have been so stupid.

EAGLE HAS LANDED

Eagle School had been founded in 1948 and its ornithological associations permeated the organisation of our lives. The dormitories were named after types of eagle, the sports houses were called Swifts, Swallows and Martins. There were 120 boys in the school when I was there, presided over by an inspirational headmaster called Claude Mellor. It was he who really introduced me to classical music. My parents used to listen to gramophone records. Radio reception in Borneo was so patchy that the gramophone was our principal source of entertainment at home. On the whole, they preferred light music, so encountering the classical repertoire at school was another revelation as far as I was concerned. Mellor used to invite us by rotation. A dozen boys at a time would join him for a light supper of something like scrambled eggs before we sat down and listened to whatever programme he had arranged for that particular evening. It was a clever thing for him to have done. Supper added a sense of occasion to the evening and the music he selected certainly made an impression on me and fostered my love of classical music that has remained ever since.

I maintained the link with my parents by way of the thin blue airmail aerogrammes we used to exchange. I wrote home avidly and my father was very good at keeping up a steady flow of replies. His letters were pretty anodyne and never conveyed very much, but it was good to have that contact. My mother did not write to me nearly as much.

However, there was one aspect of my first term at Eagle which I can honestly say they handled very badly and that was failing to tell me what was going to happen to me at the end of term. Most other boys lived somewhere in Rhodesia and there was no question about where they would be spending the school holidays. They would be going home, even if that meant a day or two travelling by train or car. But my parents were 6,000 miles away on the far side of the Indian Ocean and even at the age of eight I realised that the logistics of travelling in the mid-1950s made going home to Borneo a non-starter.

My problem was that no one had told me what would happen to me when term ended and the other boys had dispersed. I honestly thought that I was going to be spending the holiday all on my own at school. What I did not know was that my parents had asked the school which boys I was friendly with. My father then approached their parents to ask whether I might be able spend school holidays with them. Two families, the Wenbournes and the Hills, took it in turn to add me to their family groups. Richard Hill and I were in the same class at Eagle but it was close to the end of my first term before I found out what I would be doing when it ended and I remember being very worried until I was told. Frankly, simply knowing that some plan was in place was relief enough.

As it turned out, staying with either the Wenbournes or the Hills proved to be a very happy arrangement. Both families were wealthy farmers with four or five kids, so it was a novel experience to be living in a household with other children. Although their farms were fairly isolated, they had a good social life centred on a club where farming families in the area used to meet at the weekends to watch films and generally get together with friends.

The one annual trip I did make home was for the holiday at the end of the school year, which in Rhodesia fell at Christmas and for this I travelled by air. I was nine years old the first time and it was quite an adventure. To begin with, I went by train to Salisbury, where a distant cousin of one of my parents met me and gave me a bed until the first flight of my dog-leg odyssey back to Jesselton was due to depart. From Salisbury I flew up to Nairobi, where the plane linked up with the South African flight. My route then took me up to Aden to join the Asian route, where I boarded the flight to Singapore.

As it happened, the Governor of Singapore at that time was a man called Bill Goode. Although no relation, my father and he were friends through the colonial service. So, the governor's ADC was detailed to meet me off the plane and put me up for the night before loading me on to a DC3 for the final leg of my journey down through Kuching and Brunei, and finally back to Borneo.

I made that journey three or four times during my spell at Eagle and became fairly relaxed about what was still fairly crude flying at that time. Most of the planes were unpressurised and although we only flew up to a height of 6,000 or 7,000 feet, I remember the altitude giving me appalling earache. Then there was the occasion, flying in an Argonaut at night over Kenya when one of the Merlin engines caught fire. That was quite sporting, with big flames licking back over the wing. The crew, of course, were highly trained. The engines had in-built fire extinguishers, but they still had to switch off the one that had caught fire and return to Nairobi. That added at least a couple of days to the journey while we waited for BOAC to rustle up a back-up plane. Flying into Jesselton once from Singapore in another DC3, the pilot slightly misjudged the landing and we ended up off the runway with the nose of the plane buried in very thick mud.

On one of my return trips to Borneo, my father came up with the idea of flying me from Salisbury to Johannesburg and then taking the recently inaugurated South African Airways route which flew from Johannesburg to Mauritius, then to the Cocos Islands and from there to Perth (a flight of 21 hours). From Perth I flew to Singapore and finally on to Borneo. It was then one of the longest flights over sea in a DC7B! It was quite exciting for a 10 year-old!

Flying with BOAC at that age qualified me to become a member of the Junior Jet Club. Once you had flown a certain number of sectors, you were given a badge and a log book that the captain would fill in and sign to record how far you had flown on that particular flight. You got a special certificate after you had flown 25,000 miles. However, getting my log book filled in and signed was not a high priority for me on that first journey back to Borneo. I should have been in high spirits but I remember having serious worries, nightmares would be too strong a description, but I was really very concerned and upset about what would happen when I arrived back in Borneo and faced an unusual and concerning predicament.

I simply could not remember what my parents looked like. I did not know what would happen if I failed to recognise them or, worse still, if they failed to recognise me. I imagined myself wondering disconsolately around the airport at Jesselton abandoned and alone. It was completely illogical, of course, but when you are only nine, tired after a week of travel and scared, logic does rather fly out of the window.

Of course, my parents did recognise me and, in their own way, seemed happy to see me again and we went out for a special meal to mark my return. We used to go to local restaurants fairly often. They were primitive places by European standards, but the food was plentiful and tasty.

Since neither my father nor my mother were very emotional people, my return from Eagle for that first long holiday was rather low-key. I do remember my father taking a close interest in my school report, which was largely favourable. They used to give books as school prizes and during my time at prep school I picked up a respectable haul. Otherwise my life reverted to how it had been a year earlier and six weeks after getting home it was time to pack my bags and embark on the week-long journey back to Rhodesia to begin my second year at Eagle. This established a pattern that was repeated year on year as I made my way up through the school.

UNUSUAL ROUTINE

The environment created at Eagle was deliberately very hardy. We got up at 6.30 every morning and had a cold shower. In winter it was chilly and we were glad to wear pullovers during the day. Although the great majority of boys were used to having house servants at home, it was part of the school philosophy that all the manual work, including the cleaning, tidying the grounds, doing the gardening and tending the cricket pitch was undertaken by the boys. The domestic staff were all black, principally employed working in the kitchen. We may have come from privileged backgrounds, certainly as far as black Africans were concerned, but as pupils at Eagle we were made to work as hard in and around the school as we were expected to work in the classroom.

On one occasion our domestic duties and our lessons were brought together in an unforgettable and never-to-be-repeated incident. The setting was the first lesson of the day which was always Latin. Among my classmates was a mean-spirited and frankly rather horrid little boy. His name escapes me, which is probably just as well. He had returned to school with a bar of chocolate that his parents had put away from prying eyes, but which he had found. There was an understanding that we shared sweets and other goodies with friends at school. But this particular boy ignored that convention, which probably accounted for much of his unpopularity. Instead of handing round the chocolate, he scoffed the whole bar all by himself, late at night when we were tucked up in our dormitories.

What he did not realise was that the chocolate was branded Exlax for a good reason. Just one square would have been enough to sort out constipation in a child; an entire bar of 20 or so squares had truly dramatic consequences, as we were soon to discover. Back to our Latin lesson, which had not been going terribly long before the boy stood up, looking for attention. This was followed by the sound of a sort of

Eagle rugby team. I am second from the right, middle row. On the right is the excellent Claude Mellor who was a superb headmaster.

distant thunder heralding the torrent of very thin black liquid that poured out of his shorts and grew into a revolting fetid pool around him. The boy was quickly packed off to the sanatorium, where matron had the unenviable task of cleaning him up and looking after a pupil who was now really quite unwell.

It was little better for the rest of us. We were beside ourselves in a combination of hilarity and horror and laughing so much that the Latin master made us clean up the mess, which was the most awful thing to have to do. That fellow was an exception and I got on well with most of the boys at Eagle. In one comment to my parents in an early report Mellor described me as a cheerful little boy, ‘invariably covered in ink or bicycle grease’. He made a point of writing to them again when I was in my last year, offering his congratulations on my recent performance playing the title role in *Macbeth*. I enjoyed taking part in school plays and this was a performance that left me feeling rather proud. Not only had I learned the whole part of Macbeth as a 12 year-old, but I had managed to perform it without once having to trouble the prompter to feed me my next line.

FALCON RECRUIT

During my time at Eagle my father, having spent more than 20 years in the colonial office, had decided to leave not just North Borneo, but the government service entirely. After that he did not work for a year, spending the time travelling the world with my mother. They went to North America, and Europe, as well as South Africa of course. The occasional postcard from Las Vegas or some other exotic location would find its way to me at Eagle. The interesting point was that no one seemed to think taking a year off was unusual. My father was generally such a prudent man, that I suspect he already had his next job lined up and had arranged with this new employer to take an initial six months’ unpaid leave which would follow on from his official six months’ leave.

The organisation he was joining was the excellent Commonwealth Development Corporation, which had commercial interests throughout the Commonwealth ranging from large-scale agricultural programmes to emerging aviation businesses. My father’s first posting, at the regional headquarters in Rhodesia, only lasted for three months. For that short period of time, I actually found myself at school in the same country as my parents. They were soon on the move again, however, this time to the main HQ in London where my father spent a year getting up to speed on the way CDC ran things. After that my parents upped sticks once again and returned to southern Africa for my father to take up the job for which he had been recruited: running a huge ranch in Swaziland that covered upwards of 200,000 acres and employed over 2,000 people.

While all this was going on, I was concentrating on the Common Entrance exam which we all took at the end of our time at Eagle. In the normal course of events, how you performed in Common Entrance determined whether or not you would be accepted at your chosen public school. In my case, and that of a good many of our classmates, sitting Common Entrance was a formality. Eagle School was closely associated with Falcon College, near Bulawayo on the other side of Rhodesia, which was a natural destination for a lot of boys educated at Eagle. That was where I and many of my friends were heading. Home for me may no longer have been North Borneo, but at least I would continue my schooling in Rhodesia. Weighing up all the changes that were taking place, that provided an element of continuity to balance against my peripatetic family life.

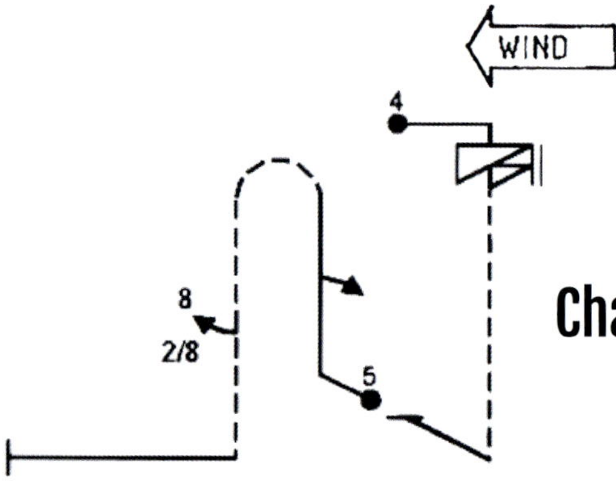

Chapter 3

SIC ITUR AD ASTRA

Where Eagle had nestled in a bowl of hills, Falcon sprawled over a large area of old mine workings, dotted with pretty basic buildings and flat-topped spoil heaps.

The ethos of self-dependence that we had come to know at Eagle carried through to Falcon. When the first pupils arrived, they found two large areas that had been bulldozed out of the virgin land and the first task they faced was collecting and removing stones in order to sow the grass seed that would grow to form their playing fields.

As at Eagle, school life was deliberately hardy at Falcon. We used to wear shorts and open-necked shirts all year round; ties were reserved for smart occasions. The houses were all converted from derelict mine buildings and my dormitory was in what amounted to a first-floor veranda, completely open to the elements. It was pretty chilly getting out of bed some winter mornings.

By the time I arrived, the school grounds were at least established and the outdoor tasks we were allotted amounted to keeping them neat and tidy. On Sunday mornings we cleaned and polished the floors of our dormitories and senior boys took it in turns to dispense food to the other boys in the dining hall. Older boys were encouraged to look after younger ones and although Falcon had a system of fagging it had none of the more brutal extremes found in English public schools at that time. Prefects at Falcon did not cane boys themselves, although they did recommend to house masters when boys should be beaten.

Self-evidently, when I went to Falcon the school had none of the legacy of traditions and values built up over decades - in the case of longer established schools in southern Africa - or centuries when compared to historic British public schools. On the positive side, this meant Falcon could cultivate its own modus vivendi suited to the cultural and social climate of the time. As a result, it developed a satisfying blend of academic and sporting achievement in keeping with the school motto 'Sic itur ad astra' ('Reach for the stars'), while equipping us for what was still the physically tough environment of living and working in the African bush, as many Falcon pupils would once they had left school.

In the decade running up to UDI (Unilateral Declaration of Independence) in 1965, Falcon inevitably reflected conflicting attitudes towards race relations in Rhodesia. Because the boys were responsible for much of the manual work, the school employed relatively few black servants with the majority of those on the payroll working in the kitchen, as they had at Eagle. We were all used to black servants at home and as uncomfortable as it makes me feel today, back then we regarded those two words 'black' and 'servant' as inseparable.

A couple of years before I left Falcon the other English-style public school in Rhodesia, Peterhouse, which had the reputation of being quite progressive, admitted two African boys as pupils. This was such an unusual and controversial thing to have done that a real buzz went round when the news reached Falcon. Come evening prayers in my own house, Founders House, we could not wait to hear whether or not our house master, Michael Woolley, would make any reference to what had happened at Peterhouse. He did.

'Some of you might have heard about a disaster at another school,' he told us gravely. 'Now, I want to assure you all that as long as I am the house master here, the only black that comes in here is in a serving capacity.' I have to be honest and admit that a murmur of approval passed through the assembled house, because at the time that was how we all thought the status quo should be.

Even then, however, there were a few boys who expressed liberal opinions. One was Robert Jackson, who would later become a fellow of All Souls and the MP for Wantage in the British House of Commons. Robert would tackle racism head-on, challenging the orthodox attitude amongst white Rhodesians towards black Africans. He had the advantage of being both incredibly intelligent and incredibly well read, which rendered him immune to any racist backlash. Robert's intellect helped him remain unscathed at school, despite the relish he took in making provocative pronouncements, so provocative in fact that, even though he was still a schoolboy, he was being watched by Ian Smith's state security officers, who invited Robert's friends to inform on him, though none ever did.

Mind you, if the security service had known what some of the boys at Falcon got up to, they might have had good reason to be concerned about possible terrorist activities. One group of boys started a kind of a territorial dispute over one of the large mine dumps in the school grounds. This covered several acres and what had

The founders of Falcon took over an abandoned mine; very isolated and some 40 miles from Bulawayo town. It was a perfect place to bring up tough Rhodesians.

begun as a series of tit-for-tat skirmishes of each other's camps quickly escalated. Barricades were built and attacks were launched with stones and catapults. It was pretty fierce combat, but it did not stop there.

This was taking place in other houses, so we did not know about it in Founders House until we began hearing the sound of distant explosions. The boys involved had started building bombs, using chemicals pinched from the school labs, and were setting about blowing up the others' encampments. The situation had got completely out of hand and one night the school was shaken by a violent explosion. A boy in another house had been putting the finishing touches to a pipe bomb he had been making, ready for the following day's attack, when the whole thing had gone off. He was incredibly badly hurt and died in the car driving him the 40 miles to hospital in Bulawayo.

That cast a bit of a pall over the territorial fighting at the mine dump, but I remember the episode being washed over along the lines of 'well, these things happen'. However, the science labs were kept strictly under lock and key after that.

SNAKE CHARMER

Catching little animals, and keeping them as pets was popular, as I had already discovered in my last year at Eagle. In one of my bush excursions I came across a very young bush baby, called a pookie. It had been abandoned by its mother, and I managed to catch it and take it back to school. Come the end of term, I thought it might as well accompany me to England, where I was going to be spending the school holiday with my parents, who were living in a flat in Hill Street during my father's year at CDC headquarters in London.

Prior to the journey, I fed my little pookie part of an aspirin, which knocked it out, and slipped it into my hand luggage to have it at my feet during the flight. That all worked well. The pookie and I passed through customs without a hitch. It was only when my father met me outside the terminal at Heathrow that things went wrong. I pulled my little companion out of my bag, whereupon it jumped up and peed all over him in the back of the taxi!

I thought he was quite a successful pet, although once I had gone back to school my mother found him a bit of a nightmare. Once she thought she had lost him when he managed to slip out of an open window. It was wintertime and bitterly cold. Our flat was on the second and third floors of a house in Mayfair and the odds of a bush baby from southern Africa surviving out in the streets were not great. My mother was wondering how she was going to tell me what had happened, when there was a noise at the window eight days after the pookie had

My mother in London with 'Pookie', the bush-baby that I had adopted. I reared it and smuggled it into the UK where it lived happily until finding a more permanent home in London Zoo.

gone and there he was, the other side of the glass, scratching at the window asking to be let back in.

Then there was his drinking. My pookie was a raging alcoholic. He would go mad for any kind of booze, shoving his head into a gin or a whisky and drinking furiously before sitting up again looking rather surprised. Once he was well and truly sozzled, he would start jumping about the room, settling momentarily to pee on his hands and rub them together, which is the pookie's way of attracting other pookies. It did not attract my mother, though. After six months she decided he was too much aggravation and we found him a new home in the London Zoo, which already had four other pookies.

Appropriately, given the name of the school, a lot of boys caught falcons and other birds of prey, which they trained and used for hawking. Then there were the snakes. There were a lot of those in and around Falcon and school rules ensured that we always carried a snake bite kit when we ventured outside the school grounds. Even though people regularly died of snake bites in Rhodesia, quite a lot of the enterprising boys would go into the bush and catch snakes such as black mambas and Gaboon vipers, which they kept in cages under their beds.

I do not mind admitting that I was terrified of them, but farmers' sons who were used to snakes took them in their stride. It was bad enough sleeping in a dormitory where a viper was incarcerated under the next bed, but one chap's viper escaped and made straight for the showers - Gaboon vipers like water – where it settled down for the night. The next morning we trooped in for our regulation six o'clock cold shower. The first chap jumped in and landed full square on the snoozing snake, which did not take kindly to being woken in

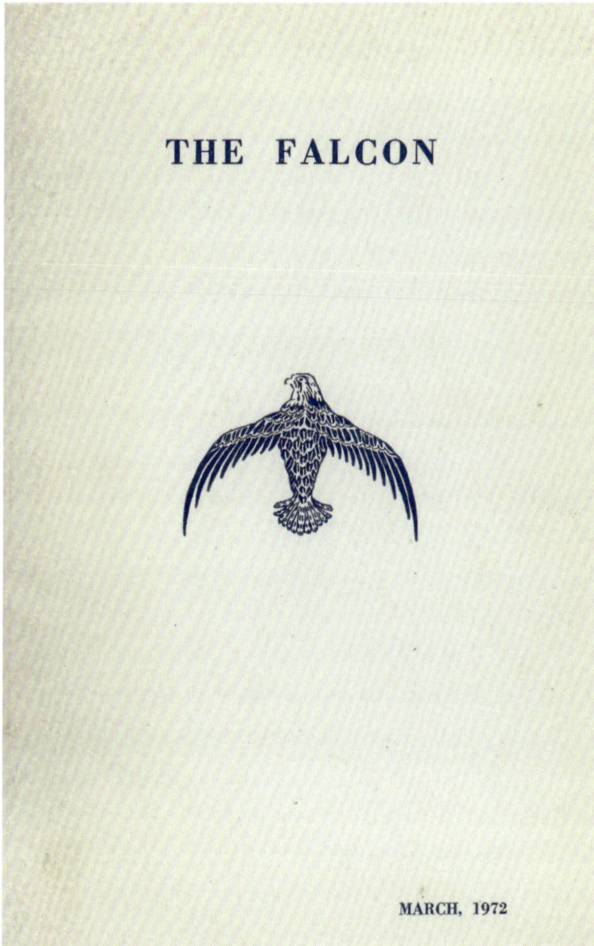

Inevitably the school had its annual magazine and somehow I have managed to keep one copy from March 1972.

this way and duly bit him. The boy was actually quite ill and, with the nearest hospital 40 miles away, it was just as well that the school had the means of treating him.

This episode did result in a bit of a clamp down by the school authorities, although it had been tacitly accepted that boys kept snakes. It was seen as part of the bush culture that was inculcated at Falcon. Keeping snakes was also a handy way of making money. Boys with the guts and steady hands to do it used to milk venom from their snakes, holding them by the back of their necks while they spat venom into a test tube, and then sold it to pharmaceutical companies which used the venom to manufacture snake-bite serum. Quite how the serum reached them from Falcon I never discovered, but there must have been a regular and reliable delivery system, because keeping snakes was a popular and profitable activity for much of my time at the school.

The prefect in charge of the part of the house where I lived had a cobra, of which he was exceedingly proud. One day he trapped a large rat and made quite a ceremony in front of us of placing the rat in the cage as a treat for the cobra to snack on. The next morning we were woken by our prefect's shriek and rushed to see what the matter was. The answer was in the cage, where the rat must have got lucky and had grabbed the cobra by the neck, killing it. The prefect was absolutely devastated; the rat had eaten quite a lot of the cobra and leftover bits were littering the floor of its cage.

IN THE MONEY

Now that I was at public school, my own finances had taken on a new dimension. That may sound rather pompous, but the reality was that from the age of 13 I was made entirely responsible for all my living expenses. This was my father's idea, his way of making me appreciate the value of money, and it has served me very well ever since. His proposition was, like so much of the way he approached life, carefully structured and thought through. He said that he would pay my school fees, my initial expenses such as my school uniform and cover my travel costs to and from home at the beginning and end of each term. He also said he would pay me 10 pounds a month, out of which I would have to clothe myself and cover whatever incidental expenditure I needed to make. He used to draw up a set of accounts, showing what he had paid me, so there would be no misunderstanding, and I very quickly realised that if I were careful, I could actually make quite a lot of money out of this system. So, where other boys might rag about in their school blazers or boaters, for example, I was always careful to take off my blazer and boater and hang them up somewhere safe before getting stuck into a rough and tumble.

Not for the first time in my life, moving to a new school coincided with moving to a new home when my parents took up residence in Swaziland. There, my father became the new head of the Swaziland Irrigation Scheme (SIS). This was a wholly-owned CDC business that involved irrigating over 200,000 acres of otherwise unproductive land and converting it into a large-sale agricultural project growing rice and sugar cane. My father did not know the first thing about farming, but that was not the point. He was a proven colonial administrator, with years of experience of managing workers from a range of ethnic backgrounds. It was a job that carried considerable prestige as well as responsibility. My father used to deal with the King of Swaziland on a one-to-one basis and he, and by extension my mother and I, were always treated with a certain deference whenever we went to the SIS social club.

The home we moved into was a newly-constructed house staffed by three servants in the house and another three who looked after the extensive garden.

Here my mother was soon busy creating flower beds filled with tropical plants and her beloved orchids. By the time she finished, the garden covered four acres with a wonderful display of colour, rich in fragrance.

For a couple of years I had my own particular pet as well, a young tame zebra to whom I gave the somewhat predictable name of Stripey. I had been driving with my parents when we found him, barely a week old, standing forlornly next to a high stock fence that ran beside the road. Stripey had been with his mother who, in her panic to get away, had managed to clear the fence and make her escape. Her baby was too small and weak to follow. We waited and waited to see if she would reappear, but when she did not we took him home to live with us in the stables and eventually rode him.

Animals that had no problem clearing high fences were impala. Our fence marked the border with South Africa and the Kruger National Park. On our side, there was plenty of lush green food for impala to graze on, unlike their side of the fence, where there was no irrigation and grazing was distinctly less appealing.

The Swaziland Irrigation Scheme was a massive project of 200,000 acres made viable through huge irrigation channels like this one under construction ©CDC.

So, impala were forever jumping over and I used to join hunting parties, made up of members of the 40 or so European families working for my father, to keep their numbers down while maintaining a supply of fresh venison.

Judging by most parents at that time, mine were incredibly liberal in many respects. The episode with my soapbox cart is a case in point. I had built this myself and was very proud of it, even though it was just a conventional soapbox with a crude brake on the rear wheels and a front axle that you put your feet on and steered with a length of rope attached at either end. Naturally I wanted to see how it handled on the road and decided that the ideal test run would be the very steep, seven-mile descent down the road from nearby Piggs Peak. The fact that this was a public road, with trucks grinding their way up in the opposite direction, did not deter my parents from letting me do what I wanted. We loaded my soapbox into our station wagon. They drove to the pass at the top, helped me unload it and then watched me set off, following behind as I raced away downhill gathering pace at a fearsome speed. They could see that achieving this was important to me and let me have my way, whatever misgivings they may have had. They were like that and I am grateful that they were. Allowing me the freedom to take risks at that early age proved to be very important through the rest of my life.

From the soapbox I graduated to a full-blown go-kart and here too my father's guiding wisdom came to the fore. The business he ran had very well-equipped engineering workshops and a team of trained engineers and fitters. I cannot have been much older than 13 when I asked my father if I could have a job there during school holidays, partly out of a growing interest in finding out how machines worked, and partly from the wish to make some money.

Being realistic, I would not have stood a chance of getting the job if my father had not been in charge of everyone working there. But because he was the boss he did not want it to appear that I was getting any special favours. Before agreeing to what I had asked, he had a word with the big Afrikaner in charge of the 40 men employed in the workshops, explaining what I wanted to do. This chap said he would take me on, although my father impressed on me that if there was any slacking on my part, or if this fellow decided that I was not up to the job for whatever reason, it would end immediately. And there were not any favours. Out of an eight-week school holiday I worked five of them, with time off at weekends and for a fortnight's holiday with my parents. I used to bicycle to the workshop to start work at the same time as the others, at seven o'clock every morning, worked a full day until knocking-off time at three and then cycle home again.

They started me on cleaning engines. After a while, as our confidence in each other grew, they allowed me to disassemble things and, as soon as I could, I began buying my own tools; my first socket set was an especially proud possession. At the end of each week I collected my pay packet with the others, not knowing that my father had actually drawn my wages himself and passed them to the Afrikaner to hand to me. As far as I was concerned, I was getting my week's pay just like everyone else and it felt good to be doing that.

A group of Afrikaners in the workshops had clubbed together to buy an old 1937 Ford V8. They let me buy a share in it too, probably because I was the boss's son, which entitled me to drive it as well. I did not have a driving licence, of course, but so far from anywhere no one really worried about that. By the time my work there ended, for reasons I will come to shortly, I was competently welding with both gas and electricity. I could do simple machining and I was able to disassemble and rebuild straightforward engines, which is where my go-kart comes into the picture.

After working for him for a year, I asked the Afrikaner in charge if I could make something of my own in my spare time. I produced drawings I had found,

My go-kart in its first iteration with a 197cc Villiers engine, which I used freely on public roads despite the clear danger of doing so.

showing how to build a go-kart. He rather took to the idea and started helping me. I bought all the parts with money I had earned, including a 197cc Villiers motorcycle engine although that was subsequently replaced by a much more powerful 500cc Triumph Tiger engine.

We had to improvise a lot of the design. We welded up a tubular frame, mounted that on wheelbarrow wheels, fitted the engine and a very short chain from the motorbike gearbox to a cog on the rear axle. The only brakes were on the rear wheels. The steering was a T-bar assembly, as found on the more primitive ride-on lawnmowers. There was no suspension and the seat was made from bent sheet metal topped off with a cushion.

It was crude, but the end result was pleasing and with the larger engine was very fast. It must have worried my parents, although they never said anything. I used to go careering around public roads reaching speeds of over 80 miles per hour, but in a vehicle so small and so close to the ground that, with the high foliage either side of the roads, other motorists had no idea I was coming.

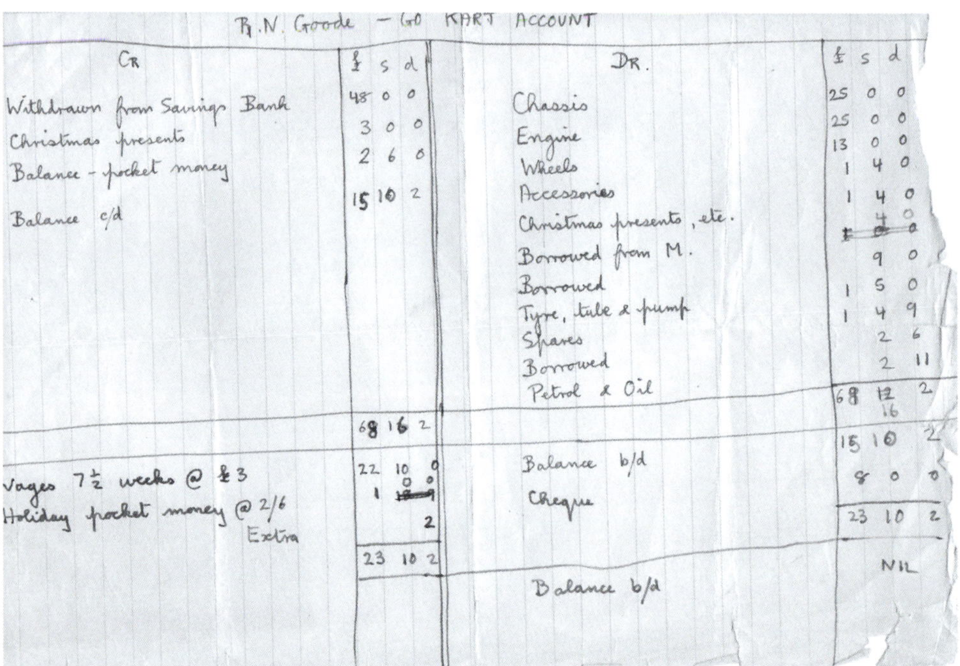

R.N. Goode — GO KART ACCOUNT

CR	£ s d	DR.	£ s d
Withdrawn from Savings Bank	48 0 0	Chassis	25 0 0
Christmas presents	3 0 0	Engine	25 0 0
Balance - pocket money	2 6 0	Wheels	13 0 0
		Accessories	1 4 0
Balance c/d	15 10 2	Christmas presents, etc.	1 4 0
			~~4 0~~
		Borrowed from M.	9 0
		Borrowed	1 5 0
		Tyre, tube & pump	1 4 9
		Spares	2 6
		Borrowed	2 11
		Petrol & Oil	
	68 16 2		68 12 2 (16)
Wages 7½ weeks @ £3	22 10 0	Balance b/d	15 10 2
Holiday pocket money @ 2/6	1 0 0	Cheque	8 0 0
Extra	2		
	23 10 2		23 10 2
		Balance b/d	NIL

For my father, financial discipline was the key and he insisted that I accounted for every detail of my expenditure. He was generous but I paid for everything in my life.

I cannot deny that there were a few hairy moments: probably no more than half-a-dozen, but they were enough. Most of the roads had gravel surfaces that built up into corrugations which made for a bumpy ride. Others had thin strips of tarmac, so when you met oncoming vehicles you had to pull to the side and bump along the uneven verge until you passed each other. Riding that go-kart certainly sharpened my driving at an early age!

A LOST SOUL

During the run-up to O-levels word reached me at Falcon of an unexpected event. The headmaster sent for me one day and told me that my mother had died a week earlier in London and news had only just reached the school. He gave me his commiserations and the usual pep talk about keeping a stiff upper lip and trying not to blub in public although in my case these were not really necessary. I could not pretend that a significant part of my life had been taken away when I heard that my mother was dead. She had been someone I had become used to seeing now and again, a fine woman in her way, but not a person I could honestly say I felt that close to.

She had been a smoker all her life and, after cancer was diagnosed, her death followed a couple of months later. I was at school and never saw her when she was ill. A top surgeon in Salisbury operated on her and then she and my father went to London where she was given further treatment, but her condition was terminal. My father took the practical decision that little would be achieved, but a considerable amount of money spent, in flying me to London to attend her funeral. The summons to the headmaster's study was the first I knew of what had happened and I did not see my father again until the next school holiday.

When I was in my early teens I yearned for an Austin-Healey Sprite and my mother had told me that if I did not smoke until I was 21, she would buy me one. Death had deprived me of my mother, but it had also snuffed out her opportunity to keep her side of the bargain.

Because my father and I seldom discussed my mother, I know nothing of his feelings after her death. He was fortunate in having a new job to throw himself into. In fact, this had been the reason why he and my mother had been in London when she died. After three years working in Swaziland he had been promoted to run a similar large-scale agricultural programme in west Africa; the Cameroon Development Corporation (Camdev).

At that time the territory of the Cameroons was divided into two colonies: one English, the other French. The vast tract of West Cameroon that my father presided over lay not far from the British administrative headquarters in Victoria. His new posting brought access to a couple of company aircraft in which he would fly to Douala to meet French officials, and which he despatched to Douala to collect me for the last leg of my journey home at the end of each term.

Flying around central Africa in those days was a bit hit and miss. These were not major routes served by big international airlines. We made do with the likes of Air Afrique, and similar small-scale airlines with tired old DC4s. It was not uncommon for all the passengers to clamber aboard only to find that one of the engines would not start.

The airfield at Victoria was just a strip of tarmac, which meant aircraft could not land at night. Not infrequently, my flight into Douala arrived too late to catch the last connecting one, which meant that I had to spend the night in a hotel by myself before my father sent his plane to fetch me the following morning.

SCHOOL'S OUT

By this stage of my Falcon career I was well established in the school and had started to acquire what might be termed an independent streak. I was part of a group that had been placed in the newly-created S-stream when we arrived in the school, which established us among the academic high-fliers who would complete their time at Falcon by sitting S-level examination papers as well as A-levels. We were the academic elite. Much was expected of us and I responded by becoming a committed swot, working as hard in the school holidays as I did back at Falcon.

My approach to school sports was equally focused. I used to get up at five o'clock every morning to go for an hour's run before the standard cold shower at six that started the Falcon day. Falcon College has the proud record of developing international rugby players for both South Africa as well as Rhodesia. Playing for the first XV was a mark of distinction and I was determined that once I had been picked to play for the first team, only I would play at hooker.

Set against this otherwise exemplary record was my growing trend towards being difficult. I remember being caned for no apparent reason. I asked why I had been given the beating and was told, 'At the moment, I'm not too sure. It's your general attitude we don't like.'

It is surprising, then, that I was made a prefect. Although, by the time I reached the sixth form I had become quite influential in the school and it would have been difficult for the headmaster not to have made me a prefect. Ironically, my reputation as a rebel may have influenced his decision. Had he not made me a prefect, there was the legitimate concern that I could have become a seriously disruptive element in the school.

The technical bent that I had developed led me towards studying Pure Maths, Applied Maths, Physics and Chemistry in the sixth form. These in turn led to a clutch of A-level results that I felt rewarded the hard work I had put into my studies. Three As, a B and two S-levels were certainly good enough grades to get me into most English universities and to try for Cambridge and I followed my father by applying to Trinity.

After working for two-and-a-half years in Cameroon, my father was now living in the UK when I was called for an interview at Trinity. He had bought a long lease on a five-bedroom flat in Cadogan Gardens, which provided me with a very useful base on that visit and in the years to come. The Head Tutor at Trinity interviewed me for three hours, but I could see he was looking for things that I simply could not provide. An understanding of English history and English culture were blanks as far as I was concerned. I was a bit of a bushman in some ways and there was no disguising that from my interviewer. I came away feeling that the interview had not gone terribly well. In a way, though, I was not that fussed. I had been offered places at other universities and if Cambridge did not accept me, Imperial, Bristol and Southampton already had. As it turned out there had been something about me that had kindled a spark of interest because in due course a letter arrived from Trinity offering me a place to read Engineering.

The Rhodesian government had a system of offering Shell Scholarships every year to the five candidates who had achieved the highest A-level grades in the country. In 1964 I had made the cut, as number four on the list as far as I remember. However, the prestige of the scholarship (and the funding that came with it) ended up with someone else. Although I had been educated in Rhodesia, my father was living in the UK when I sat my A-levels and, in accordance with the terms governing state academic awards, that rendered me ineligible to receive a Shell Scholarship.

However, any disappointment I may have felt about this was soon dissipated by my father. He felt rather bad that he had been responsible for me missing out on a scholarship which was rightfully mine and when I went up to Trinity the following autumn I did so with quite a generous allowance from him.

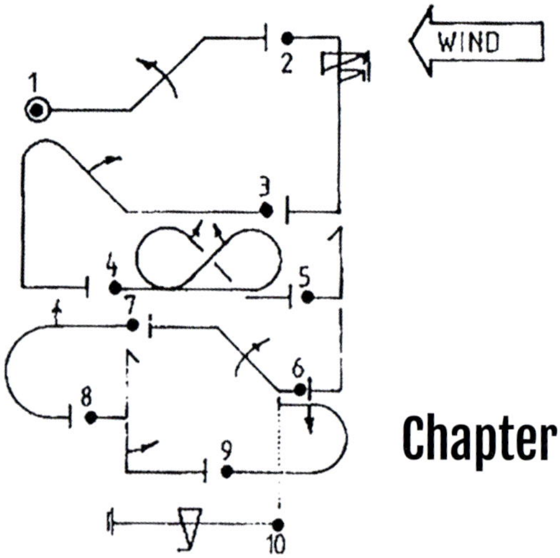

Chapter 4

FOOT FOOT FOOT FOOT SLOGGIN' OVER AFRICA

Even if my mother had still been alive, I do not think she would have tried to prevent me hitchhiking from London to Cape Town and back in the months before I started at Trinity.

My father did not raise any objections, even though I was still only 18 and there was fighting in southern Sudan, as well as the Congo. But then, for much of the time my father was terribly vague about what I was doing. Later in the year after I had gone up to university, I wrote to him periodically from Cambridge and was mildly surprised not to receive any reply; not a single word. After six months or so, I raised the subject tentatively to be told that he had written quite regularly. The snag was the he had addressed all his correspondence to me at Christ Church College, Oxford.

My father had spent a year at Christ Church himself and somehow had missed the crucial detail that I was an undergraduate at his original alma mater in Cambridge. By now I had recognised that this was not untypical of him. He could become very wrapped up in his own world, to the exclusion of almost everything else. Now that his work with CDC had moved him to London, we shared his large flat in Cadogan Gardens in the months after I left school, leading perfectly harmonious but quite independent lives.

One point my father did make clear was that I would need to fund my African adventure myself. Finding a job and making money became imperative. I actually got a couple of jobs. The first was with the pharmaceutical company Parke-Davis. I took myself off to their UK base in Hounslow, where pretty decent A-level results and a persuasive manner got me a job in their laboratory. The work was mind-numbingly boring, but it did give me the chance to develop a couple of lucrative side lines in industrial alcohol and contraceptive pills, both of which were readily available at Parke-Davis. I used to smuggle out bottles of neat ethyl alcohol, 200 per cent proof, which I sold to friends who diluted it down to more potable, but still highly intoxicating levels.

The contraceptive pills found a market with a different group of friends. There was not an endless supply, so I could not be too profligate with them but having access to several hundred pills proved to be as worthwhile with girls I knew as the bootlegged booze was with the chaps. Living in Cadogan Gardens led to my getting an introduction to Harrods and after six weeks I switched the tedious daily commute out to Parke-Davis for the few minutes' stroll round the corner to Knightsbridge.

On my way down to the south of France before catching a tramp steamer to Alexandria.

The job I was given in Harrods was in the department that chased up unpaid bills, where I soon twigged that the process of resolving outstanding invoices revolved around a sequence of four letters. The first letter politely 'drew the attention' of the customer to the bill that 'may have been overlooked'. The next letter upped the ante by 'liking to remind' the recipient of the sum outstanding. Letter number three brought the warning that the matter would soon have to be brought 'to the attention of our solicitors'. The fourth one simply stated that the matter had been 'put in the hands of our solicitors'.

Looking through some fairly hefty customer files I could see that letter number four was never sent and that a lot of files were bulging with growing correspondence that alternated between letters one and two while very few bills had actually been paid. Fresh with the zeal of the newly-recruited, I decided to shake things up a bit and went straight to letter three: 'We're getting in the lawyers'. One of my missives was addressed to Sir Winston Churchill, who had bought a set of garden furniture for Chartwell. The size of his file suggested that paying his Harrods' bill was not a high priority, so he got letter three and a huge ruction followed. Had he not died a week later, things might have become a bit tricky for me at Harrods.

To begin with, the man running the department was less than amused by my approach, but he quickly changed his tune when money started pouring in and he had to acknowledge that my immediate recourse to letter number three did deliver impressive results.

EARNED FREEDOM

I worked at Harrods until the spring, by which time I had saved enough to set off and head south. With six months to go before I was due to arrive at the gates of Trinity, I was not in any hurry. I wrote to my father during my travels wherever there was postal service to carry my missives home. In a way, I cheated slightly in the early stages. Instead of thumbing lifts all round the Mediterranean along the coast of North Africa, I hitched down to Marseilles with the aim of finding passage to Egypt, covering the length of France in just 27 hours.

That rate of passage was not continued when I boarded ship. 'Now I am on a stinking Greek tramp steamer,' I wrote to my father. 'My God, what a hell of a boat. I sometimes wonder whether it is actually moving forward!' Indeed, it was not a speedy passage and travelling on deck, with just a crude shelter at night was an interesting experience. There were several of us and my fellow deck-passengers were a pretty rough-looking band who had difficulty scraping together the pitifully small sums we had to cough up each day to pay for our meals.

Travelling through Africa meant that I could make do with lightweight clothing. I had a rather sub-standard sleeping bag. I took the portable shortwave radio I had had at school, which I usually listened to twice a day to stay in touch with what was going on in the world; keeping abreast of current affairs was important to me. This, a Michelin road map that covered the whole of Africa, and my modest wardrobe, were packed into an elderly rucksack and beyond that I lived on my wits. I imagine that my progress was not dissimilar to that of many young backpackers who have the freedom of time and the freedom of the road to pick and choose how they organise where they go and where they stay. In the days before mobile phones and internet cafes my father and I understood that weeks could pass without contact, so my letters to him were sent in concentrated batches. There were quite a few from my time in Egypt: a stay in Cairo with Egyptian friends I had made and my subsequent journey up the Nile aboard a Nile steamer.

I had to wait in Wadi Halfa, stuck in the middle of the Nubian Desert, for three days before catching the twice-weekly train south to Khartoum. It was a bit boring but people were very friendly and I never felt threatened, even sleeping outside in just my sleeping bag. It was second nature for me to eat what local people were eating and throughout my journey I took my meals at roadside stalls, where the food was tasty and terribly cheap. When I did eventually board the train, I found that it was so crowded that the most comfortable place was the luggage rack, where I spent the 30-hour journey. On the way I made friends with the cook and so had my first decent meal for two weeks. To save money I had eaten very little and scrounged what I could. I had not lost much weight, though, as I ate a lot of bread and beans. I had given up on sterilizing water and was drinking Nile water but only had a mild attack of dysentry to show for it.

After spending three or four days in Khartoum, again with some more people I had met who had offered me somewhere to stay, I intended to catch the train to Kosti. In order to get into South Sudan, I sought permission from the Minister of the Interior and with that given I travelled into southern Sudan arriving at Kosti where I transferred to a steamer the next day. This was a big vessel, well several vessels really, all tied together. At the back was a paddle-wheel steamer. Lashed to one side of this was a barge fitted out with first-class cabins. On the other side a similar barge was tied, providing second-class accommodation. In front of the paddle-wheel steamer were a couple of third-class barges and ahead of these was a further barge filled with cargo. It was a very unwieldy arrangement and frankly not terribly suited to the waters it had to navigate.

For much of its extent in southern Sudan the Nile has no finite channel. The route varied and we sometimes found ourselves having to stop and untie everything so that individual barges could be towed one-by-one around sharp corners and through winding courses between the shallows. Along the way, we used to halt at little settlements where we encountered groups of Dinka people, of whom a number of young adult men were memorable for the stones tied to their penises, presumably in the expectation that this cumbersome arrangement would enhance their manhood.

The Nile steamer that I took from Kosti, south of Khartoum to Juba on the Ugandan border. It was very primative and very slow!

For all of the time aboard the steamer the only water to drink came straight out of the river. The pretty bad dose of amoebic dysentery that I caught followed swiftly and was not sorted out until I had reached Rhodesia a good many weeks further on. Going to the loo 20 times a day, with griping tummy aches and very little to show for the discomfort and effort they engendered, was not made any more comfortable when our convoy of barges passed right through the southern Sudan civil war and we came under fire. A few bullets hit the steamer, but most flew harmlessly over our heads.

At the border town of Juba I took to the road again, hitchhiking south into Uganda. After a day, and near Gulu, I met a senior army officer at the head of a military column. He stopped to pick me up and then offered to put me up at their base. Idi Amin was in charge of the Ugandan army by then, although the coup that would usher in his murderous regime was still six years off, and the garrison where I was quartered was far removed from how I imagined a military barracks to be. The place seemed to be awash with beer with lots of good-time girls hanging around. The whole set-up was absolutely extraordinary, but my host was a genial fellow and he let me stay as long as I wanted. I had a room to myself and the girls seemed friendly, even if my dysentery was frustratingly debilitating.

My father had colleagues in Nairobi and I knew that when I reached Kenya they would have his letters for me from him. CDC also owned an apartment in Nairobi, which was empty at the time and I was given the use of that for as long as I wanted. From Kenya, I made my way through Tanzania, where I had one or two contacts, and then down to the border with Zambia, which I had known as Northern Rhodesia until the country had gained independence from the UK the previous autumn, in October 1964.

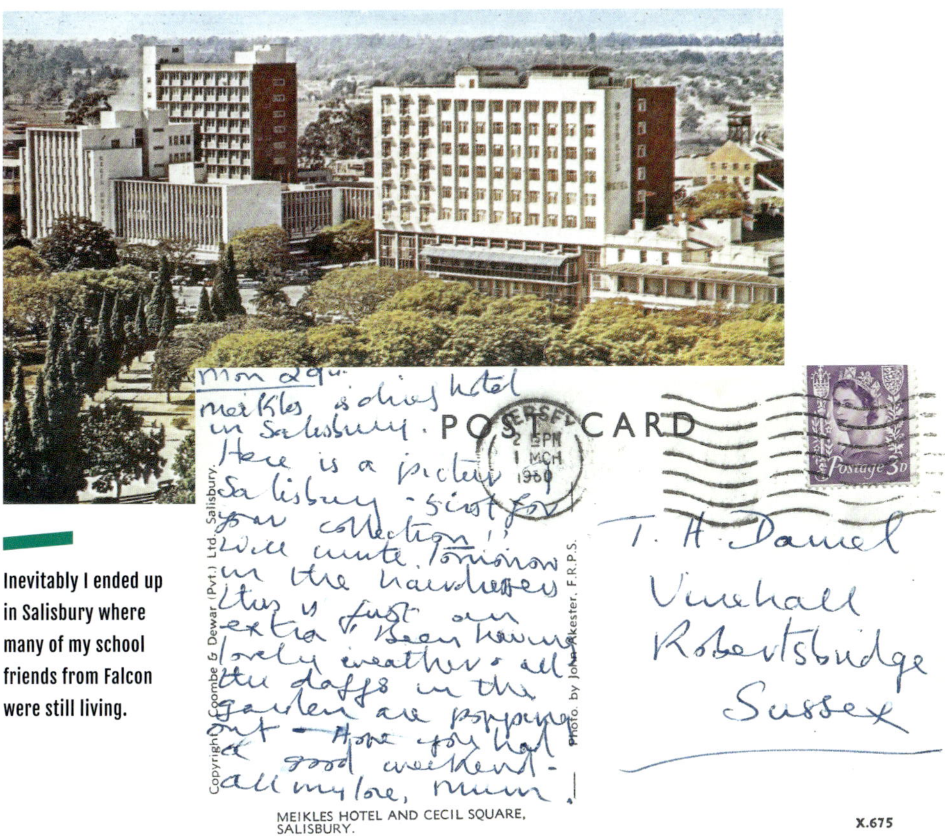

Inevitably I ended up in Salisbury where many of my school friends from Falcon were still living.

In the mining town of Broken Hill, in central Zambia, I came across a road sign identifying a thoroughfare called Goode Street. This was an opportunity I simply could not miss and, although the sign is three feet long, I liberated it from its mountings, somehow managed to shove it into my rucksack and continued on my way. I travelled with that sign for the rest of my journey, carrying it all through southern Africa. It returned with me to the UK and I still have it, prominently displayed in a window just behind where I sit in my office.

Quite a few people I knew from school were living in Zambia, which gave me the chance to spend time with them and form my first impressions of how a former British colony made the transfer from white minority, to black majority rule. The new Zambian president, Kenneth Kaunda, was enormously popular. Pictures of him were everywhere, especially emblazoned across the front of the shirts that most of the population seemed to be wearing. I bought one as a memento and did not really give a lot of thought to it until I presented myself at the border crossing into what was still the British Colony of Southern Rhodesia and had it confiscated.

Once inside Rhodesia, I made my way to the Vumba Mountains for old time's sake and one afternoon walked up the drive of a very fine house right on the edge of the escarpment, with a spectacular view of 50 or 60 miles eastwards over Mozambique. This was the home of a chap my own age called Tim Daniel, who was spending his time between leaving school (Peterhouse in Tim's case) and going to university (Nottingham) by teaching at Eagle, my former prep school, 20 minutes away by car.

Tim recalls me arriving at his parents' front door, where he greeted me never having seen me before. Apparently, I introduced myself and continued almost in the same breath with, 'I've just walked from South Kensington.' Tim, who has an ear for the dramatic, logged that as a good opening line. That meeting was the beginning of a very happy friendship. Tim had an old Morris Oxford Traveller in which we used to explore the country and cross into Mozambique to enjoy dining on incredibly hot dishes spiced with piripiri and washed down with plentiful quantities of good Portuguese beer and wine.

The final leg of this part of my journey ended in Salisbury where I stayed with the family of my school friend Gerald Gane. His father was one of the principal doctors in Rhodesia and it was he who insisted that I had tests to ascertain what form of dysentery I had contracted. When the diagnosis of amoebic dysentery was confirmed, Dr Gane put me on a course of treatment which included a brand-new drug developed by Parke-Davis. Stranger still, the principal component of this drug was paromomycin, the drug that I had been working on in the Parke-Davis laboratory and for which I had eventually isolated the active isomer!

It was with an undisguised feeling of triumph that I sent my father a summary of my travels from London to Salisbury:

> *On my journey I lost 15 pounds, wore out 2 shirts, 1 pr of shoes, gained a deep sun tan and rather bleached my hair with the sun. . . I feel a real sense of accomplishment and I feel greatly matured and very self-reliant and independent. I sort of have an innate self-confidence which always makes me most optimistic about everything.*

To avoid imposing on the Gane household, my distant cousin Gemma Pickard invited me to move into the flat that she was sharing with a friend, a gorgeous girl called Anne who was lusted after by every red-blooded male, me included. Anne also had one of the original split-screen Morris Minors, which she kindly let me drive when I was in Salisbury. At the time she was going out with a chap by the name of Mike Honey. He had been a couple of years senior to me at Falcon and his father had been the surgeon who had attempted to treat my mother after she had been diagnosed with cancer. Anne and Mike went on to marry some time later, but while I was staying with her and Gemma a very dramatic situation arose with another ardent suitor, an Afrikaner farmer who was hell-bent on making Anne his wife.

The two girls foresaw that trouble might arise from a showdown with him and Anne asked me to hide behind a bedroom door when he called round one evening. What I was meant to do if this chap had turned ugly I really do not know, because he was a big fellow. But I stationed myself as requested and through the door overheard him pleading with Anne to marry him and threatening to shoot himself if she did not say yes. If that seemed a little melodramatic, the Afrikaner farmer soon proved himself to be true to his word. Anne said no, explaining as gently as she could that marriage to him simply could not work. She asked me to see him out, to make sure that he left. Then word reached us the following morning that after leaving he had taken himself off somewhere and put a bullet through his head.

As the last person to have seen him alive, I was a key witness. The police interviewed me to ascertain what had happened and what his state of mind had been. Beyond telling them that Anne had been very reasonable in turning this chap down when he proposed to her, which had left him understandably upset, I could not enlighten them further.

I spent three weeks in Salisbury, catching up with friends and, to be perfectly honest, not behaving frightfully well. Part of the problem was that I could start

3 European youths held after alleged raid on school

THREE schools, two clothiers and a car firm were the target for burglars on Tuesday night and early yesterday morning. Three European youths were arrested at 4 a.m. yesterday following an alleged raid on Chisipite Girls' School, after a report by a night-watchman.

Thieves who attempted to smash a padlock on a door of the Girls' High School sports pavilion in Rhodes Avenue succeeded only in bending the lock.

At the Selborne Routledge School, Snowdon Road, Belvedere, intruders forced open a kitchen window and ate food on the premises before leaving.

Men's clothing worth £200 was stolen from West End Outfitters, Kingsway-Manica Road, after thieves had broken a rear window and forced burglar bars to gain entry.

When the staff of Capital Car-breakers (Pvt.) Ltd, 58 Pioneer Street, Salisbury, opened the office at 7.20 a.m. yesterday they found the till smashed and £17 in cash stolen from a desk drawer. The thieves had broken into the premises through a rear window.

Mr. G. H. Bhagat of Nagarji and Sons (Pvt.) Ltd., 55, Moffat Street, who heard the sound of breaking glass at 5 a.m. yesterday did not connect it with his own clothing store. An hour later he found that the store's front window had been smashed and clothing worth £30 stolen.

The somewhat embarrassing incident having been caught attempting to take the school bell as a trophy from Chisipite, the leading girls' school of Salisbury.

enjoying large quantities of drink again, thanks to Dr Gane's timely cure for my amoebic dysentery. I am more than a little ashamed to recall now that I repaid his kindness by getting his son arrested by the Salisbury police.

Not for the first time events began to gather pace during another boozy evening. Someone, most likely me, had the idea of climbing into Chisipite, the prestigious girls' boarding school in Salisbury, and pinching a trophy: the school bell had been our initial target. My school friend, Chris Jamieson, had a car in which we parked some distance away from the tall brick building which was the main residential block and managed to find a way to get inside. The dormitories were two or three floors up. The bell was even higher, in a little turret right on top of the roof. Pinching that was going to be out of the question.

Instead, we settled on a notice printed on a sheet of the school's headed paper, tiptoeing along one of the dormitories to snatch it, where those girls who were awake lay petrified, although thankfully for us, silent. It was a long dormitory, but at the end was a notice board from which we retrieved a piece of paper bearing the Chisipite School letterhead as proof of where we had been and what we had done.

The sound of approaching sirens told us we had been rumbled. Realising that we could not escape from the school the way we had sneaked in, we climbed up onto the roof and that was where the police searchlights found us. In the morning, we were charged with breaking and entering and intent to steal. Fortunately, Gane's father had sufficient influence that he was able to get us out on bail. Even more fortunately, he mediated with the police and the headmistress of Chisipite and reached a compromise that if she dropped her complaint, the police would drop their charges. Our side of the bargain saw the three of us going back to Chisipite to make formal apology to this august lady.

SEPARATE WAYS

The original plan that Chris and I had cooked up was that we would both travel to the UK overland through Africa. But following our run-in with the police, that idea was scotched. Chris would be travelling to London by a more conventional and far less risky means, which left me to make my own way home.

After travelling south down the eastern side of Africa, it made sense to return northwards up the western side, where I also had contacts through CDC. From listening to news reports on my short-wave radio I knew that the security situation was dicey in the Congo, through which I would have to pass on my way north. What the news failed to make clear was just how serious the actual fighting was and that only came home to me when I found myself confronted with it in Katanga.

Although I had been warned that it usually took several weeks to be granted a visa to enter the Congo, 'with my usual charm [and no false modesty in describing the coup to my father] I got one in four hours flat:'

[I got] a lift across the border with some Africans smuggling flour, soap etc. in the false bottom of a V.W. Kombi! There is a great deal of unrest everywhere, the place swarming with Gendarmes and big bomb craters in the roads, as well as burnt out hulks of cars and buildings littered around. I didn't fancy sleeping in the open in Elizabethville, and so went to the British Consulate, and through an introduction given by a chap there, I eventually slept in the flat of a girl working in the U.S. Consulate. The black market is quite incredible – one can get 8 times the official Bank Rate on dollar exchange. . . I made my way north from Elizabethville to Jadotville and finally Kolwezi (encountering traffic blocks all the way.) I've now got a job teaching a Belgian family of 7 kids English. It's great fun and I'm learning French at an incredible rate.

The delightful Belgian family who invited me to stay with them in Katanga, despite a quite serious civil war raging at the time.

Judging by my letters, I found the security situation in Katanga more fascinating than frightening: 'Still lounging in the Katangse fleshpots!' reads the airy beginning of one missive to my father from that war-torn corner of the Congo. 'I'm rather enjoying myself here and finding it, in truth, the most interesting country that I have visited. Everything is so incredibly corrupt and rotten from the Union Minière [the influential Belgian mining consortium exploiting Katanga's mineral wealth] downwards. The only thing that preserves a certain element of security in the country is the 500 or so white mercenaries – whom all the people are terrified of. When the mercenaries are in town there is no trouble at all – they kill on suspicion, and more often, without suspicion! The Gendarmerie – all Africans – are just as terrified as the populace, as are the A.N.C. – Armée Nationale Congolaise – more affectionately known as Les Animaux Non-civilisés. There are about 7 mercenaries here in Kolwezi and the place is comparatively quiet – but a few days ago a mercenary became drunk and started smashing up a bar and the unfortunate Gendarmerie were forced to arrest him. In under 30 minutes his comrades rolled up outside the jail in weapon-carriers and started blowing the place up with bazookas. I'm told that the chap was released in about 30 secs flat!!! Things are far from quiet, on the whole, despite the presence of the mercenaries who, despite their ruthlessness, are not much deterrent to the hard rebel core. An indication of this is provided by the assassination of a deputy – an M.P. – just a few hundred yards away from where I was sleeping. Notice was put outside the Gendarmerie (which I managed to steal) [it is now framed and hanging in our downstairs loo] saying ' . . . n'a pas été assassiné pour un affair politique, mais il s'agit uniquement d'un accident mortel de las chasse [basically an attempt to scotch the idea that this deputy had been assassinated for political reasons but had instead died as the result of a hunting accident!] Rather amusing all round.'

Altogether I spent two weeks in the Congo. In the end, though, studying my Michelin map made it clear that heavy fighting blocked my route north. Crucially, time was moving on and I was becoming increasingly conscious of the need to return to the UK by the middle of September, to give myself time to get ready to go up to Cambridge.

I went as far north as Kaniama [I explained, writing to my father when I was 'back in civilisation',] and my God, it was tough. One of my black friends tried to knife me in a bar, thinking that I was a Yank (they confuse them with the hated 'onusiens' (U.N.), who are still there in force . . . I also

> *got roughed up by the A.N.C. in Kamina and was offered a job with the mercenaries, which I would have taken had I more time. They make, in wages, around £250 a month, but they are such looters that their salaries are insignificant in comparison to their earnings. When I was in Kolwezi, 3 of them blew up the big bank in Stanleyville, swiped a fortune, argued about its division and 2 of them finally shot the third, stole a plane, and escaped, only to be caught when they landed at Kolwezi, thinking it was Kitwe!*

So, I turned around and retraced my steps. I got back to Salisbury reasonably quickly, which was just as well because by now I had booked passage with Chris Jamieson aboard a Union Castle ship that was leaving Cape Town bound for the UK. So, the last phase of the travelling through Africa found me hitch-hiking south from Salisbury to Cape Town. During the passage from Cape Town to Southampton we managed to cause quite a lot of mayhem aboard the RMS *Pendennis Castle*. The purser was a particularly obnoxious individual whom we soon succeeded in rubbing up the wrong way. He called us 'horrid little schoolboys' to which we responded by throwing him in the swimming pool. That earned us a summons from the captain, whose principal concern appeared to be that the purser had been dressed in his 'blues' at the time we tossed him in the water!

The ship stopped briefly in the Canaries, docking for a night in Las Palmas. Chris and I were up on aft deck having a few drinks when someone mentioned that the harbour was notorious for the number of sharks prowling around it. Tradition, rumour, hearsay – call it what you will – maintained that you would not make it ashore if you found yourself in the water. I have no idea what I had been drinking, but Chris remembers me clambering over the taffrail, high up at the stern of the ship, from where I dived into the harbour and swam to the side of the dock. The others had been watching my progress with some interest and not one triangular dorsal fin had broken the surface in pursuit of me.

Coming into Southampton at the end of our voyage, we added our own embellishment to this pride of the Union Castle line. From somewhere we had acquired a huge bedsheet onto which we painted an enormous skull and crossbones. This was kept out of sight until the last minute, when the ship was being manoeuvred alongside and the crew were otherwise engaged. That was our cue to unfurl our handiwork which flapped in gentle warning that the good ship *Pendennis Castle* had been occupied by pirates as indeed the captain and the purser may well have felt she had.

It may have been on a foray with Chris that I found myself in the Zambezi Club in Earls Court. This was the Mecca for colonials in London, popular with South Africans, Rhodesians and every other colonial from sub-Saharan Africa, not to mention New Zealanders and Australians. It was a lot of fun and a very good place to meet people and it was at the Zambezi Club that I got into conversation with an Australian girl who was about to fly home at the end of her stint in London. She was running around in a Standard 10 van, or rather she had been running around London in this van until the engine had stopped. She had not bothered to get it going again and by the end of the evening had given me the van for nothing.

Since I enjoyed tinkering with engines, I was happy to take the keys from her. This proved to be a bit of luck, because I quickly spotted that the only problem with the engine was that one of the core plugs had been pushed out; you poured

A rather scruffy lot of Rhodesians fresh off the RMS *Pendennis Castle* and taking in the sights and sounds of London.

water into the radiator and it just flowed out of the engine. With a new core plug fitted and the engine coolant topped up, the car ran well. We called the van Barry, after Barry Humphries's outrageous comic-strip Australian 'yobbo'. It was still running well when I sold it 18 months later, by which stage it had reliably ferried me through about half my time at Trinity.

Of course, undergraduates were not allowed cars at Cambridge in the mid-1960s. So I was unusual, to say the least in driving my own one there at the start of my first term. Horrid little car as it was, it was perfect for clandestine usage; it was anonymous and blended in with every other boring car parked in the side streets.

'Barry', the Standard 10 van given to me by an Australian lady that I met in a nightclub on the Earls Court Road and provided my transport to Cambridge!

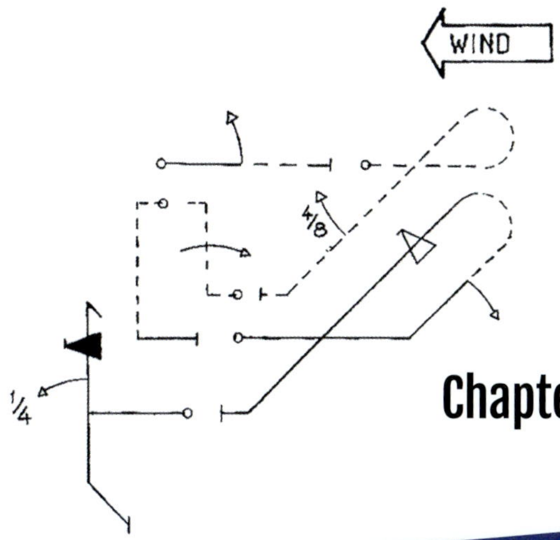

Chapter 5

THE MAKING OF A TRINITY MAN

Trinity had awarded me a place to read Mechanical Sciences at Cambridge but I had gone up to Cambridge intending to have a good time.

After just four days it became clear that these two objectives were never going to be compatible. Although my A-level results indicated that I could probably have kept pace in the Mechanical Sciences tripos, I realised straightaway that it was going to take a great deal of hard work. Fellow freshmen from English public schools had a far deeper understanding of the subject than me. Furthermore, many of them actually wanted to become engineers, whereas I had been shoehorned into engineering simply because I had studied science subjects in the Sixth Form.

If Falcon College had a shortcoming, it was in career guidance: there was virtually none. My father did not offer any thoughts on the subject either. Not for the first time I found myself on my own and unsure where I was heading. My tutor, Gareth Jones, was a nice man and very understanding. I explained my dilemma. He asked what I would like to study and between us we decided that if Mechanical Sciences was not for me, perhaps Moral Sciences would be. That degree does not exist any longer, which is a great pity because it was a fascinating mix of logic, philosophy, psychology, ethics and metaphysics. It was a course that I really enjoyed.

There was the further benefit as I quickly discovered; studying Moral Sciences would not be too demanding. All I needed to get by was a sound opinion. As long as I had that, it did not really need to be supported. I did go to a few lectures but only the ones I enjoyed. When it came to writing essays, I found that if I worked through the night before my weekly tutorial, I could knock off the requisite amount of work and keep my tutor satisfied.

With the academic side of university life straightened out, I was free to concentrate on what I really wanted to do. Rugby got off to a good start. I was soon playing hooker in the Trinity first XV, on the strength of which I was invited to go for a full university trial in my first few weeks. I was never big or fast enough to win a blue and be on the university team, but it was encouraging to realise that playing rugby at Eagle and Falcon had set me up to hold my own alongside the best players at college level.

(Left) I am sure that I looked very smooth on the balcony of my father's flat in Cadogan Gardens. Fortunately he had taken up with his new wife-to-be and moved to Hampstead leaving the flat to me for a while.

(Right) Rugby continued to be an important part of my life, and we were successful. Here is the 1968 team which finished the season of 21 matches with 19 wins.

During those three years our Trinity team was quite successful. Jumping ahead a little, we were fairly dominant in our final year: winning 19 of the 21 matches we played and with only two losses. Mind you, we did have some formidable players. Patrick Alexander, whom I came to know better when we were headhunting some years after finishing at Cambridge, had been the fastest man at Eton; he played on the wing for Trinity and ran in some scintillating tries. Packing down in our second row was the massive form of Denzil Howe, all 18 stone of him. Denzil had spent time between school and Cambridge working for VSO in Malawi, where he had been selected to play lock for the Malawi national rugby team. This gave us the opportunity for a lot of fun at the expense of opposing Oxford colleges. Before fixtures with teams from 'the other place' we used to submit our team sheet, with an asterisk beside the name Denzil Howe and the note at the bottom of the page: 'Asterisk denotes international'.

The sight of this towering figure lining up against them at kick-off was very intimidating for our opponents and served as a useful distraction for the opening exchanges, scrums and line-outs especially. Even after the penny dropped that Denzil was actually pretty slow about the pitch, he was always heavily marked. Howe also rowed in the Trinity rugby VIII. Although none of us could claim to be genuine rowers, we acquitted ourselves respectably on the river and it was thanks to Denzil that our eight tipped the scales as the heaviest college crew ever to row on the Cam. I was at my 'fighting weight' of 13 stone seven pounds and was the second lightest in the boat!

My friend from Falcon, Al Simkin, was in a different college, but we saw a lot of each other in our early weeks at Cambridge, particularly after Al had met a girl at a nearby finishing school less than a week after arriving at Christ's. With only a few women's colleges in the university at that time, the ratio of men to women was in the order of 11 to one. With girls at this kind of premium, Al faced a seven-mile bike ride out to visit his new lady friend and a seven-mile bike ride back to college. All he needed to do, though, was to mention to me that there were 10 girls holed up in her finishing school and we were heading off in Barry to pay them a visit. This soon became a regular route because among the girls Caroline Richardson, a very pretty blonde, had caught my eye.

Caroline's parents were divorced and her mother had remarried a senior barrister. He was appalled when he learned that his step-daughter was going out with me. He hauled me up into his inn of court, and gave me a very aggressive dressing down, warning that if I persisted in seeing Caroline he was going to make her a ward of court. I was polite, but took no notice and, fortunately, her own father was far more relaxed and told me not to worry. We got on well and I think he thought I was quite good news.

Caroline and I spent a lot of time together and being able to go to the flat in Cadogan Gardens from time to time meant that we were not always having to keep an ear cocked for the sound of my landlady prowling around my digs. In our second year together, Caroline moved into a flat down by Midsummer Common, which made life much easier.

Rowing the Trinity College rugby team boat. It was the heaviest ever rowed on the Cam.

Caroline Richardson (left) caught my eye early on; Marion Stevens (right) followed.

The flat in Cadogan Gardens was my base during university vacations. I would set forth from there for the highly lucrative but otherwise incongruous job I had heard about over a pint of beer in a London pub. The man with whom I had fallen into conversation had told me that if I really wanted to earn serious money, the place to make it was digging the new Victoria Line. My personal contribution to this link in London Transport's underground infrastructure began at Green Park, from where I subsequently moved to Oxford Circus. The underground tunnel itself was excavated from station to station by huge boring machines, but the escalator shafts, the ticketing halls and the platforms were dug out by gangs of men, using pneumatic picks and shovels.

DIGGING DEEP

The contractors were desperate for people and the pay was unbelievable. Where friends were earning, say, 25 pounds a week in the vacation stacking supermarket shelves, I and my fellow labourers (the majority of them Irish navvies) were earning £150 a week. And this was when I was living for free in a very fine five-bedroom flat in one of the smartest addresses in London! However, we earned our pay. The work was incredibly arduous: six days a week, alternating week by week from day shift to night shift, putting in a 12-hour day with one 30-minute break and one 15-minute break.

Initially I worked as what they called a pony man. The navvies shovelled soil into wheeled skips until they were full, when it was my job to push them along a little railway line and into the lift, to be hauled up to the surface and taken away. Pushing a combined weight of a ton-and-a-quarter, sometimes for over a hundred yards, from seven in the morning until seven in the evening, six days a week was absolutely knackering. I persuaded three friends from Trinity to give it a go, even offering them free lodging in Cadogan Gardens but only Tim Simpson, captain of the rugby team, stuck it out for a while.

Then I found out that you could make even more money from sitting in the dark banging a pipe. That at least was the gist of the job. If you study underground platforms, and I do, you will see that they are encased with huge metal rings bolted together. In the course of each shift we had to fit one of these rings and you were not allowed to knock off until the job was finished. Once the earth had been excavated, the big metal ring was lowered and bolted into place and then encased in concrete that was poured in behind it. The concrete was sent down from the surface in a convoluted way by means of a large pipe. Just to add to the joy, the concrete sometimes solidified in this pipe. Trial and error had revealed that the only sure way to stop this happening was to hammer the pipe, hard.

Volunteers were called to crawl up inside a narrow tunnel only slightly bigger than a large chimney, where they would sit for the duration of a shift, sometimes with light, sometimes in complete darkness, while water dripped over them into chilly pools. It was not everyone's cup of tea, but the pay was even higher and I volunteered.

Having taken up station in the cramped tunnel, my job was to listen out for the sound of concrete coming down from above. Once it was on its way, I had to hammer the pipe vigorously to keep the concrete moving until that batch had passed all the way to the excavation behind the metal ring at the bottom. Present day health and safety personnel would have been horrified by our working conditions. The constant din from the pneumatic picks was appalling and there were a fair number of mishaps. Two men were killed while I was working there. One poor chap found himself on the wrong side of a heavy length of railway line when it was accidentally dropped, crushing his neck. The other fellow was standing at the bottom of the lift shaft, calling up to his mates asking where the lift was, when it hurtled down out of the darkness and sent him off to meet his Maker.

The men who employed me seemed very relaxed about my having to disappear back to Cambridge at the start of each term. Once they got to know me, they were happy to let me dip in and out, working several weeks at a stretch and then disappearing for a couple of months before reappearing again.

At around the time that I went up to Trinity my father was beginning a new phase of his own life. Since he and I never discussed our personal lives, I had not twigged that he had been feeling rather adrift since my mother had died. Although they had been very independent, my parents had been oddly close and he missed her when she was no longer around.

To keep himself occupied in the evenings, he had taken to volunteering with the Samaritans. The charity had been growing rapidly since Chad Varah had started it a dozen years earlier. It needed an experienced administrator and my father was well qualified to sort out the accounts and the running of an expanding organisation. In the course of this work, he had become rather taken with Chad Varah's PA, a divorcée named Ann Meredith, who was younger than my father and who, in the fullness of time, became my step-mother.

She, like my mother, came from southern Africa: in Ann's case, from Rhodesia. So, we had a similar African background and on first meeting I liked her. She had spirit, which I warmed to. My father must have been drawn to strong women. My mother was quite forceful in her own way and Ann most certainly was similar. Her father was Air Vice-Marshal Meredith, who had been head of the Rhodesian air force during the Second World War. He was a no-nonsense character too. Ann used to tell the story of when she, as a little girl, had asked her father if she could have some dolls and a dolls' house in which to play with them.

'No child of mine plays with dolls,' was his brusque reply. Instead, he got hold of the fuselage of a crashed training aircraft called a Harvard and had this pretty big plane taken to their garden, telling his daughter, 'this is what you play with'.

A FRIEND INDEED

There is a jaded axiom that you spend your second year at university getting rid of people you met in your first year. Happily, in my own experience, the exact opposite was true. My second year at Cambridge consolidated friendships that have lasted ever since; over 50 years later a group of us remain as close in our 70s as we were in our 20s. Two factors played significant parts in this: accommodation and old Jaguar cars.

For my second year, the Trinity bursary staff installed me in another building belonging to the college: number 26, Trinity Street, which stands just outside the main gate. Here a dozen of us lived under the same roof and got to know each other really well. My main room was on the first floor and the convention we established was that its window would always be left open, so that anyone needing to get back into college after the midnight curfew, when the gates were shut, could climb through it. Access to my window did require climbing the wall of a bank right outside the college, walking across the roof and then jumping across a gap onto another roof to reach my window. None of these manoeuvres were particularly difficult; speed and success depended on how much you had had to drink.

Among the residents at 26 Trinity Street was Tony Pigott, one of half-a-dozen army officers admitted every year to read Engineering. Tony returned one night seriously the worse for wear, totally misjudged the critical jump between roofs and fell heavily into the little passageway below, running behind the bank. That was bad enough, but he landed very awkwardly and broke a leg in some style, ending up with a bone sticking out in very dramatic fashion. The rest of us were all in bed and had not a clue what had happened to him. Being a tough army chap, he stoically kept his silence and lay there in considerable pain until the morning. The bank staff got a very nasty surprise when they arrived to open for business and found a man lying, half-unconscious, in a pool of blood.

My interest in classic British sports cars began when I inherited £300 from my godmother, Aunt Muriel. She died at the end of my first year at Cambridge and I used the money to buy a Jaguar XK 150, which I used to park in the Magdalene fellow's car park. That, and the XK 120 that I chanced upon, abandoned as far as I could judge, in the University Library car park, became absorbing interests and occupied a lot of my time.

Members of 'the team' at 26 Trinity Street joined in various escapades within the walls of the college. Allan Johnson defines my approach to these episodes as 'a certain lampooning of authority'. This is an elegant legal way (he was an international corporate lawyer in professional life) of accounting for the pleasure I took in metaphorically raising two fingers to what I regarded as unnecessarily restrictive rules, or pointless and arcane procedures. The incident of the Junior Common Room elections is a case in point.

About three weeks before the end of the last term of our second year, the committee of undergraduates who had been running JCR activities were sacked. I do not remember what had brought this about and I do not think we really cared very much. What did seem ludicrous, however, was the decision to hold a formal election to elect a new committee to serve for the barely 20 days of term that remained. Nor was I alone in thinking that the people standing for election were a hopeless bunch, to put it mildly.

The election took place with pompous formality and when all votes had been cast, the ballot box was conveyed from the JCR to another room, where the votes were going to be counted. The odious little man charged with carrying the box had to pass one of the college loos, where I was hiding, complete with nylon stocking obscuring my face. To my surprise, he put up quite a struggle, refusing to let go of the wretched box, even though I was a lot stronger than he was.

There were half-a-dozen of we conspirators in this dastardly act, and while I was grappling with the box-bearer, a couple of the others, also wearing nylon stockings, were keeping the other election 'officials' at bay and preventing them from coming to his aid. When we finally wrested control of the box, we rushed down the stairs and along to the gate on Trinity Lane, where Robert Woods was waiting with the engine running in his XK 150. In I jumped with the ballot box. Off drove Robert, hell for leather into Trinity Street, where another accomplice had been stationed to hold up the traffic to ensure our getaway.

Not long after, the Trinity JCR election ballot papers were bobbing serenely down the river, from the bridge where we had tipped them into the water. We returned the ballot box quietly two days later and we were all interviewed by college authorities. But there was no evidence to back up their strong suspicions that we had been responsible. The election was annulled, which is what we had wanted, and the term eased to the end of our second year on a wave of summer balls and end-of-term parties.

RECORD BREAKER

There were other activities to keep us entertained. The notorious King Street Run was a kind of solo relay, in which you raced against the clock but instead of seizing a baton, competitors steadily took on board at least a gallon of beer. There were eight pubs in King Street and the rules of the race stipulated that each competitor had to down a pint of beer in each pub, as fast as possible, before racing to the next pub for the next pint. Assistants went ahead, lining up pints for their respective competitors. But one of the challenges of the race required runners to retain all the beer they had drunk until they successfully crossed the finish line. If you peed, or were sick, you had to go back to the previous pub and down another pint there before resuming the race. So, being able to hold a gallon of beer was a prerequisite and people used to practise to get themselves in shape.

After winning the race several times, I decided to see if I could become the first person to go both up and down King Street, which of course would involve drinking and holding in 16 pints of beer. That proved to be too much. I was sick twice and had to pee twice, with the result that when I got to the finish I had taken on board 20 pints of beer! The whole thing was rather unsightly, I have to admit, but I made my mark in the annals of Cambridge history.

For my final year I was given rooms in New Court, a quiet corner of the college beside the river and the Cambridge 'backs'. Prince Charles was a freshman on the floor below. Meanwhile Edward Woods, the younger brother of my great friend Robert had also started his first year in rooms in New Court, although he lived on a staircase on the other side of the court.

Between Edward's rooms and mine lay a sward of beautifully manicured Cambridge lawn. Placing (and winning) bets has always given me a great deal of fun, and this pristine expanse of beautifully mown and rolled grass was too good an opportunity to let pass. Over a few drinks one evening, Ed and I agreed to challenge each other to pee on the patch of lawn closest to our rooms. Whichever was most brown at the end of term would win the bet.

I do tend to take this sort of thing quite seriously, especially if prize money is at stake. It might have been bending the terms of the bet slightly, but I decided that my chances of winning would be greatly enhanced if I saved up pee during the day and added this to the nightly 'watering' of my patch of grass. I eased my conscience in rationalising that my pee was going on to my section of lawn; it was just going on in pretty hefty daily doses. So, I got into the habit of peeing into any convenient bottle and disposing of it at night as prescribed by the rules of the bet.

I do not know what Ed Woods drank in those days, but his pee was no match for mine. Not only was my patch of lawn significantly browner than his, thereby winning me the bet, by the end of term there was virtually nothing growing on it and the college gardeners had no option but to replace it with brand new turf. However, this somewhat childish wager backfired with potentially catastrophic consequences before reaching its conclusion.

At the start of our last year there was a party for Trinity freshmen to which new arrivals in other colleges were also invited, including freshers from Girton. Among the Girton first-years there was an exceptionally lovely girl called Marion Stevens who, to my great good fortune, became my girlfriend for several years.

Competition to win places at women's colleges at Cambridge was so intense back then, that every girl admitted had to be very bright. But Marion combined her intellectual prowess with selfless beauty and a delightful personality. She was great and we had a lot of fun together, even though the incident with her mother and the sherry bottle could have derailed our relationship in its early stages.

This was to be my first meeting with Mrs Stevens. We drank sherry in those days, quite a lot of it and I had already finished much of a bottle to give me Dutch courage before Marion and her mother arrived at my rooms. I made Mrs Stevens comfortable and then nipped into the little space that served as my pantry to grab a new bottle and poured her and Marion a couple of generous slugs. Marion took a sip and I saw her look rather quizzical, but her mother kept going, steadily working her way through her glass.

When my own glass was empty, I refilled it from the bottle from which I poured their sherry, drank a little and realised instantly that I had made a ghastly mistake. Trinity keeps a good cellar and even the sherry available for undergraduates to buy was quite reasonable stuff, but this was not JCR sherry.

Marion punting on the Cam with King's College Chapel in the background.

That is to say, some of it might once have been JCR sherry, but in the interim it had been through my kidneys before being peed into the nearest receptacle, ready to be poured onto what would become my bet-winning patch of turf on the lawn at the bottom of my staircase.

I snatched the glass out of Mrs Stevens' hand, apologising profusely that the batch they were drinking was corked, or something along those lines. Fortunately, I did have a fresh bottle of proper college sherry, which I was able to produce with clean glasses and just about salvage the situation. I subsequently told Marion what had happened, but she always refused to believe that her mother had drunk half of a generously filled glass of Richard Goode pee.

In addition to changing rooms in my final year, I also changed subjects. The first part of the Moral Sciences tripos lasted two years. Part Two of the tripos offered a couple of options, neither of which appealed to me. You could either study Mathematical Logic, which was dead easy if you could do it, or frankly impossible if you could not. I fell into the second camp and could see there was no point in even trying.

The other option was Ancient Philosophy. Since I did not know anything about ancient Greek and Roman philosophers and did not have any inclination to improve my knowledge of them, that was a non-starter too. I had also had a feeling that studying something that might have practical application after university could be a good idea. After giving the matter some thought, law looked a likely choice. The second part of the Cambridge Law tripos lasts two years, but I was able to persuade the college to let me take Law Part Two in one year, by putting in a summer's reading (which I somehow overlooked) and by-passing some of the law final exams. However, preparing for finals in my last term was somewhat eclipsed by the episode that gained me a certain notoriety in the university.

Marion was the kind of girl who could not pass through a place like Trinity without attracting attention. Prince Charles took a shine to her and used to enjoy chatting to her on our staircase. The college porters soon singled her out as a frequent visitor as well, which made me a marked man on the occasions that she stayed the night in my room. One night they must have spotted Marion and me walking into college together and made a note of this, so that when she had not reappeared after the gates were closed at midnight, they waited until 12.45 and then raided my room.

Marion was ignominiously turfed out of Trinity. My tutor was sympathetic, but as far as the college was concerned my conduct had been completely unacceptable and he told me that I had to leave there and then: rusticated. The

Prince Charles on his first day at Trinity being escorted by my friend Robert Woods. Charles had his rooms under mine at Trinity New Court.

story made it into the national press, when the *Sunday Express* devoted half a column to it on page three under the headline 'Charles's college bars man found with girl'.

Trinity allowed me to work in the Library, to dine in Hall and to take my finals, but I had to find myself somewhere else to live and ended up in crummy lodgings in Coldham's Lane, almost two miles from the centre of Cambridge according to the university newspaper, *Varsity*. Once finals were over, I had to leave Cambridge, and therefore miss all the post-exams fun and my last May Week. In fact *Varsity* adopted my predicament as a cause célèbre, plastering across the front page a photograph of me looking rather pathetic with my little suitcase, as I stepped through the main gate of Trinity like Adam and Eve being kicked out of Paradise.

'We deplore this action of Trinity College,' ran the Varsity *editorial. 'We do not accept that Colleges have the right to dictate to us how we run our lives. We do not accept that individual welfare should ever be sacrificed to bureaucratic legalism.'*

Other liberal voices rallied to the cause, expressing outrage that I should have been treated like this in what was fast becoming the Swinging Sixties. Interestingly, many of my very good friends took a completely different position. I think they felt I needed bringing down a peg or two and supported the college in the action it had taken. In fact, Robert Woods and several others clubbed together to publish a full-page notice commending Trinity for the action it had taken against me!

Varsity

INJUSTICE

Vol. 64, No. 3, Cambridge, Saturday, May 4, 1968, 6d.

PAGE ONE OPINION

RICHARD GOODE is a Rhodesian reading Moral Sciences in his third year at Trinity. He is 22.

On the night of Monday, April 22nd, he was in bed with his girlfriend in his New Court room.

At 12.45 a.m. a porter broke into his room, without knocking, and ordered the girl out.

Goode later appeared before the Dean of College, Mr. Swinnerton-Dyer.

According to Goode, the Dean explained that this was not a question of morality, but of breaking the rules. Trinity regulations state that all girls must be out of College by midnight. Goode had broken the rules.

This is his punishment —

● He must not sleep in his room in College, and he has had to find himself alternative accommodation. He is now living in Coldham's Lane, almost two miles from the centre of Cambridge.

But he may work in the Library or in his room. He may dine in Hall. He may take his finals.

● As soon as his exams are over, he must leav Cambridge. He is not allowed to be in Cambridge fo his last May Week. But he must return afterwards t make up his nights of residence, in order to qualif for his degree.

We deplore this action of Trinity College. We d not accept that Colleges have the right to dictate t us how we run our lives. We do not accept tha individual welfare should ever be sacrificed to bureau cratic legalism.

Mr. Swinnerton-Dyer is hiding behind a false distinc tion between rules and their moral basis. Rules ar the formalisation of the moral values of their socia structure. He claims he acted only according to th rules. But, in doing so, he cannot avoid making moral decision.

Their rules are based on principles which we do no accept. Principles which assume that students are no capable of running their own lives. Which assume tha those in statu pupillari should be more restricted tha their contemporaries elsewhere.

Parliament is about to accept the Latey Committee' general recommendations on the age of majorit People over 18 are to be recognised as full member of society, with full rights and responsibilities. Richar Goode is 22.

"This sort of thing is always happening in Trinity, said Richard Goode. And not only in Trinity. Peopl sleep with their girlfriends all over the University. Las term's Varsity Opinion Poll revealed that one in fou undergraduates have had sexual intercourse in Colleg buildings.

But we feel sure that not all Colleges would be a rigid as Trinity in these circumstances.

Last term, one Senior Tutor went on record as saying "I don't believe that we as Tutors are to set the mor patterns for the lives of our students." We recommende then that all Colleges should adopt this attitude. Trinit have not.

When will they realise what's at stake?

The front page of the university newspaper following my rustication from Trinity. The incident polarised views within the university. It even attracted interest from national newspapers (right). I learned that my friends could not be counted on (far right)!

THE SUNDAY EXPRESS, LOND

May 5

Charles's college bars man found with girl

A 22-YEAR-OLD Cambridge undergraduate must leave the university after his final exams this month because he was found in bed with his girl friend at Trinity College —Prince Charles's college.

A college porter reported Richard Goode, a Rhodesian law student, to the college authorities after entering Goode's bedroom—two staircases away from Prince Charles's rooms—at 12.45 a.m.

Goode's girl friend, an undergraduate at one of the women's colleges, was ordered to leave. Goode, in his third and final year at Trinity, was later ordered to leave his rooms and live outside the college.

Embarrassing

Drinking sherry at his digs, nearly two miles from the college, Goode said yesterday: "It was very embarrassing and upsetting when the porter burst into the room.

"Undergraduates in every college sleep with their girl friends. College rules say that girl friends should leave one's rooms by midnight.

"But my girl friend could have been asked to leave without all this fuss."

The Dean of Trinity, Mr. H. P. F. Swinnerton-Dyer, said yesterday: "Goode was told that he had the right to appeal to the college council, but he chose not to.

Reaction

"The action was taken because the college rules were being broken and because of the question of morality."

Varsity, the undergraduate newspaper, reported yesterday: "We deplore the action of Trinity College. We do not accept that colleges have the right to dictate to us how we run our lives.

"People sleep with their girl friends all over the university. Last term's Varsity opinion poll revealed that one in four undergraduates had had sexual intercourse in college buildings."

AD ADVERTISER'S ANNOUNCEMENT

JUSTICE

Justice was done in Trinity last week. Those who choose to attend the University must be prepared to accept the consequences of breaking the rules, rules essential for the running of the colleges. We therefore believe that the action of our college was beyond reproach.

The cost of this advertisement was met by the subscriptions of over 200 Trinity men.

This was not the way I had expected to conclude my days as a student, although as it transpired, my formal dealings with the University of Cambridge did not end in 1968. Forty-eight years later I was applying to become a dual citizen of Sri Lanka, for reasons that will become apparent in due course. Although I had been cheerfully presenting myself to the world at large as a Cambridge graduate for the best part of half-a-century, my Sri Lankan lawyer told me that, among a number of official criteria that I needed to fulfil, I had to provide official paperwork as evidence that I had attained a level of education acceptable to his government.

No problem, I had told him and when we returned home I had a look around for it, although I could not remember ever having seen a degree certificate or anything like it. In the end, I got in touch with the university to ask if they could send me a copy of the graduation papers that I had earned.

However, after a wait of almost a month a letter arrived in the post and it read:

> [redacted]
>
> *To whom it may concern.*
> *We would like to confirm that Richard Goode matriculated in 1965 and read Law.*

This was not exactly the fulsome confirmation of my glittering Cambridge career that I had been hoping for. So, I went back to Trinity to explain that this was not what I really thought to be the case. The upshot was that they came back to explain that they could not find any record that I had actually graduated.

Although I have no recollection of it, for obvious reasons, I must have got drunk, missed the degree ceremony and then never bothered to follow it up. So, right through life, I had been blithely labelling myself first BA, and then MA, Cantab, never knowing that both claims were a complete fallacy! What to do? The answer was perfectly simple: graduate now.

I was actually quite tempted to attend the degree ceremony in person almost 50 years later. But then I realised that I might look stupid, lining up with graduates less than a third of my age.

Was there another option? There was. I graduated from the University of Cambridge by post in 2016.

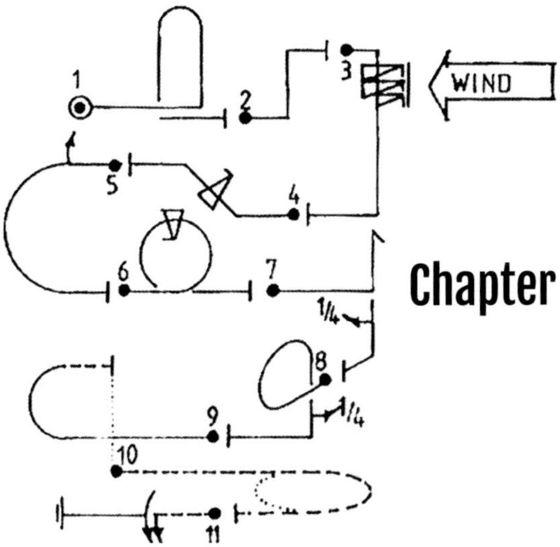

Chapter 6

ENGLISHMEN ABROAD

It was during our third term at Cambridge that the idea arose, not for the first time over several pints of beer, of going on a road trip through eastern Europe during the forthcoming long vacation.

Five of us made up the party, the other four being Al Simkin, Chris Marshall (another friend from Rhodesia) and a couple of chaps from St John's.

One of the St John's men was a serious-minded fellow who had the curious interest of collecting car registration numbers; we tired of his company and finally put him on a train in Istanbul to make his own way home. The other John's chap was Adrian Parker, who undertook the laboriously intricate work of organising all the visas, permits and the carnet de passage that we needed to travel behind the Iron Curtain. There was a great deal of red tape for him to deal with.

This was the summer of 1966, only four years after the building of the Berlin Wall, just a decade after the Hungarian Uprising and a couple of years before the Prague Spring. East-West Cold War tensions were high, at least they were at government level. Down in the everyday world, we found people we met behind the Iron Curtain to be welcoming, friendly and terribly helpful on occasions. But before we could set off to meet any of them, we needed a vehicle, and the one we chose was a London taxi. In principle, there was a lot of sense in this. London taxis were built for endurance and reliability. They were capable of carrying five people in reasonable comfort, with plenty of space for all the kit we would need for two-and-a-half months on the road. And we knew that they left service after 10 years of use.

What we had not really taken into consideration was that those 10 years had been spent on the smooth streets of London, not the rough, pot-holed roads we would encounter once we crossed into Soviet bloc countries. After 10 years our London taxi had also clocked up in the region of half a million miles, which had taken their own toll as we were soon to discover.

Comfort was something I had been deliberating before we set off and after studying the seating arrangement in the taxi I had worked out a means of removing seat-back squabs and fitting them between the fold-down occasional seats and the cushions of the rear seats to make a good-sized and comfortable bed. The others reckoned they were going to camp, although it soon became clear that mine had been the better choice. In the five minutes it took to get my bed ready each night, they had barely sorted out their pegs, poles and guy lines.

(Above) Setting off from Cadogan Gardens in the awful Austin FX-3 taxi, the most unreliable vehicle I have ever (partly) owned.

(Right) Going through Checkpoint Charlie and into East Berlin. This was easier than when we entered West Germany and the taxi broke down again.

It did not take long for problems to emerge with the taxi. Fuel vaporisation was the first to bring us to a halt and it chose to do this in the worst possible place: 100 metres just inside East Germany, surrounded by watchtowers manned by machine-gun-toting guards.

We had just passed through Checkpoint Alpha, at Helmstedt in West Germany. Ahead of us lay the 170 kilometres of the autobahn corridor running through East Germany to Checkpoint Bravo, which was the western entry point to West Berlin. Vehicles had to keep moving between the two checkpoints. Stopping was strictly forbidden, except in a few designated rest areas. So, grinding to a halt almost immediately after entering East German territory was not a smart move. It happened to be my turn to get the engine going and I kept looking over my shoulder while I was pumping the fuel pump to prime the engine with diesel, convinced that at least one of the East German Vopos guarding the border had me in his gunsight and was about to squeeze the trigger.

The gearbox held out somewhat longer than the engine, only finally giving up the ghost in Brno (home of the Bren gun) in Czechoslovakia. Again, I was at the wheel when the taxi got slower and slower as we were driving up a hill, until it reached the point where I had to pull over and it stopped completely. I was sitting in the little driver's cab, where there was a strong and very disconcerting smell of hot oil. We unscrewed the cover in the top of the gearbox to be greeted by the sight of boiling SAE30 gear oil, rather prettily flecked with masses of shiny

brass filings. Gears had been seriously shredded and it was obvious that we would be spending an unscheduled amount of time in Brno with no idea how we were going to get the gearbox repaired. That was when a chap pulled up in a rather nice late-1920s open-top Tatra and asked if we had a problem. When we explained our predicament, he introduced himself as the head of the local technical college and said he would send someone to help us.

After a bit, two tough-looking Czechs turned up on a tractor. They attached a tow-rope to the front of the taxi and then indicated that they did not have the necessary permit to tow it. 'We can drive, but we can't tow,' they explained in sign language. 'Can one of you drive the tractor?' That was how I found myself in the absurd situation as a young Cambridge undergraduate driving a Czech state-owned tractor pulling an English taxi three miles through the streets of Brno up to its technical college.

That was also how I became aware of the smell of overheating machinery for the second time that day. Our new Czech friends were perched on the mudguards beside me and they seemed unconcerned when I gestured to the tractor engine

Eastern Europe was extremely primitive in 1966 and visitors from the West were very rare. We were the objects of both curiosity and interest from the local population.

and the smell of burning. Two hundred yards short of the entrance to the technical college, it seized and a quick inspection revealed that the engine and radiator were bone dry! Everyone was very relaxed; the tractor belonged to the state, so it did not really matter. Besides which, another tractor quickly appeared and towed us through the gates where the head of the college was waiting. If we could take the gearbox out of the taxi, he said, his staff would mend it for us.

Three hours later, our gearbox was on a bench in one of their workshops, where it soon became clear that a synchro cone had jumped and the gears had gone into each other creating the shower of brass filings we had seen in the gear oil. The rooms they gave us to stay in left rather a lot to be desired, but they were free, beer was ridiculously cheap and for six days we existed in a very pleasing stupor while supremely competent Czech engineers rebuilt our gearbox with new gears, new spacers and new synchro cones. And they had to do this having converted every single measurement from imperial to metric; it was hugely impressive. What really astonished us was that, after refitting the gearbox and testing that everything worked, they did not charge us a bean for all they had done!

We had found out before leaving home that Beatles' records and jeans were a universal currency behind the Iron Curtain, and we plied our friends in Brno with some of our stock of both before driving off with our new, silky-smooth gearbox.

A couple of countries later and we were in more trouble thanks to an in-built jacking system used when changing tyres or working under the car. The system essentially featured an oil cylinder fitted with a selector that had four positions, one for each corner of the car. By selecting the appropriate position, and pumping the cylinder with a handle, you could lower a jack from the axle to raise that corner of the vehicle. Once you had finished, you turned a knob to release the hydraulic pressure and the jack was retracted by a spring.

As we had soon discovered, Bulgaria was a heavily-controlled country. We were meant to keep to a very strict itinerary, only driving on prescribed roads and spending the nights in designated places, where the authorities could keep an eye on us.

This was not our idea of fun at all and the incident with the jack occurred after we had taken on board a lot of vodka one evening, taken umbrage at the stupid restrictions placed on us and taken off into the dark to find somewhere of our own choosing to spend the night. A couple of kilometres down a side road looked like a good place to camp, and it may have been if Chris had not left one of the jacks sticking down below the axle when we set off the next morning.

Even by the standards of Bulgarian roads, the track we were driving along was very bumpy and when we struck the first pothole, the jack shaft snagged on the rim and was bent horribly out of shape. The obvious solution was to remove the damned thing and isolate its hydraulics, so that the other three jacks could still be used. But a decade of dank London weather, topped up by occasional winter doses of road salt had corroded all the nuts, while the jack itself was inaccessible to a hacksaw. We had to find a means of straightening the jack shaft. A large telephone pole seemed the obvious anchor point to which we could attach a strong rope, then tie the other end to the jack, using the momentum of the taxi to bend it straight.

I was given the job of driving, slowly reversing the taxi until the rope was taut. Then I revved the engine and let out the clutch sharply, to give it a good jerk. This caused a loud cracking noise, but not from the axle underneath me. The sight and sound of 30 telephone wires falling across the taxi revealed that while the jack had stayed in place, the telephone pole had not. A number of thoughts ran through our minds, none of them encouraging. We were in the middle of one of the most repressive countries in the Eastern bloc. We were in a place we should not have been in and we had just demolished part of the state communications system.

The sound of high-powered engines less than 10 minutes later triggered a wave of even more troubling thoughts, which grew more troubling still when three tanks appeared at the top of a rise and lumbered towards us. What kind of communications network had we destroyed? How could they have responded so quickly? And, sending tanks to deal with us? Is this the end? The chap standing in the turret of the leading tank looked like the CO, so we waved sheepishly to him. To our amazement, he waved back and all three tanks rumbled past without taking a blind bit of notice. Fortunately, no one in the tanks spotted the havoc we had caused to the local telephone network.

Obviously, we had pitched camp in a tank training area and it was purely coincidental that these three had trundled along soon after we had pulled down the telephone pole. We made sure to give tanks and telephone poles a wide berth after that.

At the end of our second year, Robert Woods and I went westwards to the USA. Robert had been invited to spend time in Georgia by a senior executive in the Lockheed Corporation, whom he had met through his father, Dean of Windsor at the time. My visit to America almost came to a premature end in Manhattan when I stepped off the sidewalk looking the wrong way. There was a terrible screeching of tyres and, spinning round in their direction, I saw the front bumper and long bonnet of a police squad car inches from my yellow-clad leg.

With the Buick that Robert Woods and myself used in Georgia, USA (left) and below on the same trip.

Yellow? I was wearing a bright yellow suit that day, which prompted the NYPD officer at the wheel of the car to lean out of the door window to ask, 'OK, buddy. Where's the rest of the band?!'

Robert and I met up in Georgia, where our man at Lockheed also helped us find work. Robert got a job in a garage with a proprietor who, interestingly in the light of the civil rights campaign at that time, still refused to serve any black

Sleeping in the desert near Las Vegas, it transpired that we had pitched ourselves right next door to a USAF base, which ensured that we were woken up very early.

man. I went to work on a golf-course, helping with the grass-cutting and general maintenance. The money was good and after digging the Victoria Line deep below ground I enjoyed working outside again.

Before leaving for the States, we had heard about the scheme in which one could drive other people's cars across the country. The owners got their cars delivered free of charge. The drivers got the free use of the cars and all they had to pay for was the fuel they used. This looked like our perfect way of heading west to California and we signed up. We were joined by a couple of slightly younger British chaps Robert knew and we four piled into a large Buick and set off for Los Angeles, following a zigzag route that enabled us to take in popular sites like the Grand Canyon along the way.

I met Jan Molen at Berkley University in California where she was a young lecturer.

Much of the driving was frankly rather tedious and to liven things up we played around with the car a bit. We had one competition to see who could get the lowest MPG out of the engine and wasting petrol was not a prime consideration bearing in mind that in Texas a US gallon of petrol cost 12 cents! Crossing the state, I managed to drop the fuel consumption to seven-and-a-half miles per gallon by keeping my foot down between fill-ups.

Before leaving Cambridge at the end of term we had been given a few introductions by a South African student called Mike Silver. He was an amusing chap, but not the most reliable person of our acquaintance. Mike had told enough cock-and-bull stories that experience had taught us to be guarded about his claims. Still, his offer to put us in touch with a gorgeous girl he knew at the University of California at Berkley, sounded worth pursuing.

Robert was going to fly home for the last few weeks of the long vacation and I decided to follow up Mike's lead. He was right about one thing; Jan Molen was stunning. A graduate student, she was working on research for her thesis when I called by to introduce myself as a friend of Mike's. 'Well, you're not a friend of mine,' was her reply, which was not the most auspicious start.

Still, I persuaded her to have lunch with me and her attitude softened. In fact, in due course it softened to the point that I moved in with her for those few weeks in San Francisco. This was the Summer of Love, of course, a high point of the hippy movement and iconic rock bands. Jan and I went to several Grateful Dead concerts, at one of which we found ourselves dancing on the stage, so close to the band that Jan's clothes got caught up on the studded clothing one of them was wearing! Two-timing Caroline had never been my intention. Maybe it was the atmosphere of free love and flower power that got to me, but Jan and I became very close. She came to visit me in the UK and I went back on a couple of occasions to spend time with her in California. I was never really into drugs, but she introduced me to LSD and used to mail me batches hidden in contraceptive pill packets when I was back in Cambridge.

PEACE IN AFRICA

As a swansong to university and before life got serious, after the end of our last term at Cambridge a group of us decided to travel overland to North Africa, to visit battle sites of the Second World War among other things. The 'expedition' comprised: Robert Woods (whose career would see him rise to become chief executive of P&O), Jocelyn Cadbury (who would become a Member of Parliament), Andrew Ritchie (who would invent and develop the Brompton folding bicycle), Tim Guinness (who has become a celebrated global fund manager) and me.

The ruins of Leptis Magna in Libya (above), and in Tunisia (left) where we discovered a derelict railway line and trolley (below).

Once again, as with our trip to eastern Europe two years earlier, a vehicle was central to our planning. And once again, the vehicle we settled on proved to be just as much of a let-down as our taxi had been. Anticipating we would face some rough desert driving, we decided to undertake our journey in an Austin Gypsy, a rather poor Land Rover knock-off, which turned out to be a seriously false economy. Robert's father's position, as Dean of Windsor, gave us access to Her Majesty's garages in Windsor Castle, where we prepared for the trip. One of the main things we did was to replace the canvas cover with a solid roof made from sheets of aluminium that we pop-riveted to the frame.

We had bought a Mark I Austin Gypsy, which was not a good move. Fundamentally, the Gypsy was a pretty inferior vehicle, but the Mark I suffered from the further impediment that the entire front-wheel assembly, including the brake drum, had a tendency to fall off. The first time this happened we were driving along towards the Pyrenees, somewhere in the region of Biarritz, when one of the front wheels went bounding down the road ahead of us while the front of the car lurched sideways and the front axle ploughed a lengthy groove down that *route nationale*.

Yet another suspension failure for the Austin Gypsy in Libya. Fortunately we found two of its sisters in a scrapyard which donated parts to keep us going.

It took us a while to find the nut that secured the wheel to the axle and a day-and-a-half later, this time on the Spanish side of the Pyrenees, a front wheel came off again. We were driving down a pretty steep descent, with a drop that looked like a thousand feet to the bottom just the other side of the crash barrier. This was not a good place for the brakes to fail. When the front wheel cartwheeled away, it took the brake drum with it. With no drum to bind against, that pair of brake shoes opened to their full extent and the brake pedal went straight to the floor. Had we been going any faster, I might not be writing this now.

We never found the errant nut, so Andrew was packed off to the nearest town to find a replacement while the rest of us spent several sweaty hours retrieving the missing wheel from the ravine into which it had careered. Andrew returned equally hot and tired bearing a couple of newly-machined nuts, but even this did not do the trick. Driving through a town somewhere in the middle of Spain, a front wheel became detached once more. Free of the car, it took off down the street at a good 40 miles an hour before hurtling into the wall of a building right beside an archetypal Spanish gentleman, complete with sombrero. Until that moment, he had been slumped in the shade enjoying a peaceful siesta.

The cause of this pretty fundamental design flaw still baffled us. Robert and I had been designated the engineers and we came up with the idea of using two nuts on each front wheel; with the second locking the first in place. That seemed to do the trick, but for obvious reasons we were on tenterhooks waiting for one of the wheels to break loose again. However, we made it to Libya where we were driving along one day when we passed a scrapyard in which we saw two Austin Gypsies. We remembered this yard, an hour or so further down the road, when one of our front wheels came adrift once again. Robert and I hitchhiked back to where we had seen the other cars to discover that the Libyan Army had placed a large order for Austin Gypsies and, crucially from our point of view, these were Mark II models in which the problem with the front wheels had been resolved.

RUNNING JOKE

Camping in the desert and largely preparing our own food with limited supplies of water meant that hygiene was a bit of a challenge. Before long, most of us had runny tummies although Andrew maintained that he had a technique for combatting diarrhoea. 'The trouble with you chaps, is that you're not holding it,' he explained. 'If you've got diarrhoea, you've got to hold it in. Whatever the pressure, you must hold it. Then it solidifies and you'll find you're OK.'

This column in Libya was not quite as high as it might seem in the photograph, so not as hazardous as one would imagine!

In his eyes, the rest of us were frankly rather pathetic for allowing ourselves to succumb to an attack of the runs. We were on the coast of Tunisia, camping on the beach right next to the Mediterranean when it was Andrew's turn to get a gyppy tummy after we had dined on a supper perhaps rather too heavily laced with chillies. 'Well, you of all people know what to do,' we commented without much sympathy. He did, although it did not work.

The next morning, I came to in the early light to be greeted by the sight of Andrew knee-deep in the blue waters of the Mediterranean, sluicing out his sleeping bag!

In seven weeks, the historical perspective of that trip ranged from the zenith of the Roman Empire to the bitter struggle against Rommel's Afrika Korps.

The Americans had built the huge Wheelus air force base not far from the Roman city of Leptis Magna, which caught our interest, mine especially, when we spotted a crashed Phantom F4 fighter that had come to rest close to the perimeter fence alongside which we were driving. The fence did not look difficult to climb and as there was no one to be seen, I nipped over and was soon exploring inside the crashed jet.

The wreckage was still pretty intact, but I had only been inside it for a couple of minutes when US military police showed up and caught me red-handed. There had not been any sign of security people, but they must have been alerted to the presence of an intruder because they were on the scene with impressive speed and I was arrested and locked up in the guardhouse almost as quickly.

The rest of the team had watched events unfolding with a blend of glee and alarm. The air base guards had got it into their heads that I was a particularly unpleasant kind of spy and it took an afternoon of fairly serious grovelling and fawning before they agreed to let me go, with the very stern warning not to try pulling that trick again.

At the end of our North African venture we made use of a shipping service from Benghazi to Marseilles, setting sail for home to start living like grown-ups. In fact, the real world had already started making its demands on Tim Guinness, who had had to leave early to start a course at MIT. For my own part, I was heading for the bar, although with nothing like the enthusiasm with which I had previously headed for any bar.

Chapter 7

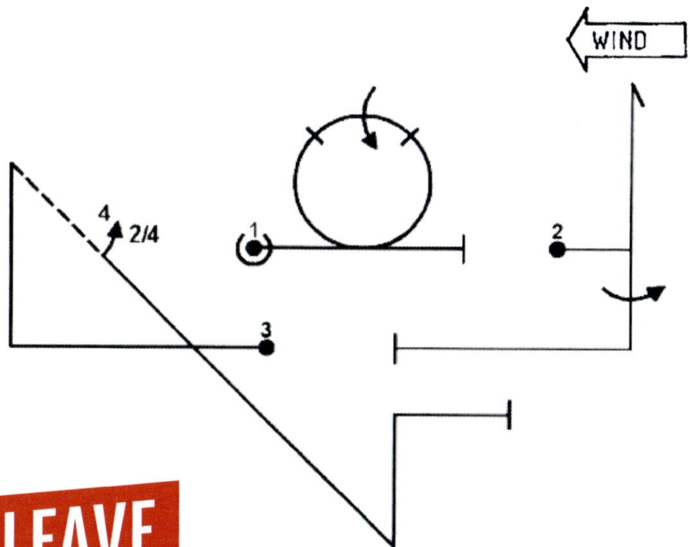

FRENCH LEAVE

Anyone studying law at Trinity in the late 1960s had the good fortune to be taught by a group of first-rate tutors.

Men like Eli Lauterpacht and Tony Jolowicz were regarded as two of the top academic lawyers of their day. So was Leon Brittan, with whom I had tutorials. They brought an intellectual rigour to my final year and they also helped me achieve a respectable second-class degree, good enough for me to enrol at Gray's Inn to start a career as a barrister.

I cannot pretend that I had any particular leaning towards the law. Rather like my change to Moral Sciences three years earlier, the Law was there and, in the absence of proper guidance about what I should do, I rather fell into it. Thus began my brief career at the bar. I started to eat my dinners and to apply myself to my studies, but a niggling doubt was growing that this was not what I wanted to do.

I suspect that things are different now, but from my perspective back then I got the firm impression that you were tied to your clerk. All your work and all your business depended on your relationship with your clerk. I knew myself well enough to see a situation arising when I might well fall out with a clerk, a state of affairs that would hardly speed my professional advancement. That prospect was bad enough, but I also envisaged the first 10 or 15 years being pretty arid, following up briefs that would be sending me off to out of the way places to represent someone who had been driving too fast.

Underlying these concerns was the freedom and independence I had been enjoying since I left school: hitchhiking down through Africa, living on my own in Cadogan Gardens during the vacations and doing pretty much what I wanted while I was at Cambridge. I had itchy feet and, fundamentally, I did not want to settle down. At that juncture what I wanted to do was go to France. My father was very relaxed when I told him. It was my life, was his answer without any hint of criticism or disappointment.

Once the idea had consolidated I telephoned Murray Kenyon, a good Cambridge friend and I asked if he fancied coming along as well. He was driving an HGV around the UK and opting to join me in Paris was not a difficult decision. So, preparations were set in motion. If truth be told, our preparations did not amount to much beyond buying a second-hand trailer, a bright yellow one that had formerly belonged to the Gas Board, to carry whatever belongings we were unable to fit in the XK 120.

We set up home in a rented flat in the Rue du Sergent Bauchat, not a smart address in anyone's book, but still within the perimeter of central Paris. With board and lodging arranged, the next thing needed was a means to pay for it and the obvious way to get a job in Paris was teaching English. Language schools were not excessively fussy about our abilities as teachers. Provided that you were a

My yellow Jaguar XK 120 lovingly restored in Cambridge and then used as a Parisian runabout.

native speaker and had a degree from an English university, you could pick up a job in a language school without difficulty.

I knocked on the doors of several and could have had a job at all of them, but the people I met at Language Studies seemed friendly and I decided to go and work for them. I roped in Murray too, and when other friends pitched up they joined the teaching staff at Language Studies as well.

Over the months, we accumulated a lot of motor vehicles with their number increasing exponentially with the number of occupants inside our flat. One that acquired a special status during our Parisian sojourn was the Mark IX Jaguar that I bought during a visit back home. This was a very fine and very commodious limousine that I picked up for a song from what was described as a 'leisure company' in London.

One could wine and dine well and inexpensively in Paris 50 years ago. We did, often, and it was unbridled consumption of liberal quantities of booze that triggered another bout of malaria. It is a curious disease, lying dormant until the liver shows signs of weakening, as it does when it is incessantly saturated in alcohol. Once a victim, always a victim and I did not help the situation by failing to recognise the symptoms. Self-prescribing a large brandy whenever I felt below par did not help either.

GLOBE TROTTING

Our forays in the Mk IX were not restricted to Paris and its immediate environs. When Marion was giving a big party in Cambridge a group of us piled into the Mk IX and crossed the Channel to join in the fun. In London, we collected Robert Woods, celebrated with a couple of pints and then started off up the A1 heading for Borehamwood, where we were collecting Andrew Ritchie from his job at Elliot Automation. On the way, we stopped at a filling station where the big illuminated glass Shell sign, on top of the pump, caught Robert's imagination, especially when he found that the screws holding it in place were loose.

'Why don't we nick this?' he whispered while I was filling up with petrol.

'Don't be ridiculous,' I answered.

But as I was paying for the petrol, Robert undid the screws holding the sign in place and then jumped into the car with this large glass object in his arms shouting, 'Go! Go! Go!'

The Mk XI had been temperamental about starting and the engine chose this moment to refuse to kick into life altogether! This gave the chaps in the petrol station ample time to write down the registration number.

Another mechanical failure, this time with the Mark IX. We worked on the basis that four heads were better than one.

We did manage to get going, after what felt like minutes. Off we shot to Borehamwood, collected Andrew, went to a pub for several more pints and then headed up to Cambridge. Somewhere on our route we approached a roundabout and noticed that a car had been parked somewhat carelessly sideways on to the road. As we got closer the car began to look like a police vehicle and indeed the chaps standing beside it did appear to be wearing police uniforms.

We were brought to a stop at their roadblock where one of the officers announced, ‘We believe you have stolen property on board.’ We tried to play innocent, which was not terribly easy with the large Shell globe sitting on Robert’s lap. ‘Oh, do you mean this?’ he asked. ‘We’ll take it back if you like. Or, you can take it back if you’re going that way.’

‘We won’t be doing that, sir,’ answered the policeman. ‘We’ve been asked to arrest you.’

Andrew, Robert and I were driven off in the police car by one of the patrolmen, while his colleague got into the passenger seat of the Mk IX and told Murray to follow the police car to the police station in Hitchin. Murray, who had had no intention of driving that day, had been getting warmed up for Marion's party by tucking into the stock of low-cost French booze we had secreted in the generous void behind the Mk IX's dashboard before leaving Paris. Apart from driving next to a uniformed traffic cop while under the influence, Murray did not have any insurance to drive the Jaguar, so it was a tense drive to Hitchin as he did his level best to follow the white lines and not to give the game away!

After some time in Hitchin, the police decided that we needed to be returned to Hendon where the crime had been committed, to be charged. So Murray, Robert and Andrew were handcuffed together and put in the back of a Black Maria, while I drove the Mk IX behind them in the company of a policeman.

At Hendon Police Station we were all charged with theft and then released on bail to appear before the magistrates the following Monday. It was gone 10 o'clock at night when we made our entry at Marion's very smart black tie party, still wearing our grubby travelling clothes. I had at least been allowed one telephone call and had rung ahead to explain what had happened, but we were not popular to say the least.

Twenty-four hours later we were on our way to appear before the bench. Robert's father was still Dean of Windsor, living at Windsor Castle, and we impressed on Robert not to give away who he was when we were asked to state our names and addresses. When his turn came, Robert told the court that he was Robert Woods who lived at Dean Close, Windsor and that is how the record stands!

Ritchie, who had played no part in this felony, of course, wanted to plead his innocence. But we others (and the arresting officers) told him to plead guilty like the rest of us because it would make everything so much easier. So, we were all, Andrew included, fined a tenner, plus five pounds costs. Regrettably it was a similarly inebriated night out in Paris that brought an end to our jaunts in the Mk IX. I was not present at the time, but the situation must have been very alarming for those who were, because they had been tootling home minding their own business when the engine suddenly caught fire. It was fortunate too that a fire station was nearby and *pompiers* were soon on the scene, having a high old time putting out the fire and not missing the chance to trash this English milord's flashy limo.

The Mark IX was a sorry sight when we towed it back the next morning and parked it in line with the XK 120, which was also incapacitated by now. The front of the car was all burned and blackened, although the fine leather upholstery in the back had escaped without a mark. Even the drop-down cocktail table was unblemished and in full working order. This was a detail that I was not alone in noticing. Only a few mornings later we came down from the flat to go to work and found a tramp comfortably ensconced in the back of the Mark IX, enjoying an early morning glass of very ordinary *vin ordinaire* and a simple breakfast that he had carefully laid out on the cocktail table.

I made the rather obvious point that he had moved into my car without asking me first, to which he replied that he had nowhere else to go. It was the principle, more than the practice, that I objected to. I did not actually mind his being there, as long as he paid a suitable rent. I cannot remember the rate we agreed on. It was pretty modest, but it established a proper commercial transaction with which we were both content. Our tramp friend gave every impression of being more than satisfied by the arrangement. There he would be every morning, raising a cheery glass to us and waving to passers-by, very much enjoying the status of his curious new residence.

Bill Begg was another friend we made at one of the weekly tea parties hosted by the Reverend Eustace Wade, father of Virginia Wade of lawn tennis fame. Bill was the son of wealthy parents who owned a plastics business in Kent. They had sent him to Paris to become more worldly, so running into us was ideal! Bill proved to be a great addition. Apart from being enormous fun, he was better off than we were and he had a new Triumph Herald, which meant there was at least one car in the household that was unlikely to break down.

Bill's car proved to be enormously useful and indeed towed my XK 120 back to Paris after it blew up on the autoroute. But having installed, on the street, the engine from the burnt-out Mark IX, we then towed Robert's XK 120 all the way to Dieppe. This journey was notable for the part played by a charming girl I had met, called Christine Lecoq. In my experience Parisian girls were a disappointment. They may have looked glamorous and soignées, but on closer acquaintance they turned out to be self-regarding and more interested in making a social impression than being good fun. Christine was refreshingly different. She had the looks. She had the style. But she was also game for all the madcap scrapes that we regularly found ourselves in.

Towing Robert's XK 120 all the way from Paris to Dieppe at night was quite an undertaking and I asked Christine if she would like to join us in the adventure. She did and arrived looking suitably chic wearing a very smart Chanel coat. Even this did not prevent her from sportingly scrambling under the cars to reattach the tow rope that kept snapping as we made our staccato progress through the dark. I was very impressed.

One of several books in our magnum opus *'Modern Business English'*. Naturally Murray and I claimed B.A. (Cantab) although as it later transpired I had failed to graduate and only did so in 2016.

WAR LORD?

Several months teaching at Language Studies had made it clear that our students were hardly being given the most enlightened materials to work with. Most of them were businessmen and women. Yes, they were keen to improve their general understanding of written and spoken English, but what they were looking for above all was tuition in business English. They certainly were not getting this from the frankly low-grade books we were using and I suggested to Language Studies that what would really light up their business would be a bespoke course in commercial English, a complete course, mind you, with an audio component to complement a teacher's textbook, and a book of exercises, oral and written, for the students.

I am pleased to say that Language Studies liked the idea. I am even more pleased to report that they commissioned me and my team of 'experienced business language teachers' to put it together. That was how Murray Kenyon, BA Cantab, became my co-author. I pulled in most of the others too. Tim Daniel was appointed editor. Al Simkin, who had come to Paris for a week and had ended up staying a year, typed the manuscript. Bill Begg played his part and gets a mention in the Acknowledgements. So does Marion, who stepped up to the plate in the recording studio we hired in London and laid down 20 hours of audio tape with me as her male counterpart.

I am sure that professional EFL teachers would find all kinds of faults with what we produced, but we have good reason to feel proud of our achievement. We were only in our early 20s when we set to and created the entire course from scratch. Bill Yates, the overall operational boss of Language Studies worldwide, was someone with whom I got on very well. We had a lot of fun together at the language school and in Paris generally. With the success of *Modern Business English*, my own star had risen in the company's eyes, and when Bill was transferred back to London, he asked me to join him there as his number two.

The scruffy bunch who inhabited number 12 Rue de Sergeant Bauchat, Paris 12.

This arrangement worked well for a while and I was able to find occasional employment at Language Studies (London) for a number of friends. Then Bill lost his job and I was rather washed out with the dirty water after he had gone. I needed something else to do and the Army looked quite a good bet.

The suggestion had already been made by the brigadier father of a girlfriend. 'It's the modern army,' I remember him telling me. 'Very different from what you might imagine.' And he kindly introduced me to the Seventh Royal Horse Artillery, which looked interesting in so far as it provided artillery support to the parachute regiments.

From my perspective, it seemed to combine the higher-calibre social life of a cavalry regiment with the operational status of an airborne regiment. The money looked good too. As a graduate, a 'fluent' French speaker and a parachutist, I reckoned I could be earning more money than friends in banking, for example. For a short-service commission of three years, it also looked like being damned good fun. I duly applied and was invited to spend a week with the regiment at Aldershot.

On my first day, they put me under the wing of a young officer a couple of years older than me. He suggested that we should have a crack at the assault course, which did not faze me because I was still quite fit; apart from regular runs, I had also played rugby for the British Rugby Club of Paris. As might be expected, a parachute regiment assault course is pretty tough, but it did require a degree of forethought as well as brute strength. That was certainly the case with a zip line we arrived at. This was the usual arrangement with a length of taut wire down which you whizzed while holding onto a slide formed from a small wheel with a couple of handles.

However, a quick glance showed this zip wire had no means of slowing when you reached the other end. The only way to arrest the rate of your descent was to twist your hands violently from side to side, forcing the bracket against the wire to create enough friction to slow you on the way down. My young officer was obviously keen to show me how fast real paras could go on this. He set off at high speed which ended with a sickening thud as he crashed into the wooden building to which the lower end of the wire was secured, breaking a leg very badly.

It was quite tricky for me, first to get him down from this building, and then to heave him the quarter of a mile to where his car was parked. It was a little MGB and manhandling him inside without causing further damage to his leg was not easy. Not so good for him, maybe, but that exercise did me no harm in the eyes of his superiors and on just my first day as well. After that we went on an escape and evasion exercise in the Brecon Beacons: the Paras v. the SAS. Although I was pretty much an observer, I found even that very exciting. I remember one chap who had been captured and had been strapped to a metal bed. He had somehow managed to flip this the other way round, so that he was face down with the bed on top of him like a tortoise with just the top part of its shell. In this position he had started crawling inch by inch and when one of his mates asked what he was doing, he replied that he was making a getaway and heading for the river!

Anyway, the senior officers liked the cut of my jib, to split service metaphors, and asked me to join their regiment. I still had to pass the RCB (Regular Commissions Board) at Warminster, which was quite a tough five days of written and physical tests. There, we 'candidates' were divided into teams and one of the members of the team I was in was a lower ranking fellow from the catering corps, who was trying for a commission. He was very large, very unfit and posed quite a problem when it came to operating as a unit.

We had to undertake a number of challenges. Getting the whole team successfully around an obstacle course was interesting and required the rest of us to haul this great lump of a man up vertical walls and slippery slopes. There was an initiative test too, in which we had to use an assortment of ropes, oil drums and lengths of timber to construct a means of conveying every member of the team across a stretch of water. Having the catering corps chap was a mixed blessing. He was a dead weight for most of the exercises, which made them even harder work for the rest of us. On the other hand, completing all the tests successfully, in spite of having to deal with him, reflected well on the rest of us. I got through these tests all right, although my nocturnal activities had a bearing on the outcome of my RCB too.

My group undergoing selection at the RCB at Warminster. All rather good fun and it nearly persuaded me to join the army. I am number 8.

I had driven to Warminster in the yellow XK 120 and it was in this that I was driving back to the RCB accommodation after a bibulous night out with other 'candidates' when I saw a flashing blue light following me. Being stopped and breathalysed was not an option, so I slowed down to let the police car draw nearer while I planned my escape. We were approaching a roundabout and in the street lights I could see that the car following me was a Ford Anglia, which gave my Jaguar the double advantage of acceleration and speed. At the last minute, I turned right onto the roundabout, steering anti-clockwise, in the wrong direction, and then accelerated away as fast as the XK 120 could go.

The driver of the police car had not expected this and by the time he had negotiated the roundabout, clockwise in the orthodox manner, and had set off up the road after me I was well away; more importantly, bends and dips in the road kept my tail lights out of sight. I remembered that there was a dark cutting on the way up to the RCB, so I turned off the engine, freewheeled into this and switched off the lights, watching as the police Ford Anglia screamed past and away into the night.

Even so, the commandant knew all too well who to call the next morning. 'We have had a report from the police,' he told me sternly, 'and I just want you to know that this is not the kind of behaviour we will accept in the Army. That is a serious reprimand.' Then his demeanour changed and before dismissing me he confided, 'but it's the kind of spirit we like'.

My night-time escapade evidently did not count against me, because I did pass the RCB and was offered a commission. There were two, almost contradictory, reasons why I turned it down. When the time came to make the commitment, army life just looked too restrictive; I valued my freedom too much to sacrifice it, even for three years. By contrast, I had a sneaking suspicion that I might find that I enjoyed army life too much and might be tempted to sign on for another period of service and then another and another, to the point where I could become so sucked in to the system that I would reach a point when it would be too late to escape.

And that was that. Her Majesty had offered me her shilling, but after due consideration I had decided it would be better not to accept it. But having turned away from career paths that could lead ultimately to my becoming either Lord Chief Justice or Chief of the General Staff, I was faced with the question of where to look next. By a surprising turn of events, the answer was back to Africa, not so much making money, as selling it.

From: Major J.E.N. Giles, Regimental Adjutant.

REGIMENTAL HEADQUARTERS,
THE PARACHUTE REGIMENT,
BROWNING BARRACKS,
ALDERSHOT.
Telephone: ALDERSHOT 24431 Extension 2895

HQPR/4274/A

1st October, 1968.

Dear Richard,

Thank you for your letter of the 24th September, 1968 which was passed to me.

I am delighted to hear that you are still interested in getting a Short Service Commission in the Regiment. After you have passed your Regular Commissions Board presumably you will go to Mons for the normal Course and during that time you will be asked to make your choice of Regiment. Subsequently, you will be required to come here for the formal Selection Board which is Chaired by the Regimental Colonel and on which two Commanding Officers of the Battalions sit. If they confirm my view of you, you will be Commissioned into the Regiment at the end of your time at Mons.

I do hope you enjoyed your short stay with us here and we all very much look forward to seeing you again.

Yours sincerely,

[illegible]

Richard Goode, Esq.,
85, Cadogan Gardens,
London, S.W.3.

It would seem that the Parachute Regiment was keen to have me and I was certainly attracted.

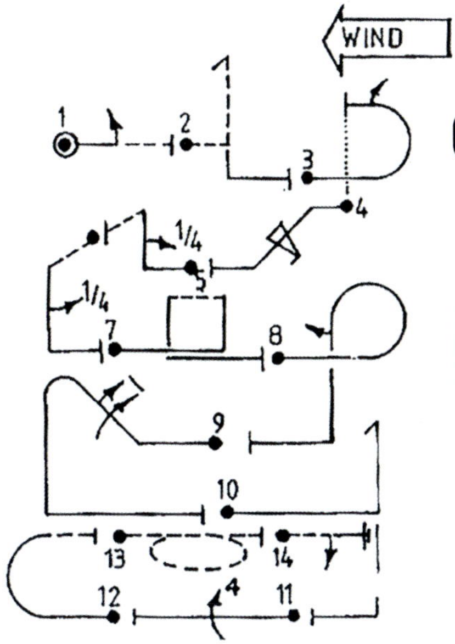

Chapter 8

MONEY TALKS

Five words caught my eye in the advertisement in The Times: *'very high-level product' and 'Africa'.*

The job on offer was in the overseas sales division of the highly-respected security printer Bradbury Wilkinson, one of the select group of engravers and printers that produced banknotes, postage stamps and share certificates used the world over. In total the workforce numbered 1,000 people, but the overseas department was tiny in comparison with just seven of us, although the very presence of my colleagues might have given the impression that there were more of us than there actually were. They all had double-barrel names; Richard Goode was the odd one out.

I worked for Bradbury Wilkinson for four years and with the wisdom of hindsight I should not really have been given the job in the first place: I was far too immature to command the position to which I had been appointed. I can see why I was given the job. I spoke very good French. I knew Africa far better than any of them were likely to know the continent and, just as importantly, I had demonstrated that I knew how to look after myself in Africa.

However, I was still only in my mid-20s, and the person they really needed to sit down to do a deal with the governor of a central bank, never mind the head of state himself, should have been in his mid-40s. But that person had not answered the advertisement and applied for the job. I had and it was me they chose to be the Bradbury Wilkinson man in sub-Saharan Africa, including Madagascar, the Seychelles and, oddly, Iceland.

I think it is fair to say that man-management was not a strong point among my employers. I spent my first four months sitting in the printing works, bored stiff most of the time, when I could have learned in just three weeks everything that I needed to know about how to print banknotes.

I had two bosses, John Bracey-Gibbon and William de Segundo, who were handing their territories over to me. Initially I travelled round with them, being introduced to everyone they knew. On my first trip to Iceland, accompanying Bracey-Gibbon, the governor of the central bank suggested to us that we should go to sample the hot baths. I had been told to anticipate this, so I had taken my swimming costume. We went into the changing rooms and then emerged out of a tunnel into this vast hot swimming pool where there must have been 500 Icelanders. Everyone was completely naked, with the exception of the two shy Brits in their bathing trunks!

The suave international banknote salesman at my desk at Bradury Wilkinson. I'm not sure why I thought it important to have a portrait of the Queen behind me.

My de Havilland Chipmunk. Although heavy and underpowered, it was a great introduction to aerobatics.

The Bradbury Wilkinson approach was always to deal with a local agent, who would be someone significant in the local business community. We made sure that whoever we chose was also well in with the minister of finance and the governor of the central bank. The ideal arrangement, naturally, was to get yourself in front of the president himself, so that you could show him a nice new banknote, while helpfully pointing out, 'You could have notes looking like these, with your picture here'.

CHANGING FACES

Over time I came to realise that one of the major frustrations of the job was that closing orders for banknotes was a slow-moving business. Bradbury Wilkinson was printing banknotes for 85 countries, but even so the processing of a new banknote order often took six years from start to finish. It was accepted that we would go off for six weeks at a time, trooping around our territories and come home empty-handed. Senior management did not seem too concerned. We were promoting the Bradbury Wilkinson name wherever we went and as revolutions and rebellions became more commonplace, replacing one African despot with another, there was a fairly rapid turnover of banknotes to keep pace with the changing presidential faces on them.

I would probably have become tired of spending this length of time travelling away from home if it had not been for the enjoyable company of Kik Woods.

He was a cousin of Robert Woods and had pitched up in London from his New Zealand home and had got a job working for Reuters, selling news information services. Luckily for me, Kik's commercial patch happened to be the same as my own and I tried to coincide my visits with his.

Kik was far more tightly controlled by his bosses than I was by mine, so a pattern evolved whereby I would wait to hear from him that he was being sent to West Africa, for example. That would be my cue to suggest to William de Segundo, 'I think it might be time we had a look at West Africa'. I am not sure that Kik was any more successful in pulling in new business than I was, but we made sure that we enjoyed those trips as much as we could. On one occasion we found ourselves in Kinshasa, more specifically in the notorious bar called the Kinois where all the mercenaries were known to go. A band of them were making the most of their down-time and we decided to join in. During that very bibulous day we had fallen in with the general manager of the huge brewery in Kinshasa, the biggest in Africa he proudly informed us. He had invited us to have a tour of his operation the following morning and we reckoned we could fit this in before attending our other, far more prestigious invitation: lunch with the First Secretary at the British embassy.

Both Kik and I slept longer than we should have and came to feeling distinctly seedy. Even so, we made it to the brewery where the tour became quite an ordeal as we trudged up and along what seemed like endless noisy iron staircases and walkways, baked by the intense tropical heat and enveloped in the sickly-sweet smell of malt, mash bins and hops.

We did start to feel somewhat better when we reached the tasting room and were invited to sample the incredibly strong export lager they produced. Things began to look a lot rosier after a couple of glasses of this heady brew. Then I remembered to check the time and realised that we were running very tight for our lunch invitation.

The taxi tipped us out at the front of the British embassy and we stumbled inside to find that the rest of the party were already making their way into the dining room. We might have got away with the fact that neither of us was too steady on our feet. People might have overlooked our none-too-fresh fragrance of stale beer and breweries. We might even have bluffed it with our stumbling apologies for arriving so late. But these all conspired against us when Kik caught his foot as we hurried into the dining room and fell right across the elegantly set table, sending glasses, china and cutlery scattering. Strange to say, we were not invited back.

Bobby Nochimson, the New York dealer in primitive art who enlivened various African trips that we undertook together.

Another companion who brightened my Bradbury Wilkinson forays was an American girl named Roberta 'Bobby' Nochimson. I met her for the first time in New York, when she was the theatre guest of the Bradbury Wilkinson man based there. Bobby and I hit it off right away. She obviously had a bit of money and when I suggested that she should visit me in London, her reply was, 'Right. I'll come next week'.

Petite, pretty and bubbling with fun, Bobby also turned out to be a very shrewd businesswoman who had developed a thriving trade in ethnic artefacts. She would take herself off to remote parts of the world, like Papua New Guinea, relying on a trim figure, a winning smile and a pocketful of cash to cut a deal that saw her buying something like a totem pole for a hundred dollars, shipping it back to the

Diana Marshall was very much part of my life when I was not living it up on endless trips to Africa.

States and selling it in New York for many thousands. Bobby was her own boss and a free agent. She had never been to Africa and it was easy for her to arrange buying trips there to coincide with my banknote-selling visits, which were always made considerably more enjoyable by her company.

From time to time, Bradbury Wilkinson agents would visit London and it was our responsibility to look after them while they were here. I remember one visit from my two Kenyan agents with particular pleasure. They were a couple of East African Asian brothers-in-law, Hasan Ratansi and Sultan Nanji, neither of whom put much effort into selecting their attire when we went to lunch in a suitably expensive Mayfair restaurant. Their rather scruffy appearance did not matter in the restaurant, although it gave me considerable entertainment on the way back to the office.

Passing Henly's showroom in Piccadilly, we spotted the new V12 E-type Jaguar, which had just been released. I had read and heard about this, but had never seen one in the flesh. Hasan and Sultan wanted to see it too, so we went in. The look on the salesman's face as good as said 'timewasters', but he went through the motions of showing us the car. We cannot have been there more than five minutes when either Hasan or Sultan announced, 'Right. We'd like two of them, please. And we'd like them shipped out to Nairobi.'

'Certainly, sir,' replied the salesman, disguising his amazement with admirable sang-froid. 'And what colours would you like them in?' Colour charts were produced and then the order form. 'What shall we do about paying, gentlemen?' asked the salesman. One of the brothers-in-law said, 'I'll pay.' To which the other chimed in, 'No. You paid for lunch. I'll pay for the cars.'

BUMP DEAL?

I had another very nice East African agent in Uganda, called Anil Clarke. It was through him that I had a couple of meetings with Idi Amin, who was president of Uganda by then. Neither of those meetings lasted more than a few minutes, but both were long enough to make me feel distinctly uncomfortable in Amin's presence. He came across as a deeply unpleasant, poorly educated, but very shrewd man. I think it is debatable whether we would actually have got a contract from him to produce Ugandan banknotes. As things turned out poor Anil got the wrong side of him, or someone else high up in the regime, and he was bumped off, in the process losing us a very good agent, never mind a potential banknote order.

The key selling tool that we took to all our meetings was the Bradbury Wilkinson banknote album. There were only a dozen of these and they were closely monitored; we signed for a copy when we joined the overseas sales department and we signed for it when we returned it at the end of our time with the firm. These were exquisitely produced examples of the firm's work: real banknotes produced on authentic paper and bound together in a set of magnificent volumes by Sangorski & Sutcliffe, the leading engravers and quality book binders.

In retrospect I am slightly surprised that it took as long as it did for someone to spot that these banknote albums had additional value. Although the banknotes were authentic in every way, including serial numbers, security features and signatures, they were still merely samples, and as such could not be printed in their genuine colours. So a high-denomination banknote was printed bright green, for example, instead of its standard pink. It was our man in Latin America who hit on the unique opportunities this presented.

He was a slightly shifty character who ran his business out of New York. I got on well enough with him, and it did come as a bit of a surprise to hear what he had been up to. I had been away from Bradbury Wilkinson for three years when the call came in, asking about banknote album number seven. I explained that I had returned it and signed for it in the orthodox way. 'Sorry,' said the caller, 'but we are having to ask everyone after what's happened in the States.'

A few calls revealed that my New York colleague had realised that a unique, bright green, but otherwise authentic note was probably worth hundreds of times its face value to the right collector. And that was just one of dozens of similarly high-value banknotes bound together in our Bradbury Wilkinson albums. So, he had sought out a dodgy New York dealer in banknotes, sold him his entire Bradbury Wilkinson banknote album, and then disappeared, never to be seen or heard of again. The rumour was that he had pocketed three million dollars for that bit of lateral thinking and that was three million dollars 40 years ago!

Quality control was something on which we prided ourselves at Bradbury Wilkinson and the incident with the Seychelles 50 rupee note is something that continues to baffle me. The order for this and the other banknotes in the series had been secured before my arrival, but it was my job to stay in contact with the governor of the Seychelles central bank and it was me he hauled over the coals when the flaw in the note was discovered.

This only came to light some time after the notes had been printed, delivered and entered circulation. The story goes that tourists had been the first to notice it. They were probably the only people with time on their hands to study banknotes closely, but once spotted the word 'SEX' is unmistakeable. The three letters S–E–X are the largest printed on the note although they were craftily disguised.

There were suggestions that one of the Bradbury Wilkinson designers had introduced this cheeky flourish to the final design, although when I took up the matter with the senior designer he assured me that they had simply followed a photograph that had been supplied by the client. Whatever the truth, we had been caught completely off-guard when the furious letter arrived from the governor of the central bank of the Seychelles who, among other things, accused us of taking the mickey out of his country which we evidently regarded as a nonentity tucked away on the other side of the world.

That was certainly never our perception, as I had to explain in a series of embarrassing exchanges. We hoped that the matter would die down, but the senior officials at the Seychelles central bank were having none of it, and the only way to placate them was to recall and scrap all the original 50 rupee notes, and design and print a completely new batch, entirely at Bradbury Wilkinson's expense.

The notorious Seychelles 50 rupee note on which you can clearly see the word 'SEX' in palm fronds to the right of the Queen.

SHIFTY CHARACTERS

One country where I thought there was a genuine possibility of landing an order was Liberia, where President William Tubman held sway. I never met the man himself, but I did spend quite a bit of time with a number of his acolytes. In the course of my negotiations, I received an invitation to the presidential palace, an enormous six-storey building not over-endowed with aesthetic charm but memorable in other ways.

There must have been 300 people attending the reception, which was held in a large salon on the top floor. Champagne was being poured in generous measures, which made up for the fact that the president had still not put in an appearance. That was until a loud fanfare sounded and one of the huge walls slid apart to reveal a large space behind, which turned out to be the top of a very big service lift. Rising into this was the president, sitting inside the presidential limousine. Perhaps I should have suggested that we could have given his official car prominent billing on a new banknote. Maybe that would have landed us the deal!

Never let it be said that Bradbury Wilkinson did not bend over to accommodate the needs of our clients, although not literally in the case of the bank governor of one particular Asian country. Word reached us that this gentleman took a personal interest in corporal punishment and, although he was nothing to do with my territory in Africa, I was going into central London on business and offered to assist my south-east Asia colleague.

My mission was to buy some whips, and I was told that Swaine Adeney Brigg were the people for whips. So I went to their shop off Jermyn Street to see what they could offer me. I explained that I needed a couple of whips and the salesman asked, not unreasonably, what sort of riding I was going to be doing. Bearing in mind that his firm had been selling high-quality leather goods to the gentry since 1750, he was absolutely appalled when I replied, 'As I understand it, they are for social use'. But it did not stop him selling me what I had gone to buy!

Having to spend more than half the year in Africa limited travelling with friends and, when the opportunity arose, I tried to cram in as much time with them as I could. On one occasion, I went with Allan Johnson and Murray Kenyon to the famous 1,000Kms race at Spa, in Belgium. They had arrived at the airport ahead of my plane and had killed time in the bar, where they were well into the holiday mood when I joined them with a Fiat 124 I had hired from Hertz.

It was the night before the race and, after a purposeful session in some Belgian bar, we decided to have a go ourselves on the 14 kilometres of public roads that constituted the 'track'. I went first and, having completed one lap, handed the wheel of the Fiat over to Murray who lost control on the first corner and rolled the car into a ditch. All the glass fell out and one door dropped off. Amazingly, the Fiat was still driveable, to a degree.

We had to return it to the nearest Hertz office, which was not easy because one of the wheel bearings had seized and could only be released with regular douches of cold water, a strategy which worked until the bearing finally locked solid 100 yards from the depot. After mentioning to the check-in clerk that we had run into a spot of bother with the car and had to leave it just down the road, we did lose a certain amount of money paying the insurance excess, although that was only a fraction of the cost of replacing a Fiat 124!

It was through friends in Lloyds that I took part in the running of the bulls through the streets of Pamplona in northern Spain. Jonny Harrison was a keen motorcyclist and the plan was that he would ride down to Pamplona where we would meet him. The chap organising the trip was Stephen Kain, whom I had only just got to know. Having worked as number three in the Peat Marwick office there, Stephen knew Spain well and we had every confidence when he assured us that all the arrangements were being taken care of by someone called Ramon.

We all piled into Stephen's 3.8 S-type Jaguar and drove down through France. Now, this was in the summer of 1975, eight months after the international arrest warrant had been issued to apprehend Lord Lucan for the murder of his children's nanny. I was wearing my moustache by this time and, without my glasses, I had more than a passing resemblance to his lordship. Somewhere near Biarritz, we were pulled over for speeding and I overheard one French policeman telling his colleague, indicating in my direction, 'C'est le Lucan'.

What remains of our Hertz Fiat 124 after Murray failed to negotiate a corner at the Spa-Francorchamps circuit late at night before the 1,000Kms race.

His chum agreed, because they immediately arrested me for being Lord Lucan and it took quite a lot of explaining to get out of it and on our way again.

Meanwhile, Jonny had been robbed at night while sleeping beside his motorcycle, leaving him with nothing but his leathers, which is what he turned up in when we met in Pamplona, by which time he was beginning to smell slightly. Ramon turned out to be rather less *au fait* with things than we had been led to believe. Having assured us that accommodation was arranged, we arrived at the house where we were meant to be staying, after dinner and getting on for half-past-ten at night, only for Ramon to be told by the owners to bugger off, or words to that effect! So, we had to set about finding a hotel, late at night, when Pamplona was at its busiest.

The actual bull running was terrifying. We took part on two successive mornings. On the first of these we had positioned ourselves 50 yards down the street we knew the bulls would charge along on their way to the square at the end, that stands outside the bullring. There were masses of Spaniards with us all and we were all dressed in white T-shirts and carrying rolled-up newspapers.

We knew the bulls were on their way when the sound of distant thunder surged towards us and these huge bulls with massive horns came charging in our direction while people fled everywhere. I managed to squeeze into a doorway as the cavalcade galloped past. The bulls are sent off with half-a-dozen cows and, not realising that they were following behind the bulls, I was nearly mown down when I emerged from my doorway thinking that the danger had passed.

Down in the square, the bulls were charging about and this was where people were gored, sometimes seriously, as they goaded the bulls to run at them, poking them with their rolled-up newspapers. The bulls rampaged about the square for 20 minutes and were then guided into the bullring, where they were corralled until the evening, when the bullfight took place. Foolish and utterly terrifying in many respects, that was truly a trip to remember.

SNOW JOKE

In 1972 a group of us went to India and again I arrived directly from West Africa. In those days imported alcohol was incredibly expensive in India. The regulations stipulated that each visitor could bring one bottle into the country, so I passed through Indian customs with one of those huge bottles of whisky, the kind that holds the equivalent of eight standard bottles. In Agra one night, the five of us improvised a bicycle rickshaw race after dinner, offering quite a decent prize to whichever rickshaw driver could cross the line first. But they were a crafty lot and after covering the course at a sedate pace finished side-by-side.

Having been outwitted, we switched places. The rickshaw drivers got into the back of their vehicles while the five of us grabbed the handlebars, lined up and then started pedalling hell for leather. It soon became clear that these rickshaws had never been propelled at anything more than walking pace. First, Robert Woods managed to turn his over, upending the driver in the back. Then the chain broke on one of the other rickshaws. I am not sure that anyone actually reached the finish line and by the time we had settled up for the cost of all the repairs it had turned into a somewhat costly evening.

Our skiing trips provided a pleasing contrast to Bradbury Wilkinson visits to sub-Saharan Africa, although I like to think that we were able to maintain a suitably distinctive British identity on the ski slopes and around the alpine villages we frequented. Skiing in tweed suits helped. There was one especially memorable occasion when we were travelling up in a cable car with a bunch of Germans. Stylish, almost certainly clad in that season's top-branded salopettes and jackets, they thought they looked fabulous. They also made no pretence in hiding their disdain for our bizarre attire, sharing audible comments about the poor Brits who could not afford proper skiing clothes and had had to make do with their grandfathers' cast-offs. However, these chaps made a grave misjudgment in taking our somewhat maverick attire as symptomatic of our skill on skis and here they were seriously adrift, certainly as far as Andrew Ritchie was concerned.

When we reached the cable car station at the top of the mountain, everyone clattered out and clipped on their skis. The Germans were still sorting out their bindings and adjusting their sunglasses when Andrew nonchalantly launched

Although I was never much good at it, I enjoyed skiing and clearly considered an old tweed suit preferable to the more modern nylon.

On a trip to India we went to a local airfield and went flying in a Hindustan Aircraft Corporation 'Pushpak' which we were allowed to fly down the Rajpath in Delhi at an altitude of 200ft!

himself over the edge of a very steep slope and descended perfectly, off-piste but with text-book precision until he disappeared from sight, racing through the powder snow down to the chair lift far below.

Our German detractors were gobsmacked. But to give them their due, they willingly ate humble pie. At the bottom of the mountain they made a point of singling out Andrew and congratulating him on the way he had skied a slope that even they regarded as very challenging. As if to confirm their admiration, one of them asked if there was a price Andrew would accept to sell him his tweed suit. Andrew said that there might be and suggested that they should meet at the end of the day to discuss the matter further.

The rest of us assumed that the German would have forgotten about this arrangement by the time Andrew went off to meet him that evening. But then it was our turn to eat humble pie, because Andrew returned with a substantial wad of cash, skiing along through the night air dressed in his underpants, socks and skiing boots and nothing more. In addition for paying some serious money for his suit, Andrew's German admirer had even bought the shirt off Andrew's back!

I could not argue that the five words in *The Times* that had caught my eye four years earlier had been wrong. Working for Bradbury Wilkinson had delivered both 'very high-level product' and 'Africa'. The job had been well paid and had given me the chance to travel pretty much when and where I wanted. My own aspirations had changed: that was the nub of it. And now my career would be altering course to follow a new heading in which 'head' would be playing a seminal role.

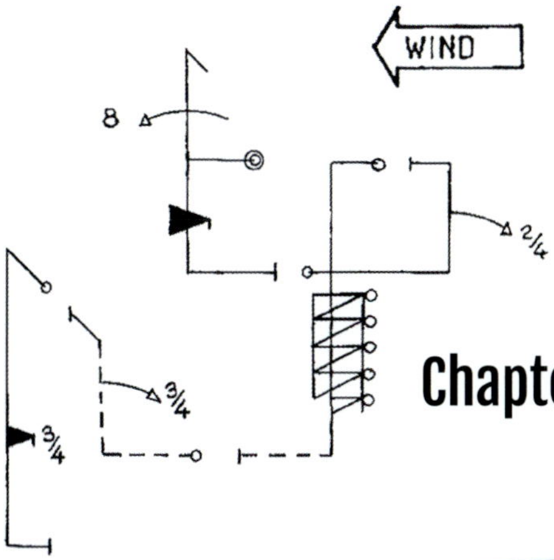

Chapter 9

THE DARK ARTS OF HEADHUNTING

Scanning newspaper pages of appointments as my feet grew itchier at Bradbury Wilkinson, one advertisement in particular had caught my eye.

It had been placed by what turned out to be an executive recruitment firm, a small company called International Appointments. The company was run by a rather curious ex-naval man named Robin Whalley who, aside from his penchant for large lunches at the East India Club, had come up with the rather good idea of placing prominent advertisements that advertised people.

Headhunting as we know it today was in its infancy back then, but Whalley used to take the back page of the *Economist* where he would post the announcement that a few unnamed top executives could be available for the right inducement, after which he presented thumbnail sketches of the executives in question. It seems such an obvious approach now, but I had never come across anyone else doing this and there was no question that it brought impressive results.

There were two other consultants and support staff working at International Appointments in W1, and I liked them all very much almost as soon as I was inside the door. The feeling was mutual, and instead of encouraging me to take the job they had been hired to fill, they suggested, 'Don't join our client. Come and work with us instead.' The proposal was ideal. By now I was becoming increasingly focused on flying (as explained in the next chapter) and bookings for my aerobatic displays at air shows were beginning to develop into a serious business. Robin and the others could see that this was important to me and we came to an arrangement that suited both parties. I was able to take days away from International Appointments to develop my aviation interests, on the understanding that I pulled my weight working with them the rest of the time. Robin and the others also agreed to let me join the firm on a self-employed basis and, no matter who I have worked for subsequently, I have been self-employed ever since.

Through placing advertisements about individual executives, International Appointments built up a very useful database of contacts. We could not call ourselves headhunters in what would become the orthodox understanding of executive recruitment but even so, we found firms were coming to us when they were looking for the right person to fill a particular position. Strange as it sounds now, none of today's big international headhunting firms had really got going at that time. The whole concept of executive recruiting was still very much a dark art. As I was discovering, no one really understood it and a lot of people in the business were experimenting with their own ideas and learning on the hoof.

SILVER TONGUES

I had been working with Whalley for about four years when I was introduced to Michael Silverman, who had just set up a recruitment firm called Merton Associates. My understanding was that Michael had to sell his former company, Lloyd Executive Selection Limited, after being diagnosed with non-Hodgkin lymphoma, and being given only a few months to live. Having sold the business, he had made an almost miraculous recovery and was now starting to work again, building up Merton Associates. As I would later discover, this summary glossed over what had really happened at Lloyd Executive Selection and if ever a dark art had been practised, that was it!

Michael Silverman wanted a partner to work with him: to be specific, he wanted me. However, even without knowing anything of his previous business conduct, I felt that he was a pretty obnoxious character: for one thing, he treated his wife appallingly, swearing at her and demeaning her in front of other people. On the other hand, my business brain told me that I could learn a huge amount from him, because Michael Silverman was so professional in the way he set about his business.

In certain ways we hit it off. I explained about my flying. He said that was not a problem and I could take time off for that, provided I made decent money for the business. And when I ended up in hospital for three months, he was understanding and helpful. He may not have been someone I wanted to socialise with, but as a business mentor Michael Silverman was exactly the kind of inspiration I had been looking for.

Merton Associates started with just the two of us, working out of an office we rented in the City. Michael had quite a big database of contacts himself. So, he was able to phone up people and say, 'I'm in headhunting. Can I meet you?' Invariably he could, and the two of us would go along to meetings where I would sit and listen and become increasingly impressed by Michael's approach and mastery of his material. It was obvious that other people were impressed too. The reason was very simple. Although Merton Associates began operating in the middle-executive tier of recruitment, the way Michael went about it was vastly superior to anything any other firm was offering. Where the top firms relied on the people they already knew, the people on their database, Michael would be far more analytical and incisive in his approach to sleuthing out promising candidates.

He would pare a new assignment right back to the core, asking questions such as: 'What people are doing that job today?' 'Who are running the major

The partners of Merten Associates. Michael Silverman (right, rear) and, to his left, Air Vice Marshal Bill Gill who had not flown a plane for 20 years when I took him up, but he was a natural flyer!

competitors?' 'What other businesses are relevant to the one under discussion?' We had very good researchers who then dug out the answers. It may seem bread-and-butter stuff now, but it was ground-breaking back then, and clients recognised it as such.

Having identified likely target candidates, we would telephone them, asking their advice and help in sourcing the right person for the job. Once into the conversation, we then asked whether they might be interested in the post themselves. The list of people we approached always looked hugely impressive when we presented it to our client.

The other secret to Michael Silverman's success, and an aspect of headhunting that I learned from him and put into practice wherever I have worked, was the meticulously researched briefs that we produced for each client. Every one of these went far further than a standard company and job description, and putative CV. Yes, there was a one-page summary to whet the appetite, but this was followed by an in-depth analysis of the company looking to make the appointment, as well as what the job itself would entail and what skills the successful candidate would need to offer. Producing this was labour intensive to put it mildly, but it always came across as a very professional, top-notch piece of work that clients were more than happy to pay for.

These documents had a similar effect on the people we targeted for each placement. As the concept of headhunting became more widely understood and accepted, the approach taken by Merton Associates, small as the company was, raised the profession to a new height and more than nine times out of 10 we were successful in finding suitable candidates for the roles our clients needed filling. And the rewards were sizeable: the industry standard is that a headhunting firm will receive a fee equivalent to one third of the salary on offer. So, if the candidate you successfully placed in a client's company was moving on to a salary of £250,000, the headhunting firm would be paid more than £80,000.

Michael's highly professional approach to the business started at his own desk. Every morning he drafted his own action list for the day, which is a practice I adopted and continue to this day. He kept up the work momentum too, based on the formula that 12 referral interviews in a week would lead to one placement. In a year, I personally looked to achieve a placement rate of 15 to 20 successful appointments. That kept me on my toes, but also kept Michael happy as the fees continued rolling in and, indeed, I earned well.

As the big international headhunting firms started to become established in London, I told Michael that Merton Associates needed to build our own international presence. He agreed and let me spend time developing Transearch, a pan-European affiliation of recruitment companies that passed searches and clients between themselves. While Michael was very helpful in allowing me a lot of space within the company to follow my own ideas and to take time away to pursue my flying, of course, he was fundamentally a nightmare to work with. I suppose we were both strong-willed people and we had some spectacular stand-up rows.

We had been working together for seven years when one of these pretty heated exchanges flared up. But where I had put the previous ones aside and carried on working as before, this time I could see that I had run my course with Michael. I told him that I thought we were growing apart and that it was probably better if we stopped working together. Michael was not very happy with this suggestion, but he could see that I had made up my mind and he did not try to get in my way. By now, he and I had been joined by five other headhunters, so Merton Associates was not going to be left high and dry.

LOAN RANGER

In the end, Michael agreed to let me take my secretary, my researcher and some of my clients to set up business on my own. We moved into a rented office in Bedford Square, trading under the name of Richard Goode. And it was at this stage of my headhunting career that I met Nigel Rugman who, as a minority shareholder of Lloyd Executive Selection, had been an innocent victim of Silverman's skulduggery. Exploiting his cancer bombshell with what amounted to emotional blackmail, Michael had persuaded the minority shareholders to agree the sale of the company, which rapidly fell into disarray, costing Nigel and the others their jobs. Meanwhile, Michael had slithered free from their investigation into his misappropriation of the firm's funds for his personal use and then experienced his sudden and rapid recovery from death's door.

Looking back, Nigel and I now agree that we would have made a good partnership and for the life of us we cannot understand why we did not go into business together. But we did not, even though I was finding running my own show rather isolated. As it happened, Nigel had been asked to recommend someone to join and run Paul Ray's office in London, and Nigel thought of me. At that stage, Paul Ray was the third largest headhunting firm in the USA, with an office in London, run by a very bright man who, unfortunately, did not know the first thing about headhunting! It was not surprising then, that the Paul Ray London office was underperforming.

I spent four days visiting Paul at his headquarters in Fort Worth and we really clicked. I liked him. I liked the people working with him. I liked their business and I was feeling a bit lonely ploughing my own furrow all by myself. So, joining his company was not a difficult decision and I simply took my little business and grafted it on to his. There were four consultants in the little Paul Ray office in St James's Street, plus the head of London operations who before long was courteously shown the door with a not-ungenerous golden goodbye. I then became the country manager.

Since I was also the manager of the only Paul Ray office outside the USA, I spent a fair amount of time travelling across the Atlantic every six weeks, for corporate meetings that rotated between the eight US offices. Although Paul observed that the methods of doing business that I had brought from Silverman were costly, he could see how effective and impressive they would be with his clients.

I knew that this was streets ahead of anything they were doing and the results were soon speaking for themselves. The Paul Ray London office turned around fairly quickly and from then we were doing well. I gave presentations to other

A partners and senior management meeting of Carré Orban.
I seem to be one of only two in a light-coloured suit.

offices in the firm, where the immediate response was that my way of doing things involved a great deal of work, and was that really necessary? However, it was not long before elements of what Silverman had taught me and what I had gone on to develop and refine, began percolating throughout the organisation.

With headhunting in general starting to gather momentum, I pushed Paul to start broadening our horizons, notably in continental Europe. Since I was based in London, exploring opportunities the other side of the Channel was an obvious fit and it gave me my first taste of developing new business opportunities and bringing together people from differing commercial backgrounds. It was stimulating and creative. At that time, Swiss-based Egon Zehnder was the largest headhunting firm in Europe. Second to them was Carré Orban, whose head office was in Brussels, and it was with Georges Orban that I opened discussions.

Very affable, very charming, Georges was slippery as hell. Although the principals in these negotiations were the heads of the two companies, Paul and Georges, I found myself geographically and strategically acting as a middleman while we gradually edged towards agreeing terms for a merger.

Carré Orban had a small office in New York and even before the deal was signed, it made sense to fold this into the much bigger Paul Ray office there. In due course the two London offices merged as well. The head of the Carré Orban London office was subsequently eased out and I took over from him running the combined UK office. Bringing together people from two quite distinctive commercial cultures was an interesting experience. In contrast to the American aggressive high-fliers working for Paul Ray, Carré Orban favoured urbane, polished consultants. There were people with MBAs, of course, but many of the senior executives came from aristocratic European backgrounds.

A BIRD IN HAND...

After protracted talks, we were very close to finalising the agreement, when Georges started hinting to his colleagues that they could probably get a better deal elsewhere. In the slightly frenetic world of international headhunting people can easily lose sight of the big picture which is precisely what started to happen with the Paul Ray/Carré Orban merger. Everyone allowed themselves to become so wrapped up in this, that they let the day-to-day business of serving clients slip, and slip badly.

With the pen poised to sign papers with Paul, Georges had been secretly having similar conversations with Korn/Ferry, the world's largest headhunting firm, then and now. The agreement with Paul was so far advanced that a joint corporate brochure had been published under the collective title: Carré Orban and Paul Ray International. But when Paul got wind of what Georges had been up to, he made a few choice remarks and told everyone that he was walking away from the deal.

By this stage the two companies had become inextricably fused in the London office, and despite the very bad blood now flowing between Paul and Georges, it was my job to keep that end of the business running. Georges then started having more overt meetings with Dick Ferry. This led to a lot of head-scratching lower down the company with the knock-on effect that work tailed off, income was reduced and the actual value of Carré Orban as a business began to slide.

I was appalled at what was going on, although there was little that I could do apart from putting all my effort into making sure that we got some kind of a resolution, ideally a merger with Korn/Ferry. However, getting to that stage was far from easy. Georges would summon us to partners' meetings in smart Swiss locations, where he would begin implying that perhaps we could be getting an even better deal than the one we were working on with Korn/Ferry – the Paul Ray debacle déjà vu.

Further Machiavellian machinations only came to light later. Georges always presented himself as a major shareholder in Carré Orban, with a serious financial stake in the company, as he might reasonably have been. But Carré Orban was structured using a curious Swiss legal formula by which Georges had a controlling interest in the business through his holding of A-shares, but only a tiny financial stake in his modest block of B-shares. The rest of the partners, like me, just had B-shares and were personally far more exposed to the financial risks the business faced than Georges would ever be.

Trying to keep the business upright on these shifting sands of innuendo and intrigue was hard going, but I did my level best to make people realise that merging with Korn/Ferry was by far the best move in the long run. Korn/Ferry was big. It was successful. It was going places.

As it turned out, Korn/Ferry sent an excellent man, Peter Dunn, to London with the sole objective of nailing the deal. Peter spent several months living in style in a smart West End hotel, while we struggled through endless late-night meetings thrashing out the fine detail of an agreement. In the end a resolution was reached. The two firms merged and quite quickly the Carré Orban name was dropped. From then onwards, I and the rest of my London team worked for Korn/Ferry pure and simple and, unknown to everyone except those at the very top, I was still self-employed, the only one in the company to be so.

(Left) With Peter Dunn, Chief Operating Officer of Korn/Ferry with whom I had endless meetings trying to complete the acquisition of Carré Orban by Korn/Ferry.

Once the dust had settled and the new organisation was up and running, Dick Ferry and Peter Dunn were generous in acknowledging my role in driving through the merger, and asked me what I would like to do in Korn/Ferry, which was very decent of them. By now I had seen enough of the inner workings of big-city headhunting to know that doing that for the rest of my working life was not for me. So, I proposed that they should give me the funds to set up new offices in 'emerging markets', which they agreed to do.

I was also perfectly straight with them about my other commercial interests, and we settled on an arrangement that gave me considerable flexibility over how I organised my time. I did enough 'headhunting' work for Korn/Ferry to cover my salary, but my main contribution to the firm would come from the income generated by the offices I was going to be setting up. To reinforce the point, I undertook to cover the cost of employing my secretary out of my own pocket, knowing I would need a PA who would work for me exclusively.

EASTERN PROMISE

Russia was the first country I went to. I already had a lot of contacts of my own through my aviation business and in the aftermath of the collapse of the Soviet Union, western firms were setting up Russian operations for which they needed to recruit able Russian executives. It was an ideal time to establish a search and recruitment business there. Headhunting did not exist in Russia, although some bright young businessmen had heard about it. Some had even made a start, setting up their own executive recruitment businesses, winging it as they picked their way

(Top) Our complete Eastern European team of Korn/Ferry. Ed Kelley (front) ran everything outside the USA.

(Above) I offered a prize to anyone who could drive my Silver Ghost without grinding the gears.

(Left) The secretarial desk to a major Russian company general director.

through the turmoil that Russian commercial life and Russian society in general was experiencing.

I was fortunate in quickly coming across a couple of these young tigers. Maxim Chouvaev and Kiril Butusov were bright and eager and both spoke English. Based in St Petersburg and trading as the somewhat grandly named Baltic Consulting Group, Maxim and Kiril were exactly the kind of people Korn/Ferry needed. However, Peter Dunn was adamant that we should buy their business as well and that was something I was dead against.

This led to significant disagreements between us. In my opinion, one that I explained to Peter, here were ideal people to work for Korn/Ferry, people we could train and fit into the firm, so why did we need their little company, about which we knew absolutely nothing? I suggested that we should pay them $50,000 each to dump their company and come to work for us instead. 'They would love it,' I tried to persuade Peter, but he dug in his heels and he was senior to me. Thus, we found ourselves embroiled in the nightmare situation of trying to buy a Russian business, from Russians, in Russia and all of this against the bureaucratic chaos of glasnost. Those who suggest that Russia at that time had more than a whiff of the American Wild West might take heart from the knowledge that Kiril, who was a bit of a wild card, kept a loaded revolver in his desk!

I found working alongside Russians in Russia immensely stimulating, quite apart from the unique insight our work gave me into how industry and commerce had operated in the former Soviet Union, not to mention how it was now adapting to the bracing winds of the open-market and free competition that were blowing in from the West. The prospect of coming to work for a big multinational like Coca Cola, or Black & Decker, which were two of our clients in Moscow, was enormously attractive to ambitious young Russians: 2,000 young executives applied for the job as Russian representative for Black & Decker alone. Indeed, Maxim Chouvaev was himself a text-book example of the kind of eager, dynamic talent we were aiming to recruit.

Maxim had a special interest in management audits, a product I had encountered at Carré Orban, which formed an important part of our work in Russia. There, and the other emerging markets where we worked, management audits were crucial for the Western firms acquiring major stakes in businesses that had previously operated under a very different corporate culture. Maxim and I conducted various management audits together, the one I remember most vividly being the very high profile assignment that required us to assess all the senior management of KAMAZ, the largest manufacturer of trucks in the whole of Russia.

Kamaz had an extraordinarily successful team racing trucks which consistently did very well at the Paris to Dakar races. Maxim and I spent 10 days there doing a management audit.

KAMAZ was based in Naberezhnye Chelny. Its huge factory completely dominated the city and the surrounding area. The population had grown 18-fold in 25 years and one of the factory halls alone stretched five kilometres: you could not see from one end of it to the other. At the peak of its power, KAMAZ employed a workforce of 150,000 and annually it produced in the region of 150,000 trucks.

For Russia, KAMAZ was a symbol of industrial might. Western investors, notably US hedge funds and the European Bank for Reconstruction and Development (EBRD) understood that, but what they wanted was a hard nosed evaluation of how the company was being managed. That was where Maxim and I entered the picture. American investors had particular concerns about the competence of the CEO and the expectation was that the professional assessment by Korn/Ferry would justify showing this gentleman the door.

This was a typical office block in Russia during the 1980s.

So, Maxim and I each spent three hours working through a rigorously structured interview with the CEO and the rest of the top brass, giving each the third degree in business terms. Having pooled our results, we reached a consensus. In fact, it was not difficult. Maxim and I both concluded that the CEO of KAMAZ was very good at his job and our professional recommendation was that he should be kept on to continue his good work.

We delivered our report and left our clients to mull over its contents. Such was the importance of KAMAZ, that our report formed part of a dossier submitted to the prime minister of the Russian Federation in advance of a high-level meeting at which the fate of KAMAZ was to be discussed with senior executives from the EBRD. When the EBRD people repeated their misgivings, they were countered by the Russian prime minister who drew their attention to our report, and reminded them that the CEO had been assessed and approved by two professionals commissioned by the EBRD, among others.

My colleague and great friend Maxim Chouvaev who helped me to build up a significant business in Russia.

That sealed it. The CEO of KAMAZ stayed where he was, now publicly endorsed by both the head of the Russian Government and the men from Korn/Ferry: Richard Goode and Maxim Chouvaev. And who was the Russian prime minister in 1999? He was a man named Vladimir Putin.

FIELDS OF GOLD

I carried out similar work with my associates in the other offices I opened and getting started in India was, mercifully, more straightforward. I had been given an introduction to Noni Chawla, who at the time was working for the Indian Tobacco Company (ITC). They had the Sheraton Hotel concession and it was Noni's job to run all the Sheraton hotels in India. He proved to be an excellent choice and, having joined Korn/Ferry, got the company's Indian operation off to a flying start. Apart from being very good at his job, Noni was also very well connected. Indeed, he took me to meet Ratan Tata, chairman of the Tata Group, one of India's largest industrial conglomerates. The fact that Noni was able to open the door to such an impressive and influential businessman was enormously valuable for Korn/Ferry.

Experience in Russia had exposed the difficulties we faced in getting a business up and running in countries where everything from the telephones to office leases had been centrally controlled by the overarching and stifling hand of the state. But when this restraint was lifted, people were not sure where to turn to get anything done and into this void stepped sinister figures like the heavy-set gentlemen who presented themselves in my Moscow office one day offering what they referred to as an 'umbrella', good old-style mafia protection to you and me, in return for regular monthly payments. 'Please understand how we work,' I answered. 'We work for companies that are abroad. We invoice from abroad. We are sent enough money just to pay the people who work for us. We have no money. So, to be honest, I couldn't pay you any money to look after us anyway.'

Then some other people came along: their competitors in the same line of business. I told them the same thing and they too seemed to accept the situation and we were not bothered after that. Buying the office car opened my eyes to another side of doing business in glasnost Russia. We were buying a Lada, like everyone else. But in those days there were no dealerships with glossy showrooms. We went to a chap sitting on a street corner, where he had a pretty scruffy lot with five Ladas, all brand new. We picked the one we wanted, took it for a drive around the block and brought it back to the salesman, at which point the warranty expired! Then we signed some papers, handed over the money and the car was ours.

Having an interest in cars, I was keen to see what this new office acquisition was like and gave it a run after work. But when we switched on the headlights, the view through the windscreen was still poorly lit. The reason became apparent when we examined the front of the car. The glass covering both headlights was in place, but that was it. There was nothing behind the glass: no bulbs, no wiring, no reflectors!

Mind you, we bought our Lada at the time when windscreen wiper blades were at such a premium in Russia that wise motorists removed their wiper blades every time they parked their cars and left them. Apparently, the one and only windscreen wiper factory in Russia had stopped making them.

My approach to spending the firm's money raised eyebrows among my colleagues, but I continued to argue my case. My offices always looked well presented with fresh flowers and well-polished furniture. But when I went to Moscow on one of my six-weekly visits, I slept on my office manager's sofa, in his flat. He was living in Kutuzovsky Prospekt, which by Moscow standards 25 years ago was the high-quality residential area populated by the social elite and the likes of John Le Carré's fictional Soviet intelligence agents. To be honest, the flat was nothing to write home about, but Jonathan Holmes had made it comfortable. It was also much more convenient for me to be with him when I was in Moscow: it saved us time and made my visits more productive and efficient than they would have been if I had been holed up on my own in a hotel.

Noni Chawla recalls a rather less successful initiative of mine to save company money in Delhi. I was due to visit the Indian offices one winter and, having discovered that the Oxford and Cambridge Club in Pall Mall, of which I was a member, had reciprocal rights with the Delhi Gymkhana Club, I asked Noni to book me a room there. He made the point that the Delhi Gymkhana Club was a Victorian establishment, largely designed to keep members and their guests cool and comfortable through the broiling heat of an Indian summer. Was it really where I wanted to stay in the middle of winter?

I told him that it was. I went there and I shivered in bed every night of my visit! However, it cost a fifth of the price I would have paid to stay in my club in London.

DRESS FOR SUCCESS

I approached starting business in eastern Europe, now fully aware of the problems we were likely to face. I did not mind these. They were a challenge and setting up offices in half-a-dozen, possibly more, countries spread across the former Soviet bloc looked like keeping me well occupied and well paid for a good few years. But was that the best use of Korn/Ferry's resources? Might there be an alternative

A publicity photograph for our corporate brochure. Would you trust this man to hire your future chief executive?

to getting a foothold in Eastern Europe? It was something I felt duty-bound to investigate and those investigations led me to the desk of Hans Jorda, a pioneer of executive recruitment behind the Iron Curtain.

That last statement is not an exaggeration. Hans was based in Vienna from where, in the late 1980s, he and his headhunting colleagues at the big European firm Neumann & Partners had been monitoring commercial developments on the other side of the Iron Curtain in Hungary. Change was on the way, there was no doubt about it and in March 1989, Hans opened a Hungarian office in Budapest, the first western headhunting business in the Eastern bloc.

However, even they were overtaken by the speed of liberation and reform. A little over six months later, the Communist regime in Hungary was toppled, the Berlin Wall was breached and then demolished and one by one, like a row of dominoes, Eastern bloc countries shook off the Soviet mantle and began to flex their muscles as independent states. By the time I met Hans in 1994, he had established an east-European office in Vienna, as well as additional offices in Bucharest, Warsaw and Prague. I suggested to Ed Kelly that we could save ourselves a lot of time and a lot of exasperation if we persuaded Hans Jorda to let us acquire his business. By doing this, we would have tailor-made offices, off the shelf, up and running and staffed by western-trained local people who understood the workings of their individual markets.

Hans knew of Edward, of course and was a bit fazed at our first meeting to find himself talking to me, rather than Korn/Ferry's head of European operations. He admitted later that he had other misgivings as well. I had presented myself in a very smart pin-stripe suit, the kind that I was used to wearing in the office. But this was not the kind of attire worn by Hans and the business people he was used to dealing with. In summary, I looked old-fashioned and Hans was not convinced that someone with what he took to be my old-school appearance had the dynamism and forward-thinking approach that he was looking for in a merger partner. In fact, as he later admitted, he was on the point of calling off the whole deal following that first encounter with me.

I picked up his scepticism and reservations, noted them and included them in the report that I sent to Ed. However, a follow-up meeting was called and I knew that I needed to get this off on a much better footing. Almost as soon as we sat down, I offered to show Hans the report I had given Ed Kelly. This was a confidential internal Korn/Ferry document, of course, summarising my assessment of our first meeting, warts and all. Hans recognised it as such, and his attitude towards me began to shift even before I handed my report to him. It changed further still when he read what I had written about his initial reaction to me.

Those two pages did the trick. Hans could see that I had logged his reservations about me personally but reading further, the report showed that my positive assessment of his eastern-European businesses and the potential they offered to Korn/Ferry were completely in tune with his own. By the end of our second meeting my business wardrobe had been pushed into the corner and Hans Jorda and I were on the way to forming a friendship that has been growing ever since.

Patrick Alexander is another friend who played a key role in the growth of Korn/Ferry in eastern Europe. Patrick and I had first met at Cambridge, where he had been the fleet-footed wing in the Trinity first XV mentioned earlier. But we had lost touch in the intervening years and were both slightly guarded when we met again in the Carré Orban London office, neither wanting to let on that we might recognise each other after 20 years. But it did not take long to pick up from our Cambridge days, not that we had been bosom pals at Trinity, since Patrick had been a year ahead of me. Once we were colleagues together at Carré Orban, we forged a close working relationship that spawned another life-long friendship. Ed Kelly was very keen on developing Korn/Ferry operations in emerging markets. Working with the excellent teams that Hans Jorda's company had established, Patrick and I were soon operating what almost amounted to a business within a business in eastern Europe.

It has to be said that we were focusing so much of our time there because the work interested us. By the 1990s the City of London, to quote Patrick, 'was going gangbusters' and headhunters in the Square Mile were making millions. By comparison, working in eastern Europe produced rather thin gruel. Most people hell-bent on earning as much as they could would not have countenanced even getting on the plane to Bratislava or Bucharest, never mind putting in a serious shift to recruit local executives so far from the seriously big money. Patrick stayed with Korn/Ferry longer than I did and consequently developed a working pattern that successfully straddled both big-city headhunting in London and breaking ground in eastern Europe.

I left when Korn/Ferry decided to go public, my decision being driven by several important considerations. If I stayed, I would be locked into working for a US public company, which was not something I wanted to do. As part of the new terms of employment, we would not be allowed to sell our shares for five or six years. However, we could leave right away at a lower valuation of something like eight dollars a share. Korn/Ferry's going public also meant that I would inevitably end up working in the London office, which again was not something that appealed to me.

Then there was my aviation business which had already grown to become a successful enterprise. Its prospects were encouraging and, when the other factors were put into the balance, concentrating on that looked like offering a worthwhile return for my full-time attention. By the time I took my leave of Korn/Ferry, I had been involved with aeroplanes in one way or another for 20 years. In them I had found an interest that had taken me around the world as a competitor in international aerobatic competitions, and had seen me forming and participating in two high-profile aerobatic display teams. Along the way I had established a business buying and selling some of the world's top Russian aerobatic aircraft. This, in turn, had led to my brief work in the MI5 surveillance of a Soviet secret agent. By a roundabout chain of events I had set up another business that sent western clients to a former top-secret Russian air base to fly the very latest Russian military jets. And, flying had almost brought about my early demise.

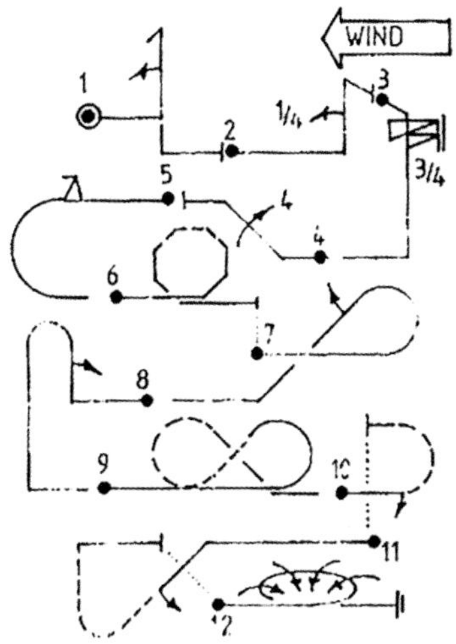

Chapter 10

PAINTING PICTURES IN THE SKY

Robert Woods's aeroplane at Sibson was not the first Tiger Moth that I had seen. When I was five years old my parents had taken me to a big outdoor gathering in Kuala Lumpur, where a Tiger Moth was being exuberantly thrown around above the heads of the large crowd.

It was exhilarating. It was thrilling. It was also incredibly reckless. As the aeroplane roared overhead, its wheels could not have been more than eight feet above the ground. I was just tall enough to make out what was happening, but one little three-year-old girl was too small. Her father had lifted her up to sit on his shoulders so she could get a proper view and that was why one of the Tiger Moth's wheels struck her head as it thundered past, killing her outright.

That was such a shocking thing to happen that it has stayed with me ever since. In all my years of aerobatic displays, the location and safety of spectators has always been the first item I have addressed in planning any aerobatic routine. Not that it should be taken as any reassurance, but the risk to aerobatic display pilots is many times greater, aerobatic display flying being one of the most dangerous activities you can do. From personal experience I know this to be true. I have witnessed five pilots being killed performing aerobatics at air shows at which I too have been giving one of the displays.

Of course, most pilots move into aerobatics having already learned to fly and gained their private pilot's licence (PPL). I would also have done this, had I known more about flying when I got started. But when my instructor began performing aerobatic manoeuvres every time we were clear of the ground, I assumed this was what flying was all about. The chap teaching me was a nice young fellow named Ray Guest. Ray did not have an aeroplane of his own. However, after I had shown a keen interest in flying, Robert Woods had asked if I would like to go 50/50 with the costs of a Tiger Moth he had bought (which he still owns registered as G-AYDI). So, when Ray set about instructing me, I already had a plane in which to learn.

Contrary to its simple appearance and widely-held reputation among people who are not pilots, the Tiger Moth is a pretty awful aeroplane to fly. It is not easy to handle and, paradoxically, that makes it quite a good training aircraft. After seven hours, trainee pilots are generally ready to make their first solo flight. If I had been sensible, this would have been the time to tell Ray that I was far from ready for the simple reason that he had done almost all the flying in the seven hours we had been together in the aeroplane. But this would not have made him look very good in the eyes of the Sibson club committee, nor did I want to lose face by looking like a wimp. Therefore, I did go solo.

Getting the Tiger Moth off the ground was relatively easy and I had taken the controls on enough occasions with Ray to be able to keep the aeroplane level and pointing more or less in the right direction once I was airborne. The tricky bit, and I knew this before I took off, was going to be landing.

I understood the theory of how to land. I was supposed to come in at the correct approach speed (60 to 65 miles per hour in the Tiger Moth), position the plane in the right attitude to the ground before touching down, ideally trying to get the two front wheels and the tail wheel to run on to the ground at the same time. As Sibson had quite a short runway, I also had to be sure that I gave myself enough space.

My problem was that my lack of flying experience meant that I also lacked the judgement that you need to bring all these elements together successfully. That was why I needed five attempts to make my first solo landing. As each one failed, more people gathered to watch what was going on. There was quite a crowd when I pulled out for the fourth time and I seriously considered taking myself off to find a quiet ploughed field, where I could return to earth without causing too much damage to either me or the aeroplane.

However, I did manage to land on my fifth attempt and in the fullness of time was awarded my PPL. This elicited an interesting reaction from my father, who

My first capable aerobatic plane, a Stampe SV-4. Here, unfortunately, I had attempted to land on a narrow track in a strong crosswind with lamentable results.

nonchalantly remarked that he had done a little flying himself when he was a young man. He told me he had been a member of the Cambridge University Air Squadron with whom he had gained his pilot's licence. My eyesight had prevented me joining the CUAS when I had been up at Trinity, but this was the first time that my father had ever mentioned his own interest in flying. I suppose that was typical of him.

As flying quickly became an absorbing passion, I wanted an aeroplane of my own. Having built up a bit of cash, I bought myself an Auster (registered as G-AMZU), a rather pedestrian, British-built plane, a version of which had been used for aerial reconnaissance during the war. The model I bought was the J5F Aiglet, which had clipped wings, making it better suited to aerobatics than the standard Auster. As the cheapest aerobatic plane one could buy, it also suited my needs and my budget in my early flying days.

By this stage, Robert and I had moved from Sibson to White Waltham, between Heathrow and Maidenhead, and it was from there that I made my first proper cross-country flight, flying the Auster over to Norfolk to visit Peter and Mel Wright: Peter was then working for the Lotus car company. I knew that I had to be on my mettle for the return, because White Waltham is situated rather too close to Heathrow for a novice pilot on only his second cross-country

My sponsorship deal with Coles Cranes involved several displays each day at the National Exhibition Centre, which would certainly not be allowed today.

flight. As luck would have it, the weather was bad. With the clouds closing in, I dropped lower and lower, hoping to get better visibility. Then, when the clouds cleared enough for me to see where I was, I found myself looking up at the walls of Windsor Castle.

In my inexperience I had not made sufficient allowance for the strength of the wind, which had blown me so far eastwards that I could have flown past the castle windows and waved to Robert's parents over their Sunday afternoon tea.

I realised immediately that I was well inside the Heathrow control zone and had committed a serious infringement of air regulations. I also realised that someone in air traffic control would have picked up the presence of my Auster on their radar, unscheduled and in the wrong place and must have been wondering what was going on. The only thing to do was to drop down to one 100 feet, treetop height, and scuttle away to the west, hoping that I could make my escape without being identified. Once I was over west Berkshire, I turned around to fly eastwards and climbed up as though making an orthodox approach to White Waltham from the west.

There were questions. I was asked where I had been and I replied without too much dissimulation that I had been in Norfolk from where I had flown westwards before approaching White Waltham in the standard way. I do not think the air traffic authorities were entirely convinced, but they had nothing to pin on me and that was the last I heard of the matter.

LEARNING CURVE

Experiences like that showed how much I still had to learn about flying in general. But I began practising aerobatics hard, flying after work and spending a lot of my spare time working on my technique. This was rewarded with quite pleasing results in national competitions, although I think the judges might have been sympathetic in their marking, because my Auster was not an easy aeroplane in which to perform aerobatics.

It was not long before I hankered for more aerobatic capability and I bought a Chipmunk (registration G-APPA), after enlisting the help of flying friends who each took a share in the Auster. The Chipmunk was a low-wing monoplane used for military training. I bought mine from an American air force officer based at Lakenheath, flew it in further national competitions and continued to do quite well with it. But the Chipmunk was still not the pure aerobatic aeroplane that I knew I really needed if I was going to improve my performance and break into international competitions. Then I got wind of the plane that would enable me to make that progress. It was called a Stampe, the French equivalent of a Tiger Moth, but a far better aeroplane. I heard about it completely by chance, when I got into conversation with a total stranger over a pint of beer in a London pub.

He and I started talking about flying, which led him to say that he knew where I could buy a Stampe, and not just any Stampe. The aeroplane he was talking about had been owned by Marcel Charollais, twice French and twice European aerobatics champion from the early 1960s. An instructor and wartime pilot, Charollais had 7,000 hours in his log book, 2,000 of them flying aerobatics.

This was definitely the plane for me. My problem was that I did not have the money to buy and restore it. However, I knew that Ed Woods did have the necessary, thanks to the generosity of the family friend and benefactor, Humphrey Whitbread, who had funded Ed through prep school, Winchester and Cambridge. Ed was keen on flying and I hoped that if he bought this Stampe, I might be able to buy it off him for my own use at a later stage. Ed understood this and agreed to the informal arrangement: that I would share flying the Stampe with him before buying it when I had put aside enough money.

Charollais's plane had been fitted with a specially-tuned Renault engine with fuel injection, of which only 10 were made. But when Ed and Murray Kenyon arrived at the airfield near Cannes to collect it, they were told that although Ed had bought the aeroplane, the engine was not included in the sale and was staying in France!

Ed was relaxed about this, rather too relaxed as far as I was concerned. He did not kick up the kind of fuss that I would have done. He and Murray simply accepted the state of play, took the Renault engine out of the Stampe and brought the plane back to England, leaving the engine in France which was a terrible shame. As it happened, this model of Stampe had been made in Belgium as well as in France, and the Belgian Stampes had been fitted with a de Havilland Gypsy Major engine. Not long after Ed and Murray had brought the Stampe to the UK, Robert and I were driving along in north Sussex when we pulled into a filling station. Behind the garage we spotted the sign for a company called Hants & Sussex Aviation, which looked worth investigating. It was just as well that our curiosity had led us to it, because round the back of the garage were 30 crates containing brand new Gypsy Major engines. Robert and I immediately bought a couple of these and sold one to Ed, to fit into his Stampe which he was in the process of completely rebuilding.

Once it was up and running again, the Stampe really got me going in serious aerobatics. It also enabled me to get the first personalised aeroplane registration in the UK: G-OODE. I bought the Stampe off Ed as soon as I could and began giving public displays. Initially I was content to receive payment in fuel alone, but more people began asking me to appear at air shows. There was not a lot of competition for aerobatic display flying in the mid-1970s and I could see a business opportunity opening before me that was well worth developing.

I believe G-OODE was the first personalised aircraft registration in the UK. I was fortunate to have an appropriate name!

I was still self-taught at that stage using a book written by Neil Williams, arguably the best British aerobatic pilot, as my manual. I would study a manoeuvre carefully, learning the procedure by heart, and then take off to practise. I was always careful to give myself plenty of space above the ground in case things did not go entirely to plan, and in this way I built a portfolio of manoeuvres from which I could make a selection when putting together a programme that fitted whatever time slot an air show organiser had given me.

At 'civilian' air shows I was paid to give my displays and the money I earned certainly contributed significantly to my aircraft costs. The situation was a bit different if I gave a display at a service airfield. Instead of taking a fee, I asked if I could have a flight in whatever aircraft were operating from the base. This had to be scheduled at a different time to the air show, of course, but the arrangement gave me the opportunity to fly in a range of front-line NATO planes. It helped me get behind the controls of a Hawk, a Phantom and a Lightning, all of which were very interesting.

COMMAND MODULE

I flew a Lightning a couple of times. One was just a jolly out of Binbrook in Lincolnshire; the other an exercise over the North Sea. The Lightning was not great on fuel consumption. On full reheat, and travelling at twice the speed of sound, it could fly for just 14 minutes on full tanks before needing to refuel. Going to Norway and back we had to refuel three times!

I did get a flight in a Vulcan, although that was slightly boring compared with other service aircraft because a partition behind the flight deck prevented one from swapping seats, so I could not have a go at the controls. Even so it was very interesting to be aboard as we flew above the Scottish Highlands at dusk, using terrain-following radar that kept us bobbing up and down at 300 feet; then we rounded off the sortie by 'dropping' a nuclear device on Liverpool.

At the US air force base at Lakenheath I was given a flight in an EC-135, a Boeing 707 which had been fitted out as a mobile command post. I was told that there are three of these operating around the world, with two more standing by as back-ups. One of these EC-135s is airborne somewhere in the world every minute of every day throughout the year. One was stationed at Lakenheath, another was based in Japan and the third was in Nevada.

During my 10-hour trip in the EC-135 we flew all over Europe and when we returned to Lakenheath they let me make several touch-and-go landings. These had none of the long approaches you have in commercial 707s. When I was at the controls of the EC-135, the flight crew encouraged me to really haul the plane round in a steep banking turn, so different to the smooth turns of a civilian 707.

In the body of the aircraft, 15 crew members were seated at keyboards studying TV monitors, while down at the back a three-star general sat at a big desk onto which three telephones were screwed, with rubber straps holding their receivers firmly in place until the time when the telephones were needed.

(Above) I flew a number of Western aircraft in lieu of fees for displays. A memorable flight was in a Vulcan over Scotland at night.

(Below) The EC-135 was a mobile command post from which a three-star general could 'run the whole of World War Three'.

The general was very affable. 'Welcome aboard, Dick,' he greeted me jovially. 'I'd just like you to know that we can run the whole of World War Three from this 'ere aircraft!'

The Americans looked after you well, offering a bed in the mess after the air show. On one of my visits to either Lakenheath or Mildenhall, I was drinking in the mess with a major who was becoming mildly over-refreshed, which led him to suggest that I might be interested to see what they had inside one of their hangars. This was well-guarded and the major had to assure the man on duty that I was a VIP attending the next day's airshow. Stepping through the side door of the hangar, I found myself facing a U2 spy plane, which they used to fly in and out at night; there were very few photographs ever published of the U2. My major friend even allowed me to sit in it which gave me a feel of the cockpit Gary Powers would have flown in before he was memorably shot down over Russia in 1960.

PATTERN IS FULL

As display bookings increased, I found myself flying pretty much every weekend of the summer, starting on Saturday morning and ending back at White Waltham on Sunday evening, having flown around the UK and appearing at maybe half-a-dozen events in less than 36 hours. This schedule was physically demanding, so to keep in shape I ran a couple of miles every day and I drank virtually no alcohol during the season, which effectively meant being teetotal for six months of the year. I made up for my abstinence during the winter. Less charitable friends might argue that I have been compensating ever since!

Flying the Stampe, starting to earn money from display flying and perfecting my technique inevitably led me to look for an even better aerobatic plane and the one I had my eyes on in the second half of the 1970s was the American Pitts Special. This was a biplane like the Tiger Moth and the Stampe, but it outperformed them in almost every way and on paper was a world-beating aircraft. Curtis Pitts, who had designed the aeroplane, had created a very powerful, but very small, aerobatic masterpiece which was capable of the most fantastic manoeuvres. Its one drawback, a significant one, was that because it was so small, it was difficult for anyone watching from the ground to follow the intricacies of its movements. Whether you were flying to entertain spectators at an air show, or to impress the judges at the World Aerobatic Championships, flying such a small aeroplane was a pretty serious setback.

These days one could probably have the choice of half-a-dozen Pitts Specials on the used-aeroplane market, but there were not many of them in the UK 40 years

My first serious aerobatic plane, a single-seater Pitts Special which was later shared with my friend Nick Ball.

ago. The one I found belonged to a professional crop sprayer in Lincolnshire. He was a bit intimidated by the plane and had decided to sell it and so I was able to pick it up relatively cheaply.

Even though I was now equipped with a really good aeroplane, I was still having to learn by myself and, without an instructor to correct my faults, I was compounding my mistakes instead of correcting them. Even simple details, such as flying at an angle of exactly 45 degrees was impossible to perfect without an instructor on the ground to watch and take accurate measurements.

Once I had been selected to fly in the British team, I used to go with Bob Mitchell, who was another team member, when he was not working on his farm south of Birmingham. He and I used to fly our planes over to my friend Joe Iliffe's airfield at Hampstead Norris in Berkshire where we would take it in turns flying, say, a six-minute sequence, while the other watched carefully and recorded notes on a dictaphone. Then, whoever had been flying would land. We would go over the notes together, before the one who had been on the ground took off to have a go flying his own sequence. This was not the same as having a dedicated personal instructor, but it was a marked step forward from trying to make improvements by oneself.

I kept the Stampe after acquiring the Pitts Special and sometimes flew both planes at displays, getting a friend to ferry the Stampe to wherever the air show was taking place. Then I would give displays in the Pitts and the Stampe myself, before my friend and I flew the two of them back to White Waltham. But owning and flying the Pitts Special stoked a burning obsession to compete internationally and reach the pinnacle by becoming World Aerobatic Champion.

THE WORLD AWAITS

The competitions in which I had been competing were largely small-scale affairs with maybe twenty competitors. Now that I was flying the Pitts Special, I graduated from these to larger events and then the British National Championships in which I came third. If truth be told, there was not a great deal of competition at the upper level of British aerobatic flying and when it came to selecting a team to represent the UK at the 1978 World Aerobatic Championships there were fewer than half-a-dozen of us who would not disgrace ourselves among the elite of international aerobatics.

Looking rather pleased with myself next to the Pitts Special. This was the plane that encouraged me to fly internationally.

Anyhow, the top three were selected, the other two being Bob Mitchell and Ian Padden, who was British but lived in the States. He had a more powerful Pitts than mine and he shipped it over to Europe for the 1978 World Championships that were to be held in Ceske Budejovice in Czechoslovakia, home of the original Budweiser beer.

Unlike many other national teams, we UK pilots covered almost all our own expenses. Clive Wilson, a friend of mine (and a fellow pilot) who was an Associate Director of the Lloyd's insurance brokers Horncastle, Crawford and West Ltd, with whom our aeroplanes were insured, managed to get us £2,000 sponsorship from Lloyd's Aviation Underwriters. But taking part in the World Championships cost the three of us the thick end of £3,000 each.

We flew our three planes in formation across Europe, accompanied by a Piper Cherokee carrying tools and spares. In theory we should have been able to reach our destination in a day, but we ran into really bad weather and had to spend the night in Germany.

The 1978 World Aerobatic Championships lasted two weeks during which time we were accommodated in an agricultural college, which was fairly basic and reminded me of the technical college in Brno where I had stayed with my Cambridge mates during our taxi odyssey through Eastern Europe 10 years earlier. Although these championships were taking place within the Soviet sphere of influence, the Czech officials running them proved to be considerably straighter than their Soviet counterparts had been two years earlier, when the World's had been held in Kiev. As a result of what some might term gamesmanship (to others, blatant cheating), in 1976 Soviet competitors filled five of the top 10 finishing positions in the Men's Championship (including first and second places). The Soviet women's team did even better; they took all top five places in the Women's Competition.

Two years on from Kiev, everyone knew what the Soviet team had been up to. Whether it is significant or not, who can say, but in 1978 the highest placed Soviet competitor in the Men's Competition was Victor Smolin, who came fifth. It has to be said that the Soviet women's team again took the top five places in their competition. Out of a field of 48, the highest placed British team member was Ian Padden. He came 30th, while Bob Mitchell and I were 40th and 41st respectively. Given my relative lack of experience, lack of practice at this level of competition and lack of proper tuition, I was not seriously downhearted although seeing how far short I was of where I wanted to be was slightly depressing.

On the upside, I started chatting up the Soviet competitors and got on well with them. I had always been fascinated by Russia and here I now found myself face to face with real Russians, who happened to be among the best in the world in a sport at which I wanted to excel. The other draw, of course, was that the Russians had fantastic aeroplanes.

In the second half of the 1970s the supreme Russian aerobatic aeroplane was the Yak-50. This was a fantastic machine. Big, with a deep growling engine that seemed to have endless power, the Yak-50 was of a size that when you did tumbling type manoeuvres it was just so impressive, the Pitts Special being tiny in comparison.

Being able to differentiate manoeuvres is critical in competitive aerobatics. Although all aerobatic manoeuvres have as their foundation the loop, roll, stall turn and spin there are thousands of possible combinations. Three thousand of these were compiled in a 'dictionary' by a Spanish aviator, Colonel Jose Aresti, published in 1961. Over the years others were added, a great many others! At one stage the Aresti catalogue ran to over 15,000 manoeuvres.

The Soviet team had KGB minders, but once I got into conversation with the team members through their interpreter, the pilots were happy enough to talk to me. They let me sit in a Yak-50 and one team member I got on with particularly well was Khalide Ajnetdinova. She had come fifth in the 1978 World Championships, although by the time she took third place six years later, she had married and changed her surname to Makagonova.

Mind you, the Soviet authorities had reason to be on their guard when their pilots mingled with their opposite numbers from the West. A great deal of state investment was put into training and equipping Soviet bloc aerobatic pilots. They were full-time professionals in all but name, very different to the likes of me who had to hold down a day job and spend my summer weekends giving displays at air shows (which required different skills to the exact disciplines of aerobatic competitions and consequently rather blunted your competitive edge), in order to fund the lion's share of my competition expenses.

Everything the Soviet pilots needed was provided for them from the very best aeroplanes to dedicated training centres: one fair-weather airfield far down in the Caucasus, in Dagestan, and another, nearer Moscow, for their use in the spring and summer. Soviet aerobatic pilots also got paid by the state at a pretty good level by the standards of salaries in the USSR.

YAK ATTACK

While I had hardly covered myself with glory at my first World Championships, I did learn a great deal. I could see the improvements I needed to make as a pilot. I also realised that I needed a truly world-beating aeroplane of my own. Top of my wish list was a Yak-50 and over the next couple of years I made strenuous, although ultimately fruitless, efforts to buy one. However, I had also been dramatically impressed by the performance, which seemed incredible to me, of the American Pitts Specials. They were so far in advance of my own aeroplane that I decided I would not be content with a standard Pitts any longer.

Working with an old friend, Bill Bonner of Aero Bonner, we set about modifying the Lycoming IO-360 engine on my Pitts Special. As well as conventional tuning, the design we came up with resulted in a much smoother, more powerful engine which, interestingly enough, proved to be rather more economical at cruise. Among other things, Bill devised a new exhaust system that comprised no less than 18 feet of exhaust pipe twisted and curved into a complex matrix that, despite looking somewhat ramshackle at first glance, proved to be very effective and robust.

With my plane flying better than ever, I entered the 1979 display season buoyed by the prospects that lay in store. Having both the Stampe and the Pitts Special at my disposal, I had 70 odd bookings that year, beginning at the Rhoose Air Show near Cardiff on 6 May and ending seven months later with a display at the Shuttleworth Collection in Bedfordshire on 28 October.

More displays brought more opportunities to perfect my aerobatic skills and gave me the form to be re-selected for the British team for the 1980 World Championships in the USA, where I was relatively pleased to be placed 17th overall. Although I came home hankering for a plane that was easier to see in the sky than the Pitts, such as the unattainable Yak-50, I felt there were still major modifications that could be done to improve the Pitts Special, and at the end of 1980 we quite literally took mine apart in order to rebuild it as the Ultimate Pitts.

I gave the engineering work to a skilled and imaginative engineer named Dave Wiltshire; the 'aircraft' side of the modifications were entrusted to Geoff Masterston. We fitted a new, more powerful engine with 220 horsepower. We improved manoeuvrability by fitting a new rudder and elevator, and larger ailerons. We also strengthened the fuselage at places where the Pitts was known to break. Creating the Ultimate Pitts took a lot of hard work and a lot of ingenuity, but the result was deeply satisfying. A stock Pitts Special would do 155 mph flat out, climb at about 2,600 feet per minute and had a rate of roll of about 170 degrees per second. The Ultimate Pitts was better in every respect: a straight and level speed of 180 mph, rate of climb 3,500 feet per minute and rate of roll of 210 degrees per second.

Although there was no escaping the fact that manoeuvres in the Pitts were still difficult to see at times, we had done our best to enhance the aerobatic performance of the basic aeroplane. Between the beginning of May and the beginning of October 1981, the Ultimate Pitts gave displays at all but nine of the 50 odd bookings I had that season; the Stampe filled in the others.

At the bottom of that season's printed schedule there was a note that read, 'Following re-selection to the British Aerobatic Team for 1981, I will be competing in the European Aerobatic Championship in Austria from 15 to 23 August'. I had no way of knowing at the time, of course, but those European Championships would mark the last time that I represented 'Team GB' in a full international competition.

The British aerobatic team of 1978. From left is Bob Mitchell, Ian Padden and myself.

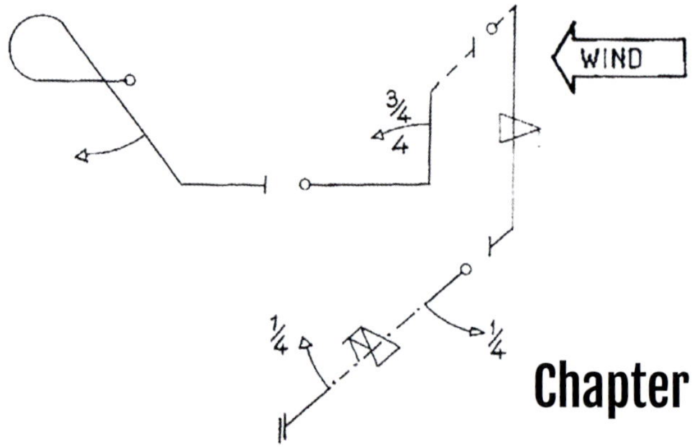

Chapter 11

FROM RUSSIA WITH LOVE

My experience of flying in international aerobatic competitions from the late 1970s to the mid-1980s was coloured by my growing admiration for the aircraft flown by the Eastern bloc aerobatic teams, principally the big Russian monoplane, the Yak-50.

I knew about the Yak-50 before I saw one flying and, if anything, the hype and admiration that surrounded this new Russian aerobatic aeroplane was exceeded by seeing it in action for the first time. Despite the underhand tactics of the Soviet team in 1976, western pilots had come back from the World Championships marvelling at the -50s, their size making western Pitts look totally insignificant, quite apart from the lovely low growl of the Yak's engine and the aeroplane's staggering performance. Victor Letsko (who was crowned World Champion on his home turf in Kiev at the 1976 World Championships) performed a dazzling freestyle sequence, landing with various rivets having popped out of the wings of his -50 through over-stressing. The rumour at the time was that he had pulled in excess of 12G!

After seeing the Yak-50 in action for the first time, I returned to the UK determined to obtain one of my own. I contacted all the avenues that I thought might be able to produce an aircraft for me. I contacted Yakovlev themselves in Moscow, the Russian embassy in London, the British Embassy in Moscow, the Russian Trade Delegation in North London and indeed the Russian pilots that I had met. Initially, though, I drew a blank everywhere.

As a corporate headhunter I was used to getting random approaches from 'senior executives' who thought that they would be invaluable to our client companies. Invariably I managed to restrict these random, one-off enquiries to a brief telephone conversation. However, one day a call came through and the voice at the other end of the phone said, 'Me, Vadim Zadneprovsky, Russian Trade Delegation. You want Yakovlev 50. I sell you.'

Of course, I met him and indeed he did actually have a brochure, in English, for a Yak-50, which made me think that there might be a genuine intention of selling, although historically the Russians had never sold any of their front-line aerobatic aircraft. However, my new friend Vadim clearly knew nothing of aircraft but superficially did seem to think that a deal might be possible.

After a couple of meetings, I then had another phone call, this time from someone who called himself Mr Witty. He suggested that we had various things in common and that a meeting might be appropriate. I assumed he was one of the time-wasting executives examining the job market, and gently tried to put him off. But he was persuasive, and when he suggested meeting at his office at 'The Old War Office' in Whitehall, it sounded a bit more interesting. So I agreed to go and see him.

A couple of days later I passed through the door manned by armed guards, not a common sight in London 40 years ago and asked for Mr Witty. The receptionist looked completely vacant, until I showed her the telephone number that I had asked Witty to give me. 'Oh, you mean Mr Witty,' she said and after a short while I was ushered into a large office to encounter the rather urbane and polished Mr Witty himself.

We discussed trivial matters until he produced a photograph of Zadneprovsky, my friend Vadim who was going to sell me a Yak-50, as I told Witty. Witty did not seem so sure, and continued that he was very pleased to meet me, since I was the one person who seemed to have got close to Zadneprovsky. He went further. He said he would like me to cultivate the relationship and of course feed information back to him.

At this stage it was becoming reasonably clear that my Mr Witty was working for MI5. I replied that I was happy to be of assistance but did not want to prejudice my aircraft acquisition. Witty then produced a file, opened it and began sharing its contents with me. That was a chilling experience. Witty made it evident that he had a remarkably intimate knowledge of me, my life, my friends, my interests and indeed my tax affairs.

Now, I would be the first to admit that there was a time in my working life when I adopted a somewhat relaxed approach to my relationship with the Inland

Revenue. This was when my idea of returning to live and work in Africa was still a viable option. I was self-employed, of course, and took the trouble of writing to the Revenue to tell them that, and I did not see it as my responsibility to contact them again after they failed to reply. Life moved on. One tax year ended and another began, and another, and another. And for a good few years the Inland Revenue and I were strangers. No correspondence passed between us and nor did any tax returns.

In the end I did go through the procedure of regulating matters, but what Mr Witty held in his hands came as an unwelcome surprise. Did I really want this additional information to be passed to the Inland Revenue? Would his having it help me to cooperate more fully? After only brief reflection, I concluded that it would. I agreed to what he had proposed, but refused to sign the Official Secrets Act, which I knew was an absolute catch-all that the authorities would always be able to use against me.

Witty asked me to meet Vadim as often as possible and encourage him to talk about his work and his colleagues. He suggested that I should also tell Vadim a bit about myself, since I was doing a lot of aerobatic displays at NATO air force bases, where I mixed with air crews from UK, the US and other NATO countries. Since I also quite often flew in whatever front-line aircraft they were operating, one can see why Witty thought Vadim might want to investigate me further.

So it was that I did as he asked, doing my bit for what I assumed was national security during the Cold War. I let Vadim take me to lunch and then allowed Witty to take me to some rather better lunches while he debriefed me. He said that I would know that I was making good progress when Vadim gave me a present, and sure enough, in due course, a whole case of good Russian vodka arrived in my office. I immediately told Witty, who was very encouraged. He told me that things were obviously going well!

However, not much seemed to be happening on the Yak-50 acquisition front. It was clear that Vadim was waiting for information from Moscow, and that that was slow in coming. After a few months, I said to Witty that I was an experienced headhunter, very good at evaluating people, and that it was clear to me that Vadim was a rather sweaty Russian engineer, and certainly no spy and so our meetings tailed off.

Then, very much to my surprise, some six months later in February 1981, I opened a newspaper to see a photograph of Vadim Zadneprovsky being escorted by burly British policemen onto a Tupolev 134 at Heathrow. Below it was the caption proclaiming 'Russian spy expelled from the UK,' followed by more detail of Vadim's 'activities incompatible with his diplomatic status'.

My brush with the underworld of state intrigue and counter espionage was interesting while it lasted, though ultimately fruitless as far as buying a Yak-50 was concerned. Still, it did give me the material for an anecdote that I have been trotting out ever since. My Russian friends especially never seem to tire of hearing about the bumbling incompetence of the unfortunate Mr Zadneprovsky. But one has to remember that the Soviet general public were never informed when one of their spies had been unmasked in the West and had been sent packing ignominiously back to Mother Russia.

For various political reasons, the USSR did not come to the 1980 World Aerobatic Championships, so the next time that I came close to a -50 was at the 1982 World Championships in Austria. Although time had passed, I had kept in contact with various members of the Soviet team, particularly Victor Smolin and Khalide Makagonova. Victor went on to win the men's championship, and Khalide came third in the women's. When the championships were over, I was one of a very small handful of Western pilots who were invited to fly the -50. As I sat in the aircraft, Victor gave me instructions, which did not take long. Showing me the undercarriage lever, he announced 'chassis up; chassis down,' and that was that.

So, with that rather brief instruction on the -50 systems, off I went. But, gosh, how different it was to aircraft I had flown! The Yak was noisy, hot and I could not get over how poorly harmonised the controls were: a very light elevator, moderate rudder pressures and yet very heavy ailerons. But these issues were relatively minor, and I came away from my flight even more keen to own a -50.

By the mid-1980s, I had still made no further progress in my quest for a Yak-50. I had also heard rumours, through my Russian friends, that because of structural problems with the very hard-flown -50s of the Russian team, the Russian authorities had put a lot of pressure on Yakovlev to come up with a new and much stronger aircraft which they did in the form of the Yak-55. This was hardly beautiful, but it was functional and immediately did well in the 1984 World Aerobatic Championships, with my friend Khalide winning the women's division and Victor Smolin coming fifth in the men's. However, the corollary of this was that instructions had gone out from Moscow to restrict the flying of -50s in Russia. Then, in early 1986, there were rumours that all -50s were ordered to be scrapped and their logbooks returned to Moscow. This was a potential disaster!

One aspect of World Aerobatic Championships is that one has plenty of opportunity to chat to other competitors, because the actual flying time is comparatively brief. One man with whom I developed a good bond was Wolfgang Jaegle, a member of the West German team. He shared my fascination and desire to own a -50, and we discussed how this might be possible. Of the 312 Yak-50s that were made, seven had gone to Bulgaria, but it was impossible to trace what happened to them. The only others exported had been eight -50s, which had been supplied to the DDR, the former East Germany. Wolfgang had contacts in East Germany, so we decided to pursue these.

Although the DDR team had taken delivery of eight Yak-50s, they had been delivered shortly before the 1980 World Championships, so they had no time to practise flying them. They then had a fatal accident in one of them. I never established the circumstances, but that led to the decision that the DDR aerobatic team would change to the Zlin 50, which had been performing extremely well in the hands of the Czech team.

However, in those days, you could not order a Zlin 50 as such. You had to supply the Czech factory with the various Western-sourced components such as the engine, propeller, battery, instruments and oil cooler, and they would then build you an aircraft. So, Wolfgang approached the East Germans with a potential deal to provide the funds for Zlin to purchase these items, in exchange for the six remaining -50s as the DDR authorities had decided to keep one aircraft for their national museum. We agreed with Wolfgang that we would take two aircraft.

The Yak-50 was the most charismatic of aircraft. I had flown one before, but it was a revelation to actually own one!

The very military cockpit of a Yak-50. Although the aircraft had amazing performance, the cockpit was a hot, noisy environment with poor coordination of controls. I was full of amazement at the capability of the Russian pilots.

We then found a potential customer in the US to purchase two more, while Wolfgang would keep two himself.

This time the deal went through and in 1987, 11 years after I had first begun picking up reports about the Yak-50 and nine years since I had first seen one in the flesh, Wolfgang began flying the aircraft to his home in West Germany, escorted out of DDR air space by East German MiGs to make sure that none of their air defences tried to shoot him down. As soon as I could, I went there and ferried the two aircraft that I had agreed to purchase back to the UK.

I decided to involve Vic Norman in the project. He had become a very good friend and was keen to get involved in anything that involved aeroplanes that was exciting. I got to know Vic through common interests in performance cars and aircraft.

He was a perfectly competent pilot but did not have the same degree of aerobatic experience as me. Vic's great strength is that he is a brilliant salesman and he persuaded Mitsubishi that what they needed to do to promote their vehicle range in the UK was to sponsor an aerobatic display aircraft, namely his Zlin 50, which he had bought through me.

DDR-

The culmination of our deal with the East German Government to purchase six of their seven Yak-50 aircraft.

Mitsubishi loved the idea and to seal the deal it was arranged that their top brass would watch the aeroplane give a display at RAF Kemble, where the Red Arrows were based and where Vic was very matey with the man who ran all the flying. Vic's problem was that he could not give the display himself but it was best that Mitsubishi did not actually know that particular detail, and so he roped me in to lend a hand.

We easily obtained West German registrations. The UK CAA seemed happy to accept those flying in the UK indefinitely. Once in Vladivar colours, we painted the registrations in Russian Cryllic script.

On the day of the display the senior people from Mitsubishi gathered at Kemble, Vic climbed into the cockpit of his Zlin, set off down the long taxiway and around the other side of the hangars, where I was waiting out of sight. Vic jumped out of the cockpit, I jumped in, manoeuvred the Zlin out onto the runway and took off to give the display. Then I landed, taxied back behind the hangars, stopped momentarily to swap places with Vic, who then returned to the Mitsubishi people to receive their plaudits and complete a good day's work.

Now that Vic and I were the proud possessors of the first privately-owned Russian aircraft in the UK, we thought about drumming up sponsorship for them. Wolfgang was keeping his purchase of the aircraft rather quiet, which meant that our two -50s were the only ones available to a sponsor, making them very newsworthy. We considered the various companies and businesses that could be interested, and one name stood out: that of Vladivar Vodka, which had rather clever advertising. Although the company was based in Warrington, they jokingly pretended that the brand was Russian, with a slogan along the lines of 'Vladivar – the Vodka from Varrington'. (The rather more prosaic reality was that Vladivar was owned by the big brewing concern, Greenalls, who also made Bombay Sapphire gin and other products).

They seemed to us an obvious fit, so Vic and I went up to meet their marketing director. We both had had quite successful sponsorships in the past and were well prepared but, as we found out, we were rather pushing against an open door and the enthusiasm was already there. In fact, the whole experience had a modicum of unreality about it. At around 11 o'clock we heard a tea-trolley clinking down the corridor of the executive offices and when it came into our director's office I noticed that, instead of pots of tea and coffee, the whole trolley was filled with bottles of alcoholic drink, with pretty much whatever took your fancy on offer. Mike, the

Having obtained Vladivar sponsorship, we painted the planes in the same basic colours as the Russian team, but with 'Vladivar' prominently displayed.

Vladivar®

IMPERIAL VODKA

P.O. BOX No. 3 · CAUSEWAY DISTILLERY
WARRINGTON · CHESHIRE WA4 6RY
TELEPHONE: 0925 50111
FAX: 0925 414445 TELEX: 629116

Our Ref : MJLD/CMP/651

29th April, 1991.

Mr. R. Goode,
28 Bryanston Square,
London W1H 7LS.

Dear Richard,

We have a reputation for original promotion so when you approached us to sponsor a Russian aerobatic aeroplane, it was natural that we should look seriously at your proposal.

In the following three years we can say quite categorically that the contribution made by you and your excellent display team was, without a doubt, a great success.

Literally millions of the public were treated to an entertaining spectacle which gave us, the sponsors, incredible exposure and the audience a terrific thrill.

On occasions when we entertained our customers at both public and private showings, the Yak and it's pilots left a lasting impression - one not easily forgotten.

Thank you for such an effective promotional opportunity.

Regards.

Yours sincerely,

M.J. LLOYD-DAVIES
MARKETING MANAGER

REGISTRATION NO. 43828

Vladivar clearly felt that we had given them exceptional value in this sponsorship deal.

marketing director, ordered a large gin and tonic; Vic and I wisely settled for fruit juice. Our sponsorship discussion continued. The trolley passed on its way, went to the end of the corridor and then, on its way back, we could hear that everyone was having refills.

At the end of a very productive morning session, we went to lunch in the directors' dining room, and that of course was preceded by a few cocktails, which in turn were followed by liberal amounts of wine with the meal. I asked Mike if much work got done in the afternoons and he said, 'To be honest, not a great deal. Most of us are having a quiet nap!' But Vladivar proved to be

Very clearly pleased with my Russian 'fighter' aircraft! Below the kind of flying for which the Yak-50 was suited.

A sponsored aerobatic team has other aspects apart from flying but, with Vladivar, helped by generous gifts of vodka!

great sponsors. They gave us huge amounts of booze and loved the exposure that we gave them in return.

We decided to paint the aircraft in the colours of the Russian team, which we thought much better than the rather drab East German version. An interesting aspect of our ownership was that we had been able to obtain West German certificates of registration and airworthiness, so our aeroplanes had German registrations. There are of course international rules governing these things, whereby all registration letters applied externally to aircraft must be in Roman script. We thought it would be amusing to have it in Russian Cyrillic script so, instead of D-EIVR, it became ДИЙВР.

Amazingly, it took the UK CAA almost nine months to spot this flagrant breach of international regulations, but we got a lot of publicity in the meantime!

Despite not having any maintenance manuals, tools or spare parts we had very few problems with the Yak-50. I had one awkward moment after returning to White Waltham from a display, when one main wheel came down and not the other. Fortunately, the airfield was all-grass and the runways were mown, leaving quite thick grass elsewhere and they provided a much softer place for my forced landing. I was able to do this safely, with the only damage to the -50 being a rather grazed wingtip. It transpired that the problem with the landing wheel was a manufacturing fault in an up-lock, which held the wheel secured inside the fuselage when the aeroplane was flying.

My other memorable mishap in the Yak-50 came about as the result of a mid-air prang the first weekend in August 1988, from which, I am hugely relieved to say, the three of us involved emerged unscathed, if somewhat shaken by the experience. I needed some aerial photographs of the Yak-50 in flight and I needed them rather quickly. So, against his better judgement I persuaded my long-standing pilot friend, Clive Wilson, to fly the two-seater Pitts we jointly owned, with the photographer, while I flew the Yak.

The consequence of a midair collision between my Yak-50 and Pitts Special that was being used as a camera aircraft. Both planes landed safely back at White Waltham.

Clive was in fact on sick leave after being diagnosed with ME from working months of very long hours at Lloyd's, and the photoshoot had been delayed to the point when I was running very close to the delivery deadline. Clive was feeling pretty rough, but my now familiar refrain of 'No. No. No – Wilson' had brought him to White Waltham, where again I exerted my powers of persuasion to get him to fly the Pitts from the front seat, so that the photographer could go in the rear seat even though the controls for the radio were mounted in the rear-seat flying position. This meant that whenever Clive wanted to talk to me, he had to get the photographer to press the RT button.

This was understood when we had the pre-flight briefing, as was the plan for Clive to fly the Pitts inverted, while I took up station right underneath, so that the photographer could slide back the canopy (while hanging upside down in his seat) to take some stunning pictures of the Yak-50 picked out against the Berkshire countryside 2,000 feet below.

After flying upside down for a minute, Clive was feeling worse than ever and, convinced that the photographer had had long enough for the necessary pictures, he rolled out, losing height in the process, without realising that I had closed up to maximize the photographic opportunity. Clive could not see what was happening, but I could and before I had time to react, the top wing of the Pitts struck the wing of the Yak quite hard and then the Pitts disappeared from my sight. The Yak wing was damaged and the ailerons were almost jammed, though moving just enough to give me the control I needed to get back to the airfield and land very gingerly.

As for Clive and the photographer, I thought they were goners because, from what I had seen, part of the top wing of the Pitts had been ripped off in the impact. However, they did make it back to terra firma at White Waltham, although Clive had a lot of explaining to do when the insurance claims were processed through his own office and it was clear for all to see that he had been off flying when he was supposed to be recuperating at home!

I was understandably shaken by the near miss that Saturday, but the next day, Sunday 7 August, I was booked to display at an air show in Belgium. With one of our Yak-50s damaged by the collision and the other in the workshop for routine maintenance, I asked the organisers whether they minded if I gave the display in my Pitts. They said that they did not have a problem with a change of aircraft, so I flew over to Belgium early the following morning.

Over lunch I got into conversation with Michel Duvivier, a major in the Belgian air force. He was also one of the country's foremost aerobatic pilots who was going

The Yak-50 was extremely newsoworthy and we achieved a great deal of publicity for our sponsors. You will see my name in Cryllic script behind the engine cowling.

to be flying a Mirage fighter that afternoon. Major Duvivier was scheduled to give his display immediately before me and I was sitting in my Pitts at the end of the runway, waiting for the word from the control tower to take off and go into my routine. Suddenly I caught sight of the Mirage no more than 150 feet from the ground going absolutely vertically down and then exploding in a terrifying ball of flame. The impact site could not have been more than 70 yards to my right and I must have been the closest person to it. Duvivier would have been killed on impact. Later investigation showed that he had tried to eject from the cockpit, but by then it was too late.

Stunned by what I had just witnessed, I now had the control tower ordering me into the sky, 'Pitts Special – take off and go into your display'. The golden rule at air displays is that the show has to go on immediately to provide something else for the tens of thousands in the crowd to focus on so that they do not rush towards the crash and get in the way of the emergency services.

After the shock of the previous day's adrenalin rush, I found myself with a bird's eye view of this scene of flaming devastation as I went through my routine with one thought in mind: completing it safely, refuelling, then flying straight back to White Waltham and home.

In May 1979 I was giving a display organised by the USAF at its base at Mildenhall in Suffolk when one of the pilots in the Italian Air Force aerobatic team crashed his Fiat G91 fighter and was killed. The team were taking part in a 'starburst manoeuvre' which involved a high-speed dive, and this particular pilot was easily a mile away from the airfield and the 80,000 spectators when he hit a tree as he came out of the dive, ripped off a wing and crashed into a ploughed field. I was airborne at the time, in a holding pattern away from the airfield waiting to start my routine and was one of the very few eyewitnesses, certainly the only eyewitness from the air. I radioed the airshow control to tell them what had happened and the emergency services were dispatched, although I could see that the pilot had tried to eject at the last minute and his body was still strapped into his seat a few yards from the cockpit of his wrecked aircraft. No announcement was made to the crowd and the air show continued uninterrupted. I learned later that during the war a bomber coming into land at Mildenhall had suffered a similar fate, when it too had hit the same tree as it approached the runway.

In all, Vic and I had three years of sponsorship for the Yak-50s, and I had the most wonderful time flying all over the UK and Europe with my aluminium, growling mistress. Our sponsorship with Greenall's may well have continued had they not been taken over by Whyte and Mackay, who were much more ruthless and efficient. The new owners also felt that aviation sponsorship was not something they wanted to be associated with. However, there were six months of the contract remaining and, being honourable people, they offered us the equivalent of the balance of our fee in alcohol at their trade prices less 20 per cent. So, I ended up with an entire vanload of booze which did take quite a long time to get through!

The warnings we had from Russia about the fate of Yak-50s very sadly turned out to be true. The authorities in Moscow ordered all -50s to be scrapped, although fortunately various regional aero clubs refused and hid their aircraft. That is why we have, at our guess, 85 left of the 312 originally made.

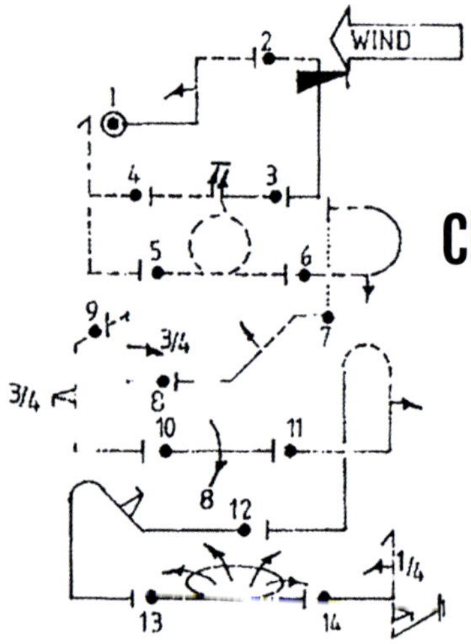

Chapter 12

PACE SPIRIT

It was not simply its size and awesome power that had drawn me to the Yak-50.

Competing alongside the world's leading aerobatic pilots had shown that those flying monoplanes were, on average, scoring half a point more on manoeuvres for the same standard of flying than pilots in biplanes. This resulted from the simple fact that judges on the ground found it easier to score a sequence in a monoplane than a biplane.

Having initially drawn a blank buying a Yak-50, I set about finding an alternative monoplane, with the aim of competing in it at the 1982 World Championships. There were a few contenders, though none seemed ideal. Then the opportunity appeared to build a new plane of my own, which allowed me to combine the best qualities of the monoplanes I liked into a single, unique design.

I did not start completely from scratch. One of the aircraft I had considered was the Stephens Akro, a kit plane that you had to assemble yourself. However, there simply was not enough time for me to build one and fly in the 1982 World Championships.

Among the international pilots I had got to know was the sometime Swiss national champion, Michel Brandt. Michel was chief engineer and test pilot for the French company Avions Robin, in Dijon, where he had been building a Stephens Akro in a quiet corner of a hangar during his spare time. Back at his day job he had spent time working with the Aérospatiale team that had developed the computer-designed wing for the French-built CAP 21 aerobatic aircraft. This was completely symmetrical, so that the aircraft flew as well inverted as it did flown erect. It was a world-beating design, as Michel well understood, so he had used the CAP 21 wing profile to fit into a Stephens Akro.

The fuselage of his new plane was pretty much welded together, the complete wing was ready as was the horizontal tail when Avions Robin hit serious financial difficulties. Fearing that his own partially-built aeroplane might be seized and confiscated as part of his employer's assets, Michel hastily removed it and then rather lost heart in the project. This is where I stepped into the picture.

After a bit of negotiation between us Michel agreed to sell me his plane and I had all the pieces shipped back to the UK where we set about finishing the project. I say 'we', because the work far exceeded my engineering skills, though fortunately not those of the inestimable Dave Wiltshire, who had helped to create my Ultimate Pitts. I also needed a licensed aircraft engineer to handle the final assembly and the official paperwork, without which my new aeroplane could never have taken to the air and the man who stepped up to the plate was Geoff Masterson.

By the time the *Pace Spirit*, as my new plane was officially called, was nearing completion it was carrying more than my aspirations for the World Aerobatic Championship. It was also proudly decked out in the promotional livery of the Pace Petroleum company, my official sponsor, and for that that I had to thank Victor Gauntlett, the founder and chairman of Pace.

He had recently come to public prominence after putting £500,000 into Aston Martin Lagonda (representing a 10 per cent stake) and then becoming executive chairman in April 1981. Given my own interest in Aston Martins, this had caught my attention, as had Victor's strong belief in publicity, which had led him to sponsor a range of motor racing events. Pace Petroleum was also sponsoring Nigel Mansell through his first two years in Formula One, so there was no doubting the commitment to the promotional ventures he invested in.

My background research had also thrown up his lifelong interest in flying, which had started when he had taken a short service pilot's commission in the RAF. He had also owned a number of aircraft during his life including a Tiger Moth, a de Havilland Rapide biplane, a C47 Dakota, a Chipmunk, a Dove and a Mk I Spitfire.

Victor once described himself as 'half overgrown schoolboy, half hard-nosed businessman,' sentiments with which I felt a fair degree of empathy. I was accustomed to sounding plausible on the telephone and my initial call obviously struck a chord, because he invited me to have lunch with him, appropriately, at the RAC. The hard-nosed businessman wanted to know what I had to offer beyond a bit of aerial excitement. I had prepared myself and replied that that year I would be doing more than 80 public aerobatic displays. On top of those I offered another 25 displays exclusive to Pace Petroleum, to be given wherever Victor wanted. With a concerted marketing effort, the promotional potential on offer was impressive.

I think it is fair to say that we liked each other from the outset and, with much in common, reaching an agreement was not difficult. Victor signed me up for three years, asking to have both of my planes, the Pitts Special and the *Pace Spirit*.

(Left) Dave Wiltshire, an extraordinarily capable and creative engineer who built much of *Pace Spirit*, as well as restoring four listed houses on my behalf!

(Below) The aircraft nearing completion with engine, propeller and fuel system installed.

Our contract ran to barely half-a-page and he paid me a set amount each month to spend as I saw fit. Beyond that he left me to run the Pace Petroleum aerobatic team without interference, which suited me down to the ground. For my part I delivered pages of cost-free coverage in the aviation and general press, which brought Pace Petroleum to the attention of a far wider tranche of the general public than it had ever achieved before.

Display bookings for 1983 rolled in and with the 1984 World Aerobatic Championship still 18 months off, I now had the aeroplane and the financial security underwriting my flying to have a serious run at nailing a top-10 place among the world's elite aerobatic pilots.

PACEMAKER

Even though I had overseen the construction of the *Pace Spirit,* it did not spare me on two occasions when mechanical problems, completely beyond my control, very nearly brought about my untimely end. The first occurred during a display I was giving at the big air show at Biggin Hill. Flying at the top of an outside loop, I suddenly felt resistance on the stick and the elevator stiffened slightly. That only lasted a moment and the resistance vanished as I came down, but it was alarming

Victor Gauntlett was a generous and enthusiatic sponsor as well as being a good friend. Our first aerobatic team was with the Pitts Special in the colours of Pace Petroleum. Pete Kynsey flew the Pitts while I flew the *Pace Spirit.*

enough. I radioed air traffic control to tell them that I had a problem, cut short the display and landed as quickly as I could. Luckily my engineer was there with his tool kit, so we removed the rear fuselage cover and looked as best we could to find out what the problem was.

I had another air show to go to and time was tight. Try as we might, though, we could not replicate the resistance I had felt. Maybe I had imagined it? All the controls looked fine. It was only when a torch beam flashed on something right down at the end of the tail that we discovered the cause: a spanner left behind by a mechanic. The next time a problem arose, it did not go away.

The *Pace Spirit* was a delight to fly. It was fast with excellent range that could take it from White Waltham to Scotland, perform a display, and return without landing.

We did a lot of work to the Pitts, now registered G-OODI and it was one of the best-performing Pitts in Europe.

Noise, or I should say the reaction of people on the ground to the noise of my aircraft, was a persistent problem. In my relatively short aerobatic career I had been banned from flying at Leicester, at Dunkeswell, from Little Snoring and even, ironically, from the Red Arrows base at RAF Kemble. In my early days I had received a very dusty letter from the chap who ran White Waltham threatening to ban me from his airfield if I did not stop performing aerobatics overhead.

Although it was a bit of a slog to fly up there, things were easier at Strathallan in Scotland and a group of us used to take our planes to this airfield north of Edinburgh where we could practise for four or five days without disturbing too many people. I was going through a display sequence in the *Pace Spirit* when suddenly the most incredible vibration started. It shook the aeroplane so violently that it broke three of the instruments and I was seriously concerned that it had damaged, possibly even snapped, some of the fuselage frame tubes. Getting back down on the ground was quite hairy and I did wonder whether the engine was going to drop out as it felt as if the whole plane was falling to pieces.

I do not mind admitting that I was as shaken up as the *Pace Spirit* when we landed, but on this occasion I saw right away what had caused the violent shuddering. One of the weights had broken off my variable pitch propeller and had blasted straight through the aluminium spinner at the front, hit one of the blades and removed a sizable length of it.

An early photograph of a test flight in the *Pace Spirit* as it was prepared for displays around the country.

The *Pace Spirit* loaded for its transport to Australia and the Philips Championship representing the UK.

ITCHY FEET

By the end of the 1983 season the *Pace Spirit* was running well, and I was feeling fairly gung-ho about the World Championship the following year. So, when the opportunity came to have a dummy run of sorts, flying in a competition for a dozen of the world's top aerobatic pilots, I was not going to turn it down, even if it did mean getting me and my aeroplane to the other side of the world to take part in a one-off championship in Australia in early 1984.

Part of the deal with Philips, the sponsors of this competition, was that I and the *Pace Spirit* and quite possibly some of the other competitors, would be flown home, at least as far as West Germany, by Lufthansa. Having made sure, then, that my aeroplane was safely loaded into their 747 Combi, I nipped round to the front of the terminal building and checked myself in aboard the same passenger-cum-freight plane for the flight back to Europe. It was a somewhat curious feeling to be riding along at 40,000 feet knowing that my own aeroplane, albeit in pieces, was riding along as well only a few feet away.

Waiting for us at Frankfurt Airport was Walter Extra, a West German qualified aircraft engineer and very accomplished aerobatic pilot, with whom I had struck up a good friendship at various international gatherings. Although

I was lucky enough to win a weekend in France with Cressida, which included our own Piper Seneca and company pilot to take us there.

our working relationship, developing planes together, was still a few years off, I had already become very impressed by Walter's design ideas, which chimed closely with my own. In fact, Walter was in the process of building an aircraft very similar to the *Pace Spirit* which, by virtue of his surname, he was able to call the Extra 200.

With typical Teutonic efficiency, we were allocated a place in the Lufthansa maintenance hangar. However, it was the consequence of a rare moment of Teutonic inefficiency that immediately caught my attention when I looked over the *Pace Spirit* after she had been unloaded. The aircraft was still bolted down onto the aluminium air-freight pallet on which she had just been flown half-way round the world. One of the checks I routinely do after flying any aircraft is to note the G readings from the flight and then reset the G-meter, which measures gravitational pull, back to zero. The instrument has two needles, one to measure positive G and one to measure negative G. Push a button, and the two needles snap back to read nought. But when I cast my eye over the cockpit instruments in the Lufthansa hangar in Frankfurt, the G-meter in the *Pace Spirit* instrument panel was reading 6.5G.

Walter I and both knew that the maximum reading we could have expected from the standard flight in the 747 Combi would have been in the order of 1.5G. Somehow then, my aeroplane had been subjected to over four times that gravitational force. There could be only one explanation for it, and that was that the whole aluminium pallet, with the *Pace Spirit* firmly attached to it, had been dropped.

In his tool kit Walter had a borescope, a long flexible device consisting of a length of optical fibres that carried an image from a lens at one end to an eyepiece at the other. On aeroplanes it is generally used for examining the inside of engines, but our interest was to look as best we could at the *Pace Spirit*'s wing. This was a one-piece wing and it spanned 28 feet. There were a few access points, but not that many, so our examination of the inside was restricted. Even so, there was no sign of any visible damage.

In hindsight I probably should have taken this up with Lufthansa, although they would almost certainly have claimed that the 6.5G reading had been left over from my last flight. I didn't really give it much thought, beyond feeling mildly irritated. Walter and I had an aircraft to put back together and that was going to take the rest of a long day, before I filled up with fuel and took the *Pace Spirit* for test a flight to check that all was well. Everything went fine, and I was set to fly back to England.

Airshow flying is not all glamour and quite a lot of time is spent in promotional activity for one's sponsor!

With a symmetrical wing and aerofoil the *Pace Spirit* flew equally well erect or inverted. The tape on my nose held my glasses in place.

WEDDING BLUES

Once back home, I started winding up for the 1984 season which was due to start in only a few weeks' time. There were the usual hours of practice, getting the display sequence slick and precise again, and I had agreed to give private displays at a couple of weddings. The first was a couple whose wedding reception was being held in Hitcham Lane, in Buckinghamshire, close to where Dave Wiltshire (now wearing his builder's hard hat) was busy converting the main section of Hitcham House for me.

The other wedding I was going to was rather more personal. In modern parlance, Rowena Hutchison and I had been quite a serious item. After a couple of years, she had eventually decided that I was not the marrying kind and had moved on, but we had stayed friends.

I had accepted the invitation to her wedding, while also apologising that I would not be able to attend the service itself in London, because I would still be on my way back from a headhunting trip to Italy. Instead, I had arranged to fly the *Pace Spirit* from White Waltham to the airfield at Framlingham close to Rendham Court, her family home near Saxmundham in Suffolk. I had flown in and out of there quite a bit when Rowena and I had been going out and I knew the lie of the land well.

So, while Rowena was getting hitched around midday on Saturday 12 May, 1984, I was aboard the BA flight from Milan to Heathrow. Within half-an-hour of landing, I was at White Waltham where the *Pace Spirit* was ready and waiting. I took off around 4.30pm for a 45-minute flight in fine weather. When the roofs of Rendham Court came into sight, I pitched the nose down at an angle of 45 degrees, aiming at a spot a few hundred yards offset from the wedding marquee and watched the speed build up rapidly: 200, 210, 220 knots, still comfortably inside the plane's safety margin, as I raced down to a height of 50 feet above the ground.

I then pulled up with the intention of doing a few vertical rolls. But as I reached 40 degrees the plane started shaking as though it was gripped by some giant hand. My mind immediately jumped to the propeller, recalling how the *Pace Spirit* had been thrown into violent convulsions when the prop counterweight had broken loose and smashed a chunk out of one of the blades over Scotland the year before.

Looking to my right, everything seemed OK on the starboard side of the aeroplane. I looked left and that was when the full enormity of my predicament became apparent. Where there should have been the smooth tapering front to the wing, there was now nothing further forward than the blunt square face of the main spar suddenly exposed for the first time since its manufacture. The entire leading edge of the port wing had simply disappeared and my mind now leapt back to the 6.5G meter reading I had discovered at Frankfurt the month before. Positioned as it had been in its padded transport cradle, the wing had been sitting upright on its leading edge and it was the leading edge that had absorbed the full force of the impact when Lufthansa had dropped the air-freight pallet.

At the same time as I was taking this all in, wedding guests were peering up at me. Some people thought I was dropping confetti. Others thought the debris streaming away behind *Pace Spirit* was strips of silver foil. But there were a number of former and serving military men with aviation experience who knew exactly what was going on. 'He's falling to pieces,' one of them told his wife as they all watched horror-struck to see what would happen next.

May 12 1984 was a dramatic and painful day in my life following a structural failure of the *Pace Spirit* that caused a violent accident. It resulted in three months in a hospital bed. The aircraft was destroyed.

From that moment *Pace Spirit* had less than a quarter-of-a-minute left. The starboard wing was still operating normally, giving maximum lift. Whereas the damaged port wing was creating considerable drag and giving no lift at all; the consequences were rapid and vicious.

Almost immediately the aeroplane flipped upside down, But before I could settle into inverted flight, the reverse happened. With the good wing now on the port side, it flicked the plane upright again.

Controlled landing was out of the question; it was time to bail out and entrust myself to the flimsy nylon bundle of the parachute. Looking down at the ground it was clear that my altitude was considerably less than a thousand feet, too low to use a parachute safely. On top of this there were seven seat belts, joined by three buckles, to undo plus the flying helmet, with a cable that attached my headphones (and therefore my head) to the radio, to remove and the big one-piece canopy to unclip and push up and over to the side, something I had never attempted to do in an air-stream of well over 100 mph. Even practising on the ground, it had taken three or four seconds to get clear of the aircraft.

I knew that there was no good outcome and I instinctively switched off the main fuel cock, the master switch for all the cockpit electrics, the radio and the two magnetos. Plummeting at an alarming rate in a steep left-hand turn, the plane turned turtle. A push on the stick just got me clear of an orchard. As I got close to the ground, I found a measure of control, but inverted at 12 feet. Beyond the orchard lay a cornfield. I tried to coax the plane the right way up and that was when the port wingtip ploughed into the soil.

There was an awful rending of wood and metal as the entire wing shredded itself, while I hit my head violently and everything went black. My first thought was to swear at British Airways when I briefly came to. I was convinced that the morning's flight from Milan had smashed into a mountain and I was now lying with my head pressed into an alpine meadow and not one of the Hutchison's wheat fields in the flat farmland of Suffolk.

Air accident investigators from Farnborough later calculated that the *Pace Spirit* had hit the ground at 120mph and come to halt in 30 yards. That impact had subjected my body to a force of 60G, 60 times the normal pull of gravity. In layman's terms, injuries from a crash like that are unlikely to be survivable.

Thirty months earlier, full of optimism and joie de vivre, I had registered *Pace Spirit* as G-OODO (GOOD OH!). Now she was lying on top of me, trapping my smashed legs, crushing the ribs on one side of my body and soaking my trousers in high octane aviation fuel, as 12 gallons slopped out through a large hole in the tank between my knees and only a couple of feet from a hot aero engine and two broiling exhausts. In just 14 seconds on the afternoon of Rowena's wedding, GOOD OH! had been devastatingly pulverised into GOODE ZERO.

By Appointment to
His Royal Highness the Prince of Wales
Motor Car Manufacturer and Repairer

ASTON MARTIN LAGONDA LIMITED

Tickford Street, Newport Pagnell, Buckinghamshire MK16 9AN. Telephone: Newport Pagnell (0908) 610620.
Telegrams: Astomartia, Newport Pagnell. Telex: 82341

Our ref: MVG/JAB

26 September 1985

Richard Goode Esq.,
25 Manchester Square
LONDON W1

Dear Richard,

I was delighted to see you performing at Finningley albeit a little sad to see you 'in a plain wrapper'.

It really is a tremendous tribute to your fortitude that you have not only recovered so well physically but appear to have no mental scars preventing you from giving 'Goode' value to your many admirers.

You, and Pete, gave us not only the best value sponsorship we ever had, but one of which we were immensely proud. I would much enjoy seeing you again for a chance to chat and will contact you shortly.

Meanwhile my very best regards.

Yours very sincerely

Victor G.

Victor Gauntlett

Directors: M. V. Gauntlett (Executive Chairman), P. G. Livanos (Joint Chairman), W. R

Registered in England at the above address. Nu

Victor Gauntlett was not only a huge support before that fateful day in 1984, but also afterwards as I sought to complete my recovery.

Farnham 724554

Pace House,
East Street,
Farnham, Surrey.
GU9 7RX

18th April 1983

Richard Goode, Esq.,
1 Manchester Square,
London, W.1.

Dear Richard,

I was at Wiscombe yesterday to enjoy yet another stunning display and thought you might enjoy a conversation I had with a chap who had also been at Silverstone on Saturday.

He reported that his brother-in-law, Tom Threlfall, who is President of the Vintage Sports Car Club and an ex-RAF pilot who had instructed in the art of aerobatics; having seen your display, said your name should not be Richard Goode but rather Richard Fan-tas-tic!

Keep up the good work.

Yours 'aye'

Victor G.

Victor Gauntlett

Chapter 13

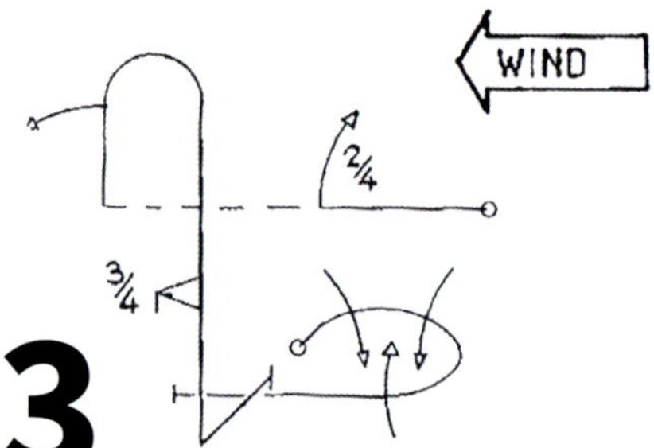

PICKING UP THE PIECES

They said I was conscious when they reached me. They also said that I had a lot to say, much of it loud and uncomplimentary about British Airways.

I cannot remember who my rescuers were, nor what they were telling me at the time. I found out later that the two who took charge were Army helicopter pilots, well trained in extracting casualties from wrecks. It was as though I was watching a film in which everything was happening to someone else. I do not even remember feeling pain, that came a couple of days later when I was in hospital, searing and relentless. Medics were less forthcoming with painkillers in those days, and I have no clear recollection of the next 48 hours.

Apparently, Rowena's new husband had taken the accident badly. 'Bloody, Richard Goode,' he had been heard to say, as though I had deliberately crashed my aeroplane and nearly killed myself to upstage him at his wedding. Rowena, though, could not hide how upset she was. It was several weeks before she could tell me herself, after she had returned from her honeymoon but I knew from Clive Wilson that she had been very concerned at what had happened. Clive had stepped in immediately to take control of things, and over the days following the accident he picked up the running of my life. And it was Clive who had first been told by Jon Wand, the young orthopaedic surgeon looking after me, that my survival was touch and go.

My body was obviously having to cope with very considerable shock and I was drifting in and out of consciousness. But when I was conscious, they told me afterwards, I was talking non-stop, most of it unintelligible. The only thing that made sense was my incessant demand to see Clive Wilson. Clive and I had arranged to meet at the little airfield near Rendham after I had landed the *Pace Spirit*. We were then going to go to a hotel to change and rest for a couple hours, before we were due back at Rendham Court for the wedding party in the evening. Clive had been puzzled that I had not shown up at the airfield as planned and had gone to the hotel, on the assumption that I would make my own way there after landing somewhere else.

The hotel proprietor was himself a former RAF pilot. By another curious coincidence, the television in the residents' lounge was tuned to a programme called *Just Amazing*. This was showing viewers the roller coaster thrills of aerobatics through the lenses of a couple of cameras mounted on the wings of an aeroplane called *Pace Spirit*, being flown by a pilot named Richard Goode.

It was the proprietor who answered the telephone call that brought news of my accident. He asked for someone called Clive and took Clive to the telephone in Reception, where he was told that I had crashed at Rendham and had been taken by ambulance to Ipswich Hospital. The caller told Clive that things did not look good and could he go to the hospital because I was asking for him. Things would have gone a great deal worse for me had it not been for the lucky chance that Jon Wand had also heard that there had been an aeroplane crash, and that the pilot was in bad shape and was on his way to A&E.

Jon too had an interest in flying, as a glider pilot. He also recognised the name Richard Goode. As he later explained, in the mid-1980s Richard Goode was tantamount to the Nigel Mansell of British flying. The other fluke, as far as I was concerned, was that Jon Wand had witnessed a friend being seriously injured in a high-G glider accident and had subsequently taken a special interest in high-G accident patient repairs and recuperation.

So, by the time my ambulance reached the hospital, Jon had rushed there to assemble an experienced trauma team. However, when Clive arrived a couple of hours after I had been admitted, he was told that they had not been able to operate because my condition was not stable. In fact my condition was so fragile that they had not even been able to clean me up. The only reason that Clive was eventually allowed in to me was because I was kicking up such a fuss. He was pretty horrified by the sight that met his eyes. I was spread-eagled on a hospital trolley with my legs at very strange angles. I was still wearing my flying suit, now

DAILY EXPRESS Monday May 14 1984

Wedding stunt air crash horror

Guests see ace pilot plunge out of control

A FLYING display to entertain guests at a lavish wedding reception ended in tragedy at the weekend when the tiny stunt plane plunged to the ground.

And last night the fight was still going on to save 38-year-old pilot Richard Goode's life as he lay in a hospital's intensive care unit.

By JOHN McCORMICK

Mr Goode was a guest at the reception for society cook Rowena Hutchison and her American husband, Thomas von Zuleger-Zabradsky.

The accident happened as Mr Goode, rated among the world's top aerobatic pilots, put his plane through its paces over the grounds of the bride's parents home at Rendham Court, near Saxmundham, Suffolk.

Pain

Ironically, when the accident happened, millions of TV viewers were watching a recording of him looping the loop on Saturday night's Just Amazing stunt show.

Mr Mike Selter, one of the first wedding guests to reach the crash scene, said last night: "He was conscious and in great pain.

"We found him some yards from the wreckage and he managed to tell us that the propellor had come off just before the plane nose-dived."

The pilot was taken to hospital in Ipswich suffering from a fractured pelvis, multiple leg breaks and internal injuries.

Mr Goode, a bachelor of Manchester Square, London, landed in England earlier in the afternoon fro ma business conference in Milan.

Last night a hospital spokesman described his condition as "stable."

A friend of the newlyweds said last night that the couple were very upset but had been urged to carry on with their honeymoon.

Two years ago Mr Nicholas Ball, the bride's 34-year-old brother-in-law, died after his microlight aircraft crashed near the scene of Saturday's accident.

muddied, bloodied and torn. He said I looked like a war casualty. But the extraordinary thing, which we both marvel at even now particularly as my memory these days is not as sharp as it might be, is that I knew exactly what I had to be doing the following day, the following week and for the fortnight after that. I then started reeling off names, telephone numbers, times of the air displays I was scheduled to do, business meetings and other work commitments that I had in my diary, rattling them out faster than Clive could note them down.

Before he went off to find a hospital payphone, Clive remembers me giving him my Rolex watch to look after. 'If I don't make it, you can keep this,' I said to him. 'But I don't want it hanging around the hospital.' Instead of enjoying the wedding party, Clive spent the next couple of hours dialling the telephone numbers I had given him and putting my life back on track. And he was able to arrange for someone else to fly in my place at the air shows where I was booked to display.

Clive got through to Michael Silverman at Merton Associates as well. Michael proved to be very helpful. Some might argue that he liked to be seen to be solving problems and there was quite a bit of 'I got Richard sorted out' in the months that followed, but it would be churlish not to recognise that he was extremely proactive and helpful in the weeks after my accident.

BROKEN ARROWS

Jon Wand and his medical team could see that my legs were obviously fractured in several places. Given the force of the accident there were almost certainly further injuries that would only become apparent when I was on the operating table. They were concerned that I might have suffered damage to internal organs. But the immediate worry was loss of blood and, until my cardiovascular status could be restored, my condition would not be stable enough to permit surgery. So, the most urgent treatment was to hook me up to an intravenous line and start restoring my blood supply.

When they were able to operate, late at night, this proved to have been a very wise precaution. Jon explained afterwards that a pelvic fracture can bleed up to six pints of blood and a pelvic fracture was just one of my injuries. The main spar of the *Pace Spirit*, which ran through the fuselage just ahead of my knees, had come back with some violence, hitting my shins with considerable force, sufficient to push my left thigh bone right through the hip socket splitting my pelvis open. The main spar also reduced two inches of my right shinbone to 22 fragments. The ribs down one side were broken as well. And, for good measure, my body was sporting a fine selection of cuts just about everywhere. I was not a pretty sight and one of the memories I do have through the grey blur of the following days was

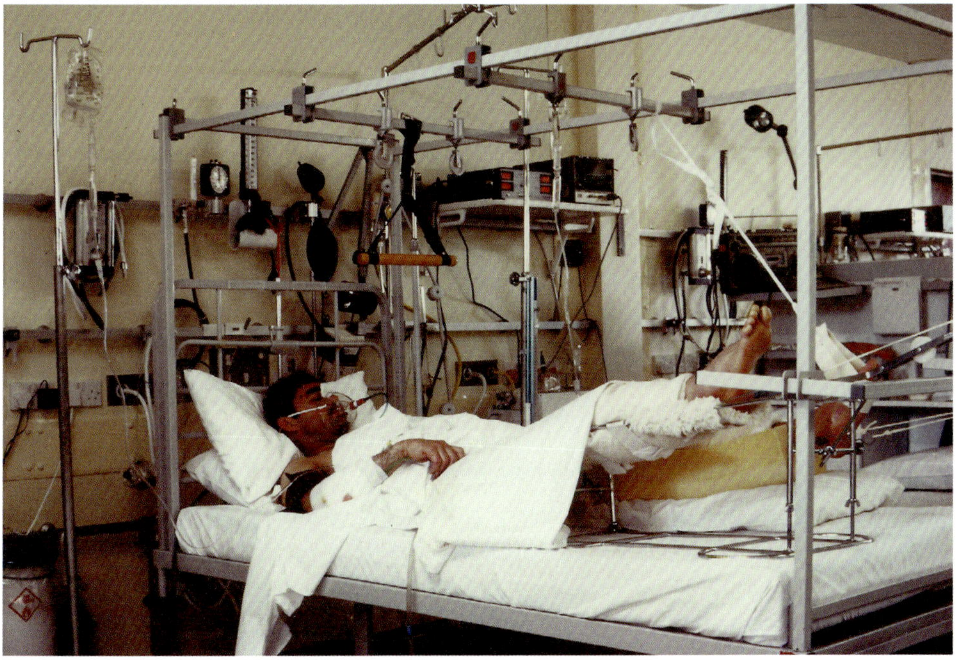

In intensive care for five days, there was a real fear that my internal organs might have been badly damaged. I was rather flattered by the number of people who came to see me although I suspect a several of them came for a last visit before I slipped into the next world!

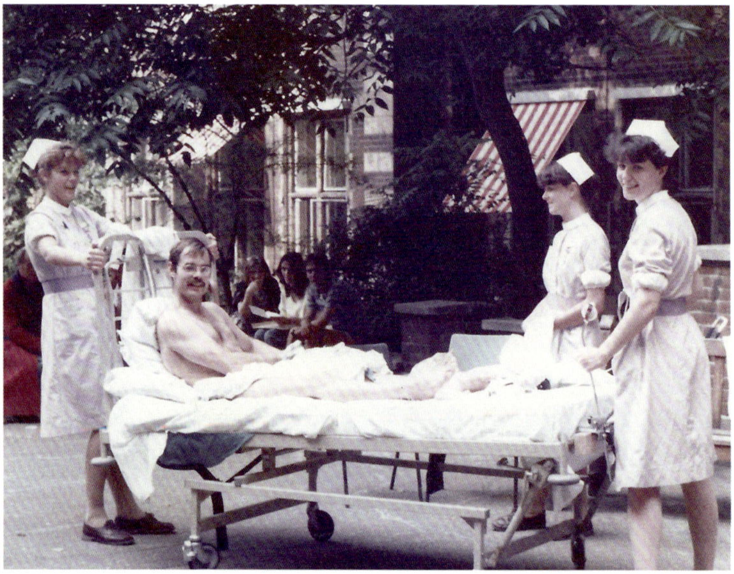

At the Middlesex Hospital in London, it was a huge pleasure when the nurses took my whole bed outside into the small hospital garden.

watching Paul Bonhomme sliding off a chair in a dead faint when the sight of me caused him, a tough, fit aerobatic pilot, to pass out and slump to the floor.

Rowena could not come to see me immediately, of course, because she was on her honeymoon. But her mother, and younger sister Isabel, visited when I was still in intensive care. It was actually through Isabel that I had met Rowena: Isabel had been going out with my flying mate, Nick Ball. Nick had married Isabel and on one visit to Rendham he was offered a flight in a friend's microlight, which he crashed into a tree. The microlight broke up around him and, in the process of extricating himself from the branches, Nick, who was not the fittest chap at the best of times, fell out of the tree and broke his leg quite badly.

He was carted off to Ipswich Hospital, where he developed a very serious blood clot. He was put straight into intensive care, in a very bad way, but died that night with Isabel, Rowena and their mother gathered at his bedside.

Imagine their shock, two and a half years later, when they went to the hospital after my accident and found me lying in the same ward and in exactly the same bed that Nick had died in. I was too groggy to hear most of what people were saying, but I was aware of them whispering this to each other. Friends rallied round and made their way to Ipswich, although I had little recollection of their visits. Harry Boggis-Rolfe drove up from London and was pretty shattered by the 'very parlous condition' in which he found me. He was so worried that he came a second time, quite possibly fearing that might be the last time he would see me before my funeral.

I was in traction for two-and-a-half months, which for anyone who has not experienced that particular delight means that you do not move from your bed whether to wash, to eat, to go to the lavatory. I had taken a shine to the lovely staff nurse in charge of the ward. I was not alone among doctors and patients in admiring Joanna Hobbs. She was very slim, attractive and unmissable. Confined to my bed and needing rather too personal care at regular intervals, I was not best placed to court her, not that that prevented me from trying.

After three weeks I was transferred down to London to the Middlesex Hospital. I was still in traction in the Middlesex when Peter Wright came to visit me, bringing his three daughters. Six-year-old Rosie ensured that her visit remained memorable when she spotted the arrangement of wires, pulleys and weights attached to my legs and gleefully jumped onto one of the weights. I could not believe the pain that resulted.

PHONE RECORDS

Fortunately, Rosie's intervention was a one-off, but after most of the discomfort faded around my body, dramatic pain remained in the big toe of my left foot. Perversely, this foot was uninjured, but the toe was at the end of the sciatic nerve, which had been crushed with my hip. The only way to relieve the incessant discomfort was for nurses to massage that toe with cold cream; it remained seriously painful for months afterwards, and is still tender today.

I was stuck in bed, of course, but was itching to get back to work. With Michael Silverman's help I managed to establish telephone contact with the outside world, long before mobile phones. We did this by sneaking in a very powerful American telephone system, the kind used to convey telephone signals across several miles of a large ranch. Over in the Mid-West this kit was ideal, but it had been banned in Europe because of concerns that it might interfere with the frequencies used by aircraft. With the powerful transmitter/receiver and its aerial next to my bed, I was linked in to the office switchboard and I am sure that most of the people I spoke to during that period had no idea that I was stuck in a hospital bed when we spoke to each other. I could not kid myself that I was making a significant contribution to the bottom line for Merton Associates that summer, but I did what I could to be useful.

As the spring of 1984 bloomed into summer my sense of frustration mounted. Other pilots were giving the aerobatic displays I had been booked to perform. All the organisers were terribly sympathetic, but inevitably I did lose quite a few

One of the nurses rather caught my eye. Joanna Hobbs, with her usual and always encouraging smile, was a perfect nurse!

future bookings. Friends were getting on with their lives. Although they were good about coming to see me and slipping in bottles of contraband booze, I began to chafe at the restrictions. I was photographed with a trio of pretty nurses being pushed in my bed out into the sunshine of the Middlesex garden, but I would far rather have been escorting them out there on my own two feet.

Things started to look up when I was finally freed from traction and allowed to start shuffling about on a zimmer frame. One of my fellow patients was a good man with similar injuries to mine. He had looked the wrong way before stepping off a pavement and had been run over. After eating NHS food for a couple of months, we both agreed that we needed a decent curry and one day, after the sister had completed her midday rounds, he and I dragged ourselves out of the ward on our zimmer frames and got into a lift. Pushing the lift buttons was not easy when balancing with all one's weight on one hand, which itself was grasping just one side of the zimmer frame.

Down at ground level, we broke out through the main doors onto the pavement and hailed a taxi. The driver could not believe that he was picking up two men wearing pyjamas and dressing-gowns in the middle of the day. He was even more amazed when we told him that our destination was only 300 yards away down Mortimer Street. I knew the Gaylord Restaurant quite well, but the other diners looked askance as my friend and I bashed through the door on zimmer frames, in our night attire, and banged our way to a table. There we consumed a lot of beer and a very large curry and the world began to take on a more positive appearance.

By the time we had finished and clattered outside we were both feeling very weak, having not stood upright for so long; being pretty drunk did not help. Another taxi conveyed us the 300 yards back to the Middlesex Hospital main entrance, from where we managed to stagger up to the ward to be given an incredibly serious bollocking. But psychologically it was very good that we had done it.

I worked hard at my physiotherapy and in the end got rid of the uncomfortable kind of splint I had to wear up my leg and inside my shoe to support the dropped foot on one leg. After a while I reckoned that the foot would only get stronger if I stopped using the splint and concentrated on exercise. Then, once I had mastered the various

At my 'it's good to be alive' party, which was well-attended, I suppose, since many wanted to see what I still looked like; but it was quite expensive in terms of champagne consumed by the revellers.

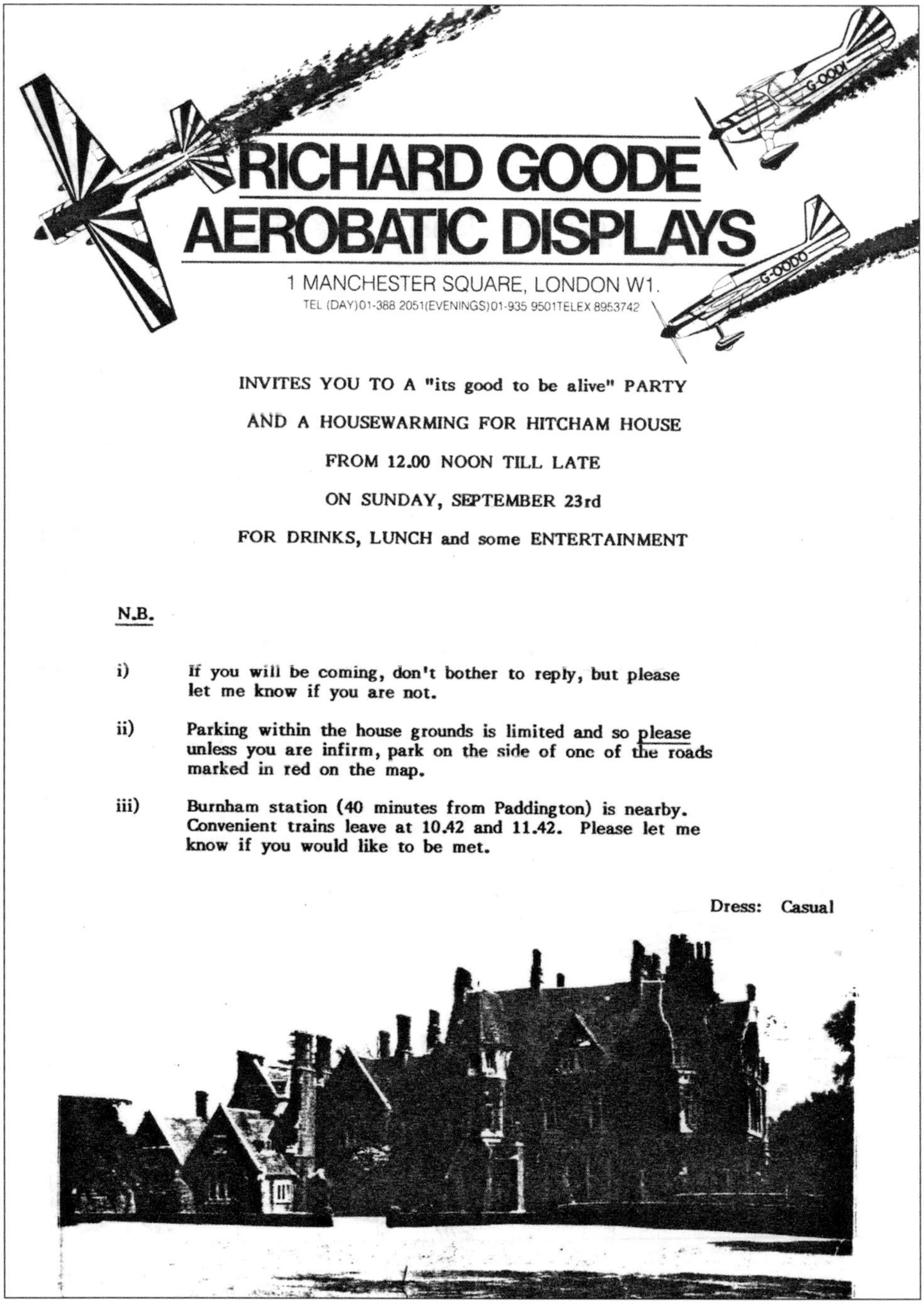

RICHARD GOODE
AEROBATIC DISPLAYS

1 MANCHESTER SQUARE, LONDON W1.
TEL (DAY)01-388 2051(EVENINGS)01-935 9501TELEX 8953742

INVITES YOU TO A "its good to be alive" PARTY

AND A HOUSEWARMING FOR HITCHAM HOUSE

FROM 12.00 NOON TILL LATE

ON SUNDAY, SEPTEMBER 23rd

FOR DRINKS, LUNCH and some ENTERTAINMENT

N.B.

i) If you will be coming, don't bother to reply, but please let me know if you are not.

ii) Parking within the house grounds is limited and so please unless you are infirm, park on the side of one of the roads marked in red on the map.

iii) Burnham station (40 minutes from Paddington) is nearby. Convenient trains leave at 10.42 and 11.42. Please let me know if you would like to be met.

Dress: Casual

The invitation for the house-warming party and celebration of not dying in the crash was typically well thought through.

exercises I needed to do, I decided I could work on these just as effectively on my own, which I did. So, I discharged myself and began getting my life back on track.

NORMALITY RETURNS

Clive and Rosie Wilson were very kind and got me to stay in their house for the first three weeks after I left hospital, converting a downstairs room into a bedroom for me. I still had to haul myself up the banisters to use the bathroom, but it was wonderful to have the freedom again to organise my own life. Another friend, my motor dealer mate Mike Elliott, fitted me up with an automatic car and I got a disabled parking badge which meant I could park right outside Merton Associates, where they let me work on the ground floor.

But if my daily life gradually got back on track, I came out of hospital with one overriding concern: flying. Everyone told me that I had lost my nerve and would not fly again. I replied reflexively that I had not lost my nerve, and I would fly again although I knew inside that was not certain. With trepidation I went down to White Waltham, where Paul Bonhomme had to lift me into a Pitts. I could barely move my legs, so flying was a joint effort at first.

But I persevered, began to get the feeling back and within a couple of months I felt quite happy about flying through a complete aerobatic sequence on my own. I started taking bookings for the next season, working on the basis that if I could not give displays myself for some reason, I now knew other people to do them for me. As it turned out, 1985 was a tough year with a lot of very bad weather. I found myself stuck in places, unable to get out, none of which helped build my confidence.

The process of mental rehabilitation took as long as the physical. The ground now appeared to be a great deal harder as I looked down on it. I decided only to perform those manoeuvres with which I felt totally happy and for a time my displays were less exciting than they had been. To force oneself to fly is a great mistake where the nature of the flying itself is very exacting. I ended up doing some 55 displays in 1985, but there was a change. Aerobatics was now something I liked very much, rather than something I loved passionately. I also had a curious feeling that in the future I would look back with a recognition that I had learned a great deal about myself from what had happened after my accident in *Pace Spirit*. In the long run, I felt sure that the benefits would outweigh the short-term pain.

The one significant bright light in that dark period was Joanna, the lovely sister from the orthopaedic ward in Ipswich. I had stayed in touch with her after my transfer to the Middlesex. To my delight she reciprocated my interest in her and visited me several times. Jo did not wait around when she had made up her mind to do something. She put in for a transfer, found a nursing job in London and moved down from Ipswich, to live with me at my flat at Bryanston Square. Jo was kind and caring and we had 18 good months together. Then one day I came back from work and found a note from her telling me that she was going back to Suffolk, sorry that things had not worked out between us. Not for the first time, a long-term girlfriend had concluded that I was not going to make the lifelong commitment to her that she might reasonably have expected.

There was an ironic twist to our story when I did make that commitment a little over 12 months later: Jo and I shared the same wedding day in October 1987. It was just that when we both got married it was to different people, and for the last 33 years it has been my good fortune to call Cary my wife.

My friend Bill Bonner was very much into power boat racing and built this boat with twin 850bhp Jaguar V12 engines. Although my legs were still weak, I agreed to join him in a major south coast race, not realising that the jolting was so severe that one cannot sit. It was a painful experience!

The remains of *Pace Spirit* went to the AAIB at Farnborough, but there was not much that they could establish since the wing that failed was destroyed. The other wing was almost intact and I kept it until it was burnt at the insistance of Cary. The structure going out to the left of the wing (pictured) was the main spar which had been pushed backwards as the fuselage collapsed and crushed my legs.

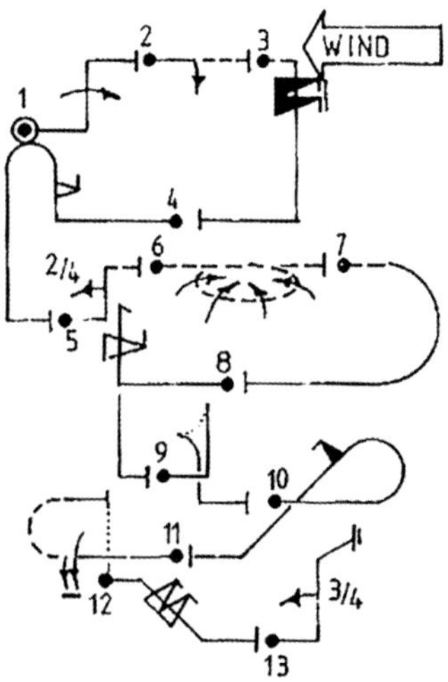

Chapter 14

MARRIAGE LINES

It certainly was not love at first sight that brought Cary and me together. We first met a good 18 years before we married, the year after I had left Cambridge.

I did not much care for her, largely because she smoked, while Cary Spink definitely did not take to me, writing off Richard Goode as a terrible show-off, who wore ridiculous clothes and always needed to be the centre of attention.

It was through our mutual friends, Mel and Peter Wright, that we first came to know each other. Peter had been my chum since Cambridge and Mel was Cary's best friend. It was inevitable that our paths should cross when the Wrights invited us both to stay with them, or at parties in London. It was also inevitable that Cary got to meet most of my former girlfriends over the intervening years.

I did once drive her back to London after one of our weekends with the Wrights, the two of us together in my racing E-type Jaguar. Cary thought I drove far too fast and too dangerously. I did not respond terribly well to this. In fact, she remembers me being very rude, turfing her out of the car at Baker Street and telling her that I did not know or care where she wanted to go but this was the closest Underground station to where I lived. For the best part of two decades, then, our lives followed different paths although we shared a number of interesting similarities.

Cary had also been born at the twilight of the British Empire. Her father had served with distinction in the Indian Army. During the war, he fought the Japanese in Burma being awarded the MC and the DSO, and at one stage became the youngest CO in the Indian Army: he was just 26 at the time. His portrait still hangs in the Punjab headquarters of the Sikh regiment he commanded.

Cary's mother had served in the Wrens, working as a signals' officer, decoding enemy signals. Her plan had been to take a secretarial course in London after the war, but she met and married Cary's father, and went back to India with him when he was posted to the staff college in Quetta. When India became independent in 1947, they had to leave the sub-continent and forge a new life back in post-war Britain, where her father joined the British Army. That was not easy. In fact, the transition was horrible. Life in India had been fun and colourful. There had been servants to take care of the day-to-day running of their home, whereas back in drab, austerity-shrouded London, Cary's mother found herself cooped up in a house, with a baby, but without a car, while her husband disappeared to the War Office every morning.

However, the War Office posting was disappointingly brief. It turned out that there were too many people doing the same job, numbers had to be thinned and a lot of officers had to leave the Army, Cary's father being one of them. Two brothers followed Cary, and Spink family life settled into the pattern shared by many former colonial families who had to make a new start after returning to the UK.

Cary shortly after we met again in 1987. We had known each other through our mutual friendship with Mel and Peter Wright.

Her parents always struggled to find enough money. Cary's brothers were sent away to board at Milton Abbey school in Dorset. Cary, as the daughter, was expected to marry and therefore needed only a rudimentary education, which is what she got. In her own estimation, the boarding school she was sent to was 'terrible, awful,' but it offered reduced fees for the daughters of army officers. Her school curriculum was limited and unimaginative, comprising botany, French, maths, English and the all-important domestic science, although even the latter had its shortcomings: domestic science at Cary's school did not include cooking.

The school did not offer A-levels either, so the girls left when they reached 15 or 16, at which stage Cary was presented with two career choices: becoming a nurse, or a secretary. She did not want to be either of these, but her father persuaded her to go to secretarial college in Liverpool; the family were then living in Lancashire. Cary completed her training, but never really threw herself into becoming a secretary largely, as she says herself, because she does not like doing what she is told. Instead of being at the beck and call of some tedious boss, she took herself off travelling and over two years worked her way down through Africa, beginning in Kenya, then moving to Rhodesia and ending up in South Africa. She also went to Australia a couple of times.

Cary took on an incredibly tough job at the National Asthma Campaign attempting to unite three separate charities.

When she was in her mid-20s she followed her father into the MOD, where she found some of the work interesting, but most of it pretty humdrum. She left after three years, commuted her pension and travelled to Australia with a friend. While they were living and working out there, Cary took on a long-distance tutorial course, studying for A-level English with a teacher friend in the UK. When she got home, she applied to London University and was accepted as the first student ever to be offered a place without having an A-level. Her offer was conditional on her passing her A-level English exam, which she did, and on passing a special entrance exam. She passed that too.

Her plan had been to take a degree to become a primary school teacher, although in hindsight that might not have been the ideal career choice either; Cary feels sure that she would have found it difficult not to have lost her patience with the children. She had other misgivings too. Most of her friends were getting married and starting families, while she, at the age of 30, was about to embark on four years of student penury, studying for an undergraduate degree, raising all the money herself which meant having to work at evenings and weekends.

The prospects for primary school teachers were not that rosy either. Just as Cary was about to begin her training, education cuts started to bite and primary school teachers began losing their jobs. Was there any point in putting herself through that? Probably not. So, Cary declined her place at London University and not long after found herself jetting out to the Gulf, where she had been offered a job running Dragonfly, a high-end shop in Abu Dhabi that sold furniture and household fittings to ex-pats with generous, tax-free incomes to spend.

When the friend who had started the business needed someone to help run it when she returned to London with her husband, Cary found herself importing furniture from firms in south-east Asia: mainly the Philippines and Hong Kong. She bought silk in Thailand, along with other fabrics and household items from manufacturers in India and Sri Lanka.

After a couple of years, she returned to the UK with a decent pot of money that enabled her to put down the deposit on a London flat and buy a car. In London, she was soon appointed as the Domestic Secretary to the Royal College of Obstetricians and Gynaecologists, running all the domestic staff, all the catering, all the cleaning and taking charge of the maintenance of the whole building at the college's headquarters on Crown Estate land in Sussex Place, close to Regent's Park.

From there, Cary was headhunted by the British Heart Foundation to lead their education division, organising conferences as well as overseeing educational programmes for GPs, cardiologists, nurses, not to mention the general public. In time her work at the top of UK medical charities earned her an entry in *Who's Who*, a publication from which my own entry still remains mysteriously absent.

THE PURSUIT OF LOVE

By this stage, however, I had come to see that there was another, more pressing, absence in my life. Now in my early 40s, I found myself, to quote Jane Austen at the opening of *Pride and Prejudice*, 'in want of a wife'. I had had quite a number of girlfriends over the years, of course. But how to find a partner for life? That was the challenge.

The answer, I decided, could be arrived at through a combination of two things in which I had a fair amount of experience: laying bets and headhunting. By now, friends had become used to me betting them to do all manner of things, most of them ridiculous. At Cambridge my bets tended to be fairly basic, such as the speed at which we could down a pint of beer. The bets matured as we matured. Which can you consume faster: a bottle of champagne or a hard-boiled egg?

So, I gathered friends at a pub in Pimlico and announced that my latest bet had an altogether higher aim: that in nine months I would be married. They could see that I was in deadly earnest. They also had my form with previous girlfriends to reflect on and before long some pretty serious money was being laid down. From the outset I was totally confident that I would win the bet. I was a headhunter, after all. How hard could it be to find someone to marry?

Therefore, I called on my headhunting experience to rationalise my approach to finding the future Mrs Goode. I drew on contacts, people with access to and knowledge of suitable candidates. I put the word about among all the women of my acquaintance, asking them in a jocular way if they happened to know of any unmarried girls whom they thought might be interested in what I was proposing. That turned out to be an excellent way of getting to meet a wide selection of delightful girls. The summer of 1987 proved to be very busy.

At the same time I needed some objective comparisons by which to make balanced judgements about the various young women I was taking out. The adage about not judging women and linen by candlelight had more than a grain of truth as I set about my task with focused and earnest application. Not only was there money riding on this but my future happiness was in the mix and helping to concentrate my mind.

I kept notes, not necessarily as detailed as those for headhunting placement or a management audit, but thorough all the same. For the most part they recorded how different girls reacted to me. It was rather like the film *Groudhog Day*. I did vary the restaurants where I took girls to dinner, but I went through pretty much the same repertoire of anecdotes and jokes, and carefully recorded how each evening's companion had responded to them.

The Covent Garden box office did well out of my research. I booked a lot of tickets to the opera, primarily because I so enjoy opera myself, but also because I hoped it would impress whoever I was taking there. And I pursued my research in finding a wife every bit as vigorously as I did headhunting the perfect senior executive for a client. To that end, I saw *Fidelio* three nights running and at one of those performances my guest was Cary Spink.

To an extent I have John Harrison and his wife Sue to thank for this key development in my search for a wife. John and Sue asked me to be godfather to the first addition to the Harrison clan. Liz Hustler was asked to be godmother and over a glass of the post-christening champagne I put to her the question that I had been asking virtually every woman I met that summer. 'What about Cary Spink?' she replied. Cary and I had not seen each other for about 12 years, but her name certainly rang a bell and Liz gave me her telephone number.

The name Richard Goode rang a bell with Cary too, when Liz called her the next day to say that she had met me and given me Cary's number. Cary thought that this was all a bit odd, especially when I called not long after and invited her out to dinner. However, she accepted the invitation. 'It's very convenient,' I continued. 'You work just around the corner from my flat, so you can come around after work.'

'I'm afraid I can't do that,' Cary replied. 'I've got two dogs and I have to come home to feed them.' She had two wire-haired dachshunds, George and Daisy who were the first of the line of dogs that would bring colour to our lives. 'You'll have to come and pick me up from here.'

'What?' I exclaimed, more than a little taken aback at being checked for the first time by Cary. 'Do you mean I have to come to the country?' Cary was living in Chiswick.

Anyhow, I did go out to 'the country' and the evening got off to a promising start when I pulled up outside her flat in what she regarded as a 'very nice' Bristol, not something flashy and brash like the E-type Jaguar in which she had been scared stiff by my driving on our previous journey together.

The intervening dozen years had wrought changes to both of us, changes that met with approval on either side. Cary was now in charge of the British Heart Foundation's very successful 'no smoking' campaign and had therefore given up smoking herself long before we met again. The changes she found in me may have been less apparent, but she detected them right away. The obsession to become World Aerobatic Champion had gone with *Pace Spirit*. I was still keen on flying, but not at the expense of everything else. I dressed more appropriately for a man of my age. I came across as driven, but less self-centred. I still had my moustache, which Cary never liked but in time that would find its way down the plughole and has never grown back. I shaved it off so that friends would donate money to charities of their choice. We raised £2,000 although I thought I might grow it back on holiday. But when the women in the office all commented on the improvement in my appearance, the moustache stayed off for good. The bottom line was that Cary Spink found Richard Goode stimulating company and fun to be with and vice versa.

George and Daisy, the two miniature wire-haired dachshunds which were an inseparable part of Cary's life. We have continued to own dogs to this day. She continued to have these dachshunds, but always outnumbered by spaniels.

Cary puts our reunion rather well. She describes it as like meeting a cousin you have not seen for a long time. We both knew a fair bit about each other. All the background had been filled in, and that allowed us to catch up on what he had been doing in our lives since we last met, comfortable and completely at ease in each other's company.

When I twigged that part of Cary's interest in me was that I had a nice house and garden and that gardening was something she enjoyed, I invited her to spend the weekend with me at my home in Buckinghamshire. There will be more about this later, but as well as my London flat in Bryanston Square, I was then living in the Manor House at Princes Risborough, which had a big garden that was tidy, but definitely in need of horticultural flair to brighten it up. Cary and I had been going out for a week when she came to stay, bringing George and

Daisy with her. This was her first exposure to my domestic arrangements and walking through the front door into the large panelled hall made an impression. The furniture, she says, looked terrible, the kind of furniture you pick up in a junk shop, which some of it was. The curtains were not a lot better as they were cast-offs from friends.

When Cary arrived, I was applying what she remembers as 'thick tan varnish' to some very nice pine bookshelves. 'You can't do that,' she told me, appalled. I stopped. Things went better in the garden. I had someone who came in to mow the lawns and trim the hedges, but the flower beds needed weeding and Cary set to on those.

In the afternoon she and I paid a visit to Arthur. Arthur had a yard and a barn filled with household items, at Maidens Green; it was not far from White Waltham and I was a regular customer. Cary bought a birdbath for her garden in Chiswick and I bought books to fill the extensive bookshelves at Princes Risborough. On the way back we stopped at a car boot sale to buy even more books. The following day I had been invited to a lunch party, not far from Cary's flat and called in to see her afterwards, to invite her to go with me to *Fidelio* at Covent Garden.

Although I did not realise it at the time that weekend did the trick. When she arrived at work the following morning, her secretary asked Cary how it had gone. It had been good, she answered, adding that she was going to marry Richard Goode. So much was familiar about our relationship, she said it felt as though we were already married. It just felt right, even though one of Cary's dogs had gone for my cat at Princes Risborough, which resulted in me getting a nasty bite which necessitated a visit to A&E.

Of course, I already knew that I was going to get married. I just did not know to whom it would be. Over the coming weeks my list of prospective candidates was whittled away as, one by one, other girls fell by the wayside, until there was just a single name left. Crunch time.

STORM BREWING

Six weeks after meeting each other again, I asked Cary if she would move in with me, to which she answered, 'No!' 'Will you marry me, then?' 'Yes,' she answered.

I should say at this juncture that our memories of exactly how events unfolded immediately afterwards vary. I maintain that I had imbibed rather freely in celebration. Anyhow, I do not have a clear recollection of how we became formally engaged.

My wife-to-be refutes that. However, there is no denying what happened the following morning, when my secretary put through a call from Cary Spink. 'I'm so pleased that we're engaged,' Cary told me brightly. I was feeling a tad thick-headed and bleary. 'The good news is that I've bought the engagement ring. The only slight problem is that I bought it with Valerie's credit card. But Valerie's a bit tight for money, so is there any chance of repaying her by the end of the day?'

Checkmate. I realised that I had met my match. Cary maintains that she bought the ring, because she knew that I would not. Using a friend's credit card also ensured that I would repay the friend for it. She felt pretty sure that if she had bought the ring using her own money, that would have been the last she saw of the £700.

On her finger, Cary had a very nice engagement ring, bought from Richard Ogden. She had told everyone at work that she was marrying Richard Goode. She had told Mel and Peter. We were getting married, there was no question about that. The only detail that remained unanswered was when. By now we had booked a holiday to Turkey and the date was in our diaries, in six weeks' time. I love

Cary and me on our wedding day accompanied by the three Wright girls in the Austin 'Chummy' that we had given each other as a wedding present.

The happy couple, now married, at the front door of the Manor House at Princes Risborough.

Istanbul and had visited the city several times with Cressida. Her father had been a senior diplomat in Ankara and Cressida had spent several months living with a very remote Kurdish community in the far east, between Lake Van and the Iranian border. When in Istanbul, Cressida and I always stayed at the Pera Palace Hotel. I liked it, so it seemed logical to go there with Cary too.

However, I really was very busy running two businesses and could not afford to take time off for a holiday and a honeymoon. The obvious solution was to turn our holiday into our honeymoon, although that did require making all the arrangements for our wedding, along with actually getting married, in just six weeks. And here I saw for the first time just how fortunate I had been when Liz Hussler had given me Cary's telephone number less than two months earlier.

Although she would have liked a church wedding, especially as the Manor House at Princes Risborough stands right next to the parish church, Cary felt that if her father was not going to be there to walk her down the nave, then she did not really mind what form our wedding took. Cary's father had died, quite unexpectedly at the age of just 71, three weeks before she and I had met again. She was very close to him and had been very upset.

So, we were married in the registry office, accompanied by Peter and Mel, and their children. However, in just six weeks Cary had masterminded the celebrations fantastically, which resulted in a sit-down dinner-dance for 220 guests, in a marquee at our own home. And not one professional had been hired to do any of it. Cary and a team of girlfriends did all the cooking. Then, two days before the dinner-dance, the Great Storm of October 1987 descended on the south of England, gathering up our marquee and dumping it in a vast, sodden heap a hundred yards away. Quite a few of our guests only managed to get to us after sawing their way through felled trees that had trapped them inside their driveways.

However, the storm disbursed. All but six of those invited were able to come to toast our future happiness and marvel at what Cary and her team had achieved. Then she and I embarked on married life together, flying out from Heathrow bound for Turkey.

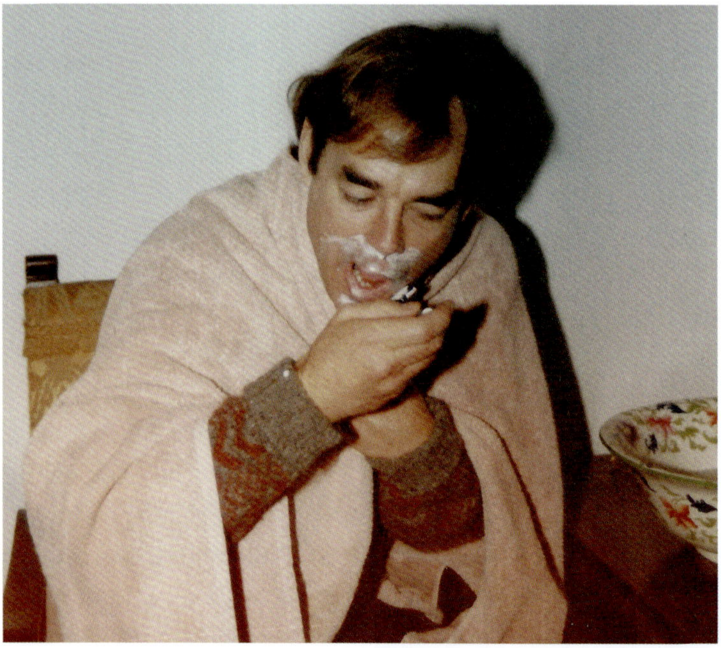

Cary never liked my moustache and cleverly persuaded a big group of friends to donate to a charity of their choice if I shaved it off. A lot of money was made for good causes, although I finished up with a large champagne bill!

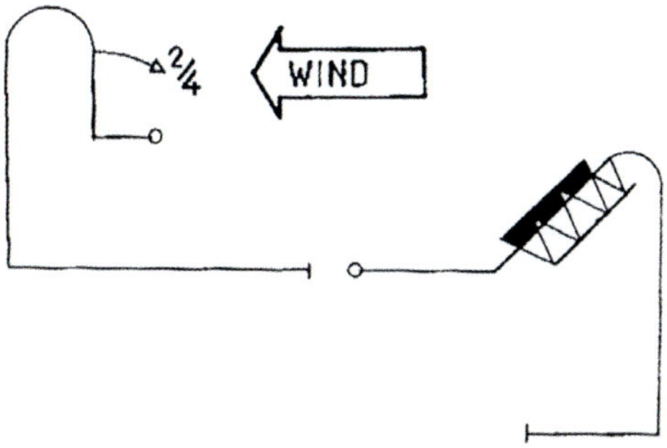

Chapter 15

A GOODE DOUBLE-FIRST

By the time Cary and I married, my own flying had undergone a pretty fundamental re-evaluation, the upshot of which was that I was now concentrating exclusively on display flying.

For me, competition flying had had its day. I could see that I was not going to better my 17th placing in the 1980 World Championships and I had come to realise that what I enjoyed most about aerobatics was sharing the thrill and excitement with spectators. There was no denying either, that being the sole focus of attention of 70,000 people as I hurled my aeroplane about and pirouetted across the sky had its attractions too.

Following the loss of *Pace Spirit*, I was giving displays in my Ultimate Pitts. I did acquire a second plane designed by my German friend, Walter Extra. However, fate and structural failure in the *Pace Spirit* port wing grounded me for so long that I never really flew his Extra 230. My friend Philip Meeson was keen to buy it from me and he added it to his aerobatic team sponsored by Marlboro cigarettes.

I always felt that Walter's plane would be improved if it was given greater power and it was at my instigation that he began thinking about putting a 300-plus horsepower engine into the Extra. What I certainly had not envisaged was that the Extra 300 would be a two-seater. The idea that a two-seater aircraft could fly aerobatics to the extent of winning a World Championship would have been unthinkable before Walter's daring innovation.

The Extra 230 (above) which we built but were persuaded by Philip Meeson to sell to him. It then carried his familiar Marlboro sponsorship.

My faithful Pitts Special, G-OODI (below), joined the Extra 300 that I had acquired for my aerobatic team sponsored by Victor Gauntlett's Proteus Petroleum.

By the time I flew the Extra 300 for the first time at the end of 1988, I had logged some 80 hours displaying the Yak-50. I had heard good things about Walter's new aircraft from a couple of pilots whose views I respected. Other reports spoke of it in glowing terms, calling it 'the Ferrari of the sky,' 'the nearest thing to strapping on a pair of wings'. When my turn came, I too was left incredulous by the way it performed and handled. That such powerful controls should be so light amazed me. There was no question about it in my mind. This was an aeroplane I had to have, and I was still working out a co-ownership deal with a couple of friends and our various bank managers, when providence smiled on me again.

Out of the blue I received an invitation to lunch from Victor Gauntlett. Our previous sponsorship deal had ended with his sale of Pace Petroleum in 1986, but now he had a new project and a new oil company, Proteus Petroleum, and he wanted to publicise it with a new aerobatic team. Opportunities of this sort do not come too often and after a while I persuaded Victor that the performance and newsworthiness of the Extra more than justified its cost! At this stage the problem of getting delivery became apparent, since the world's aerobatic aficionados were queuing up at Walter's door. When my Extra 300 finally arrived, it was on the day before the all-important Press Day to announce the aircraft to the UK aviation scene.

DISPLAY WINDOW

Once airborne, the Extra 300 was fantastic to fly and its aerobatic repertoire was only limited by the pilot's capability. That characteristic bugbear of aerobatic practice, height loss, simply did not exist. In fact, the real problem was keeping the show within sight of the crowd, and in my first practice sequence I began at 2,000 feet and found myself four manoeuvres later at over 4,000 feet, which was not going to excite the spectators much.

That first season with the Extra in 1989 was quite hairy. My display bookings were well underway by the time the aeroplane was delivered and after its arrival it became a mad rush to learn to fly it to an acceptable standard. On the upside, the Extra 300 proved to be every bit as eye-catching and newsworthy as I had assured Victor it would be.

By the start of the following season, the Extra 300 had quickly developed an awesome reputation for speed and style. So much so that *Performance Bikes*, which billed itself as 'Britain's best-selling motorcycle magazine,' organised a drag race to promote the newly-arrived Kawasaki ZZ-R1100, at that time, the world's fastest production bike, which took just two seconds to race from nought to 60 miles per hour. Astride this twin cam, 16-valve superbike was the magazine's senior test rider, Mike Forsyth. His opponent, at the controls of what was now known as the Proteus Extra, was me.

The venue for our memorable encounter was the two-mile runway at Bruntingthorpe, the aerodrome in Leicestershire where high-performance car testing was also carried out. Mike and I lined up side by side and then sped away in a cloud of smoke when the signal was given. The Kawasaki edged in front as it

A nice plan view of the Extra 300. Although lacking the charisma of the Yak-50 the Extra was a delight to fly.

Bauer Media Archives

roared up to 130mph, but I still had plenty of runway to make up the distance and gradually crept ahead as we tore down towards the end.

The Proteus Extra crossed the finish line two feet above the ground at 193mph and still accelerating, while the bike at 172mph was five yards behind. But it was at the end of the race, and the end of the runway, that the difference between our respective machines came sharply into focus. While I was able to lift the Extra off the ground to climb into the warm spring sunshine, Mike suddenly remembered that he was running out of tarmac rather too hastily. Even a gentle touch on the brakes was enough to lock his front wheel. The bike went down, sending Mike skidding across the ground at 170 mph! But he was a tough bugger, which was just as well. Although he was battered and bruised and had to be taken to hospital afterwards, part of the deal was that having raced the Extra 300 he had to fly with me in the aircraft while I went through an aerobatic sequence. Similarly I had to take his very impressive motorcycle for a spin.

That season brought Proteus Petroleum further widespread press coverage in the form of Louisa Knapp when she became the latest recruit to fly for the

I was very lucky to be introduced to Louisa Knapp, seen here with Victor Gauntlett. She arrived with a second Extra 300 and was a welcome addition.

Our team of two Extra 300s flown by Louisa and myself, and the Pitts flown here by Paul Bonhomme.

aerobatic team. Still only 21, blonde, pretty, and looking very fetching in her flying suit, Louisa was every PR department's dream signing. But the otherwise predictable brickbats about sexist stereotyping were stifled because Louisa was the only professional woman aerobatic pilot in the UK, who just happened to own her own state-of-the-art aerobatic aeroplane into the bargain. If you were looking for a sure-fire example of a young woman making it in a man's world, Louisa was a dead cert for such an accolade. The fact that she was fun, while being fully committed to learning her craft, simply added to her credentials.

When I met Louisa and her father, I made no bones about the terms of her Proteus engagement. Victor had agreed to cover all the costs of engaging another pilot. In return Louisa would be expected to roll up her sleeves and do all the unglamorous jobs around aeroplanes that airshow spectators never see. That was on top of improving her aerobatic skills in double-quick time. Louisa understood, agreed to this enthusiastically and was as good as her word. To seal her commitment, her father bought her her very own Extra 300, which gave the Proteus Petroleum aerobatic display team a total of three aircraft: my Pitts Ultimate, and the two Extra 300s, my G-OHIM and Louisa Knapp's G-OHER. When G-OHIM was still on the German register, I had registered it as D-EBTS: distinctly appropriate after its final bills had been paid.

In the wider world of international aerobatics there was no question that Walter Extra's development of the Extra 300 marked a step change, certainly among aircraft designers in the West. On the other side of the Iron Curtain, however, a development every bit as significant was taking place in Russia. It hit the wider aerobatic world at the 1986 World Aerobatic Championships, staged at South Cerney, in Gloucestershire, at which the Russian team and their quite remarkable new aeroplane pretty much swept the board.

The Yak-55s of previous competitions had been set aside and, in their place Russian pilots were parading a breathtaking successor created by the Sukhoi Design Bureau, the Su-26. This had an astonishing rate of roll of 400 degrees a second. With a carbon fibre main spar, titanium ribs and a Kevlar outer covering, the -26 was also incredibly light, yet strong, compared with an all-metal aircraft. It was quite simply the most fantastic aerobatic aeroplane I had ever seen.

SUKHOI START

It is worth mentioning at this point how the Su-26 came into being, because its evolution not only marked a turning point in the direction of my own aviation business, it was also an intriguing insight into how aircraft were developed in the former USSR, and how Russian manufacturers adapted to the commercial upheaval and uncertainties brought about by the collapse of the Soviet Union.

Essentially there were five big aircraft design bureaux, and while there were particular 'specialities' for each, such as fighters for MiG and Sukhoi, and large transport aircraft for Antonov and Ilyushin, there were considerable areas of overlap. Yakovlev had always been the sole producer of aerobatic aircraft, and probably assumed that this would continue. However, Sukhoi, whose only products to date had been military fighters, felt that they should have a go. And to do this they adopted a technique I could immediately appreciate. They headhunted the best designer for the kind of aircraft they had in mind from their rival design bureau, Yakovlev.

The man Sukhoi poached from Yakovlev was an inspirational engineer named Slava Kondratiev who, during his time at Yakovlev, had designed the then state-of-the-art aircraft, the Yak-55 and the Yak-55M. However, Kondratiev could see that the future lay in composite aircraft and, when Yakovlev refused to accept that a proper aircraft could be made from such material, Sukhoi, eager to show off their skills, gave Kondratiev a free hand to design a composite aerobatic aircraft for them.

The driving force behind this move was Mikhail Simonov, the general director of Sukhoi. In addition to wanting to be one up on Yakovlev, he could see the commercial attractions of designing and manufacturing the best aerobatic aircraft in the world. So Kondratiev was lured away from Yakovlev, where he was given 40 engineers and simply told to get on with it.

Kondratiev and his team set to work to design the very best aerobatic aircraft in the world without any regard whatsoever to cost, and very unusually to source the best components and structural material from anywhere in the world, despite the significant implications this might have in terms of foreign exchange. In my estimation, this was probably the world's last aeroplane ever to be built without cost being a factor. Many items, including the exhaust system and entire undercarriage were made from titanium, a metal that in the West was generally reserved for exotic watches and parts of Formula 1 racing cars. Similarly, components which in the West would have been fabrications from high-tensile steel were magnesium

Together with Tom Delaney who came with me for our first meetings with Sukhoi in Moscow and the Chaika limousine that provided us with transport.

My first meeting with a Sukhoi-26. Pictured are Sasha Tavaryan, commercial director of Sukhoi, Victor Smolin and Boris Raikitin, Sukhoi's chief designer.

forgings on the Su-26. Covering the fuselage with Kevlar, when glass fibre would have done the same job, added significantly to production costs although using Kevlar did strengthen the aircraft to a far greater degree.

South Cerney marked the new Sukhoi's first visit to the West. Here it was something of a sensation, as I have said, not only because of its competition performance, winning both the men's and women's team titles, as well as the outright Women's Championship, but also because of its spectacular performance in the hands of Yurgis Kairis, many of whose manoeuvres were flown directly over the spectators, to the horror of the CAA.

Mikhail Simonov's commercial nous had proved to be very shrewd. In order to create the Su-26, he had set up Advanced Sukhoi Technologies, effectively his own private company within the Sukhoi Design Bureau. Using state money to design and build what was undoubtedly the world's best aerobatic aircraft at the time, Simonov was then doing deals with himself, buying the planes privately through some strange little financial arrangement, and then selling them privately at a very handsome profit. But the profits were being funneled directly to Advanced Sukhoi Technologies, and therefore to Simonov himself, rather than the 100 per cent state-owned Sukhoi corporation.

When glasnost and perestroika came along, Simonov was perfectly placed to look for sales beyond the Eastern bloc. As in every other former state-owned manufacturing enterprise, the management of Sukhoi was desperate for hard currency and selling aircraft to the West looked like the ideal way to get it. At the same time, they were approached by the Pompano Air Center, probably the US leaders in commercial aerobatics, (where coincidentally Louisa Knapp had undertaken her training as a pilot), to ask if they could represent Sukhoi outside the Soviet Union. In the end, after protracted negotiations, PAC were appointed the agency for the USA.

From my own point of view, I did not have the burning ambition to own a Su-26 in the way that I longed for a Yak-50. Nevertheless, I did say that I would not miss the opportunity to fly one and when Boris Raikitin, the chief engineer of the Sukhoi Design Bureau, invited me to Moscow to visit the plant and to fly the aircraft I did not turn him down. At this stage an idea began developing in my mind. I could see the undoubted publicity value of having both the first Sukhoi-26 outside the USA, but also the first new Soviet aircraft of any sort to be sold to the United Kingdom. I subsequently realised that a glider had been imported, but in the publicity context I did not really feel that it counted.

So, I set out to convince Victor that the publicity a Sukhoi would generate would more than compensate for the modest contribution I was seeking towards its purchase. On top of the publicity value of the first Extra 300 to come to the UK, and bringing Louisa Knapp under the Proteus wing, I was offering him the chance to cap them both with an even more memorable 'first'. An enthusiast, as well as a hard-nosed businessman, Victor did not take a lot of convincing.

Gradually the deal to buy a -26 took shape, although I sensed that Alexander 'Sasha' Tavaryan, effectively Sukhois's commercial director, was having to fight bureaucracy at his end. Time pressures meant that I could not spend more than five days in Russia finalising everything. Apart from making time actually to fly the aeroplane, I reckoned there were two other phases to the deal: coming to a formal commercial agreement and dealing with every aspect of the aircraft's specification.

Accompanying me on the trip to Moscow was a friend from White Waltham, Tom Delaney. Tom had trained as a wartime Spitfire pilot and had then become a very successful businessman, but in many respects he led a rather dull life until he came across us and we gingered things up for him. When I suggested that he go to Russia to buy a Sukhoi, Tom did not need to be asked a second time. As I had hoped, in fact, Tom's commercial experience proved to be extremely useful in the meetings that were about to take place.

Anyone travelling to Russia in the early 1990s knew that most of the cars on the road were worse-for-wear Ladas, Moskvitchs and so forth. Stepping out of the arrival lounge at Sheremetyevo we realised that we had arrived when, in a sea of such decrepit cars, we were guided by the retinue of Sukhoi people sent to meet us towards an immaculate new Mercedes. We put our bags in the boot and made for the rear seat to be told that the Mercedes is for the luggage. We would travel in the Chaika. There, in front of the Mercedes, was one of the vast limousines normally reserved for the most serious of Politburo and KGB nobs.

Sukhoi were as good as their word and produced a lovely aircraft (below), here seen in its final stages of assembly in the factory at 23A, Polikarpov Street which was a strange address for a major military aircraft business.

Regrettably our accommodation did not rise to the same standard. The Ministry of Defence Hotel (yes, it was actually called that) was not a patch on the commercial hotels that were starting to spring up around the city. But it was where Sukhoi housed their official visitors and Tom and I fell into that category and we should probably have been flattered that Sukhoi regarded us as serious aeroplane people.

The weather the next day was as drab and unwelcoming as the hotel. Flying the Sukhoi was out of the question, but Sasha pushed us into the Chaika and we were taken to where the Russian team were practising. All the aircraft were wrapped in their massive engine and fuselage covers but the lack of flying did give me time to talk to the team, many of whom were old mates from my own competition days. I had remained very friendly with Khalide Makagonova and listening to her extolling the Su-26 had been part of my inspiration to buy one. I asked Victor Smolin for his views and his eyes lit up as he said, 'Seven rolls vertical!' which sounded pretty convincing to me.

The next day, Tom and I were taken to the design bureau and the factory for the first time and it was a real eye-opener. The design bureau housed test and development laboratories, where many thousands of engineers were at work. In the hangar, unusually for a design bureau, four aircraft were being built, each one assembled by hand by a couple of technicians. Almost everything apart from the engine, propeller, instruments and tyres were made in the factory. Because of problems of internal supply and to a lesser extent quality, Sukhoi insisted on making everything else, including all the conventional hardware and fittings, which in the West we would have expected to buy from dedicated specialists.

For the structural testing department, Sasha ushered us into a vast hangar where we were met by the sight of a -26 trussed up in a metal structure the size of a small house. This was putting the aeroplane through a +10G to –7G cycle every 30 seconds for three months. They had also tested three complete airframes and wings to destruction, with the wings finally failing at between 25 and 28G. Even at these absurd levels the fuselage had not distorted.

It was only on the third day of our visit that we began discussing the financial aspects of any potential deal. Until that point I was negotiating blind with no idea what the aircraft was going to cost. Discussions about money began with the unnerving comment from the Sukhoi side of the table that the plane cost one million dollars. However, they were not sure of their figures, as they also did not have an accounts department. Eventually it came down to a figure that began to make more sense to me: $175,000.

With the price settled, I laid out my own performance requirements for the aircraft, of which the smoke system was probably the most important. When I said that for our kind of airshow use we needed a capacity of 30 litres and the ability to deliver at least five litres a minute, the Sukhoi engineers were absolutely amazed. You need a fairly high-pressure pump to deliver diesel at that rate, but in an aerobatic aeroplane it also needs to be small. We had taken to fitting our other aircraft with a handy little pump, which was normally used to pump out the bilges of boats. Since Sukhoi did not have one of these, I provided it myself. However, I did remember to mention that they would need to re-machine the threads on the pipe fittings, because the pump had BSP (British Standard Pipe) fittings. The engineers looked at it and then smiled. That would not be necessary, they told me. Every single house in Russia has these fittings, a fascinating legacy of Victorian engineering!

I also needed a small luggage compartment, which greatly surprised them as it would, I suppose on reflection, surprise Ferrari engineers if one specified a luggage compartment on a Formula 1 racing car. I tried to explain by saying that once I had arrived at an airshow I had to pay for fuel and needed somewhere to put my wallet which also confused them. Then I remembered that I was talking to people who were used to landing and expecting the state to top up the fuel tanks in state-owned aircraft. My luggage compartment led to some three-quarters of an hour's detailed discussion with two 'airframe specialists' although, to be fair, everything we said had to be conducted through an interpreter.

I worked through my list, explaining my requirements to 'specialists' for every aspect of the aircraft, even down to a lady who was the 'paint specialist'. When it came to spares, I was relieved to see that on the first page of optional extras Sukhoi had listed a 10-ton airfield refueling truck. That made me feel that my own very modest expectations would be easily met.

We discussed delivery, and it was Sukhoi who raised the idea that they might be able to deliver my new plane by air. When I told them that would generate huge publicity, the decision was taken to lay on one of the two design bureau's massive Ilyushin-76s to bring the -26 to the UK.

I had visions of attempting to reassemble the aircraft using Russian manuals and was much relieved to learn that the delivery service would include the provision of a team of three factory engineers who would come to the UK to re-assemble the -26. Better still, the delivery package would also include the services of a factory test pilot to test-fly the aeroplane until I was totally satisfied. In the event this role was filled by Khalide Makagonova and for a week she and the engineering team would be our guests at Princes Risborough, while they worked on the aeroplane at White Waltham.

When purchasing an aircraft in the West a handshake and a cheque by way of deposit usually suffices. Not so in Russia, even in the warm glow of perestroika. Sukhoi's backroom boys produced a massive contract of sale, all 20-plus pages of it. The final signing, with both myself and the two senior Design Bureau directors, was suitably accompanied by liberal supplies of Russian 'champagne', a little sweet for my personal taste. We agreed on a delivery date of the end of January 1991, some three months off.

The Ilyushin Il-76 that Sukhoi were persuaded to use in order to deliver my aircraft. It was the first Russian military aircraft to land at an RAF base, in Abingdon.

My Sukhoi emerging from the belly of the Ilyushin-76.

Visa difficulties and the cost of travel ruled out quick flying visits to Moscow and it was therefore with a combination of high expectation and concern that the end of January approached. Sasha continued to assure me that everything was under control, but in the end I decided that a visit to Moscow would be necessary, if only to avoid the immense embarrassment of a large crowd of journalists waiting patiently at RAF Abingdon on 30 January, with no Ilyushin in sight.

However, when I arrived a very high-level, secret meeting was taking place with a bunch of foreign military people, and they would not let me into the factory to see my aircraft. Tom Delaney had come with me again and the best we could do was to go out on the road to Sheremetyevo Airport, at Sasha's suggestion, and wait beside it in a snowstorm at a designated time. Sure enough, after 10 minutes a Sukhoi lorry appeared and on it was a disassembled Su-26; unmistakably my Su-26 because it was painted in Proteus Petroleum colours.

When I finally did get to see it properly a few days later, the aircraft was outstanding. The external finish was of quite exceptional standard, but my real interest was with what lay under the skin, and there I was taken aback by the efforts to which Sukhoi had gone to produce the perfect product. Where I had expected to find the fuel tank for my smoke system inside the fuselage, Sukhoi had redesigned the inboard portion of the wing, installing two beautiful little five-gallon tanks behind the main spar. The cost in terms of design time and execution would not have been insignificant. But that was just the start.

The entire panel and all the controls, even down to those for the smoke system, had been placarded in English albeit, on occasion, rather quaintly, but a really proper job. Even my much-joked-about luggage compartment was a masterpiece of design in Kevlar, and if it weighed more than six or seven ounces I would have been surprised. Although I would have liked to have been aboard the Ilyushin that brought the Su-26 to the UK, that was not possible for bureaucratic reasons, so I flew home a few days before the delivery date.

Sukhoi did not want to have to buy any fuel in the UK, when they could get state fuel free of charge in Russia. It was decided to fill the Ilyushin with enough to fly from Moscow to Oxfordshire and back again. However, this led to concerns that the big transport aircraft might be too heavy to land on the runway at RAF Abingdon and after several days of failing to get official clearance in Moscow, the flight went ahead on the say-so of the flight crew alone. That was the way things were being done in Russia at that time. The press had gathered in impressive numbers to record the arrival of the big transport aircraft, from which my aeroplane was successfully unloaded. There was great excitement and much approval when the registered name I had given it was revealed as G-ORBY: Mikhail Gorbachev was still riding a strong wave of popularity in the UK at that time.

Robert Woods, who was now getting well bedded in at P&O, organised for P&O Roadways to lay on a truck to carry the -26 to White Waltham, and in a day-and-half Khalide flew it for the first time. After a short flight to check that everything worked, she said that she would fly a gentle warm-up, returning with

Louisa, Paul and myself on the Extra 300. Probably not good for the engine cowling but we did pretty much anything for publicity!

+10 and −7 on the G-meter! When it came to Press Day, the weather was still suitably Russian. Accompanied by flurries of light snow, Khalide showed the large crowd of journalists and general watchers what the -26 could do. As I suspected, the intricacies and technical challenges of her manoeuvres went well over the heads (in both senses) of most the crowd. But even the assembled hacks could not fail to be impressed.

'This fantastic Russian aircraft will maintain Team Proteus Aerobatics as Europe's most spectacular group of civilian airshow performers,' said Victor at the time. And so we would remain until our sponsorship arrangement with Proteus had run its course three years later. By then, however, I was already deepening my business relationship with Sukhoi and my personal friendship with Sasha Tavaryan.

Paul, Louisa and I with Khalide Makagonova, former women's World Aerobatic Champion who organised my introduction to the top management of Sukhoi.

The Su-26 (below) was far superior in all respects to anything I had flown.

The Sukhoi-26 in vertical flight. It had a power-to-weight ratio of almost 1:1 so was virtually able to hover like a helicopter!

Like the Yak-50, the first Sukhoi-26 in Europe was extraordinarily newsworthy, in the general press as well as specialist aviation magazines.

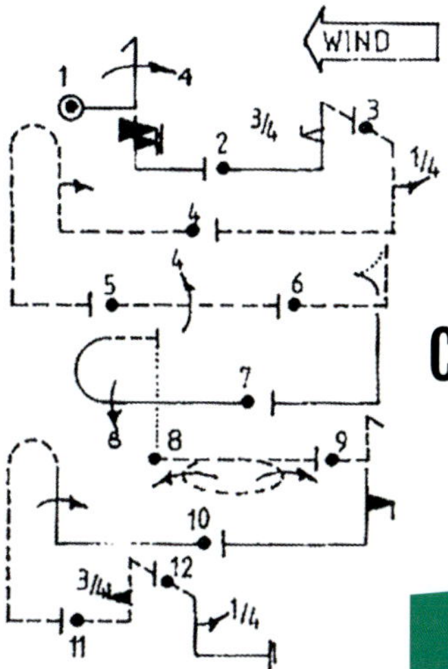

Chapter 16

RUSSIAN REVOLUTION

Opening Korn/Ferry offices behind the former Iron Curtain had shown me the challenges that the once state-controlled economy faced in turning itself into a market-driven quasi-capitalist one.

Buying aerobatic aircraft from Sukhoi had given even closer insight into the Alice-Through-The-Looking-Glass world of Soviet corporate life. But what happened next exceeded anything I had encountered in Russia thus far.

The seemingly impossible saga began unfolding when I got a call from a chap to whom I had sold one of the new Su-29 aerobatic aircraft the year before. Like some of my customers, he had served as a combat jet pilot and, knowing that I had built up a good working relationship with Sukhoi, had come to me with what would have been a simply ludicrous request only a few years earlier. Could I use my Sukhoi contacts to get him a flight in a Flanker?

'Flanker' was the NATO reporting name given to the Sukhoi-designed Su-27 which, together with its equally impressive derivatives, just happen to be what many regard as the ultimate warplanes and the best jet fighters of the 20th century. The Su-27 itself was the holder of 27 world performance records and so powerful that its 20 tonnes of thrust could send it smashing through the sound barrier in a vertical climb. And those statistics do not even begin to hint at its manoeuvrability in aerial combat.

The plane that had emerged from the Sukhoi Design Bureau in 1984 was a twin-engine, twin-finned, swan-necked masterpiece with a range of over 2,000 miles and the ability to fly at 2.35 times the speed of sound, yet blessed with previously unseen agility in a jet of its size. Thanks to its superb thrust-to-weight ratio and the sophisticated control system Sukhoi had developed, the Su-27 was found to be capable of performing exceptional manoeuvres at very low speeds. This, then, was the aeroplane that my customer was so eager to fly and, as it transpired, his timing could not have been better.

THE START OF SOMETHING SPECIAL

By this stage I was on first-name terms with Mikhail Simonov, who was then General Director of Sukhoi, and my relationship with Sasha Tavaryan was going from strength to strength. If anyone could open the door to this highly secretive sector of Russian defence technology, it was probably going to be me. Knowing that Sukhoi 'owned' three Su-27s for research and development, I asked Sasha whether it would be possible for my customer to fly one.

Unlike so many enterprises in the former USSR, Sukhoi did at least have products that people outside Russia were eager to buy. However, it shared one thing in common with all the creaky, rust-bucket state businesses and that was a desperate need for hard currency.

Sukhoi are very proud of their history and this early fighter is on a plinth at their factory in central Moscow. The back door opens out onto what was the Central Moscow Airfield and the sport aircraft, not needing much runway, were pushed out onto this airfield and flown to Zhukovsky for their formal test programme.

Sasha Tavaryan (foreground) helped me to get into a variety of commercial activities in Russia while Konstantin Mokhna, seated behind, was one of the Russian team mechanics who went on to become my agent in Russia.

Sasha got back to me swiftly. Yes, in principle, a flight in a Flanker could be arranged for my customer. How much was he prepared to pay? After buying aerobatic aircraft for a few years, I had a pretty good understanding of how the Russian aviation industry worked. While the Sukhoi Design Bureau was located in central Moscow, only the aerobatic aircraft were actually manufactured there. Once assembled, they were wheeled out of the back of the factory on to the old Central Moscow airfield, from where they were flown 40 kilometres to be tested and made ready for shipment at a place called Zhukovsky.

Zhukovsky was not just a military airfield. It was the top-secret nerve centre for Soviet aircraft testing, both military and civilian. All the design bureaux had test facilities there, Sukhoi included, and it was at Zhukovsky, I knew, that Sukhoi had its three Su-27s and, just as crucially, the highly-skilled test pilots who knew those aircraft inside out.

Having spent time with RAF and US pilots, I had a rough idea how much it cost to fly super-fast military jets like the Su-27. The figures were not for the faint-hearted. Even 25 years ago £30,000 per hour was a reasonable working assumption. On top of the tonnes of fuel the aircraft would be burning, for every hour spent flying you were probably looking at a ground-crew total of 20 working hours maintaining the aeroplane. Anyone going for a joy ride in a Flanker would need deep pockets, but it soon became clear that a joy ride was the last thing my customer had in mind.

It has to be said that the figures I was working on were based on the true costs paid by Western air forces. Vestiges of the former state-controlled system were still operating in Russia, which meant that the actual cost of running the aircraft as far as Sukhoi itself was concerned amounted to nothing. The state provided fuel for the aircraft. The state paid the pilots. The state paid the ground technicians. The state paid for the upkeep of the runways and the airfield in general. Therefore, anything that Sukhoi could earn from what my customer had in mind would be going straight into their own coffers and that fact sent a putative hourly cost of £30,000 into freefall.

It took less than a week to arrive at a figure we could all sign up to, and much of that was spent setting in place below-the-radar payments to the test pilots who would be flying with my customer, the air traffic controllers who would be turning a blind eye to who was actually in the Flanker for that particular flight and every other member of the crew who needed a sweetener to ensure that there would never be any problems.

We settled on $8,000 an hour, not an insignificant sum but well under a quarter of what it would have cost to fly in a comparable NATO jet. My customer was reasonably well off, so I did not imagine he would object to the price we quoted, and he did not. He did not want one hour, he told me straight off, he wanted eight hours! That made me sit up and take notice.

The 'Russian Connection' allowed me to fly some of their military aircraft, typically from Zhukovsky. Here I am being strapped into a Sukhoi-27 'Flanker'.

The next day he was on the telephone again, having changed his mind. Now he wanted two Flankers, and he wanted them both for eight hours, so that he and a combat jet pilot friend could take the controls in simulated air-to-air combat.

Sasha was delighted, as well he might have been. He had just earned himself, his Sukhoi colleagues, and everyone else involved at Zhukovsky a cool $128,000. To put this kind of money into perspective, one had only to look at Yevgeni Frolov, who was one of the Sukhoi Design Bureau's fast-jet test pilots, as well as being a top-flight aerobatic pilot and a member of the Russian aerobatic team. Frolov told my customer that if he had the money and did not fly Sukhoi fighters as part of his job, he would happily have paid to fly an Su-27. His problem, he continued, was that just one single flight would have him cost more than 10 years' pay.

OPPORTUNITY KNOCKS

The people at Zhukovsky could not have been more accommodating. They provided a translator to ease discussions and briefings. The Sukhoi test pilots quickly realised that they were talking to well-trained and very experienced fast-jet pilots in my

Here having my seat belts adjusted by Igor Votinsev before a terrifying flight in a Sukhoi-25 ground-attack aircraft in which we flew at 250mph at around 50ft above the Moscow river, just climbing sufficiently to miss the many barges.

MiG 29

Jonathon Whaley goes to Russia to fly their magnificent fighter, and has "more fun in sixty minutes than all the flying in the last nineteen years!"

A brief CV. I'm an ex-Fleet Air Arm fighter pilot and air warfare instructor. I last flew jets nineteen years ago: Hunters, Sea Vixens and Phantoms. My flying now is mainly in historic aircraft, doing air show displays and flying for films. I also fly unlimited aerobatics, but I gave up competitions when I found I could no longer afford a competitive aircraft as well as school fees. For a living, I have a small engineering company that has nothing to do with aviation. My wife, Annie, belongs to the small but active female branch of the 'human ingenuity over common sense' club: she's a helicopter pilot.

If asked why I left the Fleet Air Arm in '73, my answer is, "The Government was going to take all my toys away." True words spoken in jest. Morale in the Fleet Air Arm was probably at an all-time low during '71-73. As the Navy's pipeline for aircrew dried up, the squadrons' Royal Navy aircrew seemed to be out-numbered by light blue uniforms worn by people with a tendency to walk sideways—the RAF was lending us aircrew to cruise with the 'Grey Funnel Line'.

With the prospects of either transferring to helos or to the RAF (probably to be given a No.2 transport seat), I took my eight-year break point and left for the cold outside. When you leave the services, you leave one of the most exclusive clubs in the world. Your membership is reduced to 'Guest's' rights only—it's one of the many reasons I never like going to air displays unless I'm flying in them. Even then I can hardly bear to watch the jets flying—it's like being a compulsive gambler with no money visiting a casino.

So, when someone said, "Do you want to fly a MiG-29 for about $$$$$, and would Annie like to fly some Russian helicopters?" I apologised because we couldn't go that minute—I don't carry that sort of cash on me, but the next morning would be fine.

The project gathered momentum, becoming more and more off-the-wall. Annie was offered the Mi-2 and Mi-8 (NATO designator 'Hip') helicopters, and it might be possible to fly the Mi-26 'Halo'.

Then a friend of mine, an ex-Israeli Air Force A-4 and F-4 pilot, heard about the mission. He said, in effect, "If I can't come along with you, I'll break both your legs!" I was already worried that they'd baulk at my own background, but what about a combat-experienced pilot from a state that doesn't spring to mind in a 'Name Ten Russian Allies' competition? I needn't have worried, they'd welcome him as well.

Ben and I started exchanging faxes about the mission profiles we'd ask for. We soon went from thinking we'd just be taken up in the back seats for some aeros, to the fact that we may be able to fly them ourselves. By this time the whole concept and prospect was becoming surreal.

I confess to being totally addicted to flying. I can just about cope with this addiction on my own. But put me in the company of those similarly afflicted and all sense and will-power takes off in full afterburner. As Ben and I talked, the number of proposed flights escalated. We were twenty again and Daddy was going to give us the keys to his Ferrari.

I think we may have gone too far when we planned our conversation with Mikoyan along the following lines. "Now see here Ivan, we want to strap on a MiG-29 by the front seat, each have a quick familiarisation flight, then take two up at the same time. Formation take-off, did we mention that? Followed by some close formation, just for practice. Then we'll do some dummy cannon runs on each other to get our eye back in, followed by some aggressive tail-chasing. Once that's out of the way, from close formation, we'll each turn out by 45 degrees until we almost lose sight of each other, turn back 135 degrees and go for it. 1v1 ACM no holds barred. Tell us what fuel you want us to land with and we'll head on back for a formation landing." (ACM = air combat manoeuvres: dog fights, to you and me.)

The discussion on flight content was progressing in about as bizarre a fashion as the third-party routes requested to fund the flights. Even Annie had resigned herself to my outrageous expenditure. We both knew that if I turned this down merely on the grounds that we couldn't afford it, yet was still young enough to fly hard and think quick, I'd regret it for the rest of my life.

Back in 1973, if I was told that one day I'd be flying a Russian fighter, arguably with better performance than any American fighter of the same weight and class, I'd have replied, "We lost the war then?" The whole idea of the three of us playing with two of the world's top fighters and one of the world's biggest helicopters was unimaginable a year ago. For all we knew it might become unimaginable in three months time—and that's what happened—suddenly the pack of cards collapsed and the deal was off. Well, it had all seemed too good to be true anyway.

Ben came to the rescue. He has a Sukhoi Su-29 on order, and he suggested giving Sukhoi a ring to see if we could fly the Su-27. Back came the reply that a flight might be possible, but what did we want to do with the Su-27? "Now see here Ivan, we want to strap on a Su-27..."!

By chance, Evgeni Frolov, one of the test pilots for the Sukhoi Design Bureau, was coming to England to help assemble, test-fly and deliver a new Su-26M to Tim Barnby and Nick Onn. He's also one of Sukhoi's Su-27 test and display pilots. We met him at Headcorn, and convinced him that we were serious in our intentions. He kept asking us if we knew the cost. He admitted that if he had to leave Sukhoi, but had the money, he'd pay to fly the Su-27—although one flight would cost him about 140 months at his current salary!

In early November, with the weather approaching its worst, we left for Moscow to meet with the Sukhoi Design Bureau in order to discuss the program, based on four flights each. Before we left, we knew that they only had one Su-27UB available, but Ben hoped that we might get one flight under our belts. We landed in fog and snow. Four days later, still in fog and snow, we left. What we had accomplished in that time, without actually flying, was incredible.

Peter R. March photo

We were taken first to the Bureau's offices in Policarpov Street. Here we met, amongst others: Mikhail Simonov, Head of the Sukhoi Design Bureau; Oleg Kalibabchuk; Igor Emelianov, Chief Engineer and Fidail Shagiziganov, Head of Flight Testing. Fidail would be looking after us on the front line.

English was spoken in very small fly-speak amounts, no one person being able to communicate, but as a group we understood each other. Max g and Max alpha (angle of attack) graphs are the same in any language. We pored over the system manuals for the Su-27. There would be no simulator-time. From what I can gather, the Russians do not use simulators in the way the West does.

They asked us again about our flying background and what sort of flying we were currently doing. In hindsight, I'm convinced it was from the questions Ben and I were asking about the systems and operation of the Su-27 that it became an unspoken assumption by all parties that our first flights were to be from the front seats.

Then came the day to see the beasts. We were collected from our hotel and driven the one-and-a-half hours to Zhukovsky. This is the major aviation test centre to the south-east of Moscow—and the location of the MosAero Show '92. Zhukovsky town itself is one hundred per cent aviation orientated. Aviation is the only reason for its existence—from the Aerodynamics University to the Test Pilots School,

50 **PILOT**

We had little problem encouraging Western journalists to go to Russia to fly jet aircraft and they provided more marketing material than we could have hoped for!

customer and his friend, and an easy rapport was established extending from the briefing room to the cockpit. The whole venture proved to be such a success that Sasha was keen to repeat it, and I could understand why. However, I had to explain that there were not many people that had that sort of money.

While takers for eight-hour sessions were going to be few and far between, I felt pretty sure that there would be plenty of people prepared to pay for an hour's flight in a Flanker. Having visited Zhukovsky myself several times in the course of buying aerobatic aircraft, I knew that it was a plane spotter's idea of heaven. With most of the design bureaux having test facilities there, virtually every type of contemporary Russian aircraft, military and civilian, fixed wing and helicopter, could be seen at Zhukovsky at one time or another. What about offering flights in a range of aircraft, especially as many of them might be cheaper than the Su-27?

Sasha said he would look into that too, and when he came back with the green light for the project, it became obvious that we had the makings of a profitable little business for the time being. I called the new enterprise the Russian Connection and, with Sasha's help, put together flying packages to suit a range of budgets, experience and thrill seekers. Pretty much everything was on offer. At the lower end of the price range clients could take to the air to experience a few gentle aerobatics in a two-seat Su-29 for $300 an hour. Helicopter options

A 'Flanker' coming in to land at a very high angle of attack. The Su-27 and its derivatives were recognised as outstanding combat aircraft for around 20 years.

included flights in the Mil Mi-2, or the world's largest helicopter, the Mi-26. Prices for helicopters started at $500 an hour.

The legendary MiG-21 was on offer, with an hour-long flight coming in at $2,800, barely more than its fuel would have cost in the UK. For $7,200, clients could experience a sortie in a MiG-29, the ultimate Cold War dogfighter, as one friend described it. At the top of the range, clients could climb 25 kilometres to the edge of space at Mach 3 in a MiG-31, to see the stars shine in daytime.

One point we had to make clear to would-be clients was that, high-tech as their flying experience might be, down on the ground they would be living and eating in the same way as everyday Russians. They were not buying gourmet food or boutique hotel accommodation when they signed up for the Russian Connection.

They had to undergo a Zhukovsky medical as well, over which we had absolutely no control. If they failed, that would be the end of it. They would not be charged for the flying of course, but everything else including their transport to and from Russia, as well as their board and lodging still had to be paid for.

Then there was the small matter of liability. Small, because there was no liability. The authorities at Zhukovsky made that very clear. Before any of the people we sent there stepped into an aircraft, they had to sign a disclaimer that absolved everyone from the test pilot to the guard on the front gate from any responsibility should anything happen to them.

Once we had the details in place, I suggested to Sasha that the way to drum up business was to invite Western journalists to sample what was on offer.

The business end of a 'Flanker' on a frozen hard-standing at Zhukovsky being prepared for flight mid-winter.

For this to happen, the flights at Zhukovsky would have to be free. I did not enquire too deeply how he arranged this, but the reply duly came back that free flights for journalists would not be a problem. So it was that I found myself telephoning Fleet Street editors, as well as the editors of aviation magazines I already knew, asking if they would be interested in sending one of their journalists to Russia's top secret air base to fly with a leading Russian test pilot in a state of the art combat jet. The universal response was, shall we say, encouraging.

The first journalist we sent to Zhukovsky was Caroline Davies of the *Sunday Mail*, who flew in a Flanker with genial Viktor Pugachev, the first Sukhoi test pilot to execute the astonishing 'cobra' manoueve, in which this big jet rears up liking an attacking cobra and virtually comes to a standstill in mid-flight!

> *We sweep into a tight left curve, [she recalled] so acute that my body twists into a painful parabola with it. The force is paralysing, the G-suit inflates. I feel the air in the cockpit moulded like lead around my body. . .*
>
> *I'm totally stuck. But not for long. 'Zero G, Caroline,' shouts Viktor. And the pressure releases, like air hissing violently from a ball. . .*
>
> *'Okay Caroline. Now we roll,' yells the smug little man at the controls. What? You've GOT to be JOKING! Sky, land, and sky kaleidoscope as my optic nerves struggle to cling to the front of the jet. . .*
>
> *The stomach is still trying to connect with the vision when we finally swoop down on to the landing strip 20 minutes later.*

A BROAD CHURCH

A point I was keen to emphasise in the publicity that followed was that the experience offered by the Russian Connection was open to all-comers. Aside from having the funds to pay for what was on offer, the only stipulation was passing the medical.

Once we got the business up and running, whenever I was planning a trip to Russia, Sasha would ask what plane I would like to fly? I would go up in something like the Foxbat, the MiG-25 which can fly at Mach 3.1, faster than anything we had in the West.

One of the snags of being a pilot oneself, particularly an aerobatic pilot, is that it often prompts other pilots to show off when you are flying with them. On one visit to Zhukovsky I was strapped into a Su-25, a Sukhoi ground attack aircraft similar to the American A-10, widely known as the Warthog. Its Sukhoi counterpart has the equally unflattering NATO name of Frogfoot, though neither aeroplane can make aim claim to elegance when it comes down to aesthetics. These are rough, tough aeroplanes designed to operate at the lowest altitudes over the battlefield as I discovered when Igor Votinsev, one of the Sukhoi test pilots, took me for a flight in a Su-25, which included flying down the Moscow River at 220 knots, making 6G turns on the bends, and flying so low (20 feet above the surface of the river) that I watched barge crews throwing themselves flat on the deck as we screamed overhead. But then, the pilot was with Sukhoi and could do pretty much whatever he wanted without kicking up the kind of official furore that may have been faced by Western pilots flying in that hooligan fashion.

As I had hoped, the Russian Connection gleaned widespread press coverage in the UK, on the Continent and on the other side of the Atlantic. Our clients came from all kinds of backgrounds including people with average incomes, who saw this as the one opportunity in their lives to do something truly exceptional, as well as those who were seriously rich.

In the latter category I would confidently place one of the heirs to the Johnson Wax and wider pharmaceutical empire. He was hell bent on flying in a Flanker. However, he also wanted to fly his own Gulfstream executive jet right into Zhukovsky. This was not the kind of request the Russian aviation authorities were used to. It took quite a lot of setting up, but it was done.

Then poor Mr Johnson Wax found himself in the cockpit of a Flanker, waiting to take off behind a prototype passenger feeder airliner, with a dozen or so technicians and all their measuring kit on board. The prototype trundled down the runway, rose from the tarmac and then went into a stall that sent it crashing back down to earth, where it erupted in a ball of flame killing everyone on board. Horrified at what he had seen, our client lost his nerve and told his pilot, 'I'd rather not go'. The pilot was not going to lose out on the $200 he was in line to get for taking this chap for a spin and answered through the intercom: 'We fly.' And off they went.

LONE RANGER

By now the Flanker was well known in the West, having appeared at air shows on both sides of the Atlantic. I remember giving an aerobatic display at the Yeovilton show when Anatoly Kvochur brought a Su-27 to put it through its paces. He was one of the top display pilots for the Russian government Flight Research Institute, also based at Zhukovsky, where he had taken off that morning and flown straight to Yeovilton.

Apart from the flying, the really striking point was that Kvochur was there all by himself. Other nations attending an air show like that would expect to send a Hercules with a team of engineers and technicians and a whole lot of kit. Anatoly took off after his breakfast and had flown straight across Europe at 65,000 feet before arriving over the right part of Somerset bang on cue to give a stunning display. I happened to be in the control room when he popped in afterwards to meet the controller of the whole show and collect the fee for his appearance. Then he refuelled the Flanker, took off again and flew home. He was probably safely in Moscow well in time for dinner. The whole visit had been completely unsupported. Just one pilot, supremely confident in the quality of his aircraft. It was hugely impressive.

All of this certainly registered with the senior commanders in the RAF, because they subsequently approached me to ask if there was any chance of a group of their top pilots having a go in a two-seater Flanker. In due course Sasha and I arranged for a couple of Sukhoi's Su-27s to be flown up to RAF Leuchars, on the Fife coast. Five of the RAF's top pilots flew the Flankers and were unanimous in their verdict. They had to have the plane. At the time they were flying Lightnings and Tornados; the Eurofighter Typhoon had yet to enter service.

A Sukhoi Su-31 flies over the Zhukovsky airfield, home to various Russian jet aircraft including the ill-fated Tu-144 'Concordski' supersonic airliner.

Politically, it would have been impossible for the UK Government to have placed an order with Sukhoi, of course. At the time, though, the Russians thought that there was a genuine possibility of selling them, even to NATO air forces. Nothing in Russia could be taken for granted in those topsy-turvy years a quarter-of-a-century ago.

Altogether we sent 145 clients to fly at Zhukovsky, over a period of three years. Inevitably, though, people on the ground latched on to the success of the idea and, quite understandably, they started asking for more money. At the same time as I saw our margins being eaten away, Mikhail Simonov was forced out of Sukhoi. His replacement took a much tougher line on the way the business was run, and I could see that our Russian Connection was going to come under closer scrutiny.

It had gone well. All of our clients had returned home in one piece. Everyone involved in setting up and running it made money out of the venture and it seemed a good time to call it a day. At least a couple of other Western operators had jumped on the band wagon and I was happy to let them carry on in our place. What is interesting is that they both pulled out of sending people to fly at Zhukovsky within a couple of years. It was good while it lasted, but I knew from the outset that it would not last forever. Opportunities as off-the-wall as flying at Zhukovsky never can. That is what makes them so special.

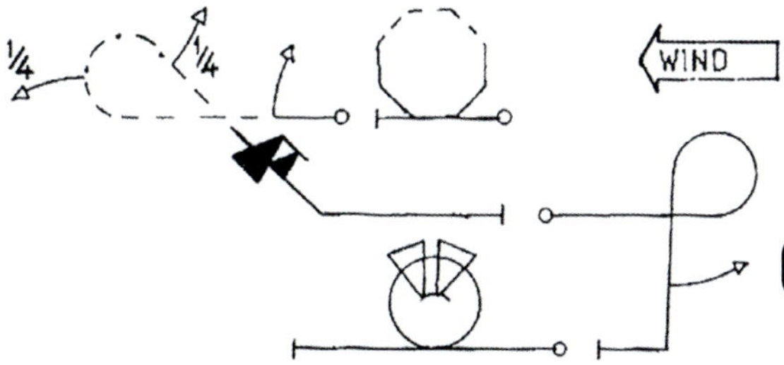

Chapter 17

OUR MAN IN THE WEST

International aerobatics is a relatively small world and following the extensive coverage of the arrival in the UK of the first Sukhoi-26, word quickly spread that this fantastic aeroplane was available outside Russia.

Since I had done all the leg work, people around the globe started getting in touch with me directly asking if they could buy from me a -26 for themselves.

I got back in touch with Sasha Tavaryan and asked if I could buy a couple more -26s. Sukhoi had no objections. In fact, they were delighted and invited me back to Moscow, where they put to me the proposition that I should become their official sales representative in the West.

When I expressed interest, they opened up a little more and explained that they were falling out with Brian Becker, with whom Sukhoi had the deal to sell their aeroplanes in the States. However, the USA remained by far their biggest market, so Sukhoi had to be wary of not jeopardising sales there. They asked if I could come to an arrangement with Brian. He and I met and formalised the situation, which left him with the US market, but allowed me to represent Sukhoi throughout the rest of the world. Brian and I were careful not to undercut each other, although the aircraft were very keenly priced anyway, considering that they were damned good aeroplanes and people were queuing up to buy them.

Between 1990 and 1996 Brian sold two Sukhois a month on average. Then Rick Massegee, one of America's top aerobatic pilots was killed in Florida when the wing fell off his Su-31. Slava Kondratiev had designed further Sukhoi aerobatic aeroplanes and they either used the same wing as the -26, or one closely modelled on it.

To say that this should not have happened is stating the obvious but the Sukhoi wing had been rigorously tested and had a flying tolerance that allowed you to push the wing to around 20G, added to which there was a further margin of safety built into the design. Subsequent tests showed that the wing on Masagee's aeroplane had failed at 13G, even though Sukhoi's prototype testing had shown that the Massegee's wing should have been capable of withstanding one and a half times the forces that had caused it to fail.

Sukhoi stepped in promptly, acknowledging structural failure and paid Massegee's family around one million dollars in reparation. Fortunately he was a single man, with no dependents.

Back at Sukhoi headquarters an investigation began immediately into what had gone wrong. Suspicion quickly fell on the main carbon fibre spar that ran the full length of the wing. The paint was scraped from a section of Massegee's wing spar. The area was sanded and polished. Then a high-power microscope got to work looking into the structure of the carbon fibre and it revealed the presence of little bubbles of air. A small batch of wings had been made by a new team that had got the process of curing the carbon fibre wrong, leaving behind air bubbles that had fatally weakened the wing. Once identified, the problem was solved and the other flawed wings were recalled, destroyed and replaced.

It had been a scandal, there was no denying that and it gave Brian the jitters. He envisaged horrendous lawsuits thundering down the American legal track heading straight for him and pulled out of selling Sukhoi aeroplanes altogether. That was a major blow and Sukhoi, desperate to keep going in the US market, asked for help.

In the vacuum created by Brian Becker's departure, I was contacted by a man from Albuqerque, New Mexico, who desperately wanted to buy a Sukhoi. He was Tom Lang, a seriously high net-worth individual with extensive business interests in real estate and publishing. I arranged the deal with Sasha and after the paperwork and payments had been dealt with, an aeroplane was shipped out to Tom. Once unloaded, it was reassembled by a couple of engineers Sukhoi had sent to the States. And, just as Khalide Makogonova had come to White Waltham to test fly my own -26 after it had been assembled, Sukhoi sent one of their pilots to test Tom Lang's new aeroplane before its handover to him.

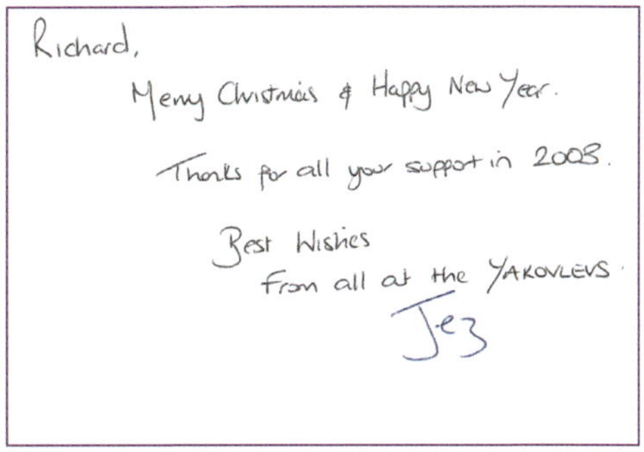

Richard,

Merry Christmas & Happy New Year.

Thanks for all your support in 2008.

Best Wishes
From all at the YAKOVLEVS.
Jez

(Above) Jez Hopkinson set up the Yakovlev display team, initially with three Yak-50s and one -52, and it went on to become one of the leading teams in the world.

(Below) Ramon Alonso became World Aerobatic Champion and stands here with the Su-31. He was very helpful, recommending our aircraft and our services.

They could not have sent a better qualified person than Yevgeni Frolov. Not only had Frolov been the test pilot who had first flown the -26 back in 1984, he was also one of the very few Russian test pilots with the skill and technical expertise to serve as a test pilot for both Sukhoi's aerobatic aeroplanes, but also their outstanding military jets.

Tom flew in at the controls of his Falcon 2000 executive jet to take formal delivery of the aeroplane, which was then taken back to Albuquerque, where Frolov was due to spend a few days teaching him how to fly it. They got on very well right away, which reflected favourably on me and led to Tom and me getting to know each other too.

I could see that while Tom was obviously very rich, he was also rather bored. Now that he had been introduced to Sukhoi and was the very satisfied owner of one their aeroplanes I suggested that he sold Sukhois. He agreed thereby solving Sukhoi's US sales dilemma.

The arrangement he and I came to mirrored the one I had had with Brian; Tom sold Sukhoi aeroplanes in the USA and I sold them everywhere else. It was a business understanding that suited us both very well. We would meet from time to time in the US, or in the UK. We also travelled to Moscow for meetings with Sasha and the other senior people at Sukhoi.

But in addition, Tom was generous and thoughtful. Cary and I would fly by commercial carriers into Phoenix, Arizona, where Tom's Falcon 2000 would be waiting to collect us. A short walk across the tarmac and we would be airborne in minutes, flying to Albuquerque where we would land at his own airfield. On a number of occasions, when we were not working, he took us down to Florida, where he kept quite a big ocean-going yacht, aboard which we used to spend several very pleasant days at a time cruising the Florida Keys.

This pilot extraction system was developed by Zvesda. In half a second the pilot's belts were cut and an extending tube shot through the canopy with a small drogue parachute which pulled out the main 'chute. It worked successfully inverted down to 200ft altitude and was lightweight.

Inevitably Tom and I began talking about future prospects and I put to him an idea that had been developing in my mind for some time. Having had insight into what went into making top aerobatic planes, principally the Yak-50, Extra 300 and Sukhoi 26, my idea was to create the world's very best.

CREATIVE JUICES

By now Slava Kondratiev had got tired of working for Sukhoi; creative flair seemed to go hand-in-hand with a restless energy. He had left, taking some of their best people with him, and had started up his own design bureau, Technoavia. I told Slava that I would cover all the origination costs for this new aeroplane, if he and his team would design it for me.

They did and, although I say it myself, the aircraft really is a masterpiece. Using the Russian M14 engine, which is still the most powerful light aircraft engine available, the design Technoavia came up with was for a very small plane, built from carbon fibre throughout, not just the wing. The Z-2000, as the plane was called to coincide with a production launch in the year 2000, would be the lightest, most powerful aeroplane of its type. If you could have propped the aircraft on its tail and started the engine, that plane would have taken off vertically.

Having received the design, I knew that Tom would have the money to manufacture the prototype, test it and get the plane launched. (The cost would have been in the region of $2,500,000 and we planned to sell the aeroplanes for the same price as a new Sukhoi, which at that time was $175,000.) But I felt we needed a name that would be recognised in the aerobatic world to give our new aeroplane the imprimatur of quality and prestige. The people I went to were Zlin, the highly respected aerobatic aircraft company in the Czech Republic.

Zlin, who had won the World Championships several times, had loads of experience of making their own top-flight aeroplanes and the proposal I put to them was simple. If we provided the design, would they like to be involved in the manufacture of this new aeroplane? The further benefit from my point of view was that Zlin had a well-established reputation among European flying regulators and Zlin knew all the ins and outs of the various complex certification criteria, which can be a minefield for the uninitiated.

However, Zlin had never made a composite aeroplane and to get around that I had one of my former customers in mind. I got to know Philippe Moch after selling him a Yak-18T. His firm, Moch Composites, were specialists in manufacturing aerospace components from carbon fibre and a range of similar high-tech materials. They make all the control surfaces such as rudders and elevators for all Airbus aircraft.

Having assembled the team, we had several meetings with Zlin to work out how we were going to put the plane into production. Work and planning progressed to the point where the Z-2000 was poised for take-off, so to speak. We had the complete design of the aircraft and the funding. All the main players were in place, primed and ready to go. A comprehensive production plan had been drawn up, right down to the detailed factory layout, and there did not appear to be any reason why we could not get started. But in the end there was a reason: me.

When it came down to the nitty-gritty I realised that I simply did not have the time needed to oversee such a major undertaking. It may come across as pathetic, but it was pragmatic. Having already put a significant amount of time and effort into advancing the project to this stage, I knew in detail what would be involved in managing the production phase successfully. It was a full-time job for a minimum of two people, whereas with everything else going on in my business life, selling new Sukhois, still undertaking a certain amount of my own display flying, not to mention holding down a pretty demanding job with Korn/Ferry, I would only be able to give it, at best, a third of one person's time, which simply was not on.

I apologised to the others naturally. I tried to find someone else to run the project and nearly appointed a chap, but in the end decided not to proceed. I have all the design plans and Slava Kondratiev even made me a model which sits in my office today, but that was as close as we got to making my evolutionary new aeroplane. Our Z-2000 would have changed the way aerobatics were flown. Perhaps one day it still will.

While the development discussions for the Z-2000 were taking place, Tom Lang and I were making our regular visits to Sukhoi in Moscow, where he regularly ran into Frolov. One of their meetings coincided with the retirement of Tom's company pilot and he suggested to Frolov that he might enjoy moving to New Mexico to take up the job of flying Tom wherever he needed to go. Frolov thought this sounded rather a good arrangement, without fully understanding what it involved. He probably envisaged flying a very smart executive jet around the US and relaxing in luxury hotels waiting for the next flight. What he did not understand was that as a US corporate pilot he would be responsible for all kinds of travel arrangements like making hotel reservations, not to mention the routine work associated with taking care of the aeroplane such as getting the radios overhauled and all the frankly tiresome things that have to be done to keep an executive jet on permanent stand-by.

Amazingly Sukhoi, not to mention the Russian defence authorities, did not raise any objections. Not only would they be losing one of their top test pilots, Frolov would be leaving for the West with a huge amount of knowledge of Sukhoi's (and therefore Russia's) principal warplanes. Even more extraordinary was the fact that no one in the States ever said to him, 'Hello, Yevgeny. Let's go and have a drink and talk about Sukhois.' Had anyone made that move, they might have struck lucky, because Frolov liked a drop or two. After a year or so, he started getting bored in America and began hitting the bottle, as quite a lot of Russians do. Seeing that things were on the slide, Tom Lang told him he could see that Frolov was not happy and suggested that he should go back to Russia, which Frolov did. Incredibly, Sukhoi welcomed him back without batting an eyelid.

RUSSIAN THINKING

When the sponsorship deal with Proteus Petroleum came to an end, I kept the -26, painted out the Proteus name and continued to use the aeroplane for my own displays although I had cut back on these a fair bit. Giving displays kept my hand in at flying aerobatics, it continued to earn a modest but steady income and it provided the ideal showcase for the aeroplanes I was selling.

I was now meeting Sasha and other senior Sukhoi people at the big European airshows such as Farnborough, where one of their top pilots always gave a stunning display. One aspect of Sukhoi's visits to Farnborough that I came to realise I could leave to them was what one might call in-hangar hospitality, and here they displayed a remarkable degree of ingenuity. Instead of hauling cases of vodka over from Moscow to offer to visitors to their hangar at Farnborough, Sukhoi made do with aeroplane de-icing fluid! This stuff is 200% proof neat ethyl alcohol and totally undrinkable on its own because it sucks all the moisture out of the inside of your mouth. However, when it was diluted with orange juice it makes the base for a pretty amazing cocktail and this was what Sukhoi used to serve up at Farnborough.

Some of their most frequent visitors were the police officers drafted in to provide security at the airshow. These were bobbies who had an interest in aeroplanes and, far from being a chore, they came from all over the country on what amounted to a bit of a jamboree. They took to the Sukhoi cocktail with enthusiasm, but without appreciating quite how strong it was. As a day wore on, the supine forms of police officers would be seen dotted around the airshow and one priceless morning I pitched up at the Sukhoi hangar to find five of the force's finest lying in the grass outside still sleeping off Russian hospitality from the night before!

It stands to reason that there is only a limited market for brand new aircraft, modestly priced as Sukhoi aeroplanes were. So, I pricked up my ears when Sasha Tavaryan put to me the idea that we might start building a business selling used aeroplanes, of which there turned out to be loads idly standing about the length and breadth of the Russian Federation. And these were not clapped-out wrecks long past their sell-by dates; many of the planes we ended up buying were brand new and still sitting disassembled in their delivery crates. In addition, each aircraft came with a box of spare parts, all the manuals and a tin trunk of tools to operate that aircraft. I was intrigued how this had come about and Sasha enlightened me.

Two of my demonstrator Sukhoi-29s flown by Paul and Warwick in very impressive vertical formation.

Right across Russia, he explained, the Soviet authorities had set up DOSAAF airfields. DOSAAF was a kind of volunteer civilian wing of the Soviet armed forces and, in true egalitarian fashion, any citizen could turn up to have a go at aerial sports including parachuting, gliding, precision flying and aerobatics. In practice, of course, most people were shown the front gate afterwards but the scheme did offer those who displayed ability the opportunity to progress.

By the time I first became aware of DOSAAF in the early 1980s, the Soviet aerobatic team had 300 world-class pilots, men and women, from whom to select their teams of less than half-a-dozen; in the UK we struggled to find 10 pilots for international competitions. So, DOSAAF had a role to play in establishing the supremacy of Soviet aerobatic teams on the international stage.

EMBRYONIC PLAN

Under the criteria established by Gosplan (the agency responsible for central economic planning in the Soviet Union), DOSAAF airfields were allocated a designated number of new aircraft every year. These continued to be delivered even as the USSR started to go down the pan. But, although the aircraft were there, funding for these airfields stopped and supplies of fuel, spare parts and overall support dried up. Therefore, the aircraft remained grounded, white elephants in the uncertainty and turmoil of post-Soviet Russia. Sasha was able to track down where a lot of these aircraft were. So, he put to me the proposition that if I could provide the funds to buy aircraft, he would set about finding them and together we could make far better use of what were now redundant aeroplanes, through selling them to pilots in the West. The airfields would welcome the cash and their future Western owners would welcome the saving on the cost of a new aeroplane, and we would benefit as the intermediaries brokering the sales.

There was a range of sport aeroplanes lying about all over Russia, even at Sakhalin at the far eastern reaches of the country, eight time zones away from Moscow. These aircraft were principally Yak-50s and Yak-52s, a two-seater (tandem) version of the Yak-50 that, although a much heavier aeroplane, was still useful for aerobatics.

Sasha and I were able to pick up these aeroplanes incredibly cheaply. The airfields were happy because they were being paid money that they had not reckoned on getting. In return they were very helpful in organising the necessary paperwork, passing a bung to some DOSAAF official in Moscow to manufacture a document confirming that such and such an aeroplane, with serial number whatever, could no longer fly because its lifetime had expired, or it was damaged in some way. Once we had this official end-of-service signing-off, it was very easy to get the paperwork we needed to export the aeroplanes out of Russia. One could never do that today, of course, but it worked in those times and we did well out of it.

REBUILDING A LEGEND

Meanwhile I had become quite matey with Slava Kondratiev; I was going to Russia pretty regularly with my Korn/Ferry work and Slava and I got on well together. I had always been a fan of the Yak-18T, a very fine four-seater aeroplane, which at the time was no longer being made. It had been commissioned as a training aircraft for Aeroflot pilots; if you flew with Soviet military you trained on a Yak-52. If you were a Soviet civil pilot, and therefore by definition flew with Aeroflot, you learned to fly in a Yak-18T. It was more than a basic trainer, though. Tough and reliable, the -18T was also a very competent fully aerobatic aeroplane and I liked it.

But for some reason lost in the complexity of one of those extraordinary Soviet decisions, Aeroflot took against the -18T and in the early 1980s announced that from then onwards all its training would take place on a Czech-built aeroplane of far greater size and complexity. The edict went out to cut the wings off all remaining Yak-18Ts.

A lot of people thought this was absolutely ridiculous and, very sensibly, hid their -18Ts, but far too many were scrapped. I suggested to Kondratiev, who had been one of the aeroplane's original designers at Yakovlev before he was headhunted by Sukhoi, that we try to get the -18 back into production. Off we went to the factory in Smolensk in western Russia, where the -18T had been made. There we found that they still had everything needed to start manufacturing the aeroplanes again: the jigs and tools, the works.

We asked them to make new ones and they were only too happy to oblige. Before long, we had brand new Yak-18Ts rolling out of the factory which we were selling for $50,000 a piece. To give some comparison, a Western-built aeroplane of similar capacity and specification, made by the likes of Piper and Cessna, would have cost five times as much! But there was always the irritating issue of official paperwork, as well as concerns about after-sales support and access to spare parts, which slightly fettered our turnover.

Still, we were doing well enough out of the deal and we made improvements to the original design. Kondratiev increased the fuel capacity to make our -18T quite a serious touring aircraft. We added a more powerful engine, which

Working with Slava Kontratiev we put the Yak-18T back into production at the Smolensk plant. It was practical and spacious and could easily be customised.

made it faster. Then there was the propeller. We changed the original Russian propeller, designed in the 1940s, swapping it for a much more efficient German MT propeller.

Production of our -18Ts continued for 10 years, with the price rising to keep in line with the increase in costs and overheads. It would have continued for longer had one of Russia's foreign military campaigns not brought an end to

While displaying at White Waltham airshow Paul became rather too exuberant and kept the aircraft inverted for more than the 15 seconds permitted and ran out of fuel at 30ft upside down. Since most of the airfield was covered with either spectators or cars his options were limited and he stalled while trying to land. He walked away with a cut nose!

With the Russian military active in Afghanistan, the Smolensk plant was later committed to manufacturing weapons; the -18T production stopped.

our successful little enterprise. It turned out that the Smolensk factory also manufactured missiles, and when it received a large order the factory's entire operation was turned over to missile production and we, and our modest Yak-18T business, were shown the door.

While much of my aviation working time was spent searching out and providing aircraft for other people, I did not neglect my own flying interests completely, especially when I came across the unique opportunity to salvage a Percival Vega Gull, the sole remaining example of a remarkable pre-war aircraft.

Percival was the leading British manufacturer of high-performance light aircraft before the war. Alex Henshaw, the famous Spitfire test pilot, chose a Percival Mew Gull for his record-breaking flight from London to Cape Town and back again in February 1939. The Mew Gull, a little single-seater aeroplane, would fly at well over 200 miles an hour.

The Percival Vega Gull was the last aeroplane Percival designed before the war. This was a long-range four-seater that again accomplished epic flights. Beryl Markham chose a Vega Gull for her historic flight east to west across the Atlantic in September 1936. No pilot had yet flown non-stop from Europe to America, and no woman had made the westward flight solo, though several had died trying. Twenty hours after taking off from Abingdon where my own Sukhoi-26 had been delivered, she force-landed in Nova Scotia after the breather pipe to her fuel tank had iced up. However, she became the first person to fly non-stop from England to North America.

When the war came in September 1939, most of the Vega Gulls were pressed into service as transport aeroplanes for the RAF. But they were generally ill-treated in the air force. As wooden aircraft, they suffered from being left outside in all weathers. As aircraft that were also quite difficult to fly, many Vega Gulls suffered further from being crashed on landing by pretty useless service pilots. Their numbers were steadily whittled away until they became extinct, all the Vega Gulls having been destroyed in one way or another.

At least, that was the consensus for a good many years until I heard of one, the only surviving Percival Vega Gull in the world, that was sitting in pieces in the archipelago outside Stockholm. I bought it and had it shipped back to the UK, in a pretty parlous condition. But it was such an iconic plane, with so much aviation history associated with it that I resolved to restore it completely. Because this was going to be costly, I enlisted Clive Wilson to share in the undertaking and we took the project to Cliff Lovell, who was the man for restoring light aeroplanes and who had tipped me off about this Vega Gull in the first place. The job we presented him with would take at least three years to complete.

Where we were very fortunate was in finding two unused de Havilland Gypsy Queen engines from the 1940s, still conserved in their cases just as they had

The unique Percival Vega Gull as I found it in Sweden, derelict but sound – the only one remaining in the world. It had extraordinary performance in the 1930s and performed exceptional feats, including the first westward flight across the Atlantic in the hands of Beryl Markham.

been when they had left the factory. We were equally lucky in finding two brand new propellers.

The finished aeroplane was fantastic. We added extra fuel tanks, so that four of us could have flown from London to Rome non-stop. Cliff fitted out the interior with beautiful leather upholstery and installed quite a comprehensive suite of flying instruments that enabled the aeroplane to be flown 'blind'. Our restoration of the Vega Gull had attracted the attention of certain aficionados, among them Roworth Spurrell, one of the top cardiologists in London. He was a keen flier and when we completed the restoration he approached me with the question, 'Richard, is there any money that would persuade you to part with this aeroplane?' He followed up this enquiry with an incredible offer for the completed aeroplane, the spare engine and the spare prop and, the last Vega Gull flying in the world became his.

Although I had no personal experience of long-distance record-breaking flights, I was briefly engaged to the well-known aviatrix, Judith Chisholm, who subsequently married my friend Murray Kenyon. Judith had a brilliant flying career, on and off the ground. A life-long aviation fan, she was the first woman air traffic controller to become a senior controller at Heathrow. When she left

After a fantastic restoration by Cliff Lovell, the Vega Gull was effectively a new aircraft and I was able to re-obtain the original registration of G-AEZJ from the 1930s.

SISTERS STAY IN JAIL
See Page 5

DAILY EXPRESS

Thursday December 4 1980 ● 12p ● Weather: Cloudy, dry

THE VOICE OF BRITAIN

WORLD BEATER

Records galore as air girl Judith flies home in triumph

Hello again England!

By PETER HARDY

HER OWN RECORD BREAKING DIARY: SEE CENTRE PAGES

WORLD BEATER Judith Chisholm flew into Heathrow last night, leaving a trail of shattered records that stretched 27,000 miles.

Thrilled but exhausted, the plucky 28-year-old pilot who circled the globe in 360 hours 22 minutes and 23 seconds, in her tiny Cessna, Express Crusader, said: "Thank God I'm home. It's been fun—but I've had enough!"

The waiting crowd gave the girl from Chinnor, Oxfordshire, a rousing cheer ... stepped onto the ...

PICTURE BY HARRY DEMPSTER

Home at last ... Judith with parents George and Audry—and dog Kipling

Judith Chisholm was not only a senior air traffic controller at Heathrow, but achieved huge publicity by completing a round-the-world flight in a single-engine Cessna. She only slept a few hours in the entire journey.

air traffic control, she became a professional pilot, flying executive jets all over Europe and was one of only a handful of women then to hold the airline transport pilot's licence. Judith ended up as the senior corporate pilot for De Beers. But her lasting claim to international fame came in 1980 when she flew a single-engine Cessna T-210 Centurion around the world in 360 hours 22 minutes and 33 seconds, breaking 28 world speed records in the process, records that had been set by the pioneering woman pilot, Amy Johnson.

UP BEFORE THE BEAK

It would be wrong to think that selling Russian aircraft was trouble-free. While that was largely true, it is worth mentioning two dark, and at the time deeply disturbing, episodes, by way of counterpoint.

Notification of the first of these came one summer day in 2002 when I was paid an official visit by the village bobby from Almeley, the village down the road from Newport House, in Herefordshire, where Cary and I were then living and working. I was not accustomed to visits from the police and what he had come to deliver was a first for him. Receiving such a document was also a first for me. What he had brought me was a summons to appear before a court in Alessandria in Italy, where I faced a charge for what amounted to manslaughter.

While the Europol arrest warrant came as a very nasty surprise, the circumstances that occasioned it sadly were not. I had sold a Sukhoi to a young Italian man, who had then crashed it and lost his life. However, Italian law makes no allowance for accidents. When someone in Italy dies in circumstances like these, someone else has to be responsible and in this case that someone was the person who had sold the deceased pilot the aeroplane, namely me.

I promptly wrote back to the prosecutors, care of the Italian consulate in London (because the warrant bore no correspondence address), succinctly explaining the circumstances of the accident and my limited role in merely selling this poor young man the aeroplane. Therefore, it was equally unsettling to receive a letter back from one of the consular staff less than a week later, enclosing all my correspondence and informing me that my letter was 'insufficient to solve the matter' and that, as the Europol warrant informed me, I had 30 days 'to state or elect a domicile in Italy and appoint a defender'. Thus began a protracted round of correspondence and litigation which has not been officially signed off even today, almost 20 years later.

From my point of view the cause of the accident was pilot error, pure and simple. But the young man in question came from a wealthy family who could not accept that their son had brought about his own death. They were looking to place the blame on me, and a lot of time and no small measure of expense followed. The aircraft had been delivered by Sukhoi to a designated airfield in Italy. Sukhoi engineers had put it together. A Sukhoi test pilot had flown the aeroplane to check that everything was working correctly and the new owner had signed for it and officially taken receipt. So far, so good.

I asked if he wanted instruction, but he had a friend who was in an Italian aerobatic team sponsored by Red Bull, to whom I had sold five other Sukhois, and this chap, who was a former Italian air force officer, did in fact instruct the young fellow how to fly the aeroplane.

However, on the day he was killed he was showing off to some friends when the engine stopped. His immediate reaction was to try to land, but in trying to do this, he pulled too much G and the aircraft spun into the ground. Had he been flying at 2,000 feet, he could have regained control but he was barely a quarter of that height and died as a consequence.

Sergio Dallan, a friend of mine, a top Italian aerobatic pilot, and a specialist in Sukhoi sport aircraft, examined the wreckage and quickly spotted what had caused the engine to stop. The dead pilot had not switched the fuel supply to the dedicated aerobatic tank before he began his aerobatics, which meant that when the plane was inverted the engine had sucked in air and stopped. When Sergio repeated the flight in an identical aircraft, videoing everything he did, the engine of his aeroplane stopped after 17 seconds, in just the same way as the engine in the crashed one. The difference was that Sergio carried out his test at a safe height and had been able to start the engine again with a decent margin of safety.

The court system in Italy is not renowned for the speed of its judicial process but eventually the case was heard. The dead young man's family were represented by a very sharp advocate, who knew the law inside out. But Sergio, as our star witness, was the only technical expert in the courtroom and Sergio just tied him up in the technology.

The case against me had been further jeopardised by the death of the mechanic who was said to have maintained the aeroplane. He had been killed in an unrelated accident two months after the young pilot's crash. But when investigators searched for the aeroplane's log books they could not find them. Nor could they come up with any record that his Sukhoi had had any maintenance whatsoever in the two years that the dead pilot had owned it! Case closed. Or at least it should have been, but the Italian justice system being what it is, I am still waiting for the file to be officially shut.

I had another nightmare experience that resulted from the sale of a Yak-52 to Dutch twins in their early 30s, who were both airline pilots for KLM. Their father was an ex-KLM captain; their mother a former stewardess.

We always made a point of telling customers that we were not aerobatic instructors. We explained that we would show them what their aeroplanes could do, but emphasised that it was up to them to get proper qualified instruction. There happened to be a highly-experienced Russian aerobatic pilot called Gena Elfimov based in the UK, who was and is an expert on teaching people to fly Yak-52s.

Our advice to these twins, then, was to hire Gena to teach them how to fly their new aeroplane. Excellent as the Yak-52 is in many respects, it does have some naughty characteristics. For example, it is quite easy to get it into a flat spin, from which it can be fairly difficult to recover. You have to know what you are doing and it can take all your strength on the stick to stop the aeroplane spinning round. A number of people have been killed because they have not been able to get their Yak-52s out of a flat spin.

But these lads did not follow our advice and did not get Gena to teach them. Instead they came across a Czech aerobatic pilot called Martin Stahalik. Stahalik was the Czech national champion and therefore an extremely accomplished pilot. It so happened that he was also a customer of mine, having bought a Sukhoi from me. Meanwhile, quite separately, I had sold another Sukhoi, a two-seater-29, to a rich Dutch businessman and this fellow had invited Stahalik to the Netherlands to teach him how to fly and display it. That was how Stahalik came to meet the KLM twins.

Knowing that Stahalik was an ace pilot, number six in the world at that time, they asked him to teach them aerobatics, which he agreed to do. So, up he went with one of the twins in their Yak-52 and deliberately put it into a flat spin. People on the ground were watching this and assumed that Stahalik was showing his novice pupil how to regain control of the aeroplane. But the Yak continued in the flat spin, and it continued coming down, and continued until it crashed straight into the ground killing both Stahalik and one of the KLM twins.

The first thought that crossed my mind when I heard about the accident was, ‘what was Stahalik doing flying a -52?’ Unlike other Eastern bloc pilots, Czech aerobatic pilots would only have flown Zlins. So Stahalik would not have been familiar with the characteristics of the Yak-52. Not long after the accident, I received a summons from the parents of the dead twin. They wanted to meet me and were flying over to Birmingham Airport. This proved to be a very unpleasant encounter.

I offered my condolences, but they were clearly after more and told me to my face that I had caused the accident, that I had not given proper instruction, and that I had sold their sons a defective aeroplane. In the circumstances the best response was to tell them that I was sorry, but I really was not prepared to talk about what had happened in detail. I stated our position politely but firmly and had to leave it at that. But the meeting left me feeling very uncomfortable.

Worse was to follow, though, when the Dutch transport safety board adopted precisely the same stance. Unlike the Air Accidents Investigation Branch in the UK, which concentrates solely on investigating aviation accidents, this agency in the Netherlands covered every kind of transport accident and therefore board members had nothing like the level of technical knowledge that an AAIB team would have brought to examine this crash.

The Dutch authorities immediately contacted me, claiming that I had failed in my duty of care to my two Dutch customers in not providing adequate tuition and when I replied pretty smartly that these chaps had refused the tuition we had offered, that was batted aside and the official response was that the transport safety board was holding me responsible for the accident. The report they published took an equally aggressive tone, stating that the fault lay mainly with the seller of the aeroplane who did not provide sufficient instruction.

I reckoned by that stage in my life that it took quite a lot to rattle me, but I did not mind admitting at the time that this situation seriously worried me. Fortunately, I had met an AAIB chap at Farnborough and had made a note of who he was. I contacted him for advice.

I explained that this was an experimental, ex-military plane and that we had offered them instruction and they had refused to accept it. I asked him to look at the report. He considered it scandalous and said he wanted to help. I asked if he would go with me to Holland to meet the transport safety board, which he very kindly agreed to do.

Over the years I have met a good number of experts in various fields who have impressed me, but this AAIB chap comes near the top. Politely, but authoritatively, he explained to the people on the Dutch board that they manifestly did not know the first thing about aeroplanes. He explained that this was an ex-military aircraft and that it is the pilot that takes total responsibility for how he uses it. It is up to him to get instruction; it is not up to the seller. The aeroplane was not certificated. The flying characteristics of this aeroplane were well known. These two owners were warned about those characteristics. He was sufficiently forceful that the Dutch board withdrew

PROCURA DELLA REPUBBLICA

PRESSO IL TRIBUNALE DI ALESSANDRIA

N. 1855/02 R.G.MOD.21

NOTIFICAZIONI ALL'ESTERO
- art.169 c.p.p. -

OGGETTO: procedimento n. 1855/02 mod. 21
N ei confronti di RICHARD GOODE
P er il reato di cui all'art. 589 codice penale, in Alessandria (Italia) il 29.4.2002, persona offesa DE FEO FILIPPO.

RACCOMANDATA con avviso di ricevimento

A L SIGNOR RICHARD GOODE

PRESSO RICHARD GOODE AEROBATICS

NEWPORT HOUSE, ALMELEY, HEREFORDSHIRE, HR3HR3 6LL

INGHILTERRA

Poiché questo Ufficio procede nei suoi confronti per il reato di cui all'art. 589 c.p., commesso in Alessandria il 29.4.2002, persona offesa DE FEO FILIPPO,

La si invita a dichiarare o eleggere domicilio nel territorio dello Stato Italiano, con l'avvertenza che, se nel termine di trenta giorni dalla ricezione della presente raccomandata, non effettuerà la dichiarazione o elezione di domicilio ai sensi degli artt.162 c.p.p., 62 D. Lv., ovvero se la stessa risulterà insufficiente o inidonea, le notificazioni che la riguardano saranno eseguite mediante consegna al difensore di fiducia o, in difetto, di ufficio.

Alessandria, 28 GIU. 2002

Il Sostituto Procuratore della Repubblica presso il Tribunale
(dott. Claudio Porna)

Si allega la traduzione del presente invito in lingua inglese.

The local Herefordshire policeman was rather surprised to be presenting an Interpol arrest warrant to me following the death of a customer flying one of our Sukhoi-31 aircraft in Italy.

their initial findings and completely rewrote their entire accident report. Meeting and remembering that man proved to be one of the luckiest chance encounters of my life. Had I not had his help, my whole aviation business could have been placed in serious jeopardy.

THE PROSECUTING MAGISTRATE'S OFFICE
AT ALESSANDRIA COURTS

N. 1855/02 R.G. MOD. 21 (Crime Records)

Services abroad
- art.169 of the Criminal Procedure Code -

SUBJECT: Proceeding n. 1855/02 mod. 21
Against RICHARD GOODE
For the crime under art.589 of the criminal code, in Alessandria (Italy) on 29.04.2002, aggrieved party DE FEO FILIPPO.

REGISTERED MAIL with acknowledgment of receipt

TO MR. RICHARD GOODE
AT RICHARD GOODE AEROBATICS
NEWPORT HOUSE, ALMELEY, HEREFORDSHIRE, HR3HR3 6LL
UNITED KINGDOM

Being this Office instituting proceedings against you for the crime under art. 589 of the criminal code, committed in Alessandria on 29.4.2002, aggrieved party DE FEO FILIPPO,

We invite you to state or to elect your domicile in Italy, and we warn you that in case within the term of thirty days of receipt of this registered letter, you will not state nor elect you domicile, pursuant to art.162 of the criminal procedure code, 62 D.Lv., or should such statement or election be incomplete or unsuitable, any notice which may concern you shall be served to your defender or if not available, to the defender appointed by these Courts.

Alessandria, 28 GIU. 2002

Il Sostituto Procuratore della Repubblica presso il Tribunale
The Deputy Prosecuting Magistrate
F.to (Dott. Claudio Poma)

This is the English translation of the original document attached hereto

SUKHOI SWERVES

The saying goes with aircraft, that when the weight of the associated paperwork equals that of the physical aeroplane, you are probably quite close to certification! Type certification is the holy grail of aviation. Without it, permission to fly aircraft can be very hard to come by, if not impossible. This is something that I have had to grapple with for as long as I have been selling Russian aeroplanes. For the most part we have muddled through with some lateral thinking, some quick thinking and a few crafty dodges, but it has been far from easy and has taken up a great deal of time over the years.

In the early days when I was buying Sukhoi aeroplanes, we got by with a buccaneering approach to certification, which we more or less made up on the hoof. Sasha Tavaryan is a bright chap, fortunately, and when I said I was going to need more than the sales receipt for an aircraft in order for it to be flown in the West, he came up with a simple solution. Sukhoi created their own certificates of registration and airworthiness, modelled on Civil Aviation Authority ones that I showed him. So, totally in contradiction to all the rules, Sukhoi printed up the necessary certificates, which they then granted to their own aircraft!

These looked very convincing with the Sukhoi crest and rubber stamps and they were certainly good enough to be accepted by the CAA and similar authorities in Europe. As the validity of the certificates expired, engineers would come from Russia to check the aircraft and authorise new certificates.

TEMPORARY MEASURE

This was a stopgap and I knew it. So, by the time European authorities began asking tricky questions about our Sukhoi paperwork, we had formulated a new system to provide acceptable certification. We had come across a Russian organisation called the Federation of Aviation Amateurs (FLA in Russian), which had the right to issue legal certification to home-built aircraft, but only in Russia.

I went to meet the people at FLA on one of my visits to Moscow and explained the problem we were facing. But FLA had all the right kind of official paper and the printing presses and, for the suitable fee, they agreed to print us whatever certification documents we needed. FLA also had a category of numbers which they were allocated by the national aircraft registration bureau in Russia. These were meant for Russian internal use alone, but FLA cheerfully gave them to all our aeroplanes, and for 13 years we continued to operate under their aegis. It was the most bizarre thing, but the documentation looked correct and everyone accepted it.

This arrangement could not last forever and of course it did not. Once European authorities started looking more closely into FLA-issued documentation, they asked the Russian authorities if this stuff was legal and the Russian aviation people, who until then had turned a blind eye to what was going on, found themselves cornered and had to admit that the documentation was bogus.

That was when all our customers around Europe began receiving letters from their respective CAA equivalents telling them that their aircraft were grounded. If that was bad news for them, it was seriously bad news for me. I contacted everyone, telling them not to panic and that we were doing everything we could to solve the problem. But the fact of the matter was that they were owners of aircraft for which they were never going get a European 'normal category certificate of airworthiness,' as it is called.

This was a time for a cool head and, turning my mind back to my final-year law studies at Trinity, I felt sure that there had to be an answer in the official legislation if I dug deep enough. In the UK we have the *Air Navigation Order*, a big book that spells out air law in the United Kingdom. To this is appended a subsidiary document, BCAR *(British Civil Airworthiness Requirements)* and it was in ploughing through this that I unearthed what I was looking for.

I discovered that airworthy ex-military aircraft in the UK were eligible for something called a 'permit to fly'. This was a tier lower than a standard certificate or airworthiness, but at least it looked like a means of getting British customers' aeroplanes legally flying again. I took myself off to the CAA and went through our aircraft one by one: Yak-52, standard Russian military trainer; Sukhoi-26, operated by DOSAAF, the sport flying side of the Russian air force therefore by definition also ex-military.

That line of thinking was bought by the CAA and a couple of other national bodies. After all, people were flying Spitfires and other ex-military aircraft that were not type certificated, so why not our Russian aeroplanes? But even I could not pretend that all our aeroplanes could be classified as ex-military and we needed to find a way of also getting acceptable documentation for the ones that did not qualify for a permit to fly.

It just so happened that at that time all European aircraft certification was being brought together under one EU-wide organisation: the European Aviation Safety Agency (EASA). The man there responsible for handling the certification issues for all light aircraft was a very helpful chap called Roger Hardy. So, off I went to Cologne, where EASA is based, to run through the whole palaver of the certification of my Russian aircraft with him as well.

EASA was not without a problem of its own in this respect because there were loads of aircraft, just the same as the ones I was selling, flying around former Eastern bloc countries which had recently joined the EU. These aircraft did not have European certification either, but for political reasons Europe was turning a blind eye to that particular detail. After all, it would not have looked terribly welcoming to have grounded these aeroplanes as soon as their respective countries became EU member states!

Roger had the authority to create a completely artificial category of what is called restricted certification. It sounded like being half-pregnant, but into this category we were able to put aircraft manufactured behind the Iron Curtain in sufficient numbers, and to a sufficient build quality to have been certificated as airworthy in the Eastern bloc, even though they had not been previously accepted in the West due to a lack of high-level bilateral agreement. So, into that new category went all my aircraft that were still looking for a certification home.

ASSEMBLY LINE

Over the 12 years or so that I was importing Russian aircraft into the UK, it made a lot of sense to establish a business that could reassemble aircraft after they were delivered, test fly them before passing them over to their new owners and of course maintain them for our customers. In turn that led us into the spare parts business and we spent a lot of money buying up Yak and Sukhoi parts.

We also brought various Russian engineers to the UK to work in this business. Bearing in mind that this was in the early 1990s, many of them had little comprehension of life in the West. One chap I remember in particular was an avid fan of Pink Floyd, even though he had had little access to Western pop music before coming to work for us at White Waltham. As it happens Dave Gilmour, the Pink Floyd guitarist and co-lead vocalist, is a very close friend of my friend and business partner, Vic Norman. So, we organised for Dave to fly his helicopter and land right next to this Russian engineer who was assembling a Yak that we had recently imported. Dave got out of his helicopter with a big box of his records and introduced himself to Sergei who was incapable of speech, such was his amazement!

In the end it was internal politics at Sukhoi that brought to a close my selling of new aeroplanes. While Mikhail Simonov was still the overall Sukhoi boss, his private company Advanced Sukhoi Technologies was able to manufacture and sell Sukhoi sport aircraft to me. But when Mikhail Pogosyan, a much younger man, and a clever, dynamic Armenian like Sasha Tavaryan was moved in to take over, Simonov was eased out. He had a couple of goes at setting up businesses making the sport aircraft, for which he still owned all the intellectual property, but these came to nothing.

I was his next port of call, not to start making aeroplanes for him but to buy his business. I told him that I could be interested, for the right price. But when he told me that the price was $12,000,000, I told him it was way too much and I was not remotely interested in paying anything like that amount of money.

That, very sadly, marked the end of the very successful manufacture of Sukhoi sport aircraft, with which I had been involved as both pilot and seller for much of its duration. Although I would go on to sell over 450 aircraft, that side of my business in Russia tailed off since, under Putin, they stopped the production of all light aircraft and he made it almost impossible to export the used ones.

Chapter 18

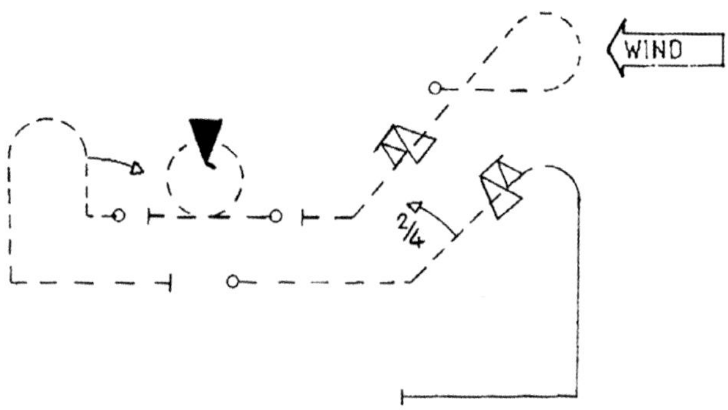

ARMS AND THE MAN

One of the Yak-52 sales led to my 'serving' for five days in the Royal Navy, flying in a Sea King helicopter operating from the aircraft carrier HMS Invincible.

I had sold the Yak to a group of Fleet Air Arm pilots, who were flying Sea Harriers aboard HMS *Invincible* when she was serving as part of Operation Southern Watch, keeping a very close eye on Saddam Hussein's military and naval deployments between the First and Second Gulf Wars.

By coincidence, the commander of *Invincible* at that time was Captain James Burnell-Nugent, the husband of the sister of my great chum, Robert Woods. Burnell-Nugent had also overlapped with Robert and me at Cambridge, where he had gone up a couple of years after us. Over drinks in the wardroom one day my name cropped up in conversation between the captain and the pilots and together they cooked up the idea that I might find it interesting to spend some time with them seeing the Senior Service in action. I received a telephone call inviting me to join them aboard *Invincible* while she was on station in the Gulf. The timing was tight, though. I had to get myself out to Oman within a matter of days, where a helicopter would collect me and fly me out to join the ship.

If not at full action stations, *Invincible* and her crew were on high alert. The ship was moving at full power all the time I was with her, tacking aggressively to avoid any potential threat from Iraqi submarines, of which there were thought to be several operating in the Gulf at that time. There was an aerial threat, of course, and in one exercise I watched a Sea Harrier carry out a simulated attack, flying straight at the bows of *Invincible*, where a huge anti-aircraft gun with a rotating barrel like a Gatling gun, had locked on to it and was moving up and down and from side to side constantly firing blank rounds as the Sea Harrier ducked and weaved.

There was one close shave when the Indian Navy arrived to lend a hand in the form of INS *Viraat*, formerly the Royal Navy's own HMS *Hermes*. Although the *Viraat* carried a complement of Sea Harriers, they were not fully compatible with all NATO communications' systems. So, an almighty flap went up after she sent off four of her Harriers to join in patrolling the skies above the other ships.

On the deck of HMS *Invincible* waiting for another flight in a Sea King. It was a rather surreal experience as a civilian aboard a warship preparing for battle but a unique and enjoyable one.

I was in the operations' control room on *Invincible* when they picked up these Indian fighters about 100 miles off and heading directly for the American task force. Radio operators aboard *Invincible* were able to call up the Indian pilots to confirm who they were and what they were doing, but the American ships had no means of doing this and, for several very tense minutes, it looked likely that American ships might shoot down the unidentified aircraft. It was in the nick of time that the American admiral received a message from his British counterpart, explaining that the Indian aircraft fast approaching him were friendly and that on no account should his ships fire anything at them!

My own Sea King flights were focused on finding and tracking hostile submarines, although the crew managed to find time to have a little fun at my expense. The Sea King is a big lumbering brute, and you need the power-assistance of the controls to make it at all manageable. Then you need what they call 'auto stabilisation,' whereby the aircraft keeps itself relatively stable. But these Navy pilots, assuming that I was a complete aviation wimp, kept switching these off when I was flying, and I can tell you that when it is incredibly unstable and the controls are extremely heavy, the Sea King is very difficult indeed to fly!

The curious reality of living aboard huge ships like *Invincible* was how uncomfortable she was. There was the constant drumming of the engines, of course, but with all the crew accommodation and work areas in lower decks, 80 per cent of the ship's company spent a large part of a day without ever seeing daylight.

The sales of two other aircraft, in this case both to the same customer, gave me first-hand experience of some of the kit used by the modern British Army in the

Firing the RPA Rangemaster which was an extraordinary and effective weapon. It was quite easy to be accurate even for an amateur such as myself.

field. This customer had a very successful business in manufacturing small arms for security forces and organised a 'weapons-fest' at a shooting range in Wales.

I was invited to join the 'shooting party' as a friend and when we assembled a couple of Land Rovers arrived. One was filled with all manner of military firearms, some up-to-the-minute present-day guns, others pretty old stuff stretching back to the Second World War. The other Land Rover was packed full with ammunition for all these various weapons. We took it in turn to shoot everything from Sten guns and Thompsons, to Uzis and the latest designs from other leading manufacturers.

Of the last, the most memorable was a new sniper rifle: a 0.5-inch calibre RPA Rangemaster with a reflex silencer. This fired a big high explosive bullet that travelled at twice the speed of sound. We were using tracer bullets which enabled us to track the course of each round we fired. The rifle was so accurate that even a novice like me was able to hit a metre-square target positioned 1,200 yards away; military snipers, firing this gun with an explosive round, can vaporize anyone they hit at a mile and a half.

When I was spending quite a lot of time in Russia setting up Korn/Ferry offices, a further sideline to my aviation business developed making new Second World War fighters, of which Yak-3s and Yak-9s were the first. I cannot claim to be the first to have done this: an American aviation enthusiast called Jim Wickersham

One of our 'new production' Yak-3 fighters. The Yak-3 was arguably the best fighter of the war. German pilots flying the FW 190 and Me 109s were told to fly away as quickly as possible if they encountered one.

had gone to the Yakovlev Design Bureau to ask if he could have the drawings and plans to make a new Yak-3 because, although 40,000 Yak aircraft had been made during the war, there were none available afterwards. Unlike in the West after the war where surplus aircraft were sold off, a good many to be conserved and flown, all surplus Soviet aeroplanes were melted down, leaving virtually no authentic aircraft surviving from that time.

I followed Wickersham to Yakovlev, where I met and got on very well with Sergei, son of the great Alexander Yakovlev, designer of the celebrated wartime fighters and founder of the design bureau. Through these contacts I too acquired everything needed to build new Second World War Yak fighters from scratch and I had them made in the big Strela aircraft factory at Orenburg, in the far south of Russia, close to the border with Kazakhstan. The factory specialised in building helicopters, but they had the machinery and expertise to make pretty much anything that flew. So they made me new Yak fighters to order, as well as other iconic aircraft from the Second World War such as Mitsubishi Zeroes.

It was during this time that the Russians pulled out of Ukraine, taking with them all their serious military aircraft but leaving behind the relatively cheap stuff such as the L-39 jet trainers, the equivalent of our Hawk. I could see that some of these aeroplanes were in super condition and, in terms of 'bang for the buck,' represented incredibly good value. We could buy and sell aircraft in very good condition for under $200,000.

One of our American customers for a new production Yak fighter was a former Marine Corps pilot named Art Nalls. During his time in the service, Art had been the principal Marine Corps test pilot on the AV-8B, the American name for the Harrier. After leaving the military he had done well in real estate, which enabled him to pursue his interest in classic military aircraft. Although he had not bought his Yak through us, we were very helpful when he needed spare parts and technical assistance. He then became interested in L-39s, and we sold a couple to his friends in the US.

During these fairly complex negotiations, he and I established quite a bond, and it became clear that he was keen and potentially had sufficient funds to purchase a Harrier. A helpful factor was that the British Government was selling off most of their Harriers. The vast majority were out of fatigue-life, and so were consigned simply to be static ornaments. I drew a similar blank after making all the enquiries I could through connections in the Royal Navy, which made it clear that the airworthy Harriers were going to be sold to India.

However, I then heard of one aircraft, designated XZ439, which had been a British Aerospace demonstrator and because of this had flown relatively few hours: around 1,100 hours in its entire life. It also had a very interesting history, having been the first Harrier to carry out a ramp take-off at sea aboard HMS *Invincible*. This Harrier then became the test aircraft for the Sidewinder missile, which proved so decisive in the Falklands War. After that, XZ439 went to the US for further missile tests where, interestingly, it shot down three remotely-flown F106 target aircraft. The F106 had served as the principal interceptor aircraft in the USAF for two decades, before its removal from service in 1980. So that performance was no small achievement for a Harrier.

XZ439 was removed from service in 2002 and entered civilian life as part of a number of aircraft and related military parts bought by a company dealing in these things, most of which they sold on for scrap. Of course, they had no idea that there could be someone with the funds, technical support and of course skill as a pilot, who could be interested in purchasing a flying Harrier.

I put together a potential deal and contacted Art, who came over to the UK. I took him to see the Harrier, which was in storage at RAF Bentwaters in Suffolk, where it was immediately obvious that he was captivated. I recently reviewed my file on the sale, which is almost four inches thick with printed emails covering a huge amount of complicated details: financial, technical and logistical but nine

The Harrier that I sold to Art Nalls in the US, one of the few who had the finance, flying experience and enthusiasm to keep such an aircraft flying.

months of careful negotiation saw the sale successfully completed. One basic problem was shipping the aircraft to the US. Even with the wings removed, a Harrier is of course far too big to put into a shipping container, and we ended up organising Ro-Ro shipment with an outsize trailer across the UK, across the Atlantic and on to its final destination.

Disappointingly, my business venture in Orenburg had a less satisfactory outcome when it came to an abrupt halt. The Strela people were building a Mitsubishi Zero for an Australian customer of mine, while at the same time building a two-seater version of a Yak-7 for a Russian customer, who had gone to them independently.

Something very serious went wrong in this Yak-7 deal to the point where one night 20 articulated lorries pulled up outside the Strela works. A team of chaps broke in, accompanied by others brandishing machineguns, and proceeded to strip everything out of that big factory. They took anything they could lay their hands on, including my 40 per cent finished Zero. I could see that there was no way I was ever going to be able to recover it, so I returned to my Australian customer his deposit and wrote it off as a bad deal.

As a lot of Western companies were discovering, doing business in Russia at that turbulent time could be unpredictable, problematic and occasionally disastrous. I was lucky that I only got my fingers mildly burned on this transaction, but it was a sobering experience.

Murray Kenyon and my aviation specialist photographer friend Peter March accompanied me on one visit to Moscow. It was early October 1993 and the atmosphere in the city was very tense following the move by members of the Russian parliament to depose Boris Yeltsin as President of the post-Soviet Russian Federation.

We had gone to Russia with two objectives in mind. I wanted to check out the Ukraina Hotel in Moscow, where we were going to be accommodating Western visitors we would be sending to Zhukovsky to fly military aircraft. At the same time, this trip gave Peter the opportunity to photograph the preparations our visitors would be experiencing and we had also arranged for him to be flown in a Yak-18T while he took aerial photographs of the new Sukhoi-31.

As on previous trips like this, Sasha Tavaryan made himself available to ferry us around. On the Sunday of our visit, Sunday October 3, 1993, we were doing the touristy things. In the morning, we went to a market and then Red Square, where we were puzzled that there seemed to be very few people about, while the guards stationed on duty seemed uncharacteristically alert. From Red Square, we set off for the hotel, but when we got to the junction where we should have turned left onto Novi Arbat Avenue, down to the bridge across the Moscow River that led to Kutuzovsky Prospeckt which runs beside the hotel, the road was blocked by a barrier patrolled by armed guards.

No vehicles were being allowed past, but the car that Sasha had provided was readily identified as belonging to the Sukhoi Design Bureau and as far as the guards at the barricade were concerned, this was an 'official car' and they let us through. Off we drove, still none the wiser, until we rounded a bend to be confronted by marching crowds carrying banners and the sight of a bus on fire. There were cars everywhere, some abandoned, others trying to get away from the area as fast as they could.

Our driver did not know what to do but Sasha did. He told the man to keep going, warning the rest of us to keep our heads down. 'Don't take any pictures,' he said to Peter, which was probably the last thing Peter had on his mind as we crouched as low as we could while the driver gunned the engine and swerved through the chaotic throng. We reached the bridge, crossed over to the other side and now found ourselves in the middle of a media scrum with television cameras, satellite relay dishes and the world's press clamouring to discover what was going on. Peter was collared by a Sky TV reporter who asked in amazement, 'Where the hell have you come from? Can't you see there's a revolution going on?'

A hastily taken photo from our car window during the Russian Revolution. It was rather dramatic but somehow in Russian context not that surprising!

Looking towards the White House, we could see what this chap was driving at. Crowds and banners were converging on the building and there were armed troops and armoured cars everywhere. Getting on with the business at hand, I went into the hotel to see the manager and make sure that everything was ready for our clients, although in the light of what was happening outside, I did wonder whether the whole Russian Connection enterprise might fail to get off the ground.

That evening we were having dinner in a restaurant in central Moscow, when the manager approached us nervously to explain that they were going to have to close shortly because a curfew had been imposed. He also told us that rumours were circulating that army units loyal to Yeltsin were going to attack the parliament building, to capture it from the opposition forces which had seized it.

We packed up hastily and left. As we were driving back to our hotel, we passed tanks and armoured personnel carriers heading in the opposite direction, rolling into the centre of the city. Come Monday morning, we listened to the gun fire as they shelled the White House.

We were supposed to be going to Zhukovsky, but we could not move out of our hotel. Transport in Moscow had stopped and things did not get going again until midday, by which time the upper floors of the White House were black and smouldering and bodies were being collected from the streets and pavement where they had fallen. According to some reports, this was the deadliest street fighting seen in Moscow since 1917. Casualty figures vary, with claims that 1,500 died in what some called 'the second Russian Revolution'. Politically, the events of those frantic days in early October 1993 marked a further erosion of communist influence and authority in Russia. From a commercial perspective, they confirmed that anyone setting up in business in Russia needed to have their wits about them: it was certainly not a place for the faint-hearted.

When I first became involved with flying Yak sport aircraft and later Sukhois, all the aeroplanes were fitted with the same tried and tested engine: a 360hp engine manufactured by VMP (Voronezh Mechanical Plant). This was a huge state-controlled organisation that occupied a 50-acre site slap bang in the centre of the city of Voronezh, 500 kilometres due south of Moscow, where a variety of aerospace products, including the Buran space-shuttle, were also made. Although manufactured by VMP, following Soviet practice, these engines had been designed elsewhere by an inspired aero-engineer named Ivan Vedeneyev, whose design bureau coincidentally happened to be in Voronezh as well.

Until the collapse of the Soviet Union, Vedeneyev continued to modify and improve his piston engines and VMP continued to manufacture them. But when the

USSR disintegrated the lavish state funding which Vedeneyev and VMP previously received stopped, as did the requirement for large numbers of engines. This made little difference to VMP, for whom the production of piston aircraft engines was a relatively small part of their business, but it created a significant problem for Vedeneyev, for whom the design of engines represented approximately half their business, the remainder being aerospace gearboxes.

This was where I entered the frame.

I could see that people who owned aeroplanes would need engine spares and on-going engine maintenance, and I proposed to Vedeneyev that he could overhaul engines for me. With a workforce of 220 people and no further central funding, they could see their business screeching to a stop and jumped at the opportunity. At the same time, I told them that we needed a more powerful engine. The Russian aerobatic team were saying the same and after discussions they modified the supercharger and increased the power to 400hp.

What was already a damned good engine had now become even better. We started fitting them to the new Sukhois we were selling and everyone wanted them. The M14PF engine remains well-proven and well-respected after more than 20 years in service. I can say this with more than a degree of confidence because I funded the upgrade and accordingly have my own revenue stream from all subsequent sales and overhauls!

As Russian industry and Russian entrepreneurs started to get used to operating without the all-enveloping mantle of state control, the long-established way of doing things started to break up and unravel. First VMP, which until now had been content to manufacture engines designed by Vedenyev, decided that they wanted to get into the engine design business themselves, encouraged in part by the Russian air force who were looking for a new Sukhoi training aircraft. Sukhoi had, by this time, fallen out with Vedenyev and had gone to VMP to ask them to design a 450hp engine to go into this new training aircraft. So, Vedeneyev found itself with a commercial competitor who was now far better funded than they were, but who also happened to be manufacturing aero engines just down the road in the same city.

Then Vedenyev was privatised in the ham-fisted way that these things were done in Russia in the early 1990s. The company was acquired by a group of venture capitalists who began asset stripping the business. The knock-on effect was not great for me. I was sending engines to Vedenyev to be overhauled, but it became clear that the quality of their work was dipping. Then financial chicanery started. Basically, they cheated me over a batch of six engines I had sent to be overhauled. Vedenyev told me that for tax reasons I should sell them the engines and then buy them back when they had been refurbished. It was very complicated and sort of made sense at the time, and I went along with it but when I tried to reclaim my engines, I was told they now belonged to Vedenyev and Vedenyev was going to hang on to them!

On the bright side, I had now formed quite a good working relationship with VMP and was selling their aero engines as well as the ones from Vedenyev. Therefore, engine supply was not an issue. I just needed somewhere else to get them overhauled.

THANK EU

Meanwhile in Hungary an unexpected opportunity was dawning. Prior to joining the European Union, the Hungarian ministry of agriculture had been using a fleet of 90 Russian Kamov-26 helicopters for crop spraying. These were very cleverly designed machines that used two contra-rotating rotors, doing away with the need for a tail rotor which saved weight and made the helicopters very manoeuvrable. A pair of rotors required two engines, one per rotor, and the engines Kamov fitted were the same Vedenyev engines as in the Yak and Sukhoi aeroplanes I was selling. Then Hungary joined the EU and EU environmental inspectors took one look at the Hungarian crop-spraying regime and brought a swift end to it, since the Eastern bloc chemicals being used were completely out of line with any crop treatment permitted in the European Union. So, Hungarian crop spraying stopped and their fleet of Kamov helicopters was cut by over 90 per cent. Today there are eight left in service.

Until this happened, overhauling these helicopter engines was good steady work for a Hungarian company called Aerometal although overhauling engines was not the only side to the Aerometal business: they had a machine shop, a foundry, an anodising unit and a plating shop all on the same site. Still, losing all their helicopter engine work more or less overnight was not great for cash flow or the company's long-term prospects.

I happened to hear about Aerometal at the time that I was being messed around by Vedenyev and flew to Budapest to meet Peter Bruller, the overall boss. It was one of those synergies that you feel was meant to be. Peter needed to replace the aero engine business his pretty sizeable workshop had lost; I had aero engines to be overhauled and needed a reliable engineering company to do that work for me. It did not take us long to reach a partnership agreement and for the last 14 years all my aero-engine work has been sent to Aerometal.

An M14PF engine fresh from an overhaul at Aerometal, my partner in Hungary. We introduced a number of updates on this superb engine and gave our customers the choice of colours to paint them!

That, today, is 90 per cent of my business, working with engines that come to us from all over the world. In time, we have tailored the product to suit the market. For example, historically all Russian military aero engines were painted green. Western pilots want something a little more eye-catching. So, we provide engines sprayed pretty much whatever colour a customer would like. We are increasing the power with different pistons and with much tighter assembly than the original Russian engineering tolerances produced. We are now fitting racing car plugs and very high-tension racing car plug leads but these are merely refinements to what have always been very good, very reliable engines.

As this part of my story shows, my Russian aviation business has been through a sequence of changes over the years. At a personal level I have moved from being an aeroplane pilot, to an aeroplane procurer, to an aeroplane maintenance provider. There have been other changes too, not ones that had any direct bearing on my business, nor the way it was run but in their own way just as significant.

The changes of address on my business stationery give a clue. And this was also the part of the business in which Cary played a key role. I have always run my aviation business from offices at home, where friends and business associates from Russia would come and stay as they continue to do today. By the time Cary and I met again properly and got married, my aviation business had already grown to much more than a sideline. With my aircraft based at White Waltham, it made sense to find somewhere to live nearby to cut down the driving to and from central London.

As Cary and I set about restoring and making our home in a succession of country houses, my aviation business moved with us. Our first married home was, of course, the Manor House at Princes Risborough but my enthusiasm for restoring large houses stretched back to a little before my accident in the *Pace Spirit*, when I began work on Hitcham House, which was conveniently just 17 miles from White Waltham.

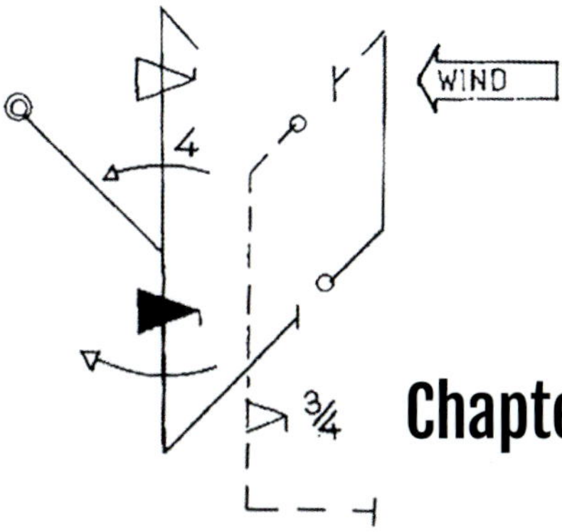

Chapter 19

AN ENGLISHMAN'S HOME

It was my flying that drew me away from central London, although I still needed somewhere to live during the working week and until only recently I kept my flat in Bryanston Square as a pied à terre.

Having easy access to White Waltham was becoming increasingly attractive. I was toying with the idea of buying an old cottage near the airfield and getting Dave Wiltshire to do it up for me. Dave had proved his versatility when we had worked together on the *Pace Spirit* and other aeroplanes and I knew that he had the skill, imagination and contacts to do a first-rate job, as later proved to be the case. However, before I found my cottage, I came across a rather good Victorian house overlooking the Long Walk running down from Windsor Castle. This had been turned into flats, one of which was for sale.

It was a very nice, very big, one-bedroom flat that required no work and into which I could move straight away. Problem solved. Allan Johnson moved in later, sleeping on the sofa, after he and his first wife parted company. Allan, by now a qualified solicitor, was an enormous help when I bought other houses. The first of these was Hitcham House itself, a massive Victorian pile that a property developer had vertically divided into eight portions of varying sizes, before selling them off. I bought the central section, which included the main entrance and grand staircase, and Allan subsequently bought the conservatory at the end of this huge house.

Probably the best location in Windsor, other than the castle itself! This photo is taken from the Long Walk, a Victorian row of houses for ladies-in-waiting where I had a ground floor flat.

A real Victorian Gothic monstrosity that possessed little architectural merit but was superbly made and provided me with a large five-bedroom house near White Waltham for the price of a local cottage.

I do not think even the most partisan owner would describe Hitcham House as attractive, but it did have some wonderfully big rooms which were perfect for large parties and entertaining sizeable groups of friends. The drawing-room alone was approaching 50 feet long. I had one very big bedroom and above that there were another five. Hitcham House was huge for a bachelor, of course, but its scale appealed to me and I could see that buying it represented a very good deal and a lucrative investment. One element of the refurbishment that was unique to my ownership was the installation of my bath, which was a massive object carved from a solid piece of stone. I was told that its former owner had been Benjamin Disraeli, in his Piccadilly house. (Disappointingly, the bath had to stay behind when I moved from Hitcham House: the floors at my new abode simply were not strong enough to bear its weight).

I was in the habit of keeping an eye on the property market and that was how I spotted an advertisement placed by the National Trust which, for the first time, was selling an 80-year-lease on one of its houses. The asking price was £200,000, which I immediately saw as a very good deal for a significant Home Counties' property, like the Manor House at Princes Risborough, and I bought it, thanks in no small measure to Allan who managed to draw out the conveyance for long enough to enable me to pull together the necessary funds.

The Manor House, a late-17th-century property that had belonged to Charles II's court painter Sir Peter Lely, had been one of the first properties owned by the National Trust. The Trust had kept the fabric in good order but it was quite primitive inside. The kitchen was basic, the plumbing was antediluvian and top -to-bottom the interior of the house needed a great deal of work. However, the long lease gave an incentive to undertake the necessary upgrades. Dave got to work installing central heating, bathrooms, a proper kitchen and smartening the whole house.

The Manor House was an attractive place to live, convenient for London and White Waltham and it had a pretty two-acre garden, which helped my cause when Cary came to visit for the first time. There may only have been a matter of weeks between her initial visit and our getting married, but in that time she had weeded out and replaced quite a lot of my less appealing furniture. The curtains were changed in a lot of the rooms and Cary bought a brand new four-oven Aga for the kitchen.

After selling her flat, she put the proceeds into further improving the furniture and furnishings at the Manor House. With my persuasion, she went for a job interview to run the recently-reorganised National Asthma Campaign, which had previously been three separate charities. The former incumbent had three secretaries, with an average age of 82! I had suggested that Cary might benefit from some interview practice and this looked a good one to start with although it appeared that here, too, I had not fully appreciated my new wife's abilities, because as well as getting some useful practice she was offered the job and accepted it!

But this required Cary to fulfil a very demanding role, pulling together what had previously been separate charities and getting them to harmonise under a new single structure. The job was extremely stressful and Cary became very run down which made her prey to a succession of debilitating conditions. But it was impossible for her to take time off work. She succumbed just once, staying at home for one day with pneumonia and soldiering on for much of the time feeling at death's door. To begin with, she did not even have the comfort of George and Daisy, because her two dachshunds had to live with Cary's mother until we found someone who could look after them at Princes Risborough during the week when we were both working in London. It was not an easy start to married life, but we got through those first six, difficult, months.

The Manor House at Princes Risborough, a beautiful house set in a fine two acres next to a pretty church.

(Above, right) Thornhill Park, graced by a pair of Rolls-Royce Phantoms and our first spaniel, Ella.

Cary worked for the National Asthma Campaign for three years and then handed in her notice so that she could devote her energy to garden design which was something she had wanted to do professionally for a long time. She enrolled on the year-long course at the English Gardening School based at the Chelsea Physic Garden. Then her replacement at the National Asthma Campaign, who had been Cary's deputy, announced that she was having another baby. While she was on maternity leave, Cary was asked to go back part-time. She spent two days at gardening school, three days back at her old job and then she had to do all the work on her course projects over the weekend.

Nice as the Manor House is, it does sit in the middle of a town. The National Trust had planted screening to add privacy, but one was always aware of other people around and about. It certainly could not be classed as a house in the country, which I knew was something Cary would have liked. She never agitated, but I also understood that she would have liked a house of her own, not the house I happened to be living in when we got married.

However, fate was looking favourably on her when, after four years in Princes Risborough, she saw a lovely house for sale in Dorset. It appealed to me too. Not only was Thornhill Park a very fine, predominantly 18th-century country house that was coming to the market with up to 200 acres of land, it was being sold at auction as a 'distress sale' brought about by the financial crisis in the Lloyds insurance market.

I was a Lloyds Name when Cary and I married, but she was always concerned about the unlimited liability that Names had signed up to. I felt reasonably secure

The garden side of Thornhill with part of Cary's hard landscaping. Taking centre stage are Ella (Bandarawela) and her daughter Amba (Ambalangoda). All the dogs were named after towns in Sri Lanka.

because friends such as Clive Wilson and John Harrison lived and breathed Lloyds and if anyone was well placed to take care of my interests they were. When the storm hit however, none of us could escape the deluge. Different Lloyds syndicates suffered different degrees of loss. Compared with many, my friends and I emerged without being hit too badly, but it was very unnerving at the time.

After a series of huge calls on the insurance market, Lloyds had come demanding money and Names had to pay up, often being ruined in the process. It was like a financial tsunami. People could see the problem building. It was slow but inexorable and some syndicates took action to save themselves, while others did nothing and were swept away. Lloyds themselves came up with a clever scheme, termed Recovery and Restitution in which Lloyds took on all the future losses syndicates might incur in exchange for every last penny those syndicates could raise up front, which was the time that Equitas, as the scheme was known, kicked in.

The premium Lloyds clawed together through Equitas came to 15 billion pounds and this was raised by every Name being contacted, in person, to be told to pay up some very serious money. I was on a business trip to Moscow when my call came one evening. Meanwhile similar calls were going out to all the other 30,000 Lloyds Names. The figure they wanted from me was £128,000. The question the caller asked was, 'When can we expect this?' I answered, truthfully, that there was no way I could possibly pay anything like that amount of money. I could, at a stretch, offer £25,000 and did so while tightly clutching my large vodka as I sat at my Korn/Ferry desk.

'I'm sorry,' replied my caller. 'That simply isn't enough.' It was less than 20 per cent of what I was being expected to pay. We got into a telephone ding dong. I dug in my heels, hoping that this chap would cave in first, because I knew he would have to make a load of similar telephone calls and was no doubt hoping by now to find other people less obdurate. In the end, he got me up to £32,000 and we closed on that. I allowed myself another large vodka after putting down the telephone receiver. With that one call I had saved myself the thick end of £100,000.

So, the mention of a Lloyds distress auction certainly chimed with me when Cary showed me the advertisement she had found in *Country Life*. The irony was that the owner of Thornhill Park was a fellow named John Rew, who, as the editor of *Chatset*, the independent magazine about Lloyds, had been issuing warnings for a long time that Lloyds was heading for big problems. Despite that, however, he had placed his wife in Lloyds, and his children. Each of them had separate unlimited liabilities and each of them had lost almost everything.

The house had been held in his wife's name and she ended up with nothing and having to live with a friend. She had even had to give away her dog; her horse had been put down. And John Rew himself? Cary and I have no idea of where he ended up.

Yet, despite its recent tragic history, Cary immediately felt a wonderful atmosphere when she stepped inside Thornhill for the first time. And here was another extraordinary turn of events: one of the previous owners of Thornhill was the grandmother of Cary's best friend at school, the celebrated event-rider, Jane Holderness-Roddam (née Bullen).

But the house was very run down and looked as if it would benefit from a lot of tender loving care. The very large room that became our bedroom had not

We bought Thornhill for £360,000 and 10 years later with the addition of some land was sold for more than £8 million, sadly not by me!

been touched, to the extent that it did not even have a ceiling! There was also a potential issue of a neighbour immediately next to us. There were two coach houses at Thornhill, one of which adjoined the squash court attached to the main house and this coach house was owned by a naval commander who lived there with his family. These problems aside, Thornhill was still a stunning house, Grade II listed, and had the makings of a seriously significant country home.

Well over 100 attended the auction, which was held in the ballroom on the first floor at Thornhill that had been used as the setting of the ball scene in John Schlesinger's 1967 film of *Far From the Madding Crowd*; Terence Stamp, as Sergeant Troy, had been shot dead on the main staircase by Peter Finch, playing William Boldwood. Cary and I had gone to a pub for lunch and I could sense that she was desperate to buy the house, and she was perturbed when we arrived in the ballroom and saw so many people. But a quick scan of the people gave me the strong feeling that most of those there were local rubberneckers. There were only a few serious bidders I assured her when we took our seats in the middle of the room.

There were two others as it turned out, but to my surprise they dropped out at a good £100,000 below the price I thought I might have to go to and, when the auctioneer's gavel fell, Thornhill Park was ours for £360,000. We also secured a couple of plots of land that together amounted to 75 acres. It was a good afternoon's work, which proved to be even better after we subsequently sold the Manor House at Princes Risborough for £500,000 and a very respectable profit.

As its name suggests, Thornhill Park had been the home of the celebrated baroque painter Sir James Thornhill, famous for his work on the Dome of St Paul's, the Painted Hall at Greenwich and the hall at Blenheim Palace. Sir James also held the official post as serjeant-painter to George I. Thornhill, the house, was the first project that Cary and I approached as a new venture together and we found that the project fell naturally towards our respective skills and interests: I took care of the structural work and the 'engineering' side of the refurbishment, while Cary's talents were employed on the overall aesthetic feel of the house and grounds, and the specifics of furniture, furnishing and décor. Of course, we consulted each other as we progressed, but by working on the house in this way we completed all we needed to do in two-and-half years by which time Thornhill Park, inside and out, had been completely transformed, especially the garden.

Dave Wiltshire had masterfully created a domed ceiling in what became our bedroom, which was then enhanced by lovely decorative plasterwork. We installed proper bathrooms. The heating system was completely overhauled, replacing the huge industrial boiler in the cellar with two of the largest domestic boilers you could buy. I had to spend time investigating architectural salvage yards to find nice old radiators and bathroom fittings, but they were still relatively cheap in the early 1990s and I always find hunting down bargains enjoyable. Meanwhile Cary got to grips with creating a fantastic five-acre garden from scratch. Now qualified as a garden designer, this was the biggest project that she had undertaken to date and the result was stunning. What had been bare grass was now one of the leading gardens in that part of Dorset.

Working with a very good friend, Cary began a very successful garden design business based at Thornhill, where she was now living full-time. Most weeks I was working in London Monday to Thursday, before flying down to Dorset from White Waltham on Thursday afternoon. That took about half-an-hour, while below me motorists would be struggling westwards on the A303. I would fly over Thornhill to alert Cary to my arrival and then land at the nearby airfield of Henstridge, by which time she would have arrived to collect me.

Living at Thornhill gave us somewhere to invite friends for weekends and we had some memorable gatherings there. The 1959 Wurlitzer jukebox that I had bought for £25, some 40 years earlier, when it was being 'retired' after 10 years of pub service, was installed in the kitchen to provide musical entertainment. Murray Kenyon moved into one of our flats following the sad death of his wife, Judith.

Then there were my business friends and associates from Korn/Ferry and my aviation business, for whom Thornhill was a wonderful place to get away from the office and get to know one another in a more relaxed atmosphere. Eastern European visitors particularly seemed to enjoy visiting Thornhill, which was so different to what they were used to at home. The thing that amazed them most was that I, a private citizen, had two armoured cars parked outside my home.

Among the diversions on offer, I used to bet visitors £20 they could not drive my 1920 Rolls-Royce Silver Ghost without once crashing the gears. The 'test track' for this bet was the main drive at Thornhill, which is three-quarters of a mile long and I only lost that bet once. The winner had been a driver in the Czech army, where he had to drive Tatra trucks. 'Compared with that, this is easy,' he said after pocketing his £20 note.

Cary is very fond of pigs, so at Thornhill we had pigs, which entertained guests. There were our dogs too: a pair of naughty Labradors to begin with, plus Cary's wire-haired dachshunds and then the first of our line of Springer Spaniels. Noni Chawla's daughter, who was making use of our London flat while studying at

SOAS, used to come to stay at Thornhill and reported home in raptures about the animals. According to her father, they, and going down to the pub by armoured car, were the highlights of her visits.

In 1727, Sir James Thornhill, erected a large obelisk in his grounds to commemorate the coronation of King George II and Queen Caroline. This, and the land on which it stands, did not form part of the sale when we bought Thornhill Park. However, it did become available a year or two after we moved in, together with another 25 acres. Here was an opportunity that I simply could not afford to let slip through my fingers. Slightly annoyingly, the most convenient way of raising the money to buy these extensions to our land was to sell the 1,500 shares that I owned in Brompton Bicycle.

My Brompton shareholding was not the result of casual, or even calculated, speculation. I had been involved with the company since its very beginnings when my Trinity friend, Andrew Ritchie, had first come up with the idea for a portable folding bicycle. At the time, seven years after we had left university, Andrew's scheme did not amount to much more than a few plans sketched out on sheets of paper, but I thought there was something in it. Andrew and I were having a drink in our regular, the Rising Sun in South Kensington, when I asked how his plans were going and he explained that they were not going anywhere until he raised enough money to pay for a prototype. He told me how much was needed and I suggested having a whip round. If we could raise £100 each from 10 friends, that would provide enough money to take the idea further.

This was not an insignificant sum for people starting out on their careers in the mid-1970s, but I managed to persuade enough people to put up the money and Andrew was able to make his prototype. Further money was needed, inevitably. But while others would drop out in time, I retained my faith in the project and became quite a serious shareholder; I also had a seat on the board while the company went through a fairly long period sorting out teething troubles.

Tim Guinness and Robert Woods were on the board as well and I could see that their interest was primarily driven by having a little business that made things. However, that was not my thinking at all. I tried to put forward the plan that since none of us knew the first thing about manufacturing, the best course would be to fund Andrew to reach the point of having a solid, marketable, product and then sell the business to someone who understood making bicycles inside out. But I was overruled and, not wanting to fall out with friends, I resigned my seat on the board. The man who really got Brompton Bicycle rolling towards a very successful financial and trading future was Julian Vereker. He had built his own hi-fi business, Naim, into an industry leader and he agreed to guarantee the £40,000 overdraft Brompton took out. Julian also brought experience of manufacturing, which none of us had, and that was critical to the company's development and success.

CLOSE QUARTERS

As mentioned above, I had always seen the proximity of the neighbours as a potential difficulty when it came to selling Thornhill. Although it did not put Cary and me off buying it, once we had finished work on the house and made it a frankly much more desirable property than it had been when we bought it, we could see prospective buyers turning away when they realised that the main house essentially had someone else's semi-detached home bolted on to it.

We got an intimation of the kind of problems that might arise when we set about converting our own coach house. The naval commander and his family lived on the other side of a courtyard, in what had grown to be a perfectly pleasant six-bedroom house, behind which they had three-quarters of an acre of garden. All of this sat like a little island right in the middle of what was now our 100 acres of grounds and formal gardens that Cary had created.

The previous occupants of the coach house had run-ins with Rew, who had taken to turning off their water supply when the mood seized him as the water pipe to the coach house ran through the cellar of the main house. Before the naval commander's time, Rew had smashed up the car belonging to the previous owner of the coach house, bashing in every panel of the body with a cricket bat.

So, historically, there was bad blood between the two houses. But we had got on fine until it came to converting the top floor of our coach house into a flat. Out of courtesy I showed our plans to the naval commander who went ballistic, complaining vehemently that he was not going to have his house overlooked. Since we owned the courtyard that divided our two coach houses he did not actually have a leg to stand on, but for the sake of harmony, we modified our plans slightly to mollify him. That issue was resolved, but it had sown a seed of doubt in our minds. Cary and I had invested a lot of money and time into Thornhill and now there was a niggling anxiety that that could be placed in jeopardy by having another property so very close to what was now quite a grand house.

But, once again, a chain of events brought an unforeseen resolution when the regional head of estate agents Knight Frank contacted us one day completely out of the blue and asked if there was a figure that would move us from Thornhill. To back up a little, he had been approached by an American couple, rather engagingly called Tom and Jerry. Tom had the money, acquired from a former partner who had owned the Perrier concession in the States. Jerry had no money to speak of, but had very good taste. Together they had made a lot of money buying, doing up and then selling large houses on both sides of the Channel. However, their last house had not worked out. On the first night in this place, just over the border in Somerset, Tom had fallen down the stairs. Taking this as a bad omen, he did not even unpack, but went straight round to the Knight Frank office to ask them to find him a similar house in the area. That was how Knight Frank came to sound us out.

With an approach like this, it seemed obvious that a buyer like Tom could easily afford to buy out the naval commander too, thereby sorting out the neighbour problem and re-establishing Thornhill Park as a unified property of considerable standing once again. The question Knight Frank needed an answer to was what the price would have to be for us to leave.

Cary and I had kept up a close interest in property values and we reckoned that after what we had done with Thornhill it was worth between £1,500,000 and £1,800,000. So, we said that we would be prepared to sell for £2,500,000 and the answer came back within 24 hours that that would not be a problem. The only condition was that we had to be out of the house within three months.

By now we had Murray living in one flat and a housekeeper living in another. When we bought Thornhill it came with a dilapidated barn, which we had converted into a separate house and were renting to a local publican, Clive Frampton and his wife Nell. Then there were our two businesses and quite a big collection of motor vehicles, including the two armoured cars. And all of these had to be relocated or found new homes in just 12 weeks. We ended up renting the clock house at Hadspen, a rather fine country house just into Somerset, but it was a nightmare scramble to meet the deadline.

NEW BEGINNINGS

On 19 March, 2004 *The Times* carried a full-page article written by the property specialist, Marcus Binney. The house he wrote about was what Binney described as one of Herefordshire's 'great ancestral seats'; the owner and vendor was a man Binney described as 'a serial country house restorer'. The property in question was Newport House, 15 miles west of Hereford, near the village of Almeley, and the owner he interviewed was me.

After Thornhill Park, Cary and I had taken on an even bigger challenge and it was this house that, in the spring of 2004, we were putting on the market after a complete restoration and us returning the building to the glory it had once known. However, between leaving Thornhill and planning to leave Newport, quite a bit had happened in our lives.

When it came to houses, Thornhill had raised the bar for our aspirations and expectations, but good houses in Dorset struck us as being over-priced. Cary and I also decided that we should look at moving to a part of the country where we had at least one well-established friend who could introduce us to people they knew. We also needed to find a house that was near an airfield. It was a limited market and for a while nothing we saw kindled our interest, although we looked very widely at houses as far apart as Norfolk and Devon. Then, one of our Herefordshire friends sent us the details of Newport House. We drove over to see it on a Saturday and bought it on Sunday.

As I told Marcus Binney, it was a rush of blood to the head. But both Cary and I loved the area from visits to friends in north Herefordshire, and now Newport presented us with a favourite location and a good project to get our teeth into once again. The potential of the house attracted me, while the garden and what it could be made into appealed to Cary. Newport was also being sold at an incredibly cheap price given the size. We bought it for around £700,000, but there was a reason for this: Newport House was not an undertaking for the faint-hearted.

Newport House on the day that we first saw it and indeed bought it the next day. We only realised later that all the chimneys had been knocked off!

Having once been the focal point of a fine 4,000-acre estate, it had fallen on hard times in the lean years that followed the First World War. In line with the national smallholder scheme, Herefordshire County Council had stepped in to buy the estate so that the land could be divided into 50-acre farms. Newport House itself had been run as a TB sanatorium until 1950. Three years later, it was taken over to provide a home for émigré Latvians, of whom there were some 8,000 living in the UK by that time. By the early 1990s, though, only an elderly couple remained. Plans to convert the main house into eight dwellings, with a further six detached houses in the grounds, had foundered, which was how Cary and I came to buy Newport with its total of 124 rooms, plus very extensive outbuildings with a clock house and a large stable-block, in which there were a four-bedroom cottage, two flats and garaging for 11 cars.

Those were the positives. The negatives had become apparent from the time we first set foot in the house. Cary and I had brought one of our three spaniels to look around the house and, the moment she was inside, the dog howled pitifully as if to tell us, 'People have died here'. Both the other spaniels behaved in exactly the same way and, as we discovered, their instinct was absolutely right. Seventy of the former Latvian residents of Newport lie buried in the churchyard at Almeley.

Tangible problems became evident after the photographs we had taken were developed. When the snaps came back from the chemist, we realised they had chopped off all the chimneys. In fact, it was even worse. They had dropped the bricks down the flues, where they had wedged and were causing dampness. Though the house looked in fair condition, once we took the slates off the roof we found that all the joists were rotten, and the whole house had to be rewired. Furthermore, there were only three bathrooms.

Newport had been empty for four years. Restoring it was clearly going to be far more challenging than the work at Thornhill and we saw that we would need a full-time, on-site manager to oversee the project. By now we had got to know Clive and Nell Frampton well. Clive was a practical, innovative chap, who was a handy builder. I had an instinct that he could be just the man to work with me on the restoration and supervise the work when I was not there. Nell was also very practical and a terrific cook. I thought she could be a great help with sorting out the house. They were just the kind of a hands-on couple that Cary and I have found so helpful and when we asked if they would consider moving to Newport with us, they happily agreed. Our first task, then, was to refurbish the Doctor's House at Newport, built during its TB sanatorium days, so Clive and Nell could move into that.

Murray was also an important part in our domestic life by this stage, looking after the dogs and keeping a watchful eye on our house when we were away or in London. He required a home in Newport too, so we needed to convert a flat for him to move into.

With Clive and me as the foremen, we recruited a dozen Herefordshire builders to work on the job, plus a specialist plumber and a specialist electrician; meanwhile Cary had a team of three gardeners restoring the gardens. We bought Newport with 16 acres of land, but that did not include the five-and-a-half-acre lake and the land surrounding it. When we were later able to buy them from the Council, they enhanced our grounds greatly. In the 19th century the gardens had been laid out by W A Nesfield, who designed the three great vistas at Kew Gardens and the Broad Walk in Regent's Park. When we arrived at Newport, his work was still evident in the form of a magnificent stone tazza with lion supports, identical to the ones he installed in Regent's Park. Subsequently the garden was extended down to the lake with fine Edwardian yew hedging and mature trees and once we had brought the lake and its immediate surroundings back into the curtilage of the main house, our vista extended to the woods at the far end of the lake, from which a stream ran on through the trees.

The one thing we were not short of inside Newport was space. The five principal reception rooms were all inter-connected, which made it the ideal venue for some great parties. We had a library, a smoking room, a music room, a dining room, a drawing-room, a family kitchen/living room. We had a separate kitchen just used for catering at parties. Even the dogs had a couple of rooms to themselves.

Cary and I had no particular plan when we bought Newport: our approach was very much 'suck it and see'. I toyed with the long-term idea of persuading, say, seven other couples who were friends of ours, to take a share in the house and move into it with us as we all got older, but I did not put a lot of effort into pursuing that and the idea fizzled away. We converted the Georgian clock-house into a private pub, which we called 'The Running Spaniel' after the succession of dogs who were now filling our lives. When it came to heating the house, I adopted the policy that had worked well for us at Thornhill and installed four of the largest domestic boilers on the market. Not only were these much better value for money than the kind of industrial boiler a house the size of Newport might need, but having four boilers meant that we could zone off parts of the house when they were not occupied, which reduced fuel consumption.

When Cary and I first slept at Newport, it was on camp beds in the clock-house. When the stables had been restored and renovated, we and the dogs transferred there, and the clock-house became offices for our two businesses. Then we finally moved into the main house, where, among other additions, we installed a pair of beautiful cast-iron French baths, side by side in our bathroom.

It took just over three years of hard work to get Newport into what we regarded as a satisfactory condition. Cary phrases our approach to house restoration well: she calls it 'efficient without being extravagant'. We do the important bits and make sure a house looks well cared for and welcoming, but we leave others to fritter their money on what we regard as eye-wateringly expensive embellishments. But having achieved what we wanted to do, it was time to take stock of where we were and what we wanted to do next.

I had stopped my headhunting by this stage to focus my energy on my aviation business, and I spent all my working time at home, when I was not travelling to Russia or Hungary. Once the momentum of restoring Newport had come to an end, we entered a less appealing management mode, in which the size and cost of running the house that had first excited us was now becoming a burden. Considering that what Cary and I needed in the final analysis was a home for us and our dogs, it did start to look too big

What we were looking for was somewhere rather smaller and more sensible, and the sort of thing we had in mind was a small farm with around 60 acres.

Newport House and gardens fully restored. Note the total symmetry of the five dogs: labradors on the outside and three spaniels in the middle. I told people that they were kept in line with wire through their jaws!

Knowing that parts of north Herefordshire have to be some of the least spoiled and most tranquil places in England, we set out to find something nearby to enjoy ourselves. This, we thought, might take us three or four years but, as luck would have it, we found precisely what we were looking for in three months, as described at the end of this book.

Of course, we had never put Thornhill on the market: the market had come to us. Even the sale of the Manor House had gone through swiftly and easily. So, Cary and I had not been exposed to the waywardness of the property market, nor people who pose as blue-chip buyers and then turn out to be anything but.

The first of this type to show an interest in Newport House was a High Court judge. He was all set to buy, full of bluster and very pleased with himself. The only thing he was not full of was money; he was our first time-waster. Others followed, showing strong interest and then mysteriously dragging their feet when it came to getting on with the sale. After putting up with this for several months, Cary and I instructed our estate agents that we would only entertain interest from buyers who would be able to exchange contracts within 30 days

The hideous but rather grand Victorian entrance portico added in 1870. We had to erect a total of 13 chimneys back onto the roof.

of our accepting their offer. Several solicitors sucked their teeth and tried to convince us that with a property of the size and potential complexity of Newport, this was a non-starter. But Cary and I were adamant and in due course a likely buyer appeared who did not baulk at our terms.

He was a big shot in the Norwich Union. He had money in the bank to buy Newport, he told us and, although we emphasized that exchange in 30 days was a red line, he still pushed ahead with the searches and other legal precursors. But it was when he asked for a survey and made the mistake of mentioning that the surveyor's valuation had better be close to the price we had agreed, that I realised he was having to borrow money to buy Newport, a detail he had somehow managed to omit before.

It was during the time that we were rapidly losing faith in this buyer that a firm called Property Vision contacted us. We knew of them through very good friends in Dorset and so understood that when they contact vendors, they mean serious business. From a vendor's point of view, Property Vision clients are genuinely blue chip clients. So, having felt that we had been messed around by people thus far, Cary and I were cheered to have serious, verifiable interest shown at last.

The man who Property Vision wanted to bring to Newport was David Watt, a British businessman close to my age, who had become very successful and wealthy working in the Far East, first in Hong Kong and after that in Malaysia. He arrived to look over the house with Jenny, his much younger half-English, half-French wife, their three small children, the nanny and his mother-in-law.

I had no illusions about Newport. It looked splendid superficially, but the Victorians had messed about with it and for a house of its size, the land was rather limited at 34 acres. The French side of Jenny Watts made her quite outspoken and when they were leaving after a pretty thorough tour, she told me, 'Well, I can see that David is quite taken with the house, but I can tell you that I'm not. But thank you for showing us around.' That was a bit disappointing, but we still had the Norwich Union man, although we had our doubts about him. Then, to our surprise, six days after the Watts had come for their viewing, we got a call from Property Vision to tell us that after looking at lots of other houses in the meantime, the Watts had decided to buy Newport.

This was excellent news, naturally. But given our previous experience, I did emphasise the requirement to exchange contracts in 30 days. I also explained that we had agreed a sale price of £2,500,000 with the man from Norwich Union, but that Cary and I seriously doubted that he would be able to fulfil his side of the agreement, given that there were only a couple of days to go before his 30 days were up. Property Vision noted these points and said they would come back to us after consulting their client. They were back on the phone within the hour. Mr Watt would pay the price we had agreed with the other purchaser, plus an additional £100,000. The caller added that Mr Watt would also exchange contracts in three days, not 30.

Here was a deal we could not turn down, even if the three-day commitment did look a little far-fetched. Although we were under no obligation to do it, I offered to cover all the Norwich Union's buyer's costs, even though it was manifestly clear that he had not been straight with us. With rather poor grace he accepted and Cary and I waited to see what would happen next with the Watts. They did exchange contracts pretty much as promised: in the end, it took them three-and-a-half days!

The Watts were on their way back to Malaysia, but now that the sale was confirmed they asked if they could come and stay at Newport before leaving.

An aerial view of Rhodds Farm in 2016. From the left is a garage, foreground the offices and a large Victorian barn. The garden was still a work in progress.

That was slightly unusual, but Cary and I had no objection, so the whole charabanc reappeared: mum, dad, three kids, nanny and mother-in-law. In they came and down came the heavens. I had never seen rain like it in all the time we had lived at Newport. We had our own mini-sewage plant, the sort of thing that you might find treating the effluent from a small village, and this was completely overwhelmed by the torrents of rainwater and overflowed spewing its foul contents far and wide. There was water flowing into the house. The whole situation had the makings of an absolute nightmare, but David was completely relaxed. The sale went through without a hitch. He and Jenny took over from Cary and me and continued to reinstate the prestige Newport had enjoyed in past centuries. David bought back adjoining farms and woodland that had been hived off after the First World War, and has given Newport the kind of acreage one would expect for a house with its status and situation.

Meanwhile, the sale had liberated funds for Cary and me. Although there was work to be done and money to be spent on Rhodds Farm, our new home only a few miles from Newport House, our horizons were by no means restricted to a rural idyll in Herefordshire. Having enjoyed a number of holidays in Sri Lanka, we were drawn to the tropics, especially during the dank, drab months of an English winter. So, our next significant property venture would not be in the rolling hills of the Welsh Marches, but in the central uplands of the island I had known since my childhood as Ceylon.

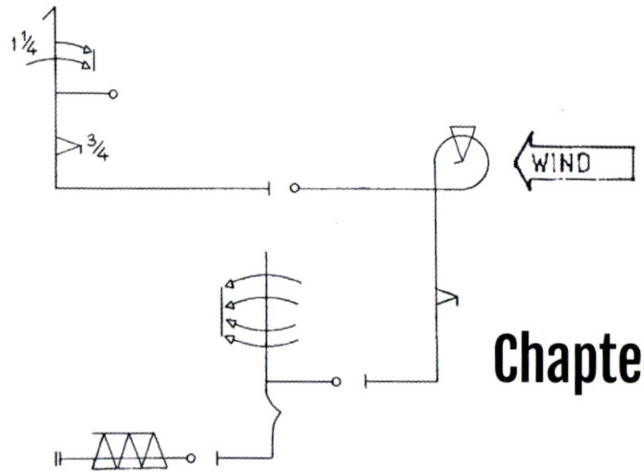

Chapter 20

HIGH IN THE HILLS ABOVE KANDY

It was not so much that Cary and I bought a house in Sri Lanka on a whim and being us, we gave no thought to what we do with it or how often we might go there.

It was more the appreciation that we had bought Thornhill, and especially Newport, largely on the spur of the moment coupled with the gut feeling that we would make them work one way or another.

We did set ourselves some broad parameters, though. We knew we wanted to be within an hour of Kandy, ideally placed between the coast, which can be very hot, humid and crowded with people, and the highest parts of the hill country, which at 6,000 feet can get jolly cold. Being close to Kandy also gave good access to shops and services such as doctors and banks.

So it was that we found ourselves arriving there on Boxing Day 2004, the day of the Indian Ocean tsunami. The internal news services in Sri Lanka leave a lot to be desired and to begin with the only hard news was coming from Western news agencies, who were helicoptering people down to the south coast, parts of which had been totally devastated. Like almost all other tourists in Sri Lanka, Cary and I were met and were ferried about by a driver and it was he who told us that there had been a storm on the south coast and 20 people had died. When we soon found out that the scale of the disaster was immeasurably worse, we went to a bank, along with a lot of other tourists, and donated to a disaster relief fund although how much of that money, if any, found its way to the people most in need, I would be interested to know.

House hunting in Sri Lanka is not the same as house hunting in Herefordshire, or anywhere else in the UK for that matter. There are people who set themselves up as property brokers but, as we quickly found out, they frequently knew very little about the houses they purported to be selling. Details such as who actually owned a property, or how much land it had, the sort of things that prospective buyers generally find quite important, frequently eluded these agents.

However, we were very fortunate to have a friend who knew Sri Lanka very well. As David Blackler told his story, he had been working in London in the mid-1950s (he was in his mid-20s at the time) and was earning £800 a year, when someone suggested that he take a new job in Ceylon, getting paid £2,500 a year and benefits which included a large house, a car and three indoor servants. David accepted the offer, but the people who had made it had been shrewd, because less than 40 years later he had become chairman of John Keells, the biggest public company in Sri Lanka.

David had a house, modestly called Chatsworth, where Christopher Worthington, an old Ceylon planter for 50 years or longer, who could not face going back to the UK, had an arrangement with the Blacklers to live in part of it and keep an eye on the place when they were not there. Cary and I went to stay with him at Chatsworth when we were looking for a house of our own.

We saw more than 22 houses, a couple of which were definite possibilities; our problem was that Cary and I had no experience of living in Sri Lanka for any length of time and therefore were not sure what we really wanted. But our gut feelings had served us well in the past and they did again when we were taken to see what was then known as Seetha Valley, a small tea estate, centred on a typical bungalow about six miles from Chatsworth. The moment we walked into it, we felt immediately at home. The house was a bit tatty and needed work on it, the gardens were overgrown and there was an ugly tea-processing building very close by but, even so, everything about it just felt right.

The property was being sold by a rather slick chap called Sarath Ranaweera. We were never entirely sure what had happened, but as well as Seetha Valley (we changed the name to Ellerton after discovering a reference to the name some time back in the title deeds), Ranaweera owned a tea-factory just up the hill. He was very entrepreneurial and had evidently persuaded some European investors to put money into a new venture for growing bio-organic tea. However, it did not take them long to conclude that this was not a great deal for them. The bio-organic business was not making any money, the house was run-down, there was no hot water, there was no swimming-pool, the cook was useless, and there was a noisy

tea factory right next door, with trucks coming in and out all the time. I could understand why they lost heart pretty quickly.

Nevertheless, when we met Ranaweera, he tried to convince us that the business was thriving. But I reckoned that if a sharp local operator like him could not make a go of it people like Cary and me, who did not know the first thing about tea, could lose some serious money. I told him that we liked the house very much, but we would only buy it with its 10 acres of land; we did not want the tea factory or the responsibility of the people working in it either. He declined our offer, so we left him our contact details and set off to look at our next property.

Ukuwela was a similar bungalow to the one Ranaweera was selling, though not as nice and not as well situated as far as Cary and I were concerned. It was north of Kandy, and to get to it one had to drive through some pretty unattractive industrial sprawl. Travelling southwards from Kandy to Ellerton was very different: the drive took you through the delightful 1,700 acres of tropical grounds that formed the campus of the University of Peradeniya, famous for its botanical gardens, before you climbed into the hills that led to Ellerton.

Although Ukuwela came with 14 acres, the house was parked at one extremity of the land. Ukuwela also came with a ludicrously complex divided ownership, which was not uncommon in Sri Lanka. It did not have one owner, or at best two. Ukuwela was owned by nine people, all siblings and the offspring of the previous owner, who, incidentally, had previously sold off 140 acres of land to 62 different people. Just to complicate matters further, as a devout Muslim,

(Left) It was difficult to get a good photograph of Ellerton from the air due to the jungle surrounding it. The main part of the hotel is in the background, foreground on the left is our apartment, centre and right are the staff quarters.

(Right) The infinity pool was popular with guests but I worried in heavy rain it might slip away!

he had sold all these little plots to fellow Muslims in accordance with sharia law so none of them, nor the owners' respective titles, were officially registered. Nevertheless, we engaged the services of a lawyer named Jiffri, who had the endearing trait of peppering his conversation with terms like 'vagabond' and 'scoundrel'. More to the point, Jiffri had been at school with two of the brothers who each owned portions of Ukuwela, so he knew the family and vice versa. Even he warned us that trying to buy Ukuwela would not be easy, but we pushed on regardless.

Having no legal status in Sri Lanka, we contrived a deal of sorts by sharing £3,000 in cash equally with the nine owners as a kind of deposit. Then one of the brothers, who had already served time in jail for fraud, tried to persuade his siblings to renege on our agreement. Cary and I were all set to walk away, when one the sisters, in an effort to preserve a degree of integrity, offered to sell us her one ninth of Ukuwela

Meanwhile, Ranaweera had got back in contact. He had had a change of heart and was now agreeing to sell us Seetha Valley and its 10 acres but without the tea business; the workers would be deployed elsewhere and he was going to remove the ugly factory close to the house. This now left us with the option of buying one complete property in Sri Lanka and one-ninth of another, so we bought both.

Buying Ellerton was an obvious thing to do. But a small share of Ukuwela? My feeling was that owning a portion of someone else's house was going to be quite valuable when he wanted either to live there, or to do something else with it.

So, we instructed Jiffri to draw up proper legal documents and we bought our one ninth of Ukuwela.

That done, I turned my attention to Ellerton and Ukuwela drifted to the back of my mind until I happened to bump into the property broker who had first shown us Ellerton and he told me, 'Did you know that Ukuwela has been sold?' 'Well, I know that part of it has been sold to us,' I replied.

But this chap continued, and from what he told me it was clear that a wealthy Anglo-Sri Lankan businessman called Roman Scott had been sold Ukuwela under the impression that he now owned the whole property. My telephone call informing him that we already owned part of it was news to him. Jiffri knew Scott's lawyer, so we went to see him and asked to see the sale documents for Ukuwela. He dug them out and, on the Deed of Transfer, everything was explained. There were the names of the nine vendors, as one would have expected, but vendor number six, the sister who had sold her portion to us, had a line drawn through her name with a note explaining, somewhat self-evidently, 'Vendor No. 6 has been deleted'.

Roman Scott's lawyer seemed very relaxed and assured us that we would sort out the situation, which sounded like mañana to me. I spoke to Roman Scott himself saying that, although Cary and I were not in a hurry, he might like to rectify matters and we left it at that.

Christopher Worthington introduced us to a good local builder, Perry Jacobs. He was indeed a very good builder when he was sober and that was not a lot of the time. Even so, he did a pretty good job on the house considering that the roof timbers were riddled with termites and the whole roof structure had to be replaced. Another basic problem we uncovered was that the walls at Ellerton had been constructed from big granite boulders held together with mud. Trying to make openings for doors and windows was a nightmare because the granite was impenetrable to normal masonry tools. We then installed a caretaker couple, Lucky and Pia, to live in the house to look after it while Cary and I were back home in England, and to keep a check on how many builders were working each day and what they were doing.

When we bought Ellerton, we did not expect to end up running it as a hotel. We liked its serenity. It was somewhere we imagined we would go to with friends to enjoy holidays in matchless scenery. In the main house, we had three bedrooms and, making use of the concrete foundation that Ranaweera had installed for his tea processing machinery, we built what we called the Valley House. Ranaweera's tea processing factory had been removed of course, but the substantial concrete floor and footings remained. Once the sale of Ellerton had gone through, however,

Ranaweera insisted that this lump of concrete was his and demanded that we should pay him for it. I knew this was just a ploy and told him that we did not want it, so he should take it away. However, if he left it on our land, I pointed out, we would consider it to be ours.

Of course, Ranaweera made no attempt to remove the hundreds of tons of concrete that constituted this substantial structure and the slab provided very serviceable footings for us, the only drawback being that the ground plan of the Valley House was constrained by the proportions of Ranaweera's concrete footings. However, thinking that was where Cary and I would have our own accommodation, we created a very nice suite of rooms with a big master bedroom, a nice bathroom, a smaller bedroom and a study.

Then word began to spread that Ellerton had had a very good makeover and, since it was well-placed on the tourist route around the island, we began getting

I was continuing to do my normal aviation business from Ellerton although one initial challenge was the slow internet! There can be few nicer places in which to work.

enquiries, asking if we would let out rooms. People started coming to stay and liking Ellerton as much as we did. Local travel agents got in touch to ask if we would consider taking paying guests. There was only one nice, small hotel in the area called Kandy House, to the north of Kandy itself. Steadily, without any effort from us, a flow of paying guests started to pass through our door and, before we really knew it, we found ourselves running a hotel.

Cary says the trouble with me is that I always try to turn everything into money if I can. But, in the case of Ellerton, I really did feel that we had the makings of a profitable enterprise. Besides which, we found that we were also spending quite a lot of money on the house and garden. Building the Valley House and constructing a swimming-pool on quite an appreciable slope were just a couple of our major outgoings. And they came after the cost of the work we had had to do on the main house, and the kitchen, which itself required completely new equipment. We were already into serious outgoings and I thought that it would be good to see some money flowing the other way.

We had our own veranda on the back of our apartment with this wonderful view across the valley and to the distant hills. It is a very spectacular country.

There was a pragmatic consideration as well. We realised that you cannot simply leave a big house over 5,000 miles away in Sri Lanka for four months at a time in the care of staff. As soon as your taxi has left for the airport, the staff will be running a hotel of their own there. This did happen in fact. Friends of ours arrived at their house 24 hours ahead of schedule and found the place full of Sri Lankans to whom their staff were letting out rooms! We had been warned.

Therefore, the decision was taken that Ellerton was going to begin operating officially as a hotel. Correspondingly, that was going to require some adjustments as far as we were concerned although neither Cary nor I envisaged how much of our own time and effort would be required.

We wanted the experience of staying at Ellerton to be special. Even though it would be run as a commercial concern, we were very keen that guests should feel that they were staying with friends in an English country house with the important distinction that this was a country house with fabulous weather and glorious views over unspoiled tropical jungle. We also structured our rates so that everything

Meals at Ellerton were had in this open-sided dining pavilion where guests could either sit at their own table or mix with other guests at dinner or evening cocktail parties.

(Above) The Valley House was an old tea factory that was demolished leaving the foundation on which we built an office and two large bedrooms, plus a veranda.

(Below) Ellerton was a traditional tea-estate manager's bungalow. It was extraordinarily welcoming and on walking in for the first time I knew I had to buy it!

(except lunch and dinner) was included, from borrowing bicycles to having a beer or a gin and tonic beside the pool, to sipping a brandy after dinner. Everything guests wanted once they had arrived was covered in the cost of their stay at Ellerton. This looked generous and guests appreciated it, with very few abusing the system, but there was a practical reason too. Guests at Kandy House had to sign chits for every last extra and three members of staff were employed dealing with these pieces of paper. Then, when guests came to leave, they had laboriously to check through all their chits to make sure that their bills were correct before paying. We had none of that at Ellerton and our system worked well.

While a lot of guests came on the personal recommendation of people who had already stayed there, we were very lucky to become ensconced with Audley Travel who cater principally for the holiday needs of well-off British clients, largely aged 55 to 75. Ellerton had just the kind of old-worlde, colonial charm that Audley travellers loved. Our rooms had no televisions and no air conditioning. At 2,400 feet above sea level we did not think it was necessary, although a small number of guests thought otherwise. Instead, we had fans in the ceilings, and portable fans if the weather did start to get uncomfortably hot.

With a hotel, one needed staff. We had inherited a fairly useless cook from Ranaweera. Since we did not know anyone in Sri Lanka to begin with, and we were never there for long enough to spend time recruiting properly, we did make a few injudicious appointments at the start. Our first manager, a chap called Rohan proved to be an out and out crook, as we later discovered. But he was very personable and was used to catering for the needs of Western visitors because his principal occupation, before we engaged him, was as a driver whose job it was to chauffeur tourists around the island for the duration of their stay. Cary and I did not have a very high opinion of these Sri Lankan tourist drivers, for reasons which I will come to in a moment, but Rohan spoke good English and, although he was lazy, it was reassuring to have him keeping an eye on Ellerton when Cary and I were back in England.

We knew that he was not a satisfactory appointment from the outset, but for the first couple of years we muddled through, and then things did start to go wrong rather seriously. We used to send out money every week so that Rohan could pay the next week's bills. He would email us a list of outgoings and we transferred the necessary funds to his bank account. On our next visit, we would then go through his receipts checking that they matched with the money we had been sending him. The system was not watertight, but it was the best we could devise.

Then came the visit, three years into his time with us, when Rohan met us at the airport looking very shifty. He drove us to Ellerton and then announced that he needed to go back home to see his mother, who lived near Colombo. He had asked to do this a few times and we thought nothing of it until he had not reappeared after several days. We made a few enquiries and that was when we discovered that Rohan had emptied the house bank account, making off with £5,000 of our money. He had been well paid by Sri Lankan standards, but it turned out that he had fallen in with some very disreputable people who were making a lot more money than him from nefarious goings-on that involved prostitutes and a lot of drinking.

We asked about, seeking advice, and the universal advice was to steer clear of the police. However, Cary and I were employing quite a number of people by now and we felt it was crucial that we made it clear that if anyone stole from us, they were going to end up in court. So, off we went to the local police station, where we had a farcical meeting during which the police told us that they could arrest him, but could we lend them a car so that they could go and pick him up?

We did not provide their transport, but Rohan was arrested and was then subjected to due process, which in Sri Lanka is very long-winded. In all, he made 14 court appearances stretching over two-and-a-half years. Frequently he appeared before a different magistrate who had not a clue what the case was about. In the end, though, he was found guilty. He was given six months in prison, reduced for time already served, and was ordered to repay the money he had stolen from us, which we knew he never would.

As I have mentioned, Cary and I did not have a terribly high regard for Sri Lankan tourist drivers and this was not just because of our run-in with Rohan. The way things worked was that most of our guests would be met at Colombo airport by a driver, who would then be with them for the duration of their holiday, ostensibly to ferry them around although, as we were to find out, there were darker motives at play. It was also understood that the drivers would get free board and lodging wherever the guests they were driving were staying. In a lot of hotels this amounted to a scruffy room with three-up bunk beds, a cold shower and pretty basic food. We did it differently. Drivers staying with their guests at Ellerton were given a decent-sized room, with beds, hot showers, television, food and a big bottle of beer every night, and still they were ungrateful. This was pretty outrageous considering that without the visitors coming to Ellerton, and everywhere else in Sri Lanka for that matter, the drivers would be out of a job.

It took us a while to cotton on to one of the unspoken truths of Sri Lankan tourism: that drivers made a big chunk of their income from taking tourists to particular shops where the proprietors paid the drivers a generous commission on whatever their tourists bought. It was a system so ingrained in the country that, as I subsequently discovered, at the start of the season big travel agents would each decide which shops would be favoured by their drivers' patronage.

In every tourist centre a travel agent would select the jewellery shop to which all tourists travelling with their travel agency would be taken – another would be the batik shop, another the wood carving shop and so on. The travel agents, or their representative, would then go to each of these shops to share the good news before asking for a sizeable payment up-front as a fee for the commission the shop owners would be earning from the trade the drivers would be bringing them and we are talking of a payment equating to several thousand pounds. I could see that the whole thing was a racket controlled right at the top.

Kitty, born in the drain from Ellerton courtyard and a real survivor, but Pinky, her sister, was sadly ran over by a tuk tuk.

We had personal experience of this when Cary went shopping with Ken Hetti, who succeeded Rohan as our manager at Ellerton, fairly early on in his tenure with us. Unlike Rohan, Ken was utterly trustworthy and totally above board when it came to money. Cary was buying decorative furnishings for Ellerton and had asked Ken to help her transport all these bits and pieces. The shop they went to was one that Cary knew well, although Ken had never been there. She bought a lot of things, big stone jars and the like, but before they started back to Ellerton, Ken handed her a big wad of cash that he had been given by the proprietor of the shop which was the bung to Ken for taking Cary there even though Ken had not set foot inside the place until that day!

Shopkeepers handing out backhanders did not come as a surprise to me, but what did was how liquor control in Sri Lanka operated in a not dissimilar fashion. Alcohol consumption is a serious problem in the country and the statute books have incredibly strict laws as a consequence. No one can sell alcohol without a licence and nor can you transport or store it.

Calling again on my three terms of law studies at Trinity, I got hold of the actual legislation, read it and realised that it was all predicated on one basic assumption: that people would be selling booze. Since we were giving free drink at Ellerton, I did not see how the law could touch us, except that we were transporting it and storing more than the one case of alcohol permitted by the law. Having been told by everyone I spoke to that getting a liquor licence was a nightmare, I decided that we would not bother and would carry on as we were and that was an arrangement that lasted satisfactorily for 12 years.

Then someone ratted on us, tipping off the liquor police in Kandy, who raided Ellerton. The first thing they did was to help themselves to 15 cases of drink and then the officer in charge took our by now excellent manager aside and told him they were going to meet later to come to an arrangement. They did indeed meet. A deal was struck and we were left alone to continue handing out drinks as we always had. Nine months later, when I happened to be staying at Ellerton, a minibus pulled up in the drive and seven substantial men got out and introduced themselves as the liquor police from Colombo. They had obviously had another tip-off and the same thing happened all over again.

We explained that we already had an understanding with their colleagues in Kandy and that the scope of our understanding really could not stretch to coming to a similar understanding with them too. The upshot was another sit-down, this time with both the senior policemen who had raided Ellerton and we reached a collective understanding.

That, we thought, had to be the end of it. But five months later Ellerton had another liquor raid, this time from the police station at Gampola, a tinpot little place just down the road from the hotel. I think they knew they were chancing their arm, because they lacked the swagger of the chaps from Colombo. The Gampola raid, by comparison, was almost timid. Anyhow, they had to be brought into the arrangement as well. Apart from being scandalous, the whole situation was bordering on the farcical.

Another area of Sri Lankan legislation that I boned up on was employment law, specifically Employers' Provident Fund (EPF), the Sri Lankan equivalent of National Insurance. From my reading of the legislation, however, it was clear that EPF did not apply to us, since employers in private houses were not obliged to pay it and I reckoned Ellerton could still be classified as a private house.

This was what I told the smartly-dressed man who presented himself one day and said that he was from the Labour Office. Why was I not paying EPF for our staff, he wanted to know? And when I gave my reason, he protested that I had paying guests staying. As a guest in their country, I had a moral obligation to be paying EPF, the man told me. That was a fair point, I acknowledged, and asked if I could see him in his office in Gampola a couple of days later.

In I went as arranged, taking with me a list of all our staff and their salaries. My EPF man placed this on his desk and then opened a big ledger in which were listed all the staff on other tea estates in the area and the salaries that they were being paid and he began to compare my list with the ones in the ledger.

It did not take him long to announce his conclusion that we were paying our people too much! As far as I was concerned, we had met our moral obligations, but there was a new problem. He could not have such salaries in his area. His solution was to lower the official returns to show a 40 per cent reduction in Ellerton salaries!

To make sure that our staff understood the situation, I asked if he would come to Ellerton to explain his proposition. That all made sense and we then moved to recording the duties of the staff. Here things proved to be less straightforward. As a civil servant, the EPF man had a fixed way of doing things and since Ellerton was listed as a tea estate he tried to match our hotel jobs with the ones on his tea estate model.

From this, quite heated arguments developed. Never mind that they might end up paying higher levels of EPF, our staff were adamant that the level of importance and the status of their jobs should not be down-graded in any way!

In the end a settlement was reached, everyone was happy and for the rest of our time at Ellerton that continued to be the case. It was only when we were very

Much of the success of Ellerton could be attributed to the staff. We made a few mistakes along the way, but once we recruited Athula as our manager (second row, middle) he developed an exceptional team. Ben (front) was a perfect hotel dog, always ready to walk with the guests.

close to securing a sale at the end of our tenure that our would-be purchasers spotted that we had been paying less EPF than we should have been and asked me to deal with the matter in order for the sale to go through. The fact that it did not, and that in the end we sold Ellerton to someone else, does not diminish what I can now see was a serious mistake on my part.

Doing as our potential purchaser had asked, I presented myself at the Labour Office, explained that we had been paying less EPF than we should have done and asked if we could settle the balance to rectify matters. To begin with the EPF officials told us not to bother, that an arrangement had been reached, we had kept to that and there was nothing more to be done. This was when I should have backed off, should have explained their reply to our buyers and then suggested that we put a covenant in the sale contract to the effect that if the Labour Office ever demanded unpaid EPF contributions, I would pay whatever they were asking for.

But I did not do this. Instead I asked the Labour Office repeatedly to let me pay what was owed until they reluctantly agreed. Then it took them over a year to arrive at a figure, which could have been calculated in an afternoon. The sum demanded was not insignificant, being equivalent to £25,000. But with this calculation was the additional demand for a penalty payment of 50 per cent of the sum due!

I protested the injustice of this penalty charge, pointing out that it had been me, not the Labour Office, who had first raised the shortfall in our EPF payments and it had been me who had offered to pay what was outstanding there and then. It gives me no pleasure in reporting that our dispute with the Labour Office remains unsettled to this day!

In contrast to the somewhat irregular practices of dodgy officials, it is worth saying that one aspect of Sri Lankan government service that never failed to impress us was its health care provision. When Bandara, one of our two guards, was diagnosed with advanced cancer in his chest, no effort was spared in treating him. He was given radiotherapy, chemotherapy and a full range of cancer treatment that kept him alive for three more years. He was in and out of hospital a good deal during that time and none of his treatment cost Bandara a penny. This was deeply impressive.

Visiting Bandara was not my sole experience of Sri Lankan healthcare. On one occasion I found myself on an operating table after I had popped into Kandy to get some cash from the bank for the weekend. This was not the result of an accident that had happened while I was there; as it turned out my hospital admission in Kandy tracked back to two accidents in the UK.

Jon Wand, the excellent orthopaedic surgeon who had organised my treatment and care after the crash in *Pace Spirit* in 1984, had warned me that my hip had been so badly damaged in the crash that I would need a replacement within a few years. However, thanks to his good work and my own efforts to keep myself fit, the hip lasted until 2010. In the intervening quarter of a century Jon had moved hospitals and was now the senior orthopaedic surgeon in Cheltenham, not a million miles from our Herefordshire home. So, I went into hospital in Cheltenham where he gave me a replacement hip.

Eighteen months later, I was clearing decades of bird muck from our dovecote at Rhodds Farm, when I fell through the floor, severely wrenching and damaging both shoulders as I crashed down between the floor joists. So, once again Jon came to my aid. He had developed a speciality in treating shoulder injuries and sorted out mine just before Cary and I were due to leave for a visit to Ellerton.

Although I had become used to it, I had been feeling unwell since my hip operation. I kept going, hoping whatever it was would sort itself out, but I felt pretty rough for much of the time and it was clear that something was not right because my skin would erupt with boils for no apparent reason. The local clinic in Kington offered antibiotics, which I really do not like taking, but not once did anyone do a test to see what the problem might be.

Three years on from my hip operation, and one-and-half years after the shoulder one, Cary and I were staying at Ellerton when a big septic area developed underneath my thigh. Cary told me that I really had to get that seen to. So when I was next in Kandy I went to the slightly run-down Suwasevana private hospital. It was very efficient, though. I paid the equivalent of £2 to be seen by the duty doctor, who did not like the look of my thigh one little bit and sent me up to see the consultant, who happened to be on duty as well. He was an older, London-trained man, who examined me and said, 'We need to operate'. In other words, he needed to cut deep into this abscess to drain it.

Cary was mildly surprised when I telephoned her to explain that my brief shopping trip to Kandy would have to be extended because I was going under the surgeon's knife. And, within an-hour-and-a-half of walking into the hospital I was unconscious in the operating theatre. The cost for the entire procedure, plus dressings for a couple of days, was £214! There was an American surgeon staying at Ellerton at that time. When I told him what I had paid, he remarked that in his hospital back in the States the bill would have been $15,000.

The next day I went back to see the surgeon to have the wound dressed and he told me something very interesting. He had diagnosed what was wrong with me and had been making me feel sick for three years, caused the periodic eruption of boils and most recent abscess that he had treated.

He explained that for all that time I had been suffering from MRSA, a condition of which they had little experience in Sri Lanka because they saw it as a European problem. There were two courses of treatment. The most effective involved sitting in hospital for two weeks having doses of an intravenous antibiotic every six hours. That did not appeal to me in the slightest. Option two was a far less effective oral antibiotic. I opted for that and my MRSA was indeed cured.

When I got back home, I asked the local clinic why on earth no one had thought to test me when I had visited them on and off over the previous three years. They did not have an answer, apart from being extremely embarrassed. Jon was pretty sheepish too. Not only had I contracted MRSA when I was in hospital in Cheltenham having my hip replaced, when I was back in the same hospital 18 months later to have my shoulder seen to, no one had thought to test me then. After contracting MRSA, I had taken it back into the same hospital and back into the operating theatre and all because no one at any time had thought to test me.

Our cats and dogs, and their health and wellbeing, were an important part of our life at Ellerton. The cats were ahead of us because Kitty, our first cat was born in the space under the kitchen. A couple of years later he introduced his little brother Pinky, having extracted him from the wood pile and depositing him in the house, where he quickly made himself at home. In the same way that dogs had followed cats back home in the UK, Cary and I decided it would be good to have the company of dogs at Ellerton too. We thought it would be nice to give a home to a village dog and in part of the University grounds at Kandy a fantastic woman called Champa Fernando ran a charity called KACPAW that rescued dogs. She had masses of pens and sheds in which she housed over 200 waifs and strays she had taken in. She had rescued them from all over the place, had sterilised them, inoculated them and was now trying to find them homes; the University of Peradeniya itself had the principal veterinary school in the whole of Sri Lanka.

So, Cary and I arrived at KACPAW to be met by 200 dogs, all barking, all brown and white. My initial comment was, ‘Cary, how in hell do we choose?’. She spotted quite an attractive looking bitch and asked to look at her. We agreed that she would do and the deal was done. The dog was free, and we paid the equivalent of 75 pence for the collar. It was only when the dog was with us in the car, driving back to Ellerton, that it began frothing at the mouth.

We thought it could be rabies, or that the dog was just sick, as it was all over the car. Back at Ellerton, I opened the back door, and the dog got out to reveal that one back leg was just hanging limp and listless. The dog had been on the ground when it had been picked up and given to Cary, so neither of us had seen that it had a game leg. That setback was quickly followed by another: when I went to pick up the dog, it responded by biting me really hard, leaving a big wound on my hand. Given that it had been frothing at the mouth only half-hour earlier, this was not an auspicious start. Quite clearly it was not suitable to have around hotel guests, so the three of us piled into the car and back we went to KACPAW to arrange an exchange, once my hand had been bandaged.

Champa was back at the charity when we returned and explained that the dog that had bitten me had just arrived from the streets of Colombo, so she did not know anything about its history. And, by the way, I needed to go to the hospital to have the bite seen to. What about a replacement dog, I asked?

There was no problem about this and we were shown a very pretty dog, which we chose and called Polly (for Polonnaruwa in north central Sri Lanka). Polly was housed with a rather less appealing sister, but feeling pretty shocked from the bite, I decided that one dog was enough for the time being. So, we dealt with dog paperwork for a second time that day and, once Polly was ours, off I went to the Suwasevana private hospital where the duty doctor confirmed that having anti-

Our first dog was Polly, typical of a village dog who was friendly but whose loyalty was to herself!

Ellerton was perfectly suited for biking on a range of tracks and roads with spectacular scenery. It became an attraction for many guests staying with us.

rabies treatment was important. This comprised of five inoculations, all but the last of which I had there at Suwasevana, for the princely sum of £8 each. The final jab, in our local Kington clinic, cost £135.

Polly proved to be the perfect hotel dog. She was welcoming and friendly, but totally independent. In fact, she was such a success that when we saw an advertisement for Labrador puppies we decided one of these would be good to have at Ellerton. An irresistible litter of black, podgy Labrador puppies, obviously in very good health, were just living on a flat roof in Kandy. We bought one and he became Ben, after Bentota on Sri Lanka's southwest coast.

Unfortunately Polly was still coming into season, which was sending poor Ben to distraction, so Cary arranged for her to be fully sterilised at the university vetinary department. They were taken straight into the operating room with not one but eight operating tables all occupied by dogs in various stages of surgical procedure. It was not a sight for the faint-hearted and Cary, fortunately, was not perturbed by the blood all over the floor and dogs howling and yelping as they objected vehemently to being held down while their anaesthetics were administered. Cary had to help pin Polly to her table when the vet came along to anaesthetise her. Then she had to hold Polly while the operation took place with blood pouring everywhere. But, with Polly sewn up and groggily coming around, the bill came to just £8.

Ben took his duties seriously and one day he had gone for a walk with some guests when their driver went looking for them, since Sri Lankan drivers always want to have control of their guests. He went ballistic when he was told that they had gone off with Ben. The driver went charging around Ellerton, swearing that he would sort out that Ben well and truly for pinching his tourists and in his unspoken imagination taking them shopping and collaring the backhander from the shop owner that was rightfully his. He kept up his effing and blinding until a member of our staff brought his tantrum to a halt by pointing out that the Ben his tourists had gone off with was the hotel dog!

With Ben on the steps of Ellerton. He established himself as 'top dog' in the area, mainly because he was rather larger and better fed than the local village dogs!

If you had taken Ben in his prime to a smart shoot in England, people would have commented on what a handsome dog he was and Ellerton guests were not the only ones to think so. Lady dogs in the area thought Ben was a bit of all right and when he was about two-and-a-half he took up sex incredibly seriously. There was one night when a terrible cacophony of howling broke out around Ellerton and when this was investigated five bitches were found staked out on the veranda at two o'clock in the morning all demanding Ben! We had not realised, but apparently if one bitch is in season, she can turn others to be in season at the same time. No wonder Ben would come home looking well and truly exhausted from some of his forays! The morning after this episode with his visiting fan club, Cary took Ben down to the vets to have the procedure that would put a stop to his rampant wanderings. It was the only sensible thing to do, although our staff thought it was appalling to deprive a 'man' of his natural urges.

Ben lived up to expectations in every respect: he was indeed just the kind of friendly Labrador you would expect to be greeted by when you arrived to stay at an English country house. Cary and I never lost sight of that original idea and there was a time, when I envisaged us having much longer stays at Ellerton, that I looked into shipping one of my old Bentleys out there to serve as our car. This was not such a curious idea as it might first appear to be. Cars in Sri Lanka were eye-wateringly expensive because of a 270 per cent import tax that was slapped on cars brought into the country, but that was based on their cost when new! The Bentley was also a tough old car and easy to maintain, so I felt sure that running it in Sri Lanka would be no more difficult that running it at home. Then there was the obvious tie-in with Ellerton's colonial past. T he Bentley would be the perfect car to evoke bygone years that appealed to a great many of the people who came to stay.

So, I took myself off to Colombo to look into how much it would cost to bring the Bentley into the country and keep it there. One of the first problems I encountered was that you are not supposed to import cars that are more than three years old. My Bentley was getting on for 70. I spent a totally frustrating day-and-a-bit speaking to various government officials. I went to talk to the head of the customs division, the minister of finance and to the chap who ran the port and to the Automobile Association of Sri Lanka but I could not persuade anyone to get their head round the issues of importing a 70-year-old Bentley.

In the end, it proved to be too difficult and the Bentley remained with its fellow cars in my garage back home, enjoying the occasional outing around the country lanes of Herefordshire, rather than spending its sunset years meandering through the tropical byways of Sri Lanka.

Chapter 21

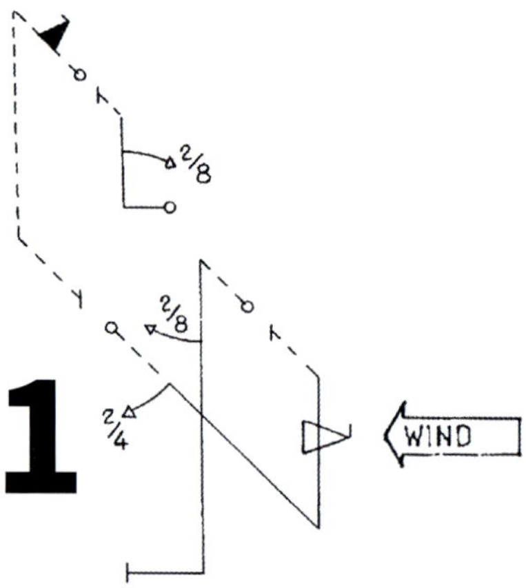

GRACE, SPACE, PACE

I have very good reasons for being grateful to Cambridge: lifelong friendships that started there, a degree of course (even if it was formalized somewhat later than it should have been) and the beginnings of my enthusiasm for cars.

Cars have been an important part of my life ever since my undergraduate days, and at a rough count I have owned around 80 to date, many unremarkable and some downright awful!

As has been described elsewhere, I drove to Cambridge in a Standard 10 van, but it was hardly a memorable vehicle. However, late in my first year, my Aunt Muriel's bequest of £300 gave me the only money, or indeed anything else, that I have ever inherited. Then, as today, Jaguar sports cars probably gave the best combination of performance and cachet for the money, so I went out and bought an XK 150 Drop Head. Thus 675 HPC entered my life: bright red, slightly tatty, but at the time perfect for me, and one of the better undergraduate cars, particularly given that undergraduates were not permitted cars unless there were exceptional circumstances.

Interestingly, Robert Woods bought a 150 Fixed Head some months later, and then we heard that there was another 150 Fixed Head owned by a Selwyn undergraduate. We did not think much of Selwyn, mainly because it had a strong background of educating people for the Church, but our view of the car's owner radically altered when we heard that he had changed the engine and gearbox by himself. This is a major job, and certainly one that we would not have attempted solo. That was how we came to meet James Mehew and how he became a lasting friend.

All three of our Jaguars were pretty rough and ready: none of them had bodywork in great shape. In fact, James was driving with his girlfriend, slowly thank goodness, when he went around a bend, the passenger door sprang open and she slid out sideways to be dumped unceremoniously at the side of the road.

A very interesting development in my life began in the car park of the University Library when I spotted a 120 roadster (registered LXH 6), again bright red, which had clearly been sitting there for some time. It looked very unloved with not even a tonneau cover to protect the interior. I felt it a shame to leave a car like this to decay further and with Murray Kenyon decided to see if it could be made to go. With clean fuel and a charged battery, we short-circuited the ignition key and, rather to our surprise, it leapt into life! It had good oil pressure, water remained in the engine and radiator, and it did seem that the engine had survived the neglect.

A couple of days, and a few pints later, it seemed a shame not to see if the car would move. Murray and I removed a couple of the wheels which had flat tyres, pumped them up, restarted the engine and did a couple of laps around the car park. Everything had gone well, so we retired for a celebratory beer. The car clearly needed

675 HPC, my first Jaguar was an XK 150 Drop Head of which I was extremely proud. It was noteworthy in Cambridge as undergraduates were not allowed cars. It certainly seemed to impress Caroline Richardson!

some exercise and we concluded that it would be very short-sighted simply to leave it where it was. We hatched a plan to check everything a bit more thoroughly, change the oil and then take it to the disused airfield at Bourne, which had a good perimeter track where we felt the XK could be given a proper run. This plan was put into action and we drove to Bourne (of course not actually stealing the car since we had every intention of returning it) and spent a good hour or so around the track before driving the 120 back to its now familiar home at the University Library.

Inevitably this jaunt was repeated a couple more times, until it became apparent that we were probably not being that wise. The car of course had no road tax or insurance and even I felt that it would be prudent to regulate the position. After making discreet enquiries of the various college porters, I discovered that it was registered to an Ernest Wolfgang Brauch, a former postgraduate student in John's, who had gone down a year before. Further detective work revealed that he was now running a business called International Colloids, on the Charing Cross Road in London.

I wrote to him, asking if he remembered an old Jaguar that he seemed to have left behind in Cambridge and whether I could simplify his life by taking it off his hands. He invited me to meet him. So I went to London and found that he had rather smart offices and seemed to be running a not insignificant company for a relatively young man. This was partly explained when he was subsequently charged with major financial fraud, which imprinted his name on my mind. Anyway, after a certain amount of negotiation, the princely sum of £60 was agreed; I paid and LXH 6 was mine!

A more detailed inspection followed, and it became clear to me that bodily the car was excellent, although the paint was faded and dull. The engine ran well but was tired and, of course, the interior was finished. However, my new purchase was certainly the basis for an excellent car. The next problem was that the library porters finally woke up to what was going on and presented me with an ultimatum. If the car was mine, I had better remove it from Cambridge; if it was not, then I should keep my hands off it!

At that stage I found a friendly man called Eddie Welch, who ran a small car repair business outside Cambridge. Eddie had little time for undergraduates, but he did rather approve of an undergraduate who owned not one XK but two, even though both cars were far from immaculate and, more than that, an undergraduate who was prepared to get his hands dirty working on them. So, we came to an agreement whereby he would restore and paint the bodywork and, in exchange, would give me space in his workshop to restore the mechanics.

I had never done anything like that, but my experience in the Swaziland workshops had given me the confidence to tackle almost any mechanical work. Compared with working on classic cars today, back then there was very little support for their restoration, both in terms of parts and expertise, so one was very much on one's own. I realised I needed quite a lot of spare parts, but also wanted a good engine, and indeed wire-wheels. Hunting around in south London, I found a roadworthy but somewhat tired XK 140 Drop Head, with a rather good registration OLO 9. So, I bought this, took it to Eddie's yard and began dismantling it firstly to get the engine, which was one of the quite desirable 'C-types'.

In the meantime, Eddie had done an excellent job of the body and, after a few months' work which had somewhat inhibited my studies, my 120 was ready for its maiden test drive. The first problem occurred after about six miles, when the right-hand front wheel detached itself at 60 miles an hour, shot across the road and through a fence, ending up well off the road. It transpired that we had made the fairly fundamental error of putting the entire right-hand front suspension onto the left side and vice versa so the 'knock-off' simply unwound itself. After a while, I decided that the 120 was a much nicer car than the 150 besides which running two XKs was somewhat of an extravagance for an undergraduate. So, 675 HPC went, but it had served me very well.

Having left Cambridge, I decided to go and live in Paris and took the 120. It was a perfect car for Paris, and of course rather glamorous to the fairer sex. I also took it on a number of continental tours, including a celebrated one when Robert Woods drove out to Paris in his 120 (HBL 128) and we set off together for the Monaco Grand Prix.

We followed a very roundabout route, with a lot of pretty competitive driving between the two cars. Some 60 kilometres short of the Mediterranean coast, an ominous rumbling could be heard from the engine of HBL which became worse and worse until it was obvious that a big end had failed. So, LXH became a tow car to take HBL into Monte Carlo, where we had arranged with some family friends of Robert's to sleep in an annexe of their house.

Having installed ourselves, we began working on the car in their drive. We removed the sump, found the destroyed big end and concluded there was nothing we could do to repair it. With a little lateral thinking, however, we did come up with what seemed to be the brilliant idea of converting the car into a five-cylinder XK, by totally removing that piston and connecting rod and simply blocking the crankshaft oilway with rubber and jubilee clips. However, as those

The consequences of drink and over-exuberance. Peter Wright, later of Lotus Grand Prix fame, had his arm out of the left-hand door and still feels twinges of pain.

who know Jaguar engines will confirm, you cannot extract a piston downwards which means you first have to remove the cylinder head.

This seemed far too much work and, knowing that the piston was aluminium, we thought it a good idea to attempt to smash it into pieces, through the spark plug hole! Extraordinarily, this worked and, after a lot of hammering, the entire piston, now reduced to small pieces, was removed. The sump was then reinstalled and the engine started, naturally with vibration, but the solution was quite acceptable! Sadly, though, we had missed a small piece of the piston. This was sucked into the oil pump, which broke open and that was it. So, HBL was towed again, this time to the SNCF station where we had to leave it to be transported back to Paris.

Then, driving overnight back to Paris, a valve dropped into the combustion chamber of LXH, and that was that for my 120. As a result of an unfortunate mishap, related later, we did happen to have a 3.8 Jaguar engine sitting in the partially burned-out wreck of a Mark IX, which was now marooned outside our flat. So, I found a man with a large tripod and a block and tackle and in the Paris street we put that 3.8 engine into the XK!

This amalgamation of parts continued as my faithful companion. It put up with a lot, including very amateur club racing and serving as my everyday transport for several years. It was with Peter Wright and his girlfriend (soon-to-be-wife) Mel that Marion and I drove down to Spain for a holiday one summer. I was still working in Paris and, for reasons that I cannot remember, decided that the car for the trip was a Mk I Jaguar, which I had just bought in south London for 50 quid. Two days before we were due to leave, I telephoned Peter to tell him this. 'The good news is I've bought a Mk I Jag,' Peter recalls me announcing. 'The bad news is that we've got to change the crank on it!'

My rather fast and tuned XK 120. From my dress you can see that the car was extremely exposed and also note the Andorran licence plates which seemed to be accepted by everyone, including the police!

This meant that I had to drive the car up to where Peter and Mel were living in Lincolnshire, where we took out the engine, suspending it from the branch of a tree, and removed the crankshaft. Somehow, somewhere, we managed to get it reground and fitted with new bearings. Back in went the engine. The four of us piled into the car and off we drove to Spain. In those days I took a somewhat relaxed approach to vehicle registration and on this trip to Spain I 'acquired' a set of Andorran number plates which proved to be very useful on various cars I would later own. The Mk I had a split front bumper and I had the first part of the registration number attached to one bumper and the second half attached to the other bumper. Inevitably, I suppose, somewhere on the way to the Channel I was pulled over by the police for having an inadequately number-plated car. After a certain amount of 'persuasion' they gave up and let us go, on the grounds that I lived in Paris and I was taking the car to France.

MOD JOB

I was now getting pretty serious about the Jaguar Drivers' Club and, on one trip back to England from Paris, I went to a Jaguar Drivers' Club meeting at Silverstone where there was a cheerful but somewhat rough bunch from Wales. It turned out that they owned a Jaguar garage in Risca, west of Cwmbran, and were racing a very modified XK 120. This car was clearly quick in the Modsports category, where you were allowed to do quite a lot of modifications. It had extremely wide wheels, but with crudely chopped-out wheel arches, a modified E-type engine and six exhaust pipes exiting menacingly and noisily just behind the left-hand front wheel. However, it was becoming less competitive against E-types, which were then appearing and in consequence had been put up for sale. I could see that it would make a marvellous road car and duly bought it.

Towing it back to Eddie Welch's garage on the other side of the country was an interesting exercise, for which I enlisted the help of Allan Johnson. It was going to be a long drive home, with me in my 120 and Allan at the wheel of my new acquisition, registration number TAL 81. To minimise the inevitable jolts and jerks, I had brought along a tow rope with a degree of elasticity; quite a generous degree as it turned out. This proved to be very satisfactory until we came to our first and really quite sizeable roundabout. I was used to the smart acceleration of my 120 and, spotting a gap in the traffic, shot off. Still completely stationary, Allan watched in fascination as I whizzed round the roundabout. It was only when the tow rope was taut, pretty much bisecting the roundabout, that its elasticity gave out. Off shot Allan, as if fired from a catapult, frantically wrestling with the steering wheel in the days long before power steering, as he grappled with the enormous tyres to keep the car on the tarmac while circuiting the roundabout and not bounding across the grass in the middle.

Eddie Welch did a marvellous job in making really elegant wheel arches, while we preserved TAL's more streamlined positioning of the headlights directly into the front of each wing. With the car came a set of D-type aluminium wheels, but significantly wider than those on a normal XK, and these were fitted. The boys from Wales obviously had good contacts at the back door of Jaguar's racing department and offered me a very special (but not wide-angle) cylinder head as a separate deal, together with three large Weber carburetors. It was quite a job fitting the carburetors, which involved cutting away part of the wing and fabricating a cold-air scoop, rather like the Weber-equipped C-types.

With the work finished, as hoped the car proved to be a great one and served me well. I took it on a number of Continental trips, one of which was to the Nürburgring, where I raced against a variety of cars (Mercedes Gullwings, Ferrari 250 SWB, et cetera) whose value today is enormous. With the new cylinder head, it was extremely quick, but, frankly, both noisy and very wind-swept with only aero-screens.

I sold it to a very keen Frenchman who asked me to bring it to Heathrow and meet him off a Paris flight. We took it up the slip road to the M4, on which we reached somewhat over 120mph. Turning round at the roundabout, in a matter of minutes he was back at the terminal, where he delved into his briefcase and gave me a plastic bag filled with a lot of sterling notes at a time when the French had strict exchange controls and said that I must deliver the car to Paris within four weeks! Of course, I did.

HEAD SPACE

It is probably appropriate at this stage to mention Lord's Garage. Robert Woods and I met a charming and elderly Jewish businessman at a drinks party, and he told us that he owned a defunct garage on the main road going north through St John's Wood, very close to Lord's Cricket Ground. He was waiting to get planning permission to develop it, and indeed subsequently made a huge amount of money when it became the Wellington Hospital! But he said that we were very welcome to make any use of the site in the meantime, which was an absolute revelation.

Lord's Garage provided us with a large central workshop where we could work on four cars at one time and up to 40 or so lock-ups that we could use. So, Robert, James Mehew and I moved our car operations there, established a company called

GWM Motors to enable us to get trade discounts on purchases, and none of it cost us a penny! The garage was also a good social gathering point and perfect for rowdy parties, although we tended to meet there at least a couple of times a week in any case.

In the end, we were there for seven years before our benefactor asked us to leave, now having got his planning permission. Having been given notice, we duly packed up. But there were a few of the lock-ups which had been very firmly locked during our time and so we had never investigated them. Given everything was about to be bulldozed, I asked our benefactor for permission to open these up, and he told me to help myself.

Incredibly, in one of them I found a well preserved HSM (High Speed Motors) from the mid-1930s. The story is complex, but the Alfa Romeo 8C 'Monza' was the sports-racing car of the '30s with an extraordinary specification, having eight cylinders, twin overhead cams, twin superchargers and a very impressive record in international racing. Triumph in the UK came up with a proposal, engineered by Donald Healey, whereby Triumph would take the design of the 'Monza' and Alfa Romeo would manufacture Triumph motorcycles in Italy. Healey brought the designs and, with some modifications, a few were constructed. It is believed three complete cars and six engines were built before Triumph's financial problems caused the project to be cancelled.

Two of the cars were rebodied as HSMs, and what I had discovered was one of them. Of course it had been sitting in the lock-up for years and was covered with dust, but even then clearly had value. I asked our benefactor what to do, and he said that the owner had long since disappeared, had not paid rent for years and I could help myself. But I already had a problem with garaging three cars and reluctantly I had to leave it. More recently that car was sold at auction for, I recollect, more than £600,000!

Apart from the Mark IX we had in Paris, I have owned a number of saloon Jaguars including Mark Is and IIs with various engine capacities and several of the big saloons, mainly Mark VIIs.

Over the years, I owned a number of XJs. These were incredible cars, particularly considering the limited resources Jaguar had to develop them. The XJ 6 was a bit anaemic, and the XK engine was definitely getting long in the tooth. But the XJ 12 was a fantastic achievement, and arguably the best saloon car in the world in its day. Shortly after the XJ 12 was announced, Mike Elliott, my North London motor dealer friend, was able to borrow a demonstrator from a friend in the trade which we took to Alsace for a wine tour. So, five-up, with beers chilling

A very rare Daimler Double-Six coupe, an extraordinary long-distance car in which I averaged 97mph from London to the Lake District one Christmas Day.

on the air-conditioning outlets and sitting at 120mph on the autoroute, fuel consumption barely into two figures, we sped across France. What a car!

Probably the only XJ worth an individual mention was my last one, a Daimler Double-Six Coupe. Absolutely the top of the range, this version was fitted with rather better seats and trim, obviously with the V12 engine and the very rare two-door coupe body. I mildly tuned the engine and suspension and decided to put in a sunroof.

One Christmas I had been invited to stay with my girlfriend, Cressida, and her family in the Lake District and had agreed to arrive before lunch. However, I got up very early on Christmas morning; the Daimler was full of fuel and I set off well before five o'clock. I recollect that the distance, door to door, from my flat in Manchester Square to the other side of Keswick was 304 miles, and, including a fuel stop, it took me three hours nine minutes – not quite 100 miles an hour average. My hosts were rather surprised when I arrived well in time for breakfast.

Of the E-type Jaguars that I owned, the most distinctive was unquestionably the modified one that had formerly belonged to Dick Protheroe. He was a very capable racing driver (almost always in Jaguars) who had four E-types which he raced very successfully and typically with the registrations CUT 7 and CUT 8. Sadly, he was killed at Oulton Park driving a Ferrari and I heard that his widow, Rosemary, was selling his last E-type. I went to meet her and found that it was indeed a very interesting car with a Fixed Head body, a high-performance wide-angle cylinder head but I believe uniquely, it had a 4.2-litre block and a synchromesh gearbox, with overdrive. The car was pretty lightweight with a glass fibre bonnet and doors; the rear door was replaced by a sheet of Perspex. Behind the doors were air scoops to duct air to the inboard rear disc brakes, always a weak point when racing E-types.

I immediately fell for it, and bought the car for a very reasonable £875. My aim was to use it as a road car so I put in sound-deadening, replaced the plastic doors with steel ones, but otherwise left it very much as I found it. What is very curious is that there have been a number of articles published about the 'Protheroe E-types' and none has ever mentioned this particular car although it clearly was an E-type that had belonged to Dick Protheroe and I bought it from his widow! It certainly was an epic car to drive and was faster than almost anything on the roads in the early 1970s.

The principal drawback of this E-type was that it liked to drink as much as we did. When it was being pushed, the fuel consumption seldom rose above 12 miles to the gallon! So, when a group of us drove to Sicily to watch the celebrated Targa Florio, I drove the E-type as far as Rome, where I was able to leave it with Robert Woods's cousin, who was then the New Zealand ambassador in Italy. With my E-type and Robert's 120 in safe hands, we carried on down to Sicily in the Mk VII Jaguar owned by the ambassador's brother and our great mate, Kik Woods, and James Mehew's 120.

The Targa Florio was a classic road race that took place over 40 or so miles of mountain and village roads in Sicily. It was incredibly exciting to watch and more than a little dangerous at times, because spectators used to crowd the roadside as these high-powered GT cars tore past in clouds of dust and sometimes no more than a few feet away. We were in a trattoria the night before the race having a few drinks and something to eat when a couple of chaps sauntered in carrying Thompson sub-machineguns. James, Allan and Marion decided that they were not going to hang about and left in James's 120 but the rest of us stayed and had quite a few drinks with these guys conversing in a kind of pidgin English.

In the very early 1950s, Mike Salmon was an apprentice at Jaguar, but clearly better off than most since he was able to buy a new XK 120 off the production line. He raced it with some success, aided by his close relationships with the right people in the Competitions Department, who provided him with the parts that he needed for extra performance. However, he soon began hankering for even more performance, which inevitably meant a C-type Jaguar, so the 120 was sold.

It went through a variety of hands and had one quite major accident, before ending up with a fellow who decided to make the 'ultimate XK'. He totally restored the car and then fitted a proper D-type engine with slightly modified suspension. The engine was somewhat mongrel, although the individual parts were completely genuine. It had one of the very rare 3-litre cylinder blocks but taken out to 3.8 litres, correct inlet manifold and 45 DCOE Webers. He used it very little, became bored and sold it to a London motor trader from whom I bought it. Rather like TAL, it was very quick, but also rather noisy, and with the basic problem of having original 120 drum brakes which were not up to the performance of the car. I always saw it as a car that I would keep for the very long term, but after some 25 years was approached by a Continental motor trader. He seemed very keen to purchase it and was prepared to pay what then seemed to be a huge amount of money at the time, although it was rather less than I would have got today!

SWITCHBACK

If you taxed and insured an XK 120, but actually owned two, it was simpler and cheaper to use one at a time and move the registration plate. It was during my Bradbury Wilkinson days selling banknotes when I was making frequent visits to Africa, that the germ of an idea came into my head. On my next trip I took

My ex-Protheroe E-type Jaguar, not one of the genuine 'Lightweight E-types' but it was a delight to drive. It went from a dawn start in Boulogne to dinner in Rome that evening.

Here is the yellow E-type going over the St Gothard pass in spring, still with lots of snow.

the papers of my E-type with me. Finding myself with time on my hands one morning in Kigali (the capital of Rwanda), I went to the local vehicle licensing office and asked if I could register the E-type.

Naturally the official I approached asked me where the car was and when I said it was in England, he explained that it would be impossible to register it in Rwanda. However, a 50-dollar bill slipped across the counter gave him pause for reflection and I ended up with a complete set of paperwork and indeed a pair of licence plates from Rwanda! When I got home, I put these onto the car and drove around the UK and Europe, oblivious to the attention of the police. Of course when I sold the E-type, or more accurately swapped it for my first Aston Martin, a DB5, I kept the plates and have them still.

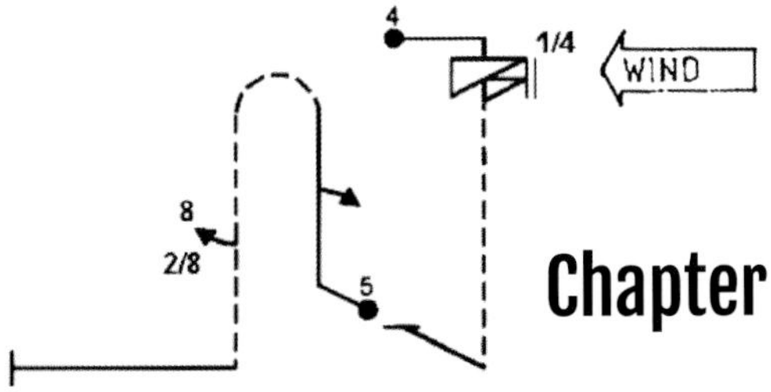

Chapter 22

KEEPING THE WHEELS TURNING – FOUR AND TWO

The Tata Safari that we used at Ellerton was like many of the cars I have owned, in that it was a pretty awful but pragmatic solution to circumstances at the time.

This Tata was an Indian apology for a Discovery and I bought it mainly because it was relatively cheap in an environment where cars are subject to such a punishing import tax. But it was a tough old girl. I crashed it once and our staff did so twice, but it kept going. However, the interesting part was that, after eight or so years, pretty much every mechanical part was totally worn out and by coincidence I came across a little business which would import from the UK the front half of an accident-damaged Land Rover and then the rear half of another one. They would then buy up an old army Land Rover chassis which had a serial number, so legitimising the vehicle, and buy engines, gearboxes, axles, et cetera from crashed Mitsubishi Pajeros and assemble a car out of the pieces. I explained that my Tata still had a reasonable body but was dying mechanically and came to an agreement whereby they would remove the entire body, throw away all mechanical parts, replace them with Mitsubishi parts and put the body back on again. The idea was good, and to an extent worked, although inevitably all sorts of parts did not quite fit with each other, but at least it gave another few years of life.

When it comes to cars, my first love has always been the Jaguar marque which is why my Jaguars have been given a chapter all to themselves. This does not mean to say that I do not have fond (and some not so fond) memories of other cars and other vehicles over the years, going right back to Barry, the Standard 10 van I owned in 1965.

Cars have been such an important part of my life that although I could write reams about different marques and models that have come my way, it would be unwise, not to say unkind to readers to do that. What follows are A to Z snapshots of the cars (and the friends associated with them) that are most firmly lodged in my memory.

When we got married in 1987, Cary and I gave each other a little 1926 Austin Chummy, which I had persuaded Robert Woods to sell. He had owned it for over 20 years, so it has had only two owners for the last 50. It was such a sweet little car, but of course incredibly slow. On the other hand, who is in a rush to get anywhere?

A much more exciting Austin 7 followed later, an 'Ulster', a real giant-killing little car that did terribly well in contemporary racing. With all of 32hp, rather than the anaemic 13hp of the Chummy, it had a reasonable turn of speed. And 60mph in an Ulster is rather more exciting than 130mph in a Ferrari, particularly with the brakes of an Austin 7 which do little to alter the speed of the vehicle!

I have had a love-hate relationship with Aston Martins, which I can say with a certain amount of assurance having owned quite a few. When people see the astronomical prices that are demanded and indeed seem to be offered, for

The little Austin 'Chummy' that Cary and I gave to each other as our wedding present. It is extremely slow and the brakes leave much to be desired but it is immensely charming.

One of the many Aston Martins that I owned, here in a rather undignified role competing in a muddy autocross at a Welsh village fair. The locals found it hard to believe that such a car should compete!

old Astons, there would seem to be an underlying assumption that they were incredibly good cars. In many ways they were not too bad in the sense of gorgeous looks, fine leather interiors and reasonable performance, but like so many limited-production cars they suffered terribly from a lack of development. And of course, I am somewhat jaundiced since in the 1970s we were buying quite good DB5s and DB6s for around £1,500.

But they did have problems not least of which was that the bodies were built on the Italian 'Superlegerra' principle, whereby there was a steel platform chassis and then a framework of tiny steel tubes onto which hand-beaten aluminium panels were laid. The idea was good, but unless the steel and aluminium were kept well separated, one inevitably got electrolytic corrosion, with the aluminium suffering first. Also, there was lamentably little corrosion proofing on the steel chassis which corroded appallingly. Dynamically, these Astons were not much good either, and certainly they were far from being a genuine sports car.

At one stage I owned an Aston Martin with a truly unique history. It was a DB3 that had done 24,000 miles when it came into my ownership. Interestingly, it was

(Above) The DB3 with extraordinary pedigree having been owned by three separate custodians of Aston Martin! One could not do much better than that.

(Below) An Aston DB5 in a very non-standard bright yellow. They were, and are, extremely elegant but are now, I feel, absurdly overvalued!

not a car that I bought: this Aston was given to me (along with an aeroplane that I did not particularly like) as payment in lieu of money for my aerobatic display flying for Proteus Petroleum. Proteus had been formed by Victor Gauntlett who was also the owner of Aston Martin at the time. Indeed, the car I was given had belonged to him. What made it particularly special, though, was that it had also been owned by Alan Curtis and Peter Livanos, the two previous owners of Aston Martin. So, my DB3 had been owned by the three men who themselves had owned and transformed the fortunes of the Aston Martin company. This was a pedigree that caught the attention of Simon Draper, Richard Branson's cousin, Branson's partner in the founding of Virgin Records, and the owner of the world's best collection of Aston Martins. He made me a very good offer for that DB3, and now owns it.

One of my DB5s has embedded itself in my memory for somewhat different reasons. I was living on the Fulham Road at the time I owned that particular car and, driving into work one day, I had just come off a roundabout and was accelerating along a dual carriageway vaguely aware of a pedestrian bridge that crossed above it about 100 yards in front. It was just as well that my eyes were on the road ahead because I suddenly saw at the side of the road an elderly man, who was rather laboriously heaving himself over the Armco barrier before stepping out into the fast lane. I swerved and just avoided running into him but went into the Armco and three other cars piled into the remains.

With the rear quarter of one side of my Aston written off, feeling pretty shaken and really very angry, I assailed the old boy who had caused the accident, asking what on earth he thought he was doing walking across a dual carriageway in the rush hour. I pointed to the bridge and suggested he use that. 'Sorry, governor,' he wheezed. 'I've got this heart condition'!

I have always had a soft spot for Bentleys and I believe that the best car of the 1930s was the Derby Bentley. Bentley went bust in 1930 and was bought in a very underhand fashion by Rolls-Royce who were keen to stop the 8-litre Bentley, which was arguably a better car than the Rolls-Royce Phantom II. However, as part of the deal, Bentley himself had to work for Rolls-Royce for five years and a plan was developed whereby the Rolls-Royce 20–25 was significantly improved into a 'silent sports car', using the Bentley name. And of course, being made in Derby, these cars became known as Derby Bentleys. Some other cars of the 1930s might have been faster, some had better brakes, et cetera, but on balance, there is a very good case for saying that it was the best.

Rolls-Royce was seldom innovative, but were extraordinarily thorough in the development and perfection of a car and it really shows. Also the 1930s were the

The Derby Bentley, made by Rolls-Royce, was in the view of many the best all-round car of the 1930s. This saloon was followed by two open-top Derbys, which are among my favourites.

pinnacle of British coach-building and some truly beautiful bodies (of course all were 'coach-built' and Bentley only made the chassis) were mounted on these cars. I began with a Thrupp and Maberly saloon (the saloons have always been less desirable than the open and more sporting bodies), into which the previous owner had poured money, not particularly judiciously, and then ran out of funds and enthusiasm.

One problem with most cars of that era, of course long before motorways (except in Germany), is that they tend to be very under-geared. A ready solution is to fit an overdrive, a small gearbox behind the normal gearbox, giving a 'longer' fifth gear. I then bought an open Derby, a 'Continental Tourer' from Van den Plas, one of the prettiest Derby bodies, but still very light giving good performance. The car had had a remarkable history, in that it had been the everyday transport of David 'Bunty' Scott-Moncrieff, whose company tag-line was 'Purveyors of Horseless Carriages to the Nobility and Gentry since 1927'. He called the car 'Charlotte' and I have of course retained the name. Under his ownership, it completed some epic journeys including right around the Mediterranean, around Albania and indeed a long way across Russia. He had sold Charlotte to buy a twelve-cylinder Hispano-Suiza which he bitterly regretted after a couple of days.

Charlotte was then joined by an H J Mulliner 'concealed drophead'. Rather than having a big hood-bag sticking up at the back of the car, luggage and interior space were sacrificed with the hood folded and hidden under a streamlined metal cover. Additionally there were no running boards with long sweeping wings.

The first of these cars was the star of the 1934 Motor Show, but I suspect it was simply too radical for the average and rather conservative buyer, and only four were made. However, to modern eyes it is a gorgeous car and of course has all the other advantages of a Derby.

In the mid-1980s BMW came up with the concept of 'M' cars with the first BMW M5. The idea was a modest saloon car body, but with racing-car-derived engine, brakes and suspension. The first two generations of M5 were literally hand-built. They took a new body shell to a separate 'motorsport' plant where two highly-skilled specialists would build the car by hand. In addition to the mechanical improvements, the interiors were more luxurious with extra leather. But they were expensive. My first M5, bought in 1987, had cost £34,000 when new in the UK a couple of years before. But what a car it was, one which was capable of outrunning any other saloon car, while looking totally modest on the outside. They were built in very small numbers and are now very sought-after.

BMW then extended the programme with the new M5, featuring a later body, more power, but again hand-built. Very rare were the estate-car versions (all left-hand drive), and I bought one of these in around 1995. Sadly, it was stolen in central London and I was lucky to be able to replace it very quickly with another. This was one of the equally rare 'Elekta' limited-edition cars built for the Italian market. Only 20 were ever made: 10 finished in green with brown interior and the other 10 silver with dark blue interior, which was totally leather, even covering the roof. In those days, I found that it was much cheaper to buy a German-supplied car a couple of years old than a similar car in the UK, and there were various motor traders in north London specialising in importing these used cars.

I owned my last M5 in the late-1990s, again a fantastic car and certainly quicker than any saloon car of its day. However, the first few cars made had a problem with their pistons which led to them being recalled by the manufacturer but, since I had bought mine in Germany and brought it into the UK, no one told me about this. The piston problem did not affect the performance of the car, but did make it very greedy with oil. In the end my M5 was suffering a little through ferrous acne and I advertised it for sale. It was bought by a curious Chechen, who paid with a bag full of cash, filled the car with fuel and set off for Grozny where being a left-hand drive car was presumably going to be an advantage.

I owe a special debt of thanks to my Bristol. It was the car in which I picked up Cary when I first took her to dinner and the car that began to persuade her that Richard Goode might be somewhat more civilised than the petrolhead E-type owner who had scared the wits out of her when he drove her back to London, too fast and too dangerously, from a weekend with friends in the country.

I owned two Bristols. The first was a rather nice 403 from the early 1950s. Beautifully made and obviously a product of an aircraft business, it used a development of the pre-war BMW two-litre engine which Bristol took as its own version of war reparations; but it was quite a big car for a relatively small engine.

Later I had a 411 (Series III) as everyday transport for a number of years. Again, this was beautifully made, but with a six-litre Chrysler engine which gave it a very respectable performance, although it returned somewhat ruinous fuel consumption if the performance was used. In their day, these cars were marketed as being suitable for four six-foot men and their luggage, and certainly it was capacious and an ideal car for long-distance journeys.

This car subsequently involved me in a rather bizarre murder case. At White Waltham airfield I was approached by a very pleasant Australian called David Martin, who had set up a very successful business making the sound systems for rock concerts. We fell into conversation; he was clearly admiring the Bristol and asked how much something like that would cost. I added 50 per cent onto what I thought my car was worth. Within a couple of minutes, he asked if he could buy it and a few minutes later it was sold!

My second Bristol, a 411 was a real 'gentleman's carriage' and served me well, implying to Cary that I was more civilised than she remembered from our first date.

However, David Martin was a curious and somewhat lonely man. He would often phone in the middle of the night just to chat, and would come up with curious propositions such as saying that he had hired an executive jet to go to Paris for dinner the next day and could I go but, with him, everything was always at the last minute. As we got to know each other better, I got him interested in flying. I could see that he had serious money and persuaded him to buy a Hawker Tempest, which had been rescued from India but needed a total, very expensive restoration which he made a start on. Again through flying, David got into a business with a partner selling helicopter parts. He told me on several occasions that there were problems with this new venture and his relationship with his partner and, one Saturday, I opened a newspaper to see a headline reading 'Millionaire presumed murdered – but no body!'

It transpired that David and his partner had met at David's house. The partner maintained that they had had a big argument, but that he had left. However, there was a lot of David's blood in the house, although the only definitive evidence against the partner was that he had subsequently been seen washing his shoes. The police took the case very seriously, however. Something like 80 detectives were put on the case and they followed up every single social contact David had, including me. A major issue in the investigation was that there was no body, and indeed none has ever been found. Despite the weakness of the evidence, the partner was convicted of David's murder and he lost the case again when it went to appeal.

I had always admired the extraordinary excesses of American cars of the late 1950s, the most dramatic example of which was the 1959 Cadillac with huge wings on each side of the back of the car. Even more impressive were the twin 'rocket-style' tail-lights mounted high on each side of those wings. These cars were such a ridiculous aberration and of course absolutely vast and I felt I had to have one.

As a car my Cadillac was pretty hopeless to drive, with incredibly vague steering and soft suspension but it did have reasonable performance from a big V8 engine. Delightful features included a rubber pedal cover on the foot brake on which was embossed 'Power Brake' and a very early self-seeking radio with a button on which was printed 'More Stations'.

The brakes, though, were unreliable and required a considerable amount of forethought when you wanted to slow down. Not only did you have to pump the ill-named 'Power Brake' to get enough pressure for the brakes to bite, but this pressure gradually faded as you pushed on the pedal and it slid to the floor so you had to remember to pump the pedal again in order to stop in time. Bringing the Cadillac to a halt was a multi-phase process.

Anyhow my passengers at the time recall that I was somewhat distracted by operating the radio on the occasion that I failed to 'charge' the brakes soon enough, leading to a fairly major accident on the London Embankment, during Friday evening rush hour, on our way to France for Le Mans one year. Realising that we had no brakes as we were coming up to stationary traffic, waiting for a traffic light, I had to take to the right-hand side of the road. This caused a collision with two cars coming in the opposite direction, both of which were written off. But the Cadillac took the smash well and with the aid of a large jack, we were able to prise the front wing and bumper off the tyre.

Having missed our ferry, we ended up docking at Ostend at six o'clock in the morning, from where we drove straight into France until it dawned on us that we did not have insurance. So, we swung around and headed back to the border to arrange suitable cover. However, a beady-eyed Belgian customs officer had spotted the 'B' on our registration plate; it was there because this Cadillac had originally been imported into Belgium. On the assumption that we were Belgians trying to sneak home after an accident in France, we were arrested and spent several hours in a police station until the penny dropped that we were heading for the 24-hour race at Le Mans. 'Ah! Le Vingt-Quatre!' exclaimed our arresting officers, before sending us cheerily on our way.

A curious and impulsive purchase, this Buick was previously owned by the Kuwaiti embassy in London. It was smooth and spacious but had few other redeeming virtues.

My 1959 Cadillac after the brakes failed on the Embankment on our way to France. Two other cars that were hit were written off, but this was roadworthy again after a little hammer work!

We did not have tickets for Le Mans; we never had tickets. But there were various places where one could climb in and watch the race. It was while we were scaling one of these illicit 'entry points' that Tim Daniel got his boot entangled in the barbed wire at the top, leaving him suspended like a piece of game outside an old-fashioned butcher's shop.

Drink was cheap in France in those days and we imbibed liberally. At some stage during the night, Tim felt the call of nature and left to relieve himself. He returned, somewhat blearily, and after quite a lot of thought opened a rear door and clambered inside. The first we knew about this was when quite a commotion began in the big Citroën parked in front of us. Then a rear door burst open to be followed by Tim, forcefully ejected by the French couple he had inadvertently joined in their backseat amours!

I have owned three Ferraris, one awful and two fantastic. Of course, with their incredible racing record and beautiful bodies, Ferraris have always had an extraordinary allure. But inevitably with small production runs and quite complex machinery, they were generally poorly developed by the standards of mass-produced cars. Then, assuming that their average purchaser would want to drive flat out immediately, the factory tended to install very soft piston rings which would 'bed-in' quickly, but of course would not last. And, more alarmingly, rust protection was absolutely minimal. Indeed for years Ferrari never bothered to paint anything on the inside of the doors, so while the outside might look gorgeous and glossy, within a year significant corrosion would be developing!

My first Ferrari, shared with my friend Andrew Cox, was a 365 BB generally known as the Berlinetta Boxer. This had been developed after Ferrari had become very alarmed by the success of the Lamborghini Miura and thought that they had to go mid-engined to compete; this was their answer. The car was very heavy on the controls, visibility from it was limited and the designers had chosen a curious layout in which the engine sat on top of the gearbox, which resulted in quite a high centre of gravity and a frightening tendency for the back of the car to overtake the front in a corner.

The 365 BB certainly was not reliable. I discovered this in truly dramatic fashion when I was driving it for what turned out to be the last time. The irony is that I was driving relatively gently when there was an appalling noise from the rear. I stopped, got out, saw pools of oil descending from the gearbox, looked underneath and was met with the sight of a huge crack splitting the gearbox in two!

I phoned up the Ferrari concessionaires and told them of my problem, and the first question they asked was how many miles it had done. I recollect that it was 28,000, to which the person I was speaking to responded, with what seemed to be a genuine reaction, that they were surprised that the gearbox had lasted that long. Even after wheedling with Ferrari in the UK, and having the installation work done by someone who was definitely not an official agent, the new gearbox and installation cost something like £7,000, a lot of money in the early 1980s. However, we sold it to South Africa and just made a minute profit, but it was a relief to see the last of that 365 BB.

On the other hand, the two Maranellos that I have had are absolutely excellent cars. When Luca di Montezemelo took over the direction of Ferrari in the early 1990s, he quickly became aware of the quality problems. He stopped all new car production and went back to the drawing board. The first car produced after this shake-up was the 550 Maranello which was a huge success. This car was given an all-aluminium body, so there were no corrosion issues. It had absolutely bullet-proof mechanicals, a gorgeous and traditional Ferrari V-12 engine, lovely handling, good balance since the gearbox was in unit with the differential at the back of the car and it had a really high-class interior.

In 2002, the Maranello was updated to the 575, very much the same car but with a number of detail improvements. I decided to have one and, totally fortuitously bought the first one I saw, which happened to be a manual transmission 575, very few of which were made.

Not only is the 575 a superb car and a great pleasure to drive, it is a marvellous car for a long journey. And the great thing about manual transmission 575s is that all the right-hand-drive cars came to the UK although there were not many at that. So, the other right-hand-drive markets such as India, Japan and Australia came and plucked at least half of the UK cars, meaning those that remained escalated dramatically in value!

My other Maranello is a 575 HGTC, of which Ferrari produced around 90 at the end of the Maranello production. They were designed with slightly less weight, a bit more power, huge wheels and carbon brakes. I was doing business in the Czech Republic when I heard of one that was for sale, seemingly at a very cheap price. It transpired that it was owned by a rich enthusiast, who had a saloon-car racing team. Since he had his own engineers on his payroll, he never took his car anywhere near a franchise dealer, getting his own chaps to maintain the Ferrari for far less cost. But with these cars, a service history is what people tend to be paranoid about, and since this particular car did not have a service history I was able to negotiate what seemed to be a very good deal.

I actually offered the owner more money than he wanted, but that was on the understanding that he would take the car to the official Ferrari dealers in Vienna, where I had a contact, so that they could go right through the car carrying out all the work on it that they thought necessary. That turned out not to be a great deal for the vendor, but all the work was done and I went to collect the car when it was ready in the eastern part of the Czech Republic.

It was quick but did have harsh and uncompromising suspension. Even so, it was an absolutely captivating car to drive. Setting off in the early morning I did the 1,200 kilometres (750 miles) to the French coast very easily within the day.

My Iso Grifo was another Italian car that gave me enormous pleasure. Although Iso produced cars in limited numbers, the ones they made were unforgettable. They were created by Renzo Rivolta, an Italian count, but also a shrewd businessman, who developed a series of bubble-cars in the 1950s, before becoming somewhat more ambitious and moving into high-performance cars. Cleverly, he got the best Italian coachbuilders, such as Bertone, to design the bodies, but for simplicity and convenience used off-the-shelf mechanical components, principally Chevrolet V8 engines and associated gearboxes.

Insofar as most of the mechanical components were made in large volumes, the cars were genuinely good, and far better than most limited-production cars. Rivolta began with the Rivolta saloon, and then made his most exciting and best car: the Grifo two-seater GT car. When tested by experienced journalists, the Grifo was almost universally commended. It was not a cheap car at about three times the price of a contemporary Jaguar E-type, but they did sell. I was determined to have one, and found one being sold by a North London motor trader named Mike Elliott. I quickly bought it. It proved to be an excellent car: powerful, smooth, with lovely interior trim and devastating good looks! And, it introduced me to Mike with whom, possibly more than anyone, I shared so many extraordinary events in my life.

Mike was quite unlike any of my other friends, but he had an easy charm, a ready wit and was always full of fun, which made him excellent company to be with. He was a great character even if he did sail the wrong side of the law from time to time! The first occasion that he fell foul of the authorities and was caught by them came when Mike was persuaded by his ne'er-do-well brother that they could make a load of easy money from smuggling hashish into the UK from India.

The first stage of their plan saw Mike's brother land at Geneva Airport, directly from India, carrying two suitcases packed with cannabis. At the same time a woman flew into Geneva from Paris, accompanied by her little girl, and carrying two identical suitcases. The suitcases were swapped inside the airport and, working on the assumption that no one would stop a mother and child, the woman walked out of the terminal with the two cannabis-filled suitcases, which

The Iso Grifo was, in its day, arguably a better car than contemporary Ferraris. It was good looking and had the power and usability of a big Chevrolet engine.

she passed to Mike, waiting outside with a big Volvo estate car. For good measure, his 11-year-old son was with him!

The next stage of this absurdly complex heist found Mike, skulking somewhere in the countryside of Savoie, where he removed all the internal panels of the Volvo and stuffed the cannabis behind them. I would have thought that there were two essentials to achieving success in a criminal activity that involves driving from one side of France to another: you keep to the speed limit and you have cash. Mike failed in both of these. Some distance short of Boulogne he was caught speeding by a police radar trap and given an on-the-spot fine amounting to something like £150 in today's money.

Of course, Mike did not have that kind of money on him, so he offered to leave his son as security while he drove into town to get the necessary cash. The last thing Mike wanted to do was to leave the car with the police in case they brought in a sniffer dog and his stash of cannabis was detected. But the police answered that the car was not going anywhere, which left Mike in a bit of a jam. He was desperately racking his brains for a way out when down the road bowled a sky-blue Rolls-Royce convertible heading away from the coast. Mike saw that this had a British number plate and stepped into the road to stop the driver. There was another man in the front seat beside the driver and two rather tarty girls in the back.

They were able to help out from a briefcase seemingly filled with money and, when Mike enquired how to get the cash back to them, they gave him a business card bearing the name of a London jewellery shop in Hatton Garden called Pussy Galore. Mike paid the police, who could not believe that he had just stopped a complete stranger and blagged the fine off him. And that was that in France at any rate.

For the next part of the plot, Mike had to meet another driver somewhere outside Dover to transfer the cannabis to him, and this was where the smuggling operation really started to become unglued. The man given the task of receiving the stash from Mike was not the sharpest knife in the box. Although he had been given plenty of money to buy the kind of respectable car that would not attract any attention, he had hung on to a good chunk of it, buying instead a clapped out old van, with a headlight more or less hanging out of the front wing. Worse still, this idiot had also written down all his instructions and all the details of what was due to happen.

So, the police could not have believed their luck when they pulled him over for driving an unroadworthy vehicle and found that they had stumbled across a drug-smuggling operation in full swing. Meanwhile, Mike's brother and the other ringleaders were sorting out how dispose of their illegal haul and what share everyone was due to get, when the door of their house exploded into the room (courtesy of a police hydraulic ram backed up outside) followed by the massed ranks of Scotland Yard's drug squad. Mike's brother then tried to swallow the incriminating evidence, but one of the policemen shoved a hand down his throat and retrieved it. Off they all went to the police station to be charged and then let out on bail.

But it took a day or two for the police to work out Mike's involvement and he and I arranged to meet for a drink after he had been to Pussy Galore to return the £150 he had borrowed. When he got to the shop, he found that the Met had got a team of men with pneumatic drills digging up the floor. Mike made enquiries among associates who knew about Hatton Garden and grew very alarmed when he found out that the owner of Pussy Galore, the chap in the Rolls-Royce he had waved down outside Boulogne, was none other than Kenneth Noye, one of the key figures in the notorious Brink's-Mat robbery.

Mike was sent down for three years. He started serving his time at Ford Open Prison where he quickly spotted that there was a huge demand for pre-paid telephone cards. So, he telephoned his mates in the north London motor trade and before long shoeboxes jam-packed with phonecards were sailing over the security fence at Ford, where Mike was lurking to catch them and start making a killing on the prison's phonecard black market. He saw out the rest of his time in Parkhurst.

I have always been fascinated by military vehicles, to an extent because you can buy an incredible amount of quality engineering for so little money, and indeed, within the UK, there is the strange ability to use armoured vehicles on public roads. I began with a Ferret, a small scout car made by Daimler with a six-cylinder Rolls-Royce engine. Although weighed down by armour, it had quite good performance and, like all smaller British armoured vehicles, had a pre-selector gearbox, a strange invention but very popular even with racing cars, such as ERA, before the war. The Ferret was made in different versions, but I had what I think is the nicest one with a small turret and a Browning machine gun – sadly deactivated!

My Ferret was followed by a Fox, a later and rather more sophisticated vehicle. Considerably larger and weighing six tons, this was powered by a Jaguar XK engine, and again had a pre-selector gearbox. It had a rather effective 30mm Rarden cannon, and normally operated with a crew of three. But I stripped out most of the internal radios, ammunition boxes and other military impedimenta, so we could easily take five on a short trip to the pub. The only major snag with the Fox was that the visibility for the driver was very restricted, which led to an

My Fox armoured car, not a great success militarily as they tended to topple over on rough ground, but an unbeatable vehicle to take friends to the pub.

amusing incident when I was coming out of the drive of Thornhill. I was turning onto what was quite a busy public road, and of course the cannon preceded the vehicle by a fair amount, which made it tricky to see oncoming vehicles. One of these did an exaggerated swerve around the Fox and then stopped in the middle of the road when the driver observed me following behind.

He got out and came to me demanding to know where the commander was. I explained that the Fox, of course in full military colours, was my own and that I had no commander. To which he replied, 'Don't be ridiculous; you cannot drive a Fox without a commander!' To an extent he was right. Having someone in the turret with an intercom was extremely helpful.

Earlier, I had an ex-US Army Dodge 'Weapons Carrier', a 4x4 and very tough three-quarter ton truck. It would go anywhere, and carry pretty much anything!

The fourth military vehicle I owned was a Volvo 'Suga' Command Car. Suga translates from the Swedish as 'a sow'. I was looking for another 'go-anywhere' vehicle that was a more interesting alternative to a Land Rover and, while I suspect that purists might have objected, I stripped out all the radios and the partition that divided the 'other ranks' from the capacious rear where the Swedish general sat commanding his troops. This created a large space for four people to ride in comfort and as many dogs as one wanted. It was very tough and would take any amount of abuse, but was appallingly slow, although great fun.

Of course, the name Rolls-Royce says it all, and there is probably no other car with such a story and such achievement. Rolls, although an aristocrat and playboy, but serious businessman, and Royce, an extraordinarily demanding and obsessional engineer, made a number of very limited production cars, but their first 'proper' car was the 40-50, popularly known as the Silver Ghost, which was introduced in 1907. I still have the Ghost that I bought some 30 years ago, and never tire of the extraordinary quality of every part of the car.

In those days, the most demanding automotive competition was the Alpine Rally, which involved two weeks of racing up and down what were often poorly-made tracks in the Alps. Rolls-Royce could see the publicity value of success and entered three cars in 1912. Sadly, they were ill-prepared. Most critically, they had a three-speed gearbox with a very high first gear and they were simply unable to climb the steep Alpine hairpin bends. After this disappointing experience, they went to work back at Derby and produced a far better car with more power, a four-speed gearbox, longer fuel range and better cooling. Altogether there were some 150 improvements.

The ultimate Edwardian sporting vehicle; my Rolls-Royce 'Alpine Eagle' Silver Ghost

These cars then dominated the 1913 Alpine Rally, coming first and second, and indeed would have come third had the final team car not been driven into (the general opinion is deliberately) by another competing car. Inevitably sporting motorists began demanding replicas of these team cars which became known as 'Alpine Eagles'. However, the First World War put paid to civilian car production, but, post-war, production continued and my car was produced in 1920, effectively the same as the pre-war cars.

Importantly it has what is known as the 'Speed-model' engine, but also was re-bodied with a very light open four-seat body, exactly as the 1913 team cars. So, it is a big car and, for one that is almost 100 years old, very sophisticated. It has one fundamental weakness of only having rear-wheel brakes in a car where most of the weight is on the front wheels, so stopping is always a worry, particularly on narrow roads. Many books have been written about the Silver Ghost, and certainly it is one of the most charismatic cars ever made. There were over 6,000 originally made, and around 500 remaining; so Ghost ownership is quite an exclusive club.

I also owned two examples of the Phantom II Rolls-Royce – the 'PI' being the successor to the Ghost, and the 'PII', launched in 1929, being an altogether more sophisticated car. The pinnacle of the PII is accepted as being the 'Continental', which was a higher performance and much more sporting car with a short-chassis; it was a car intended for what was amusingly called the 'owner-driver'. I bought an early Continental made in 1930, which came with its original 'Build Sheet', showing the vast amount of choice owners had in their specification from the strength of the springs, to the size of the steering wheel, and including such obvious touring necessities as a horn, a klaxon and a siren!

In my ignorance, I did not realise that the body had been quite significantly modified while it had been in New Zealand, and then had not been brilliantly converted back to a body like the original Barker open tourer. But it was not a bad car: it had been quite cheap and had been looked after well mechanically during its sojourn in New Zealand. We undertook a certain amount of work, including fitting an overdrive, which transformed its ability to cruise, and had some rather good continental holidays with it.

Then, still thinking that the PII Continental was the ultimate pre-war car, I bought another, this time a Barker close-coupled saloon. This had quite an attractive body and was mechanically good; and again its performance was transformed with an overdrive. But I began to realise that not many people want a car that is so big, heavy to drive and unwieldy however stylish it might be. So, it went in favour of an open Derby Bentley!

Inevitably, with my enthusiasm for speed and excitement, I was drawn to motorcycles, and in Africa, long before obtaining any licence borrowed a variety of motorbikes from friends.

But once I took up motorbikes, I did so fairly seriously and went through quite a lot of them. I began with Norton Commandos (this being just before the Japanese showed Europeans how to build motorcycles) which sounded great but were mechanical nightmares and extraordinarily unreliable. Going back to my office one day in the rain I lost control of a Commando in the Hyde Park Corner underpass. Fortunately, it was the uphill part joining Piccadilly, so I slid rather uncomfortably to a halt, but it did not do my City suit much good.

As soon as I could, I bought a Honda 750-4, the first really sophisticated motorcycle with four cylinders. It was very smooth and, importantly, totally reliable. I then came to meet Dave Degens who was a somewhat legendary figure making special frames for both racing and road bikes, under the name 'Dresda'. His approach was to take standard motorcycles, tune the engines and then put them into lightweight frames of his own design. I had a headhunting client who was quite keen on motorcycles, and we came up with the scheme of obtaining a licence from Dresda for the USA – clearly a large motorcycle market – and selling them there. We made a couple of trips, sold a few motorcycles, but we both had more important businesses and allowed the whole thing to fizzle out.

My next motorcycle adventure when I obtained the first production 1,000cc motorbike, the Kawasaki 1000, before getting a Laverda Jota, probably the best motorbike I owned. Those who knew their bikes called them the Ferrari of motorcycles: beautifully made, had loads of power and handled impeccably.

Another motorcycle worth mentioning is a Suzuki GS1000. Through Mike Elliott we were able to buy a couple of new ones relatively cheaply. I registered mine in the normal way, but Mike could not see much point in paying to do the same so he simply got identical licence plates to mine, put them on his motorbike and never bothered! It did, however, somewhat restrict our ability to ride them together!

Later, I became attracted to the six-cylinder Honda which was probably the most incredible motorcycle engine ever made, but was installed in a very mundane frame. All the same, it had 1,100cc and six cylinders (stretching across the frame and indeed sticking out substantially each side), and it made a glorious noise. It was also pretty quick although rather hopeless around corners.

(Above) My first proper motorcycle, a Norton Commando. The 750cc engine was totally unreliable but the bike handled well.

(Below) For a while the Suzuki 1000 was the performance bike to have so Mike Elliott and I bought one each. I registered mine; Mike got an identical number plate and used that!

My first six-cylinder Honda was stolen within a few months of ownership as they were rather attractive to thieves, so I quickly went out and bought another one. I took delivery the day before I was due to go to RAF Binbrook to go flying in a Lightning. So, that evening saw me on the A1M heading north, at a steady 85mph (the motorbike's maximum running-in speed), when I espied the most incredible sight of a car reversing from the central reservation into my fast lane! I just had time to touch the brakes before hitting the car, as it transpired an estate filled with firewood. The impact tore the back of the car off, spreading firewood over the road. I suspect on any other motorcycle I would have lost my right leg, but with the Honda, the huge engine sticking out took the blow. Nevertheless, we tumbled down the road together for about 60 yards, during which the motorcycle fell onto my foot.

One of my three Honda 'Six' motorbikes, the most superb engine housed in a hopeless frame. The width of the engine saved my leg from amputation when I hit a stationary car on the A1.

The A1M is quite a busy road and I could see lights of other northbound vehicles heading in my direction, so I hobbled to the central reservation and hid behind the Armco barrier. Various cars started losing control when they reached the accident, skidding and running into the car that I had first hit. In the end, there were another seven seriously-damaged cars before people started slowing down sufficiently. I was taken by ambulance to hospital where they X-rayed my foot and leg. I was told that the results showed there was nothing wrong apart from general bruising and I was collected by Ray Guess, my first flying instructor, with whom I had arranged to spend the night.

However, I was in great pain and his wife, a nurse, could see that something was quite badly wrong. Inevitably I cancelled my flight in the Lightning (but was able to do it later), and, given the pain, decided to take a taxi from the Midlands straight to the Middlesex Hospital in London, where they X-rayed me again and said that I had six quite badly broken bones in my foot!

A couple of weeks later I went back to the scene of the accident and saw what had happened. The very respectable driver of the estate car had crossed the northbound carriageway (in those days you could do that) and was waiting on the central reservation to go south. But the reservation was very narrow, and I suspect she was worried that she was sticking into the southbound fast lane and reversed backwards. But this was at night and I almost certainly did not realise that she was backing straight onto the northbound fast lane.

She was charged with dangerous driving and I was asked to appear as a prosecution witness. This good lady had last seen me in frayed motorcycle leathers and clearly assumed that I was a motorcycle thug, so she was somewhat surprised when I appeared in a City pin-striped suit. In order for me to succeed in my claim against her insurance company for 'pain and suffering', it was quite important that she was convicted and, fortunately, she was.

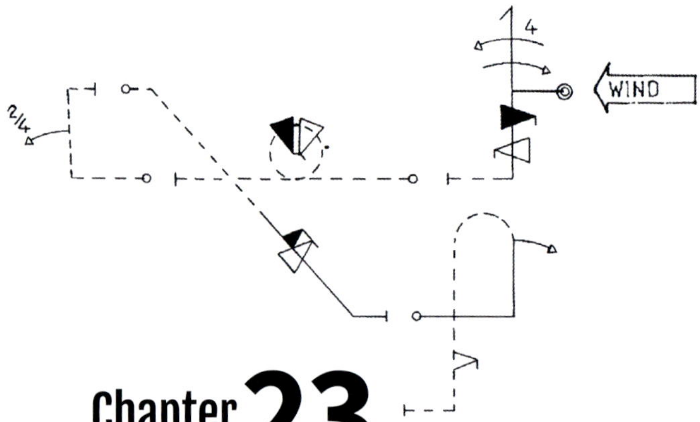

Chapter 23

WHY STICK AT SEVENTY?

I turned 70 on 1 March 2016 and four days later Cary and I held a party for over 200 guests in a marquee at Rhodds Farm.

The menu carries a picture on the front cover showing me at the wheel of my Silver Ghost; beside me sits Lulu, one half of our current pair of Springer Spaniels. Each table was identified by the name of one of our dogs, the majority of whom had themselves been named after places in Sri Lanka and many of the guests at that party had also been guests at Ellerton.

By this stage, however, our days at Ellerton were numbered and we would be looking for a new owner. The end of an era was drawing to a close, not just with Ellerton and Sri Lanka in general but the close affinity I felt with south-east Asia that stretched back for all of my 70 years was approaching its terminus too. The change would take some getting used to, there was no doubt about that. There would be things I would miss with the passing of Ellerton that could not be replaced or even replicated.

I would miss our staff. Most importantly, I would miss Athula, our wonderful manager who had entered our lives as if by magic and who did so much to make running Ellerton comparatively smooth and straightforward for Cary and me. After our bad experience with Rohan, Cary and I were on our guard. It was when things were going seriously wrong with Rohan that Ken Hetti entered the picture.

Ken came from a well-to-do family in in Kandy and they had been able to send him to the UK to take an engineering degree. So, he spoke good English and was also very personable. He had been installing a generator at Ellerton when he picked up the vibes that Rohan's days with us were numbered and had put himself forward as a replacement manager.

Ken had many worthy qualities. Apart from being totally straight when it came to handling money, he was good with guests. But he lacked the detailed experience necessary for the efficient running of a hotel. The answer, we decided, was to appoint a house manager below Ken, who would do all the things he was not doing, leaving Ken to meet and greet guests and generally act as our front of house man when Cary and I were not there. The man we appointed as house manager was Saman. He came with experience of the hotel industry and he also came with a long-held wish to join his family, who had all emigrated to Australia. However, Saman's own application had been turned down three times by the Australian immigration authorities and he told us that he was resigned to not being given leave to emigrate to the country. And, for two-and-a-half years, Saman did an adequate job at Ellerton. Indeed, he would probably have continued doing an adequate job had it not been for the news that rocked us all one February, at our busiest time of the year. He had applied for and been given an Australian visa, and was leaving immediately.

We were furious, but he introduced us to Athula, who turned out to be everything our previous managers had never been. He was very good with the guests, and so motivating with the staff that he transformed a lot of things at Ellerton for the better. As far as Cary and I were concerned, Athula was totally reliable and efficient to the extent that we felt completely comfortable leaving him in charge when we were not there and he liked Ellerton. Although he was married, the hotel became the focus of his life.

Meeting guests and sharing our experiences of Ellerton with them was something else I knew I was going to miss very much. My office window in the hotel overlooked the drive and main entrance and I used to enjoy greeting guests personally when they arrived. Many were friends, of course, but a lot were people of similar age to Cary and me who were attracted to Ellerton for the very reasons that we had been.

For a small hotel, our guest book included entries from a number of distinguished international guests. The leading Parisian fashion designer Christian Louboutin visited with a couple of friends. I greeted some British guests, having first checked I had their name right before welcoming them to Ellerton, although I did wonder if we had made a mistake with the booking because the chap who had made it seemed slightly unsure when I called him 'Mr Swan'. Over a drink a short time later, he explained quietly that 'Mr Swan' was one of half-a-dozen identities he used quite legitimately, with passports and bank cards to match because he was one of the UK's leading intelligence chiefs. Travelling under one of his alter-egos spared him the unwanted attention of local intelligence agencies when he was on holiday.

John Myatt, the celebrated art forger, was another of our memorable guests. He was very open about his unusual line of business. He was sentenced to a few months in Wandsworth for his part in a major criminal case although his time inside was not entirely wasted. His fellow lags included a number of quite serious criminals, who, when they heard that John was a gifted painter, commissioned him to paint their portraits at the going rate. So, he ended up making some useful money while serving time.

Two Chiefs of General Staff came to stay at Ellerton as well. And, at the time that the Sri Lankan 26-year-long civil war was coming to an end in 2009, we happened to have staying at Ellerton the UN representative to Sri Lanka, the head of the Asian Development Bank and a key European ambassador. Their mobile phones were ringing almost non-stop as the fighting reached its crescendo in the north, before the final battle and massacre of Tamil Tigers and many more innocent Tamil civilians brought the war to an end.

After the civil war it was quite a problem to get your hands on even an air gun. However, I did manage to buy a .177 in the end, which our gardeners fired at monkeys to send them skipping back into the jungle if they ventured into the hotel grounds, to stop them becoming a real nuisance pinching mobile phones and wallets, and even snatching handbags and cameras.

Then came the occasion when one very bold monkey decided that breakfast one morning looked particularly appetising. The gardener on air-gun duty was alerted and he responded swiftly, if not wisely. Instead of stalking the monkey around the outside of the hotel, this chap rushed pell-mell into the dining pavilion, brandishing the rifle. Children screamed, tables were upset, chairs knocked to the ground and pandemonium ensued as the gardener charged past. The irony is that he never got in a shot. There was no need. The uproar in the dining pavilion had been enough to send the monkey scuttling back into the undergrowth.

My working day at Ellerton was not dissimilar to my working day here at home, with the exception of popping out to welcome guests or seeing to anything else in the hotel that needed my attention. I ran my aviation business as usual, allowing for the fact that the office at Rhodds Farm opened for work five hours later than the start of the working day in Sri Lanka. Come the end of the afternoon, I would set off on my bicycle for a ride of between one and three hours. I had put together a range of 10 cycling routes of varying lengths, which I took guests on if they were keen to explore the area on two wheels.

One of my destinations stood at the summit of a hill from where one could take several routes back to Ellerton. Up on the hill is the memorial to Robert Knox, a 17th-century English mariner who had been shipwrecked at the end of 1659, along with his father (the captain of the East India Company merchantman) and 14 of the crew. They were taken prisoner and incarcerated by the King of Kandy. In time, though, those who survived malaria were allowed a degree of liberty within the closely-guarded kingdom. Knox and three of his crewmates were given land around the hilltop behind Ellerton (where the memorial stands) where they were allowed to farm and trade. After 19 years of captivity, Knox and one of the other captives managed to escape, finally returning to England in September 1680, where Knox became something of a national celebrity. The following year he published a book about the island of Ceylon, where he had spent more than half his life. This included detailed descriptions of the Kandyan people, their way of life and that part of the island in general. *An Historical Relation of the Island Ceylon together With somewhat Concerning Severall Remarkable passages of my life that hath hapned since my Deliverance out of Captivity* – to give Knox's book its full title, gained its author international recognition: Daniel Defoe drew heavily on its contents when he was writing *Robinson Crusoe*. Interestingly, Sri Lankan friends have said to me that if you want to understand the Kandyan mind, you should read this book, even though it was written well over 300 years ago.

In 1908, the stone memorial I cycled up to was erected to commemorate Robert Knox and three of his shipmates, but over the years this had become dilapidated: the roots of a big bo tree had undermined it and the huge stone slab was listing to one side. We had several vaguely amusing, but otherwise unproductive, meetings with people from the Ministry of Antiquities. In the end, we went ahead by ourselves and set the memorial upright on a secure foundation, where it now stands.

Another favourite bicycle sortie was to take a group by minibus down to the railway station at Gampola, where we caught the train for the stunning three-hour journey through the hills up to the station near Nuwara Eliya, in the heart of the hill country. There we would be met by the minibus with all our bicycles, which would take us to have lunch at the Grand Hotel. Afterwards, we bicycled back to

Ellerton 63 kilometres away, much of it downhill. There was a sting at the end, though – the final four-kilometre climb back up to the hotel, by which time you were feeling pretty bushed!

One of our guests, with whom I was cycling, came face to face with rather more local colour than he might have wished for when he came across a line of several hundred Tamils, all dressed in their finery, marking Thai Pongal, their harvest festival. My cycling companion and I worked our way gently through the crowd to the head of the procession, which was being led by three trucks. The front truck was carrying the long trunk of a coconut tree and from the coconut tree a man was suspended from big hooks pushed through his flesh. He was looking a bit glazed, as one might imagine. Alongside him was a second chap, similarly hanging from large hooks in his flesh. But the third fellow hanging from the coconut tree easily trumped the first pair. He was also suspended from meat hooks digging into his flesh, but he had gone one better and was sitting in a chair – so not only his own weight, but that of the chair too were pulling down on the hook and his flesh

The memorial to the intrepid Robert Knox who was a captive King of Kandy, together with his shipmates for many years. The memorial was erected in 1908 and we restored it.

supporting them! The extraordinary thing was that not one of them was bleeding, nor was there any sign that they were in pain. Even so, my cycling companion was absolutely horrified and could scarcely believe what he was seeing.

Cycle past quiet forest lay-bys in Sri Lanka, as I have done countless times, and you will see tuk tuks and mopeds pulled over while furtive sales of illicit arrack, the local spirit derived from coconut juice, are being transacted. And it is the illegal production of arrack that takes up much of the time of the courts in Sri Lanka, because so many people are distilling the stuff at home. Drive by a courthouse in Sri Lanka and you will see stacks of assorted bottles of this moonshine, confiscated by the police.

As one might imagine, most illegally produced arrack is a distinctly acquired taste: pretty revolting is close to the mark. On the other hand, legally-produced arrack, distilled in proper facilities and under carefully controlled conditions is a very different and far more palatable entity. Some of it is matured for six years in French brandy casks and the spirit coming from these is as smooth and rewarding as a nice cognac. I have conducted blind tastings with friends who know a fair bit about wines and spirits. But, presented with unmarked glasses containing arrack, cognac and something similar, they often could not tell which was the arrack.

Over the dozen years that I was cycling in the area, the local dogs became fitter and faster as they chased after me hoping to sink their teeth into my leg, which they did twice resulting in each case in a visit to hospital and a course of five anti-rabies injections: sure signs that the dogs' owners were able to feed them better! During our 13 years at Ellerton, we could see prosperity growing among local people. Our own staff used to walk to work when Ellerton began operating as a hotel but, by the time we left, they all had either motorbikes or tuk tuks.

The other pointer was the cause for a certain *schadenfreude* on my part, because it tracked back to a detail I had insisted was inserted into our purchase contract when we bought Ellerton from Ranaweera. The clause I demanded concerned water. I am paranoid about water. Having lived in Asia and Africa, I attach much greater importance to a stable water supply than most people brought up in the UK, who assume water will appear whenever they turn a tap.

Ranaweera took a similar view, laughing when I raised the issue of water at Ellerton. 'We have fantastic water here,' he assured me. 'The estate supplies it. It has done for 120 years.' But I insisted that the water supply to Ellerton had a legal safeguard and a covenant was inserted into the contract that if Ranaweera's estate had water it had to supply Ellerton with water too. Even so, as soon as we were the legal owners, I had a borehole sunk to ensure our own water supply. Oddly enough, the one place where the drilling expert reckoned we could drill the well and find a decent aquifer was very close to a stream, although the two were separated by 100 feet of granite. So, installing the borehole had not been a cheap exercise, but at least we had a guaranteed water supply.

For the time being, though, we were using the estate water because it was free and plentiful as Ranaweera would delight in telling us. However, Ranaweera had failed to take into account the changing lifestyle of his neighbours who also drew their water from his estate supply. They were starting to shower more, and collectively they were using more and more water, to the point about seven months after we acquired Ellerton the estate water supply suddenly dried up for the first time in 120 years.

We switched to drawing our water from our borehole and carried on as before. But Ranaweera was stymied, and for two years we used to watch his men driving a tractor and trailer carrying a huge bowser down the road to the stream close to our borehole. They then had to fill the bowser by handpump, before driving it back up the hill, where it had to be pumped into a tank to be used in Ranaweera's tea factory and this was something that had to be done many times a day! More recently, he has come to an arrangement that allows him to pump water from the stream, but nowhere on his land is there now water.

To return to the beginning, there was never any forethought as to how Ellerton would develop. Like a number of things Cary and I have done in our lives, Ellerton evolved with events. We certainly never planned to run Ellerton as a hotel: that just happened. But as it happened, it grew to the point where we were handling over 2,500 guests a year. We had a division of labour, as we have on all our projects. I took care of the marketing, the legal work, the technicalities of building and running the hotel, and dealing with local administrators and contractors. Cary took care of all the aesthetic and culinary aspects of running Ellerton: anything requiring a bit of taste. At a more prosaic level, she also handled the bookings, the banking, the book-keeping, dealing with all the enquiries to the point when she would be handling several Ellerton emails every day of the year. If she was lucky, these could be knocked off in three quarters of an hour; at other times she might be at her desk dealing with them for five or six hours.

By now, Cary was also running a garden tour company alongside her garden design business and, with the three businesses on the go simultaneously, there simply were not enough hours in the day to do everything that was needed. So, with reluctance, she sold her garden tour business. But, after owning Ellerton for approaching a decade, Cary was wanting to travel to places other than Sri Lanka. In addition to which, Ellerton was no longer somewhere she and I could go to relax: our staff would save up problems to present to us when we arrived.

Personally, I do not like 'relaxing', but I understood that Cary wanted downtime to enjoy her garden and simply unwind. So, we decided that the time had come to sell Ellerton, a process that would take us two-and-a-half years in the end. We came close to closing a couple of deals: one to a big Indian consortium, the other to a wealthy Indian family, but these both foundered for various reasons. The present couple took over the ownership of Ellerton in the spring of 2018. She is Sri Lankan, her husband is Swiss and, judging by reports, Ellerton is in good hands.

With Cary, Lulu (short for Luluwatta, a village near Ellerton) and Kandy, as well as Crocus the dachshund, in the garden at Rhodds Farm.

However, our contact with Ellerton did not entirely end with the sale. The issue of our one-ninth share of Ukuwela remained unresolved after 13 years. It still had a value, so Cary and I decided to give it to Athula, as a thank-you for all he had done for us. In 2018, Athula, who is a would-be frustrated farmer, bought about 10 acres quite close to Ellerton and began putting up cattle sheds and a house for a farm manager. Cary became enthusiastic about the idea, mainly, I suspect, because we like Athula as a friend as much as a trusted employee, and said that

The painting very generously organised and indeed paid for by our staff at Ellerton when we left. Inevitably Polly had escaped, so had to be taken down to the artist's studio in Kandy to be incorporated into the painting. Cary feels that it is not very flattering and so it now resides in my cabin in the woods at Rhodds Farm.

she would like to buy his first cow. Athula gratefully received this news, and then Cary said that she wanted the cow to be called 'Cary'. Athula was horrified and said that he could never do that, so the compromise was agreed whereby his first cow would be called 'Madam' which is what the staff always called Cary.

When we left as owners for the last time, our staff presented us with a large oil painting. It shows Cary and me at Ellerton, with Ben and Polly. The painting was based on a photograph that had been taken two years before and Polly, single-minded as ever, had got bored posing for the camera and had wandered off, leaving Ben with Cary and me. When the staff decided to give us a painting of this touching scene, Polly had to be added to the group. So, Athula had to arrange for her to be taken down to the artist's studio in Kandy to be added alongside Ben and the two of us. The painting that resulted was very much a case of, 'It's the thought that counts' and we were both deeply touched by the kindness of their gesture. The picture hangs here, at Rhodds Farm, but not in the main house; I have it in my wooden cabin, up in the trees. Ben, sadly, has also finished his last tour of duty at Ellerton: he passed away in the middle of 2018. Cary and I paid for his headstone and he now lies at rest in the garden he loved and patrolled, missed by everyone who knew him.

Rhodds itself was another of life's serendipities. Having decided to move from Newport, we were slightly caught off guard when we discovered the little haven of tranquility we were seeking after just a couple of months and only a few miles from Newport.

The house itself was a very modest Herefordshire farmhouse. Beside it was a ramshackle barn, some disused byres and a granary. After our first viewing of Newport House with its 100-plus rooms, this looked like a serious come down in the world and I was not at all sure how well I would adapt. However, both Cary and I loved the setting of Rhodds Farm. We loved the woods, 18 acres of mixed broadleaf trees. And we loved the peace. If we had made Thornhill and Newport work, surely we could do the same here? We still had Newport to sell, of course, but we secured Rhodds by paying the owners a 20 per cent non-refundable deposit. Our only stipulation was that they allowed us to convert the byres into offices before we completed on the sale. By doing that, we would be able to transfer our businesses directly into new premises, to carry on work seamlessly while we set about major works on the other buildings.

However, the sale of Newport House did not draw a line under our financial dealings with it. I had made the naïve assumption that there could be no question of paying capital gains tax. But my complacency ended with a polite letter from

(Above) I would like to say that this is a rare moment of transient relaxation.

(Below) Biking has always been part of my life and an amusing annual event is the Huntingdon Chase of bicyclists versus horses versus runners.

a Revenue inspector asking for plans of Newport House. Once these had been provided, I was asked to define my dwelling house. This was then followed by the assertion that only the principal house was the dwelling house, while the large clock-house and extensive stables – only yards away – were not within the curtilage.

The stakes were high with a gain of something like £600,000, only a portion of which I could reasonably attribute to the main house. I researched the law and found it to be vaguely worded and imprecise and it took six months to demonstrate that the clock-house and stables were part of the curtilage. I had considerably more difficulty with the two other houses, mainly because they were further from the principal house, one at 26 metres and one at 51 metres.

I tried the 'permitted area' argument, which required research into the acreage of the gardens and grounds of similar houses to Newport in 'the locality'. I found 14 houses of similar size, and 17 smaller, but still significant houses, and established that on average their houses and grounds exceeded 20 acres. So, I felt reasonably confident that the permitted area for Newport House must be at least six acres, the area that would have included all the buildings. To my surprise, the district valuer established an area of only four acres, conveniently excluding the larger and more valuable of the remaining two houses.

However, her plan of the proposed area was bizarre and did not even give access to the front door of the house. Nor did it allow for the need to walk between the various houses, which, I suspect, rather weakened her argument when reviewed by HMRC. In the end, I won, but it was not easy and I would not go through it again.

Dealing with issues that occurred at Rhodds Farm was relatively straightforward in comparison. There were the inevitable run-ins with the planners, which we managed to resolve largely to our advantage. In time, we were able to buy the fields in front of the house, securing a cordon sanitaire around our home. And Cary set to work, creating another fabulous garden which attracts many visitors from all over the world.

These days my own travels tend to be visits to Budapest and Vilnius in Lithuania, to meet with my partners in my aero engine business, or to seek out opera around Europe.

It has never been in my nature to spend too long dwelling on the past: writing this book is a notable exception. Another Cambridge man – if relevant records are correct, quite possibly another rusticated Cambridge man – (J. Milton, Christ's 1625–32), put it aptly, when he signed off one of his best-known works with the closing line, 'Tomorrow to fresh woods, and pastures new'. As I contemplate the view through the trees and over the fields here at Rhodds Farm, that does give me pause for thought.

The future?

Well, for a start, ideas running through my mind are: at Rhodds Farm, Jaffna, another springer to join Kandy and Lulu; in Argentina, the eight Sukhoi aircraft that we originally sold to the Argentine air force, now to be purchased back; in Sakhalin, at the far east of the Russian Federation the 12 absolutely brand new Yak-52 aircraft and in Hungary, the new engine we are developing with Aerometal which will be the most powerful light aircraft piston engine ever made, with a power output approaching 500hp. And, further automotive purchases? Now, there's a question!

And finally Kandy, my adored springer spaniel.

CAST LIST (Restricted to those not mentioned in more detail within the text)

Ramon Alonso Spanish and World Champion aerobatic pilot. Also a loyal customer.

Nick Ball Very old friend and sharer of aircraft. Killed in microlight accident.

Harry Boggis-Rolfe Cambridge contemporary and barrister. Very close friend.

Bill Bonner Brilliant engine designer and tuner who worked wonders on my engines.

Michel Brandt Skilled aircraft designer who created the wings for Pace Spirit.

Peter Bruller The owner of Aerometal, my partner since 2006.

Noni Chawla Exceptional Indian businessman we recruited to run Korn Ferry offices in India.

Judith Chisholm Outstanding lady aviator to whom I was briefly engaged.

Maxim Chouvaev The principal consultant for our headhunting offices in Russia.

Sergio Dallan Top Italian aerobatic pilot and engineer. A huge help in my battle with Italian courts.

Tom Delaney WWII Spitfire pilot and great support in my aviation ventures, both psychologically and financially.

Peter Dunn. The chief operating officer of Korn/Ferry with whom we had endless negotiations to purchase Carre Orban.

Walter Extra. Brilliant German aircraft designer with whom we worked on various projects.

Yevgeni Frolov Sukhoi test pilot for both military and aerobatic aircraft.

Victor Gauntlett Owner of Pace and Proteus petroleum companies and Aston Martin, good friend and sponsor of my aerobatic teams.

Jez Hopkinson Very successful aerobatic team owner and loyal customer.

Rowena Hutchinson Charming girlfriend at whose wedding I had my dramatic accident.

Wolfgang Jaegle German aerobatic pilot who organised our deal to buy the East German Yak-50s.

Hans Jorda The first headhunter into Eastern Europe and key to my building the Korn/Ferry network there.

Stephen Kain A smart accountant turned scrap-metal dealer and incredible fun.

Ed Kelly My boss at Korn/Ferry who gave me great support.

Slava Kondtratiev Russian who was probably the world's best light aircraft designer, and with whom we worked on many projects.

Tom Lang Very successful US industrialist who became the Sukhoi dealer for USA, and a very generous friend.

Khalide Makagonova (née Ajnetdinova) 1984 Women's World Aerobatic Champion. Opened the door for me into Sukhoi and always helpful.

Geoff Masterson Leading UK aircraft engineer and mechanic.

Philip Meeson Aerobatic team competitor, good friend and later a very successful businessman (Jet-2).

James Mehew Cambridge contemporary and part of our 'GWM Motors' - much joint automotive fun.

Philippe Moch Very successful French manufacturer of aerospace components, but also a customer and friend.

Konstantin Mokhna Ex-Sukhoi engineer who came to work for me in the UK and then became my full-time representative in Russia.

Vic Norman Very old friend and partner in aviation adventures. Historic car specialist and operator of a wing-walking team.

Cressida Pemberton-Pigott Very dear friend for many years.

Mikhail Pogosyan Subsequent general director of Sukhoi.

Viktor Pugachev Sukhoi test pilot and inventor of the 'Cobra' manoeuvre.

Boris Ralkitin Chief designer of Sukhoi sport aircraft.

Paul Ray Jnr Chief executive of the eponymous company and for whom I ran the London office. Became a good friend and mentor.

Andrew Ritchie Cambridge contemporary, very good friend and inventor of the very successful Brompton folding bicycle.

William de Segundo My West African mentor for Bradbury Wilkinson and still close friend.

Mikhail Simonov The general director of Sukhoi with whom I had my first dealings.

Victor Smolin Top Russian display pilot and subsequently manager of the Russian aerobatic team.

Martin Stahalik Leading Czech display pilot, sadly killed in one of our aircraft.

Sasha Tavaryan The commercial director of Sukhoi sport aircraft with whom we had many exciting adventures in Russia.

Dave Wiltshire Incredibly talented engineer who helped me to build aircraft, houses and cars.

Peter Wright Cambridge contemporary and very successful Formula One racing car designer.